Undoing Coups

About the author

Antonia Witt is a Senior Researcher at the Peace Research Institute Frankfurt (PRIF), Germany. She has a background in International Relations, African Studies, and Peace and Conflict Research. Her main research interests are: international and (African) regional organizations, authority and legitimacy in the international realm, and societal effects of interventions in Africa.

Politics and Development in Contemporary Africa

Published by one of the world's leading publishers on African issues, 'Politics and Development in Contemporary Africa' seeks to provide accessible but in-depth analysis of key contemporary issues affecting countries within the continent. Featuring a wealth of empirical material and case study detail, and focusing on a diverse range of subject matter – from conflict to gender, development to the environment – the series is a platform for scholars to present original and often provocative arguments. Selected titles in the series are published in association with the International African Institute.

Published in partnership with the International African Institute

The principal aim of the International African Institute is to promote scholarly understanding of Africa, notably its changing societies, cultures, and languages. Founded in 1926 and based in London, it supports a range of seminars and publications, including the journal *Africa*.

www.internationalafricaninstitute.org

Managing Editor: Stephanie Kitchen

Series Editors: Jon Schubert (Brunel University) and Elliot Green (London School of Economics and Political Science)

Editorial board

Rita Abrahamsen (University of Ottawa); Morten Boas (Norwegian Institute of International Affairs); David Booth (Overseas Development Institute); Padraig Carmody (Trinity College Dublin); Neil Carrier (University of Bristol); Fantu Cheru (Leiden University); Kevin Dunn (Hobart and William Smith Colleges); Amanda Hammar (University of Copenhagen); Alcinda Honwana (Open University); Paul Jackson (University of Birmingham); Gabrielle Lynch (University of Warwick); Zachariah Mampilly (Vassar College); Henning Melber (Dag Hammarskjöld Foundation); Garth A. Myers (Trinity College Hartford Connecticut); Léonce Ndikumana (UMass Amherst); Cyril Obi (Social Science Research Council); Susan Parnell (University of Cape Town); Mareike Schomerus (Overseas Development Institute); Laura Seay (Morehouse College); Howard Stein (University of Michigan); Mats Utas (Uppsala University); Alex de Waal (Tufts University)

Already published

Mobility between Africa, Asia and Latin America: Economic Networks and Cultural Interactions, edited by Ute Röschenthaler and Alessandro Jedlowski

Agricultural Reform in Rwanda: Authoritarianism, Markets and Spaces of Governance, Chris Huggins
Liberia's Female Veterans: War, Roles and Reintegration, Leena Vastapuu and Emmi Nieminen
Food Aid in Sudan: A History of Power, Politics and Profit, Susanne Jaspars
Kakuma Refugee Camp: Humanitarian Urbanism in Kenya's Accidental City, Bram J. Jansen
Development Planning in South Africa: Provincial Policy and State Power in the Eastern Cape, John Reynolds
Uganda: The Dynamics of Neoliberal Transformation, Jörg Wiegratz, Giuliano Martiniello, and Elisa Greco
AIDS in the Shadow of Biomedicine: Inside South Africa's Epidemic, Isak Niehaus
Negotiating Public Services in the Congo: State, Society and Governance, Tom De Herdt and Kristof Titeca
BRICS and Resistance in Africa: Contention, Assimilation and Co-optation, edited by Justin van der Merwe, Patrick Bond, and Nicole Dodd
Ironies of Solidarity: Insurance and Financialization of Kinship in South Africa, Erik Bähre
Africa's Shadow Rise: China and the Mirage of African Economic Development, Pádraig Carmody, Peter Kragelund, and Ricardo Reboredo

Forthcoming titles

Malawi: Economy, Society and Political Affairs, edited by Matthias Rompel and Reimer Gronemeyer
Entrepreneurs and SMEs in Rwanda Conspicuous by Their Absence, David Poole
Contesting Africa's New Green Revolution: Biotechnology and Philanthrocapitalist Development in Ghana, Jacqueline Ignatova
Youth on the Move: Views from Below on Ethiopian International Migration, Fana Gebresenbet and Asnake Kefale
Politics of Fear in South Sudan: Generating Chaos, Creating Conflict, Daniel Akech Thiong
Decolonizing Civil Society in Mozambique, Tanja Kleibl
War, Women and Post-Conflict Empowerment: Lessons from Sierra Leone, Josephine Beoku-Betts and Fredline M'Cormack-Hale
Angola's Securitized State: Reframing Hegemonic Power and National Identity, Paula Roque
Economic Diversification in Nigeria: Fractious Politics and an Economy Beyond Oil, Zainab Usman

Undoing Coups

The African Union and Post-coup
Intervention in Madagascar

Antonia Witt

ZED

LONDON • NEW YORK • OXFORD • NEW DELHI • SYDNEY

Zed Books
Bloomsbury Publishing Plc
50 Bedford Square, London, WC1B 3DP, UK
1385 Broadway, New York, NY 10018, USA
29 Earlsfort Terrace, Dublin 2, Ireland

BLOOMSBURY and Zed Books are trademarks of Bloomsbury Publishing Plc

First published in 2020
This paperback edition published in 2022

Copyright © Antonia Witt 2020

Antonia Witt has asserted her right under the Copyright,
Designs and Patents Act, 1988, to be identified as Author of this work.

For legal purposes the Acknowledgments on pp. xv-xvii constitute
an extension of this copyright page.

Series design by Burgess & Beech
Cover Image: Prison guards at Marofoto Prison, Mahajanga, Madagascar.
(© Robin Hammond/Panos Pictures)

All rights reserved. No part of this publication may be reproduced or
transmitted in any form or by any means, electronic or mechanical,
including photocopying, recording, or any information storage or retrieval
system, without prior permission in writing from the publishers.

Bloomsbury Publishing Plc does not have any control over, or responsibility for,
any third-party websites referred to or in this book. All internet addresses given
in this book were correct at the time of going to press. The author and publisher
regret any inconvenience caused if addresses have changed or sites have
ceased to exist, but can accept no responsibility for any such changes.

A catalogue record for this book is available from the British Library.

ISBN: HB: 978-1-7869-9683-1
PB: 978-1-3503-4994-0
ePDF: 978-1-7869-9686-2
ePub: 978-1-7869-9685-5

Series: Politics and Development in Contemporary Africa

To find out more about our authors and books visit
www.bloomsbury.com and sign up for our newsletters.

Contents

List of illustrations ix
List of abbreviations xi
Acknowledgements xv

    Introduction 1
1. Norms, intervention, and the making of orders 21
2. Crafting an African anti-coup manual 45
3. What 'crise malgache'? 72
4. The intervention scenario 99
5. The logic of intervention 142
6. Reproducing old, legitimating new orders 180
7. Politics and power of post-coup interventions 198

Notes 218
References 235
List of interviews 268
Index 273

Illustrations

Figure

4.1	The intervention scenario	113

Tables

2.1	Ideal-typical problematizations of infringements of legitimate order	68
7.1	Cases of post-coup interventions by the African Union (2004–2019)	207

Abbreviations

3FN	Three National Forces (*Trois forces nationales*)
ACHPR	African Commission on Human and Peoples' Rights
ACJHR	African Court of Justice and Human Rights
AfDB	African Development Bank
AGA	African Governance Architecture
APRM	African Peer Review Mechanism
APSA	African Peace and Security Architecture
AREMA	Association for the Rebirth of Madagascar (*Andry sy Rihana Enti-Manavotra an'i Madagasikara*)
AS	Other Sensibilities (*Autres sensibilités*)
AU	African Union
BIANCO	Independent Anti-Corruption Office (*Bureau indépendant anti-corruption*)
CAPSAT	Army corps for personnel and administrative and technical services (*Corps d'armée des personnels et des services administratifs et techniques*)
CCM	Malagasy Construction Company (*Compagnie de construction malagasy*)
CDE	Club for Development and Ethics (*Club développement et éthique*)
CENI-T	Independent National Electoral Commission for the Transition (*Commission électorale nationale indépendante pour la transition*)
CES	Special Electoral Court (*Cour électorale spéciale*)
CNOSC	National Coordination of Civil Society Organizations (*Coordination nationale des organisations de la société civile*)
COI	Indian Ocean Commission (*Commission de l'Océan Indien*)
COMESA	Common Market for Eastern and Southern Africa
CONECS	National and Economic Social Council (*Conseil national économique et social*)
COSC	Coalition of Civil Society Organizations (*Coalition des organisations de la société civile*)
CRN	Committee for National Reconciliation (*Comité pour la réconciliation nationale*)

ABBREVIATIONS

CSC	Roadmap Implementation Monitoring and Control Committee (*Comité de suivi et de contrôle de la mise en œuvre de la Feuille de route*)
ECOWAS	Economic Community of West African States
EISA	Electoral Institute for Sustainable Democracy in Africa
EITI	Extractive Industries Transparency Initiative
EKAR	Catholic Church of Madagascar (*Eglizy Katolika Apostolika Romana*)
ESCOPOL	Space for Consultation of Political Organizations and Parties (*Espace de concertation des organisations et partis politiques*)
EU	European Union
FEDMINES	Federation of Professional Mining Associations (*Fédération des associations professionelles de mines*)
FFKM	Malagasy Council of Christian Churches (*Fiombonan'ny Fiangonana Kristianina eto Madagasikara*)
FFM	Malagasy Reconciliation Council (*Filankevitry ny Fampihavanana Malagasy*)
FISEMA	General Confederation of Malagasy Workers' Unions (*Firaisana Sendikaly Malagasy*)
FJKM	Church of Jesus Christ (*Fiangonan'i Jesoa Kristy eto Madagasikara*)
FNOIM	National Federation of Malagasy Engineering Organizations (*Fédération nationale des organisations d'ingénieurs Malagasy*)
FNS	National Solidarity Fund (*Fonds national de solidarité*)
FPVM	New Protestant Church in Madagascar (*Fiangonana Protestanta Vaovao eto Madagasikara*)
FRELIMO	Mozambique Liberation Front (*Frente de Libertação de Moçambique*)
GIS-M	International Support Group for Madagascar (*Groupe international de soutien à Madagascar*)
HAT	High Authority of the Transition (*Haute autorité de la transition*)
HPM	Rally of Political Forces (*Hery Politika Mitambatra*)
ICG	international contact group
ICG-M	International Contact Group on Madagascar
IO	international organization
IR	International Relations
KMF/CNOE	National Election Observation Committee – Citizen Education (*Komitim-pirenena Manara-maso ny Fifidianana*)

ABBREVIATIONS

MAP	Madagascar Action Plan
MBS	Malagasy Broadcasting System
MDM	Movement for Democracy in Madagascar (*Mouvement pour la démocratie à Madagascar*)
MONIMA	Nationalist and Independent Movement of Madagascar (*Madagasikara otronin'ny Malagasy*)
NDI	National Democratic Institute
NEPAD	New Partnership for Africa's Development
NGO	non-governmental organization
OAS	Organization of American States
OAU	Organisation of African Unity
OIF	International Organisation of La Francophonie
PACEM	Support Project for the Electoral Cycle 2012–2014 in Madagascar (*Projet d'appui au cycle électoral 2012–2014 à Madagascar*)
PAP	Pan-African Parliament
PSC	Peace and Security Council
QMM	QIT Madagascar Minerals
R2P	responsibility to protect
REC	Regional Economic Community
RFI	Radio France Internationale
RFN	Rally of National Forces (*Rassemblement des forces nationales*)
SADC	Southern African Development Community
SeFaFi	Observatory of Public Life in Madagascar (*Sehatra Fanaraha-maso ny Fiainam-pirenena*)
SPDUN	Solidarity of Parliamentarians for the Defence of Democracy and National Unity (*Solidarité des parlementaires pour la défense de la démocratie et de l'unité nationale*)
SSR	Security Sector Reform
TGV	Young Malagasies Determined (*Tanora malaGasy Vonona*)
TIM	I Love Madagascar (*Tiako I Madagasikara*)
UDR-C	Union of Democrats and Republicans for Change (*Union des démocrates et républicains pour le changement*)
UN DPA	UN Department for Political Affairs
UNDP	UN Development Programme
UNECA	UN Economic Commission for Africa
WTO	World Trade Organization

Acknowledgements

This book is the outcome of a long journey. As most books probably are. It was an intellectual journey, a physical journey, a challenging, joyful, and enriching journey. But first of all, it was an accompanied journey, even if sometimes it felt like a lonely endeavour. It is to all those who visibly and sometimes invisibly accompanied me throughout this time that I am deeply indebted. My thanks go first of all to Ulf Engel and Klaus Dingwerth, my PhD supervisors, for having had trust that I would find my way through empirical and theoretical jungles and for having been safety nets in case I threatened to get lost. The result of this is the basis of this book.

This research would not have been possible without the strong support I received particularly during field research. I am very thankful to Sirak Tesfaye, Chedza Molefe, Kirubel Getachew, Milka Mkemwa, and the other staff members of the AU archives and library whose efforts for keeping the organization's records are admirable. I also thank my former colleagues from the EU Delegation to the African Union in Addis Ababa for being great teachers, informants, and friends. It was this time of diplomatic apprenticeship which convinced me that there exists a world of AU practices that is not yet reflected in academic writing. And it encouraged me to take the risk of trying to write it down.

I am deeply indebted to the team of the Friedrich-Ebert-Stiftung in Antananarivo for a sheer endless list of contacts, for inspiring discussions, and for letting me learn a lot about Malagasy political culture. My particular thanks go to Jean-Aimé Raveloson and Marcus Schneider, whose support during this time was invaluable. And I am grateful to Baovola and Narison Radanielina, Anne and Erich Raab, Toavina Ralambomahay, Tatiana Eddie Razafindravao, Friedrich, Giovanni, Bruno, Tops, Jan, the musicians of Mahaleo, and the people from Tany Malalaka for being very instructive company throughout my stay in Madagascar and beyond.

My greatest thanks, however, go to the many interviewees in Addis Ababa, Antananarivo, Pretoria, Johannesburg, Gaborone, Paris, and elsewhere who patiently shared their experiences, memories, opinions, personal diaries, letters, and newspaper collections with me. They may not be happy with everything I made of it. And not every detail of their stories may be covered sufficiently. But without their availability and openness, this book could not have been written.

The coming together of this book has also benefited from crucial academic support. The DFG-Emmy-Noether Junior Research Group 'Changing Norms of Global Governance' was a source of great inspiration and discovery that made me think differently about global order and international organizations. I am very thankful for (heated) discussions and great company to Klaus Dingwerth, Ina Lehmann, Ellen Reichel, and Tobias Weise. The German Research Foundation (DFG) also provided the financial means that made all of this possible in the first place. For critically engaging with parts of this book, for thought-provoking comments, critique, and suggestions, I am also grateful to my former colleagues from the Institute for Intercultural and International Studies at the University of Bremen, to my colleagues at the Cluster of Excellence 'The Formation of Normative Orders' at Goethe University Frankfurt/Main, and to Nicole Deitelhoff and Christopher Daase in particular. In 2014, I was lucky to spend two months as a guest researcher at the Department of International Relations at the University of the Witwatersrand, Johannesburg. I thank Malte Brosig for his great support during this time, as well as Gilbert Khadiagala, Anthoni van Nieuwkerk, Amy Niang, Mopeli Moshoeshoe, and Rod Alence for asking the right questions while I was slowly bringing order into a universe of observations and ideas from field research. Throughout the long journey, I presented several draft chapters and papers drawing on this research at academic conferences and workshops. I am particularly thankful to Linnéa Gelot, Christof Hartmann, Anna Holzscheiter, Simon Mason, Joel Migdal, Laurie Nathan, João Gomes Porto, and Klaus Schlichte for constructive feedback at different stages in time. While I revised this book manuscript, the Peace Research Institute Frankfurt (PRIF) became my new academic home. I am indebted to Sabine Mannitz and the entire institute for intellectually, financially, and administratively supporting the finalization of this book.

I want to express my gratitude to Anna Emil and Lilli Hasche for their support in transcribing interviews and to Maike Wäscher for invaluable help during the finalization of the manuscript. And I thank Felix Anderl, Kai Striebinger, and Micha Wiebusch, as well as the anonymous reviewers, for their wise thoughts and critical reading of previous versions of this book. Kim Walker and Melanie Scagliarini from Zed Books, as well as Megan Symons, have accompanied me very patiently and professionally through the different stages of the publication process. I thank them as much as I thank Felix Pahl for his remarkably thorough language editing, from which I learned a lot about the depths and facets of the English language. I finally thank my parents for letting me find my own path, even if it took me to faraway places, and for giving me the strength to pursue my own goals, even if they looked zany at first glance. And I thank Gabriel, who has been a constant encouragement and support in bringing this project to an end and not forgetting the other journeys life holds for us.

Introduction

Addis Ababa, 27 January 2014. The Peace and Security Council (PSC) of the African Union (AU) gathers for its 415th meeting. The Council expresses its 'appreciation to the Malagasy people, as well as to all political actors and institutions of the country, for the smooth and peaceful conduct of the elections and the completion of the transition process' (AU PSC 2014a: 1). These words marked the end of almost five years of international efforts to re-establish 'constitutional order' in Madagascar. The reason for such an intervention was a political crisis that culminated in the ouster of President Marc Ravalomanana in early 2009. This intervention involved numerous rounds of negotiations held in Antananarivo, Maputo, Addis Ababa, Pretoria, and the Seychelles, several negotiated agreements, the deployment of special envoys from more than five international and regional organizations, an international contact group, targeted economic sanctions, capacity-building for local mediators, and more than 800 international election observers to accompany transitional elections. At its end, the PSC registered that 'constitutional order' was successfully restored. All this took place in the context of the AU's anti-coup norm, which mandates the continental organization to condemn and 'undo' coups, called 'unconstitutional changes of government' in the AU's language.

Antananarivo, around the same time. A group of Malagasy activists gathers on a weekend in one of the crowded *quartiers* of Madagascar's capital. The group wants to collect signatures in support of the AU's Charter on Democracy, Elections and Governance so that the newly elected Malagasy president will finally sign and ratify it. In its preamble, the Charter is defined as an instrument to nurture, strengthen, and consolidate democracy on the African continent (AU 2007). It was adopted in 2007 in order to give the AU's anti-coup norm legal clout. Asked how the campaign is going, the activists respond with frustration:

> It is very tedious. Nobody wants to sign. The majority of the passers-by are very suspicious. They say that signing the Charter would mean that Malagasies will lose their right to stage a coup, to get rid of our government if we don't want it anymore.[1]

What for some was the successful re-establishment of constitutional order and the result of Malagasies' ownership for others felt like an external imposition that robbed Malagasy citizens of the opportunity to actually decide how and by whom they want to be governed, so they would rather avoid a similar experience in the future.

This book traces the rise and consequences of the AU's anti-coup norm based on an in-depth reconstruction of the post-coup intervention in Madagascar. By answering the question of what it actually means to return a country to constitutional order, I show that African interventions to 'undo' coups are an effective form of transnational order-making that reconfigure power relations in and beyond the state concerned. This is not only relevant for scholars interested in understanding the domestic effects of the norms and policies of regional organizations, and those of the AU specifically; it also holds valuable insights for International Relations (IR) scholars more generally who are interested in the changing fabric of the international, in particular the rising authority of international organizations and how this affects politics within states.

Togo (2005), Mauritania (2005 and 2008), Guinea (2008), Niger (2010), Mali (2012), Guinea-Bissau (2012), Egypt (2013), the Central African Republic (2013), Burkina Faso (2014), The Gambia (2016), and the Sudan (2019). Madagascar is not the only country that experienced what the AU calls unconstitutional changes of government. Since its establishment in 2004, the AU PSC has condemned unconstitutional changes of government in all these countries, followed by concerted international efforts to re-establish constitutional order. As in Madagascar, reactions to these instances usually included public condemnations, the suspension of the respective country from the AU, special envoys, international contact groups to coordinate the various reactions, negotiations over power-sharing agreements and inclusive governments, sanctions against putschists, national dialogues with civil society groups, and financial and technical support to organize transitional elections (see Engel 2012a; Witt 2012a; Vandeginste 2013; Nathan 2017). Apart from the AU, such efforts involved donor countries and other international and African subregional organizations, such as the Southern African Development Community (SADC) in the case of Madagascar. All these efforts are signs of the AU's proclaimed 'zero tolerance' against unconstitutional changes of government (AU Assembly 2010a). They underline that the anti-coup norm is not merely a declaration on paper; rather, it has given rise to a variety of intervention practices that – as this book demonstrates – come with tangible consequences.

However, in contrast to this political and practical relevance, scholarship has until today paid little attention to these developments. And in the few existing studies, scholars have tended to view the continental outlawing of coups as an example of regional norm diffusion or democracy promotion by regional organizations such as the AU (Tieku 2009;

Leininger 2014; Souaré 2014). This forms part of a more general and burgeoning research agenda on the role of regional organizations in promoting and diffusing norms and policies in their member states (see, for instance, Pevehouse 2005; Cooper & Legler 2006; Börzel & van Hüllen 2015). But so far, this scholarship has mainly been concerned with determining how consistently and effectively the AU has invoked its anti-coup norm – as seen from a top-down, institutionalist perspective. What has divided this nascent scholarship so far is the question of what effects these reactions have. 'Afro-optimists', on the one hand, see the regular application of the anti-coup norm as evidence for the AU's functioning as a regional norm entrepreneur and the AU as playing an ever-greater role in the successful promotion of democratic norms in its member states (Souaré 2014; Tieku 2016: 138). To 'Afro-pessimists', on the other hand, these developments are mere window dressing, designed mainly to appease international donors. As far as they are concerned, therefore, all the AU will do is reinforce existing regimes and help tighten incumbent elites' grip on power (Sturman 2008; Omorogbe 2011). At a more global level too, scholars see regional anti-coup norms either as an instrument for promoting democracy (Powell 2014: 223; Shannon et al. 2015) or as a measure to restore authoritarianism (Tansey 2017). Indeed, a brief look at those countries in which constitutional order has been restored under the AU's anti-coup policy appears to suggest that the promised land of more democracy is yet to come. Madagascar, as will be elaborated in this book, at first sight seems to confirm this impression – as also reflected in the above short scenery from the streets of Antananarivo.

However, this book challenges both accounts, those of Afro-optimists and those of Afro-pessimists, and proposes an innovative perspective for understanding how AU norms are implemented and what they do on the ground, beyond the binary of success and failure. Instead of starting with predefined assumptions on what efforts to re-establish constitutional order ought – but often fail – to do, I suggest an open investigation of what such efforts actually *do*. This also requires taking a different perspective on what they *are*. The book therefore offers a thorough empirical reconstruction of the actual processes and practices involved in returning a country to constitutional order, but also proposes a more general shift in the conceptual vantage point from which to do so. In the conclusion, I also integrate the insights generated from the case of Madagascar into a bigger picture of post-coup interventions in Africa, arguing that there is indeed evidence for viewing the effects of post-coup intervention in Madagascar as reflecting a much broader pattern of transnational order-making through the AU's anti-coup norm.

Return to what?

On 12 July 2000, African heads of state and government took a far-reaching decision. In Lomé, the 36th summit of the Organisation of African Unity (OAU), the AU's predecessor, ended with the observation that 'coups are sad and unacceptable developments in our Continent, coming at a time when our people have committed themselves to respect of the rule of law based on peoples [sic] will expressed through the ballot and not the bullet' (OAU 2000a: 1).

The OAU Assembly decided to reject 'any unconstitutional change as an unacceptable and anachronistic act, which is in contradiction of our commitment to promote democratic principles and conditions' (OAU 2000a: 1). It was decided that governments that come to power through unconstitutional means shall not be recognized and shall therefore be suspended from participating in the continental organization. The following situations were defined as unconstitutional changes of government:

> i) military coup d'etat against a democratically elected Government; ii) intervention by mercenaries to replace a democratically elected Government; iii) replacement of democratically elected Governments by armed dissident groups and rebel movements; iv) the refusal by an incumbent government to relinquish power to the winning party after free, fair and regular elections. (OAU 2000a: 3)

The definition of 'unconstitutional changes of government' thus explicitly referred only to acts committed against democratically elected governments. However, unlike their Latin American counterparts, African heads of state and government refrained from bindingly defining what 'democratic' means (Legler & Tieku 2010: 471). As a result, how to interpret this condition became a recurring topic in the ensuing debates about the adequacy and refinement of the African anti-coup norm, as Chapter 2 elaborates in more detail.

More crucially, however, the OAU Assembly also decided to mandate the organization to actively work for the respective country's return to constitutional order. It established that:

> [a] period of up to six months should be given to the perpetrators of the unconstitutional change to restore constitutional order. (...) The Secretary-General should, during this period gather facts relevant to the unconstitutional change of Government and establish appropriate contacts with the perpetrators with a view to ascertaining their

intentions regarding the restoration of constitutional order in the country; the Secretary-General should seek the contribution of African leaders and personalities in the form of discreet moral pressure on the perpetrators of the unconstitutional change in order to get them to cooperate with the OAU and facilitate the restoration of constitutional order in the Member State concerned. (OAU 2000a: 3)

In this so-called Lomé Declaration, African leaders thus defined governments coming to power by unconstitutional means as deviance from the orderly norm, a path that has to be corrected. As observed by Stef Vandeginste (2013: 23), the continental organization thereby moved from being a mere 'registrar' to playing the role of a 'judge', setting terms and limits for what counts as legitimate authority and 'good order' within its member states. However, the mandate to facilitate the return to constitutional order also meant that beyond being a mere judge, the continental organization and those acting on its behalf in fact became active parties in re-establishing constitutional order.

Since this decision, the African continent has seen an unprecedented reinvention of regional and subregional organizations and the development of policy instruments to promote peace and security, democratic governance, and human rights in African states. After the transformation of the OAU into the AU in 2002, the organization's mandate to address and prevent political crises in member states was gradually expanded and integrated into a more robust institutional framework, the so-called African Peace and Security Architecture (APSA). The AU was given an explicit mandate to promote democracy, protect human rights, and suspend any government that comes to power unconstitutionally (OAU 2000e: Art. 30). The PSC was set up and mandated to institute sanctions against perpetrators of coups (AU 2002: Art. 7(1g)). With the African Charter on Democracy, Elections and Governance of 2007, the anti-coup norm was even given a legally binding status (AU 2007: Art. 23). It was also decided to likewise outlaw constitutional manipulations, with the recognition that not only putschists, but also incumbents, can be a threat to the ideal of people's right to political self-determination, as once declared in Lomé.

As will be elaborated in Chapter 2, the Lomé Declaration was meant to provide the OAU/AU with a clear manual on how to handle disruptions to what was defined as 'normal' and to avoid arbitrariness both in access to power in the organization's member states and in international reactions thereto. It was an attempt to discipline both politics within the state and politics within the OAU/AU and the wider international community. In the imaginary of the Lomé Declaration, returning a country to constitutional order therefore follows a rather mechanistic and legalistic path: condemnation, facilitation, completion (see also Tieku 2009: 76).

However, contrary to the hopes at the time, neither more elaborate legal scripts nor continental institutions were able to eradicate the politics of defining what it means to restore constitutional order. The Lomé Declaration itself outlawed coups, but the above-quoted mandate to 'facilitate the restoration of constitutional order' (OAU 2000a: 4) left rather open what that entails. The anti-coup norm outlawed deviance from an assumed constitutional normalcy, yet without determining on what grounds, with whom, and for what purpose constitutionality is to be reinstated. Moreover, in this mandate, constitutional order should not only be 'restored', but should also prevent future crises. The Lomé Declaration therefore stipulated that 'the strengthening of democratic institutions will considerably reduce the risks of unconstitutional change on our Continent' (OAU 2000a: 2). The rationale of the Lomé Declaration thus entailed both a claim that the organization *should* and *can* 'undo' coups, as well as a promise that the new orders will be somewhat *better* than the preceding ones, that 'undoing' was not only temporal but sustainable.

What we know so far

Despite a growing academic interest in the AU, the African anti-coup norm and resulting efforts to re-establish constitutional order in African states have so far received little academic attention. Besides general overviews on African reactions to coups (Engel 2012a; Witt 2012a; Souaré 2014; Nathan 2017), there are only a few more detailed case studies, usually in the form of book chapters or policy briefs (Cawthra 2010; Yabi 2010; Asante-Darko 2012; Nathan 2013; Hartmann 2017). This relative indifference on the part of academia not only contradicts the political and practical importance attributed to the phenomenon; it also contrasts with how detailed other AU practices, military interventions in particular, have been studied so far (see, for instance, Söderbaum & Tavares 2011; Brosig 2015; de Coning et al. 2016). Overall, discussion of these engagements has been confined to area specialists or scholars interested in regionalism and regional organizations more specifically. Neither scholarship on international interventions nor that on IR more generally has adequately taken note of these developments. In general, interventions are still mainly considered as something Western states or global actors such as the UN do. Despite increasing efforts to decentre the study of interventions (see Schroeder 2018; Turner & Kühn 2019), the empirical relevance of non-Western, particularly African, interveners has so far not been adequately reflected in academic research. Moreover, a substantial part of the available literature on the AU's reactions to coups stems from decidedly policy-oriented research. In fact, there is – in sharp contrast, for instance, to the Americas – a clear dearth of theory-driven and theory-generating perspectives on regional reactions to coups in Africa.[2] Unsurprisingly, this lack of theory-informed empirical engagements with the AU's anti-coup norm also affects how these developments have been analysed and what we know so far. On the one hand, the dominant policy orientation favoured a perspective on post-coup engagements 'through the eyes' of the AU, which paints a rather top-down and often apolitical image of what these engagements are about. On the other hand, this also meant that the effects of African reactions to coups have mainly been studied and evaluated based on the terms provided by the interveners themselves. In order to situate this book within the existing literature, I will first summarize how the latter has so far conceived of and analysed the processes of returning a country to constitutional order (i.e. what post-coup interventions *are*) before I turn to a discussion of the answers the existing literature provides on the aims and effects of post-coup interventions (i.e. what they *do*).

What post-coup interventions are: policy, mediation, or what?

Existing works on the AU's post-coup interventions broadly conceive of these engagements in two ways: they analyse them either as diffusion and implementation of AU policies (Leininger 2014; Souaré 2014; Powell et al. 2016), or as AU-led mediation efforts, defined as impartial external assistance to parties in conflict (Engel 2012a; Nathan 2017; see generally Moore 2003: 15). Both perspectives, as will be elaborated over the course of this book, are inadequate lenses to grasp the processes and consequences of regional reactions to coups.

A key insight of several overviews on AU reactions to coups is that they follow dissonant paths and that the AU implements its norm inconsistently: what counts as a successful return to constitutional order is measured according to different standards. In some cases, for instance, putschists were allowed to stand in transitional elections, whereas others have been banned from doing so (Souaré 2009: 11; Engel 2012a: 80; Nathan 2017: 17–18). Also, some putschists were granted amnesty arrangements while others were not (Ndulo 2012: 267). Moreover, when and on what grounds countries have been readmitted to the AU has not been consistent (Nathan 2017: 14–15). In a similar vein, those analysing the AU's reactions to coups through a mediation lens show, for instance, that the means invoked, such as sanctions or the convocation of an international contact group, differed from case to case (Engel 2012a: 73).

Also, several works stress conflicts between mediators and the sending organization, the AU or the respective subregional organization, as well as rivalries between competing mediators and sending organizations (Witt 2013b; Nathan 2017: 17–18). Thus, contrary to the mechanistic manual, how constitutional orders have been re-established so far was not mechanistic and rule-governed at all (Witt 2012a).

These accounts of inconsistencies all point to the politics and complexities involved in efforts to undo coups. However, the dominant analytical perspective in this literature still looks at such efforts mainly as something the AU *does* (be it as policy implementation or mediation). This means that post-coup interventions tend to be narrated in the organization's own terms, often based on publicly available documents. By way of consequence, apparent inconsistencies are considered as failures in the successful implementation of the script of the Lomé Declaration, a fact requiring correction.

In such a top-down perspective, the processes and consequences of these engagements that unfold 'on the ground' remain more or less invisible. What is missing is an understanding of the local dynamics, the struggles and contestations, triggered by the AU's invocation of its anti-coup norm and the demand to re-establish constitutional order in a given country. If at all, these dynamics have so far been registered as a hindrance to successful norm implementation and as acts of spoilers (cf. Sampson 2012: 239). Moreover, while some of the above contributions are based on interview research, this rarely extends to the negotiating parties or other constituencies in the respective countries (exceptions are Cawthra 2010; Kotzé 2013a). As a consequence, the perspectives of those affected by the efforts to undo coups have been widely neglected. There is therefore fairly little understanding of both the local dynamics of post-coup interventions and the societal, political, and economic figurations that led to what then became labelled as an 'unconstitutional change of government' in the first place. Moreover, a top-down perspective also conceals how the various organizations, including the AU, actually act 'on the ground', which more often than not diverges from the self-descriptions in official documents. Making these processes and dynamics on the ground visible requires more empirical depth, but also another analytical lens for what efforts to re-establish constitutional order actually are.

What post-coup interventions do: democracy versus regime security – change versus status quo

The adoption of the African anti-coup norm has been widely hailed as a positive development and as a break with the continent's past of shielding autocratic rule. As in other cases of norm change on the African continent, these developments are often interpreted and assessed in light of preceding experiences, in this case the OAU's deplorable history of recognizing whoever was able to control the capitals of African states (Omorogbe 2011). Against this background, the African anti-coup norm has been predominantly discussed as an instrument to promote and defend democracy on the continent (Tieku 2009; Leininger 2014; Souaré 2014) and as a measure to prevent conflicts and build peace (Dersso 2017). For Issaka Souaré (2014), the decision to ban unconstitutional changes of government underlines the AU's role as a continental norm entrepreneur, evidenced by a decreasing number of coups since the turn of the millennium (see also Powell et al. 2016). Others stress that the anti-coup norm even grants the AU the power to sanction member states that deviate from established political norms (Sturman 2008; Eriksson 2010). The various forms in which the AU became engaged in re-establishing constitutional order are subsequently referred to as 'pro-democratic interventions' (Levitt 2008; Edozie & Gottschalk 2014: 117). In large part, this reflects the liberal-constructivist perspective that dominated the debate on the AU's so-called shift from a culture of non-interference to one of non-indifference, as well as the generally positive expectations of the AU's capacity to affect politics in Africa that underpinned this perspective (Williams 2007; see also Witt 2013a).

Yet there has also been a more sceptical reading of these developments. Some authors challenge the uncritical pro-democratic lens through which this normative innovation was interpreted. They employ a more cautious language which points to the multiple and conflicting meanings that merged in the AU's decision to ban unconstitutional changes of government. Kathryn Sturman (2008: 100), for instance, remarks that it was in fact Robert Mugabe who was one of the most fervent supporters of the anti-coup provision. Considering Mugabe's track record in democratic governance, she concludes that in its current form, the anti-coup norm may 'have more to do with entrenching the status quo for many AU member states than it has with fostering democracy' (Sturman 2008: 105). In a similar vein, others note that while the Lomé Declaration rejected the unconstitutional *acquisition* of power, there was no intention to sanction or even assess the *conduct* of governance by incumbent governments (Souaré 2009: 11; Dersso 2017: 658). In fact, leaving out such a provision had been a conscious decision of the OAU Assembly (Ikome 2007: 33; see also Chapter 2). Even after the African Charter on Democracy, Elections and Governance, adopted in 2007, corrected some of these shortcomings, some analysts remain cautious vis-à-vis the actual commitment of member states to the ideals of democracy and good governance (Kotzé 2013b: 4; Engel 2019).

In a nutshell: while some champion the AU's decision to ban unconstitutional changes of government as an expression of a liberal normative shift and a commitment to the defence of democratic governance on the continent, others remain sceptical as to how this promise shall be realized under the given political realities. The highly ambiguous democratic record of AU member states as well as the norm's indecisiveness between being an instrument to defend regime security and serving to protect people's right to democratic self-determination gave reason for a more sceptical view vis-à-vis the potentials of the AU's official promises.

By reconstructing almost five years of re-establishing constitutional order in Madagascar, this book seeks to provide a more nuanced answer to this debate: I show that post-coup interventions are indeed an effective way of reconfiguring power relations, but neither necessarily lay the foundations for more democracy nor merely work in the service of incumbent governments and regime security.

Introducing the case

For the AU PSC, the political crisis in Madagascar became the fourth situation that the Council treated as an unconstitutional change of government. It turned out to become the longest-lasting effort to re-establish constitutional order in an African country until today. However, what suddenly appeared on the PSC's agenda in 2009 did not happen without warning signs.

Since the beginning of 2009, a broad popular protest movement had formed against the incumbent regime of President Marc Ravalomanana, holding regular demonstrations in Madagascar's capital Antananarivo. The protests were led by the mayor of Antananarivo, Andry Rajoelina, and supported by parts of the Malagasy military. Several attempts by the Malagasy churches to mediate between the protesters and the incumbent government, later supported by international and African diplomats, ended without result. On 17 March 2009, Marc Ravalomanana bowed to the public and intra-elite pressure, handed over power to a military directorate, and fled into exile to South Africa. The military directorate, in turn, installed Andry Rajoelina as President of the Transition. The AU, SADC, and most of Madagascar's international donors condemned this act as an unconstitutional change of government and demanded the rapid restoration of constitutional order (AU PSC 2009b; SADC 2009b). They decided to suspend Madagascar's membership and cut development funds. In the following weeks, several mediators and special envoys were sent to Antananarivo in order to engage Rajoelina and his High Authority of the Transition (*Haute autorité de la transition*, HAT) to relinquish power and organize elections. Despite varying international interpretations of what constituted 'la crise malgache' and how to end it, a consensus soon emerged around the demand for a 'consensual and inclusive transitional period' and an 'inclusive, transparent and credible dialogue' (AU PSC 2010b: 1; SADC 2010a: 3). It was decided that this 'dialogue' to effectuate the re-establishment of constitutional order should be held among the so-called *quatre mouvances* – the four movements – referring to the groupings around Rajoelina, Ravalomanana, and the two former presidents, Didier Ratsiraka and Albert Zafy. Several rounds of negotiations in Antananarivo, however, ended without result. In additional negotiations in Maputo and Addis Ababa in August and November 2009, respectively, under the auspices of SADC mediator Joaquim Chissano, the parties decided on a power-sharing agreement. But fundamental questions about the division of posts and the role of the two protagonists remained unsettled. In late 2009, Rajoelina therefore declared the negotiations suspended. In March 2010, the AU PSC applied targeted sanctions against 109 members of the HAT government and demanded implementation of the agreements mentioned above (AU PSC 2010a). Yet the sanctions did not have the expected effect. In September 2011, the so-called SADC Roadmap for Ending the Crisis (SADC 2011a) was signed by eight political parties and two of the former mouvances, paving the way for an 'inclusive' transition. It was also decided that neither Rajoelina nor Ravalomanana would run for office in transitional elections. After a tumultuous transition, presidential and legislative elections were held in December 2013 and were won by Hery Rajaonarimampianina, who had run as Rajoelina's replacement. Following the inauguration of the newly elected president, the AU PSC in January 2014 officially declared that constitutional order had been successfully restored (AU PSC 2014a).

This book follows an inductive and exploratory approach. The selection of Madagascar as case study was therefore driven less by theoretical than by research-pragmatic criteria (Schwartz-Shea & Yanow 2012: 70). Nevertheless, this choice crucially influenced what kind of insights this book presents, and thus it requires transparency and reflection. Chapter 7 will discuss in more detail to what extent the case can be regarded at the same time as unique and as part of a larger pattern of post-coup interventions. There were three reasons that made studying the case of Madagascar particularly advantageous when I started researching for this book in 2011. First, the fairly long duration of re-establishing constitutional order in Madagascar and the high number of international, regional, and national actors involved in this process meant that there was an abundance of empirical material to be gathered in textual form but also in the form of direct accounts of the protagonists involved. This made the case particularly suitable for single-case research. Madagascar is also one of the few cases that was dealt with twice under the AU's anti-coup policy (in 2001/2002 and 2009), allowing for a historical comparison but also for reflection on how preceding experiences shape both interveners' practices and perceptions and trust on the part of local parties, as I explain in Chapter 4 in more detail. Second, unlike some other countries that have experienced African regional post-coup interventions, in Madagascar there was neither a situation of violent conflict (as in Mali or the Central African Republic) nor was the country affected by the Ebola crisis (as Guinea later was). In short, not only the abundance, but also the accessibility, of empirical material was crucial. Third, and most importantly, the choice of Madagascar allowed for studying post-coup interventions synchronically (i.e. while the intervention happened). Concretely, this meant, for instance, that my field research in Madagascar (see further below) coincided with the official re-establishment of constitutional order, which made it possible to gather conclusive narratives about the parties' experiences with and assessments of the almost five years of re-establishing constitutional order in the country. It also allowed me to participate in events such as press conferences of international election observers and the first meeting of the international contact group on Madagascar after the official return to constitutional order. These were events of collective interpretation and assessment of what had happened since March 2009, which also allowed for observing and encountering interveners on the ground. So, apart from availability and access, the expected quality and comprehensiveness of the empirical material also played a crucial role for choosing the case of Madagascar.

The argument in brief

This book offers an empirically rich and methodologically rigorous analysis of the effects of the African anti-coup norm, based on a reconstruction of the processes, protagonists, and rationalities that played a part in re-establishing constitutional order in Madagascar (2009–2014). The book demonstrates that the post-coup intervention was a consequential moment of reordering both within the Malagasy polity and beyond. In Madagascar, what the intervention essentially served to do was to restore the ideal of a liberal polity, even though realities on the ground proved the opposite. Although it did not necessarily succeed in establishing a more democratic order, the intervention did (re)configure power relations. It did so by narrowing the re-establishment of constitutional order down to a technical transition based on default international peacebuilding cures such as power-sharing and elections. This approach was undoubtedly effective in depoliticizing the search for solutions and gradually excluding all actors and voices who believed more profound change was needed if 'la crise malgache', as it came to be known internationally, was to be resolved. At the same time, however, the intervention opened up opportunities for sections of the Malagasy elite to use the international demand for an 'inclusive' and 'consensual' solution in order to regain access to state institutions. By upholding the myth of the liberal polity, the intervention thus both re-legitimated old and established new power relations – belying both Afro-optimist and Afro-pessimist expectations. The reason for this lies in a merger between international norms on sovereignty and on popular legitimacy that underpin internationalized efforts to undo coups and by consequence heavily shape the realm of possible action for all those involved in this process.

Even more revolutionary were the order-constituting effects that the intervention had beyond Madagascar. Although the international interveners were in favour of the narrow, depoliticized, technical interpretation of transition, they also began to plan development programmes to tackle hitherto unaddressed 'problems' once constitutional order was restored. Many of the international and regional organizations involved in 'assisting' Madagascar's return to constitutional order used this experience as an opportunity to experiment with new norms and practices, and thus to gradually extend their spheres of responsibility – a development of relevance well beyond the actual locus and time of the intervention. Crucially, the post-coup intervention in Madagascar thus also contributed to the creation and expansion of regional and international orders as it expanded the reach and changed the fabric of the international.

All this, the book shows, is not what the AU does. Also, it is neither mediation nor mere policy implementation. Rather, I use the conceptual lens of 'transboundary formations' (Latham et al. 2001: 5) in order to show that the re-establishment of constitutional order is in fact the result of a complex and contested interaction between a variety of international, regional, and national forces that all seek to define what re-establishing constitutional order ultimately entails. The AU and other internationals are neither merely assisting, nor are they bystanders to this process; they are active parties in negotiating and setting the terms for how constitutional order is restored. However, this transnational interaction would not have been possible if AU heads of state had not decided in Lomé that coups should be outlawed and constitutional order preserved. The various reconfigurations of power relations through almost five years of post-coup intervention in Madagascar are thus proof of the tangible effects of an AU norm and the emergence of an African international that affects politics and order in AU member states.

In developing this argument, my aims with this book are threefold. First, to the literature on AU and other regional organizations' anti-coup policies I seek to contribute an in-depth case study on efforts to undo coups that adds a more nuanced account of the consequences of such policies. The particular perspective developed here pays attention to the politics and interactions of these engagements, which have hitherto remained largely ignored. This requires going beyond the 'view from Addis' and giving voice to those participating in and affected by these efforts. Focusing on different national and local actors, the book analyses the latter's interactions with, and resistance to, the AU-led efforts to re-establish constitutional order. In so doing, the book garners firsthand empirical insights about how these efforts take place that often tell a different story from the one recounted in official policy documents.

Second, I integrate current developments on the African continent into theoretical debates, drawing on IR, African studies, and peace and conflict research literatures. I thereby seek to overcome the largely atheoretical way the AU and its practices and consequences have been treated so far (Edozie & Gottschalk 2014: xxix). On the one hand, drawing on these debates allows developing a different perspective on what the AU's anti-coup norm and the resulting practices are – in short, *theorizing* them differently. On the other hand, I seek to show that current developments on the African continent do indeed bear insights that should be of relevance for a much broader audience than they currently seem to be, including for mainstream IR (see also Death 2013: 786). This links up with Amitav Acharya's (2014) call for a global IR in which so far ignored non-Western experiences should serve to theorize a 'multiplex world'.

Third, I seek to provide a reading of the consequences of post-coup interventions beyond the dominant binaries of failure/success or democracy promotion/regime protection. This will also offer another vantage point to articulate critique that is based neither on ideal policy statements nor on the analyst's own implicit assumptions of what a 'good order' should look like. Rather, a critical interrogation of post-coup interventions, such as the one I demonstrate in this book, allows the consequences of AU norms and practices to be assessed not on the grounds of *what they fail to do*, but on the basis of what the intervention

INTRODUCTION

has *actually done* according to the narratives and experiences of those affected by it.

Methods and data

In order to develop a different account of what African post-coup interventions are and what they do, this book was based on a great variety of sources gathered in the course of multi-sited fieldwork between 2011 and 2014 in Madagascar, South Africa, at the SADC headquarters in Gaborone, Botswana, and at the AU headquarters in Addis Ababa, Ethiopia (see generally Marcus 1995; Shore & Wright 1997: 15). This research strategy was underpinned by the principle of exposure – that is, the pool of empirical material evolved as part of the research and was assembled according to a logic favouring contradiction rather than convergence (Schwartz-Shea & Yanow 2012: 84). This followed the rationale that it is only through surprise and the 'fine grain of empirical detail' that new stories, including new theorizing, arise (Lobo-Guerrero 2013; Neal 2013: 43–44).

The empirical material consists of over 90 semi-structured interviews conducted (in French and English) with: international diplomats; officials from international and regional organizations; members of the mediators' teams; Malagasy parties to the negotiations; representatives of Malagasy political parties, churches, civil society organizations, and the security forces; and Malagasy academics and journalists (Kvale 2011; Fujii 2018; see list of interviews in the annex). Where possible, the interviews were recorded and transcribed afterwards. In all cases, interviews were followed by thorough note-taking on the content, course, and context of the interview, which then also formed an important part of the data analysed. As the content of the interviews touched politically sensitive issues, all interviewees were guaranteed anonymity, so that when quoting from interviews, I use broad descriptions instead of the interviewees' real names. Particularly during field research in Madagascar, accessing interviewees was fairly easy, and apart from one case interviewees were surprisingly open and willing to share their accounts of what happened in Madagascar in the aftermath of March 2009. The timing of most interviews – early 2014 – coincided with the official re-establishment of constitutional order, which was an opportune moment for many people involved and affected to reflect on how and to what extent 'la crise malgache' was resolved. As I elaborate in Chapter 6, this moment also brought up many of the contradictions that had shaped the process of re-establishing constitutional order in

Madagascar, which once again underlined to what extent this process had been infused with politics. I therefore felt a certain eagerness on the part of many of my interviewees to share their experiences and evaluations of the processes concerned, often paired with a certain curiosity and appreciation that such knowledge now enters academic research and writing. While this situation translated into a great wealth of data, it also challenged me to constantly communicate and explain my position as a neutral researcher who tries to *understand* all sides but does not explicitly *take* sides with any of those involved in re-establishing constitutional order in Madagascar (see also Ansoms 2013).

The information culled from these interviews was complemented by data from primary documents such as letters, minutes of meetings, strategy papers, and internal reports – notably from the Malagasy parties to the negotiations and the international mediators. All these primary sources were augmented by and checked against media articles from three French-language Malagasy newspapers (*Midi Madagasikara*, *L'Express de Madagascar*, and *Madagascar Tribune*). In addition, this study also draws on primary documents on the historical evolution and institutionalization of the African anti-coup norm gathered at the OAU/AU archives in Addis Ababa.

Apart from bringing unique empirical material to the debate, the book thus demonstrates that research into the impact of AU norms and policies without solely relying on official documents and narratives is both feasible and instructive. However, the effort to base this book on a set of sources as diverse and comprehensive as possible does not eliminate a certain degree of selectivity. In fact, moving beyond a narrative of post-coup interventions merely based on official policy documents also requires acknowledging and indeed appreciating the specific circumstances and sense-making practices that shaped how this particular narrative came into being (Schwartz-Shea & Yanow 2012: 2). First, despite thorough planning and conscious strategies for how to select and contact interviewees, encounters during field research still also follow their own rules: who has how much time, who knows whom, who is willing to share personal diaries, and so on usually lies far beyond what is plannable and steerable, and yet this can have a profound effect on whose and what kind of stories become heard (Fujii 2018: Chapter 3). For instance, the great number of internal memoirs and letters between the mediators and the Malagasy negotiating parties that I received from interviewees opened entirely new perspectives to me on the processes that happened at and beyond the negotiating table; they also added a depth to my analysis that interviews as such would not have permitted. For me, to receive these documents was pure luck, and for this book it was crucial. However, it also meant that my knowledge about, for instance, the four mouvances – the main Malagasy parties negotiating the return to constitutional order – was not equal for each mouvance, since not all of them produced internal memoires or shared them with me.

Second, positionality obviously matters (Kvale 2011: 14; Fujii 2018: Chapter 2). As a white female researcher, my own background shaped the relationship to my interviewees and affected to whom I was able to talk and how. Language skills, for instance, played a crucial role both enabling and constraining what kinds of stories ended up in this book. On the one hand, many of my Malagasy interlocutors immediately noted that French was not my native language. In several instances, this encouraged interviewees to spontaneously express solidarity, stressing that we share a certain fate of having to operate with a (colonial) language that isn't really ours (see generally Jackson 2013: 126). In some instances, this was also accompanied by very explicit statements of relief that I was not of French nationality, but from a country whose relationship to Madagascar is usually seen as positive and as serving the interests of the island. This gave the interview situation a sense of trust that shaped interviewees' willingness to tell their account of what happened in Madagascar post-March 2009. However, it also reflects how present global power hierarchies are in a postcolonial setting such as Madagascar and to what extent they infuse the everyday possibilities of doing field research. On the other hand, my lack of Malagasy language skills also constrained the pool of interviewees, newspaper articles, and online discussions whose narratives finally entered this book, which would certainly have been different if such voices could have been considered. In this sense, there surely remains a certain elite bias in the accounts provided. However, since I started this research by following (and interviewing) those involved in re-establishing constitutional order in Madagascar, the analytical elite bias also bears an important insight: it only echoes the actual elite bias of these efforts in the first place.

Third, the final narrative presented in this book stems as much from the various sources consulted as it is of my own making. The explicitly iterative approach with which I analysed the data required a constant navigation between the puzzles currently debated in existing academic literature and the story that stems from the material itself (see Schwartz-Shea & Yanow 2012: 27). The ensuing chapters therefore necessarily deviate from my interviewees' own stories, as they bridge and translate these stories into an academic discourse that has its own meanings, rules, and priorities. The result is hence *a*, not *the*, story of post-coup intervention in Madagascar. Yet it is a story that is based on a comprehensive set of consciously selected and diverse sources, triangulated and critically checked against existing accounts. So, this is not a plea for arbitrariness; quite the opposite. It is rather meant as an instruction to read the following chapters as an account that is as much assembled and subjective as it is reliable and comprehensive.

Outline of the book

This book is divided into seven chapters. Combining literature from IR, African studies, and peace and conflict research, Chapter 1 discusses how to think of the links between international standards of legitimate authority and the constitution of orders. From this, it develops two 'conceptual resources' (Howarth 2009: 311) for this book. First, inspired by the works of Michel Foucault (1982; 2004) and related contributions to IR, the chapter elaborates a perspective in which international organizations (IOs) such as the AU are conceived of as sites where principles defining what counts as legitimate order within states are formulated and institutionalized. This allows one to plot the emergence of particular knowledge regimes that determine what counts as legitimate order, and to see how these change over time, how they become institutionalized, and how they are enacted in specific IO practices such as mediation or election monitoring. This permits seeing the AU's anti-coup norm as part of a much broader phenomenon and contributing to its theorization. The second conceptual resource developed in this chapter allows interventions to be construed as concrete instances of the enactment of the knowledge regimes in question. However, in line with critical peacebuilding and intervention research, interventions are conceptualized not as top-down enactments of a 'pre-written script', but as a 'transboundary formation' (Latham et al. 2001: 5), a transnational interactive space in which a variety of actors vie with one another to determine the 'rules of the game' – and thus also the outcome of the intervention. While itself drawing on key IR and peace and conflict literature, the chapter points out that both areas of study have largely ignored developments on the African continent, particularly those at regional level – an issue taken up again in the concluding chapter.

Chapter 2 reconstructs the contested making of the African anti-coup norm, from the preparatory work on the Lomé Declaration of 2000 to the negotiation of the African Charter on Democracy, Elections and Governance, and beyond. By reconstructing developments over more than two decades, the chapter shows that the continental outlawing of coups was an incremental though contested expansion of the scope of ideas that define 'good' political order and their legalization (i.e. enshrinement in continental law). Moreover, the chapter also demonstrates that the idea to outlaw coups was intimately tied to a process of authorization (i.e. attributing a particular responsibility to the AU).

INTRODUCTION

Over time, I argue, this process in fact subverted a deeper engagement with the more general dilemmas and contradictions involved in the idea to prescribe and defend standards of legitimate authority through a continental organization.

Chapter 3 provides context for the events of March 2009, which led to the ouster of Madagascar's President Ravalomanana. For this purpose, the chapter reconstructs the multiplicity of conflicts as experienced and expressed by various Malagasy social and political actors from both rural and urban settings, and shows that 'la crise malgache' was in fact a multifaceted and deep-rooted phenomenon occurring at a time when the legitimacy of the order then in place was very much in question. The chapter also acts as a foil against which the limitations of the international solutions ultimately proposed, and the parties and issues they excluded, are made visible.

Working on the assumption that interventions are a transnational space in which international, regional, national, and local actors come together to negotiate an outcome, Chapter 4 provides a detailed analysis of the protagonists of the post-coup intervention in Madagascar. On the one hand, the chapter scrutinizes the aims and strategies of key Malagasy players invited to take part in the re-establishment of constitutional order and shows how they came about as a result of the intervention. On the other hand, the chapter explores the various international and regional bodies that became involved in supporting Madagascar's return to constitutional order. It analyses their mandates and interests, as well as how they organized their respective involvement in re-establishing constitutional order in Madagascar. A closer look is also taken at the individuals dispatched as mediators or special envoys to Madagascar. The chapter shows that at various levels, the intervention, rather than resolving conflict, in fact itself created conflicts, which meant that resolution became more elusive. Apart from conflicts among the various international actors – which other studies on the case of Madagascar have already stressed – the chapter specifically identifies conflicts between the Malagasy negotiating parties, on the one hand, and the various international actors, on the other, and shows the crucial (physical, institutional, and ideational) disconnect of the latter from what happened on the ground.

Chapter 5 reconstructs the logic underpinning the re-establishment of constitutional order in Madagascar, which ultimately shaped how and what kind of order was to emerge from almost five years of post-coup intervention. It does so in relation to: (1) the objects of intervention (i.e. the problems and issues considered relevant to resolve 'la crise malgache'); and (2) the subjects of intervention (i.e. those actors given a particular role for resolving the crisis). The chapter's detailed reconstruction of the logic of intervention sheds light on a gradual depoliticization of what it meant to re-establish constitutional order and resolve the crisis, ending in a technical transition driven by the president whose sole purpose was the holding of transitional elections. Although many more Malagasy political actors became included in this transition than initially planned, inclusion was based on rather arbitrary terms. Moreover, the chapter also demonstrates that this depoliticized solution was not a coincidence, but that it was sustained by a particular mode in which the various international actors approached the situation on the ground.

Following on from the analysis of the logic of intervention, Chapter 6 looks at the order-constituting effects of almost five years of post-coup intervention in Madagascar. It does so by tracing how the intervention reconfigured power relations both in and beyond Madagascar. With regard to the first, the chapter shows how the five years spent in re-establishing constitutional order served primarily to re-legitimate old power relations and the ideal of a liberal polity – however much at odds the latter was with the realities on the ground. Yet at the same time, the re-establishment of constitutional order also deepened the spaces for international intervention: problems identified but not addressed during the post-coup intervention were translated into development programmes and thus became the subject of new international aid and capacity-building projects. More revolutionary, however, were the changes that took place internationally. Citing the examples of, inter alia, the AU, SADC, and the Indian Ocean Commission (*Commission de l'Océan Indien*, COI), the chapter shows that the process of re-establishing constitutional order in Madagascar offered these organizations an opportunity to explore and institutionalize new norms and practices, which in many regards expanded their hitherto limited radius of responsibility and action. The chapter thus demonstrates that post-coup interventions are consequential and have order-constituting effects, in that they (re)produce power relations and (re-)establish order both within and beyond the actual site of intervention.

The concluding chapter summarizes the book's main argument. It integrates the findings on post-coup intervention in Madagascar into a discussion of other cases of post-coup intervention in Africa. From this, a pattern emerges in the logic and approaches employed by African regional interveners to address (very different) post-coup situations. On this basis, the chapter argues that it is reasonable to assume similar ordering effects in other affected countries, caused by the AU's anti-coup norm and its enactment in practice. The chapter discusses the implications of the book's findings for the study of the AU and other regional organizations, as well as for IR and its agenda to take non-Western worlds more seriously.

1
Norms, intervention, and the making of orders

Research always implies a perspective. This chapter introduces the theoretical vantage point from which this book analyses the evolution of the idea and the practices of re-establishing constitutional order in African states. The chapter situates these engagements, what they are and what they do, within broader theoretical debates in IR, African studies, and peace and conflict research. The aim of this chapter is hence twofold. First, it introduces the 'conceptual resources' (Howarth 2009: 311) that underpin this book: (1) to think of IOs as sites for the definition and dissemination of knowledge regimes that define 'good order'; and (2) to conceive of interventions as moments of actualization of such knowledge regimes that open up a transnational space of interaction in which orders are renegotiated and reconfigured. Second, the chapter links current developments on the African continent to broader theoretical debates. It thereby aims at overcoming the largely atheoretical approaches that have hitherto dominated the literature on the AU (Edozie & Gottschalk 2014: xxxv) and seeks to interpret the AU and its anti-coup policy as part of more general phenomena that are more broadly of interest to IR scholarship. In doing so, the chapter connects both to recent calls in IR for a more global study of international politics and to demands for a more theory-inspired engagement with politics in Africa as advanced in African studies.

As demanded by Amitav Acharya (2014), in order to truly become a discipline of *global* international studies, IR needs to engage more thoroughly with empirical and theoretical pluralism – 'multiplexity', in Acharya's own terms. He argued that 'regional worlds', while in themselves highly diverse, may serve as a starting point in this endeavour. But according to Acharya, such a focus on regions should clearly transcend the hitherto established division of labour between the regional, often non-Western 'periphery' and the discipline's 'core', where the former contributes the material while the latter provides the theory (Acharya 2014: 648; see also Comaroff & Comaroff 2011).[1] He therefore pleads for a different approach to theorizing, aiming 'to develop concepts and approaches from non-Western contexts on their own terms, and apply them not only locally, but also to other contexts, including the later global canvas' (Acharya 2014: 650). 'Regional worlds', Acharya demands, should thus become objects for theorizing and concept development, rather than sites of allegedly atheoretical empiricism or experience-distant theory-testing.[2]

A lack of interest in theorizing experiences in and of the non-Western world has also been problematized from the other side. Rita Abrahamsen (2003), for instance, criticized African studies' indifference towards their own theoretical and thus also political underpinnings (see also Bryceson 2012; Death 2015; Abrahamsen 2016: 129). She argues that theory, and in particular critical and postcolonial perspectives, are too often dismissed for their alleged practical irrelevance and their failure to generate tangible, policy-relevant knowledge. Theory here seems to be contrary to the practical demands that, for some, ought to drive academic engagements with the continent. In this view, poverty and injustice require practical, not theoretical, knowledge; theory and lived reality are two separate worlds. The dominant reading of the AU's reactions to unconstitutional changes of government, as outlined in the introduction to this book, is reminiscent of this binary between knowledge that is allegedly relevant to policy and life, on the one hand, and theory, on the other.

This chapter seeks to overcome this binary and to stress that, as argued by Abrahamsen (2003: 190), it is exactly the endurance of poverty and injustice that requires a more thorough engagement with the links between power, discourse, political institutions, and dominant political practices (Gabay & Death 2014: 15). In this sense, policy is itself an inherently political enterprise whose impacts on the world need to be analysed in terms other than those policy employs to describe itself (Bacchi 2009: 7; Stepputat & Larsen 2015). The role of theorizing and the purpose of repositioning conceptual lenses is thus to allow for a different perspective on the assumptions underpinning and consequences emanating from currently dominant answers to very practical challenges – such as coups. Theorizing in this sense is not antithetical to, but part of a concern for, (political) practice in that it may serve to provide the terms for a redescription of existing forms of government, understood as a particular mode of regulating and governing problems (Foucault 1994). In James Tully's (2002: 534) words, such a redescription of existing forms of government may serve to transform 'the self-understanding of those subject to and struggling within it, enabling them to see its contingent conditions and the possibilities of governing themselves differently'. This is the explicitly critical approach this research is based upon. Its practical consequences will be taken up again in Chapter 7.

What, then, is the function of theory? It seeks to establish 'an alternative set of relationships between dimensions of international social life' (Reus-Smit 2004: 14) that are deemed relevant to seeing a given phenomenon in different lights. In this sense, the role of 'conceptual resources' (Howarth 2009: 311) is to guide our gaze towards particular aspects of an empirical phenomenon – here, processes of transnational order-making – and to render them visible and intelligible. The notion of 'conceptual resources' underlines that the theoretical vocabulary developed here is used in a constructive way. The rationale of this chapter is hence to explicate a certain *perspective* – a vantage point – whose merit should be judged by the community of readers in terms of its coherence and its contributions to seeing a particular social phenomenon at all, or differently than before.

The remainder of this chapter proceeds in three steps. It first integrates the idea and practices of outlawing coups into a body of literature that interrogates the links between international standards of legitimate authority and the constitution of orders. This has been a concern for IR and African studies alike. But the two disciplines addressed this question from rather different angles: while IR scholarship has mainly been concerned with the historical constitution of *international* order and changing membership criteria for 'international society', scholars in African studies mainly focused on the consequences of international state recognition for *domestic* order. This book seeks to integrate these two perspectives by scrutinizing the simultaneous making of orders in and beyond the state. To this end, the chapter second turns to recent IR scholarship on the role of IOs as sites for the definition and licensing of principles of legitimate authority and corresponding practices of intervention. Such a perspective raises the important question of how this affects the relationships between states, societies, the individual, and the international. Contemporary African experiences may contribute valuable insights to this debate. Third, the chapter proposes a heuristic for analysing reactions to coups not as policies or mediation, but as sites of transnational interaction and order-making. I suggest for this purpose the term 'intervention' in order to describe a transnational space of interaction between a variety of agents, interests, and rationalities that is shaped by both politics (i.e. conflict and negotiation) and power, and in which authorities, responsibilities, and subjectivities are reconfigured – hence in which orders are made.

Legitimate authority, the international, and the constitution of orders

The question of how to establish standards for legitimate authority – what counts as 'good order' – has been one of the centrepieces of political theory and philosophy. Indeed, as argued by Anne Orford (2011: 206), it has been its 'core concern'. Generations of political theorists offer a variety of normative standards upon which to assess what is needed for an order to be considered legitimate: the capacity to provide security, recourse to established cultural norms, the rule of law, or the provision of justice and welfare, to name but a few. Max Weber (2006), for instance, identified his famous three ideal types of legitimate authority on the basis of their underlying principles of legitimacy: the characteristics of the ruler (charismatic rule), the fit to established cultural norms (traditional rule), or the rule-bound character (legal-rational rule). What Weber underlined with this distinction is that the terms of legitimate authority, the legitimacy principles, may change over time and depend on social context (Weber 2006: 218). What counts as legitimate authority is thus contingent, contextually and historically bound, and subject to interpretation. One might add that this also means that different principles of legitimacy may coexist at a given point in time and that indeed the core of politics is a struggle over which principles should prevail (Schlichte 2012). This book is not interested in establishing principles of legitimate authority or to assess their relative normative validity. Rather, it investigates the consequences of an increasingly internationalized effort to establish what counts as 'good order', as revealed when the perceived normalcy of 'good order' experiences a sudden rupture.

In a world in which the state has become the dominant form of political organization, the question of what counts as rightful authority is of concern not only for those subject to a particular system of rule or those seeking to establish their rule. It is also of importance for those deemed to recognize the state from without. As argued by Mlada Bukovansky (2002: 211), 'an entity that deserves the name "state system", even if it displays a degree of heterogeneity, enshrines certain modes of authority and order, privileging some forms of rule over others'. In this regard, Christian Reus-Smit (2001: 520) observed that what counts internationally as legitimate authority serves as 'the dominant rationale that licenses the organization of power and authority into territorially defined sovereign units'. Thus, what counts internationally as legitimate order has tangible effects. Indeed, the state itself is one of the most overt examples for this. The globalization of the state as a form of political organization can be regarded as a very consequential effect of a particular international definition of 'good order', which henceforth became normalized as a dominant mode of political organization (Herbst 2000; Migdal & Schlichte 2005: 17).[3] While over time, as will be elaborated below, statehood has become more substantially defined, the international still retains a crucial role in licensing the organization of authority within states. This constitutive link between international norms of legitimate authority and the formation of orders has also been a key concern for scholars in IR and African studies alike, yet the two disciplines approached this issue from rather different angles, as the remainder of this section will elaborate.

IR scholarship: sovereignty principles and international order

In IR, scholars traditionally studied the links between the international and statehood using the concept of sovereignty. But for a long time, the dominant realist perspective assumed sovereignty to be an ontological fact, a natural accompaniment of the state (Biersteker & Weber 1996: 2; Krasner 2001: 1; Agnew 2009). As a consequence, IR scholarship has largely ignored the question of how the principles underpinning notions of sovereignty contribute to the formation of orders as a relevant *problematique* for the study of international politics.

With the rise of (critical) constructivism in IR theory, another analytical perspective on sovereignty became possible.[4] Thomas Biersteker and Cynthia Weber (1996: 1) called for an understanding of sovereignty as a *social* concept. This implies recognizing both how notions of sovereignty have been subject to changing meanings over time and how each of them had constituting effects on dominant forms of social and political organization (Biersteker & Weber 1996: 4; Murphy 1996). Sovereignty therefore defined what Reus-Smit (1999: 31) called the 'moral purpose of the state' based on hegemonic 'reasons that historical agents hold for organizing their political life into centralized, autonomous political units'. What counted internationally as legitimate authority was thus not taken for granted, but regarded as being 'presented, debated, and applied in the context of particular events in international history' (Clark 2005: 1; for a critique, see Bartelson 2014).

For constructivists, ideas about sovereignty *constituted* rather than merely described the state (see also Murphy 1996: 87). This perspective allowed investigating how dominant notions of legitimate authority have changed over time, how different referents of what counts as good order entered the realm of international legitimacy principles, and how this enabled and constrained politics within states, constructed particular subjectivities, and empowered certain actors over others (for overviews, see Barkin 1998; Roth 1999). Analytically speaking, sovereignty thus became historicized and subject to concrete practices: a matter of making rather than an empirical fact. Such a perspective not only underlined the generally amenable and historically contingent meanings of sovereignty; it also revealed the constitutive linkages between dominant notions of sovereignty and the nature of international order itself. Evolving legitimacy principles defined both rightful membership and rightful conduct for the members of 'international society' and thus shaped the very nature of this society (Clark 2005: 5). Shifting notions of sovereignty and the normative structure of the international thus also structured what kinds of conduct were possible and legitimate among the actors of the international system. They served to define what was possible in international politics by establishing who was a legitimate participant and by providing the overall purposes, the rationale, for their conduct (Aalberts 2012). As summarized by Samuel Barkin and Bruce Cronin (1994: 128), changing principles of legitimate statehood 'affect the ways in which states are constrained and enabled to act in their international relations' and by way of consequence what was considered deviant behaviour or a threat to international order (see also Finnemore 2003).

Altogether, the critical constructivist thinking on sovereignty in IR introduced three fundamental tenets: first, that principles of legitimate statehood are subject to international definition; second, that such principles are historically contingent; and third, that changing notions of legitimate authority also define the particular form of international order. So, from an IR perspective, international norms of legitimate authority mainly affected the constitution of *international* order: they defined membership, set the conditions for state recognition, and prescribed certain rules of rightful conduct and, in case these were infringed, of conflict resolution. This order was largely considered as an international order in which states are the primary agents. In short, IR scholars were mainly concerned with the question of how the primary units of the international system (i.e. states) relate to that system and how constitutive principles shape their conduct (Aalberts 2012: 238). As will be elaborated further below, more recent IR scholarship also seeks to describe how changing notions of legitimate authority affect the 'making of the international itself' (Walters 2012: 7) and thus transcend the state-centric and inter-national imaginary of previous works. Scholars in African studies, in turn, have mainly focused on studying the domestic effects of changing international principles of legitimate authority.[5]

African studies: sovereignty and the struggle for domestic order

For scholars in African studies, the international principle of sovereignty has been a concern with tangible consequences for the very nature of the state itself. Here, sovereignty was not only a matter of law or power politics, but, as famously argued by Robert H. Jackson and Carl G. Rosberg (1982), the very reason for which Africa's so-called weak states persisted

NORMS, INTERVENTION, AND THE MAKING OF ORDERS 27

(see also Grovogui 2002). The authors distinguished *de facto*, positive sovereignty, the capacity of a government to exercise effective control over its territory, from *de jure*, negative sovereignty, which derives from external recognition and membership in IOs. External recognition and the internationally upheld principle of sovereignty was thus much more relevant for the constitution of African states than their *de facto* capacities to exercise the role and functions international sovereignty principles imagined them to exercise. Membership in IOs, the two authors argued, provides African states with the opportunity to 'both influence and take advantage of international rules and ideologies concerning what is desirable and undesirable in the relations of states' (Jackson & Rosberg 1982: 21). International recognition has thus become an ordering device with very powerful consequences for the persistence of a particular form of political organization: the state. As shown by Frederick Cooper (2008) with the example of the Mali Federation, on the eve of independence, the power of international principles of statehood also foreclosed other potential forms of political organization.

In contrast to IR, African studies thus mainly focused on the imprint of international legitimacy principles on the constitution of and struggle over the state itself – thus on *domestic* order (Cooper 2008: 186). In this sense, the external constitution of African states has been one of the core tenets for understanding both persistence and change in African politics (see, for instance, Clapham 1996; Bayart 2000; Englebert 2009). Christopher Clapham's (1996) foundational book *Africa and the International System* interprets politics in Africa as interacting with and integrated into an international system that provides both normative and material incentives for the maintenance of order and the 'politics of survival' in which most African states and their leaders came to be entangled (see also Herbst 2000). Others provided a more nuanced account of individual agents and forms of agency that stem from the rents of international recognition. Jean-François Bayart's (2000) theory of extraversion and Pierre Englebert's (2009) account of the 'legal command' as a consequence of internationally recognized authority, for instance, reinterpret the imprint of the international from a more agency-based perspective. Both investigate how African actors – governments, rebel groups, 'civil society', and local authorities alike – make use of the rents that derive from international norms and recognition as rightful authority (see also Piccolino 2012; Fisher 2014). Here, Africans are not passive victims caged in their state because of dominant international principles of sovereignty. Rather, international norms are a vehicle for agency, despite their structuring (and thus constraining) effects. As particularly stressed by Bayart (2000: 255), more often than not, this agency comes with ambiguous consequences and thus defies an interpretation as the mere realization of external, postcolonial role expectations.

In short, tracing the consequences and investigating the transnational links that sustain orders on the continent is anything but a novelty in African studies (Death 2015: 5). Instead, international norms of legitimate authority – and their changing meanings – provide a crucial avenue for African studies scholars to understand political dynamics within African states, and there is a set body of literature that has for a long time taken this analytical path. Yet what often remains missing in these accounts is a more thorough engagement with the changing contours of 'the international' itself, particularly with the role of African actors therein. Despite Clapham's (1996: 110) discussion of the OAU as sustaining a system of mutual recognition and preservation, what remains largely unaccounted for are African actors' *own* contributions to providing and disseminating the international normative structures upon which domestic struggles over the state are fought out (an exception is van Walraven 1996). Thus, the international has often been depicted as if its nature and agents were self-explanatory, static, and above all external to the continent. African studies scholars' sensitivity to local dynamics and agencies is not mirrored in a similar sensitivity vis-à-vis the nature and constitution of the international itself, described on the basis of current African experiences (see also Abrahamsen 2016).

Summary

In summary, scholars in both IR and African studies have been interested in understanding how international norms on legitimate authority affect the formation of orders. In IR, this has mainly been debated as historically changing legitimacy principles that defined rightful membership and conduct in the international society of states and thus constituted *international* order. African studies scholarship, in turn, has been more interested in understanding how international legitimacy principles affect both the very persistence of states and power struggles within them. Its focus has hence been on *domestic* order. In this sense, the two disciplines have been reproducing the (misleading) international/domestic divide and the dominant division of labour between IR and area studies, which attributes to IR an expertise about the 'general' (here, the international system) while the area specialist holds intimate knowledge of a particular case (here, a specific domestic context). Although much of African studies scholarship transgresses at least the international/domestic divide by conceiving the international as constantly present in the struggles in and about the state, there has been less interest so far in reading current developments in Africa as a 'window on the contemporary world' more generally (Abrahamsen 2016: 127) – that is, in delineating the actual nature of the international based on African experiences and identifying the role of African actors in making and enacting this international.[6] This book aims at developing such a perspective and making it resonate with both disciplines. For this purpose, I will again turn to IR and recent scholarship on the role of IOs as sites and agents for the definition of international legitimacy principles, as discussed in the next section.

International organizations and the dissemination of legitimacy principles

When studying historically changing international principles for what counts as legitimate authority, critical constructivists have mainly focused on changing grounds upon which peoples were granted a *right to* a state. By contrast, this book is interested in the emergence and consequences of changing meanings of legitimate authority in *existing* states. As will be argued in this section, at least since the end of the Cold War, one can observe a general international trend towards legalizing, universalizing, and expanding ('thickening') the internationally disseminated meaning of legitimate authority. The African anti-coup norm is but one example of this trend. Second, this more recent 'thickening' of international norms of legitimate authority also expanded the powers and practices of IOs, which, like the AU, increasingly serve as sites to define what counts as 'good order'. Together, both developments raise questions as to how this affects the relationship between states, societies, the individual, and the international, to which this book seeks to provide some answers based on an in-depth study of the post-coup intervention in Madagascar and the consequences of the AU's anti-coup policy.

The expansion of international legitimacy principles

Already in the early 1970s, Martin Wight (1972: 2) observed that international principles of legitimate authority evolved from the mere recognition of allegiance to a matter of rights, a history in which the referents and scope of these rights gradually changed and expanded. Over time, what counts as legitimate authority has increasingly become *legalized* and couched in *universalized* terms.

While since the eighteenth century legitimate authority was thought to be based in 'the people', as opposed to the divine ruler, the global spread of liberal norms gradually enlarged the scope of who counted as 'the people' and what was required for the effective realization of the ideals of collective and individual self-determination. Historically, this is reflected in a gradual expansion of internationally enshrined rights: from a right to a state for people under colonial rule, to the effective protection of minorities in existing states, to the international guarantee of political and civil rights vis-à-vis the state (Roth 1999). One may therefore add to Wight's observation cited above that international legitimacy principles also became much 'thicker' over time (Neumann & Sending 2007: 690; Bartelson 2014). Today, a government's mere claim to 'effective control' alone does not suffice any more as a criterion for membership in the international society of states. In this sense, David Scott (2012: 197) diagnosed a 'normative sea change', a paradigm shift by which with the end of the Cold War legitimate authority became increasingly based on more substantive conditions. This paradigm shift is usually attributed to both the rise of international human rights principles and the spread of democracy as the international standard for recognizing legitimate authority. As argued by Clark (2005: 173), '[S]ince the end of the cold war, rightful membership has been expressed, not simply about *states*, but about certain *types* of state' [emphasis in original]. More precisely, the shift introduced a new thinking by which the 'internal political character of a regime ought to have a bearing on its standing in the international community of states' (Scott 2012: 199). The internal make-up of states was thus opened up for more consequential international scrutiny and evaluation.

To be sure, international human rights norms such as political rights, internationally enshrined, for instance, in the Universal Declaration of Human Rights and the International Covenant on Civil and Political Rights, did exist before. This new conditioning of statehood, however, addresses the state's political order in its entirety and thus goes beyond the mere international enshrinement of individual rights (Sandholtz & Stiles 2008: 290; Scott 2012). Moreover, unlike before, today these rights are pursued in a much more consequential way. The rise of the idea of the responsibility to protect (R2P) – however one may assess its legal status and normative validity – is probably the most widely cited and hotly debated outcome of this 'normative sea change' (Bellamy 2014; Hofmann & Zimmermann 2019). The AU's own Article 4(h), which allows for military intervention in cases of genocide, war crimes, and crimes against humanity, is another case in point (Mwanasali 2006; Wilén & Williams 2018). Much of the academic debate on the status and consequences of this apparent normative shift has been focused on questions relating to the legitimacy of the use of force in addressing the most severe infringements of these principles (for an overview, see Seybolt 2016). This book, in contrast, is interested in the more subtle ideas and corresponding practices that resulted from the rise and expansion of international norms of legitimate authority. In this sense, the expansive internationalization of what counts as legitimate authority is not only to be found in changing norms of military intervention and the use of force in cases of large-scale atrocities. It also gave rise to a great variety of international practices and the responsibilization of agents that affect state–society relations on a more subtle and more everyday basis. International mechanisms to promote good governance and democracy, the conditioning of development aid, election observation missions, international human rights monitoring, the expansion of international sanction schemes, and the internationalization of conflict resolution, peacebuilding, and state reconstruction after violent conflicts are all fields in which expansive international ideas on what counts as legitimate authority affect how societies are (made fit to be) governed and how order in states is upheld and legitimated (Abrahamsen 2000; Jabri 2013; MacMillan 2013). All these efforts provide evidence that statehood has become defined on more substantive terms and is increasingly conditioned on internationally set standards. Even though these standards have rarely been criteria for effective exclusion from the society of states, they nevertheless provide the rationale for a variety of efforts to establish the conditions of possibility of their fulfilment.

In normative terms, scholars across different disciplines have since engaged in a lively debate as to how to interpret and assess these developments. While some see in the expansion of international legitimacy principles the global fulfilment of a liberal utopia (Franck 1992), others fear that we are witnessing a new version of the 'standards of civilization', which in the eighteenth century demarcated the boundaries of the society of (European) states and defined the external Other – the land of 'barbarians' and 'savages' – as an a-legal space and thus open to arbitrary and coercive intervention (Roth 1999; Paris 2002; Bowden 2004: 45; Jahn 2007a; Jahn 2007b).

In analytical terms, scholars have since been debating whether and how the expansive list of legitimacy principles affects sovereignty as such. In this regard, several authors have stressed that changing international principles of legitimate authority are *transforming* rather than replacing sovereignty, and with this the state, both as an idea and as an empirical fact (Hameiri 2010; Bartelson 2014; for an overview, see Deitelhoff & Zürn 2015). The liberal utopians might thus be mistaken in conflating the rise of individual rights with the decline of the state both as an idea and as an agent in international politics (see also Latham 1999: 49; Reus-Smit 2013). Empirically, this has raised the question of how exactly changing notions of legitimate authority contribute to the reorganization of state–society relations (see, for instance, Duffield 2001; Hameiri 2010; Jabri 2013). This book takes this question about the consequences of expanding international legitimacy principles as a starting point in order to investigate in an empirically open way how exactly the enactment of such principles affects and potentially reconfigures notions of statehood and order, as well as how to assess this normatively. As I will argue in the remainder of this section, the realization of international principles of legitimate authority is intimately tied to the role of IOs as locales for the definition and dissemination of such principles and their enactment in various practices of intervention. Understanding the effects of their enactment thus also requires seeing IOs in different analytical terms.

International organizations: producers, disseminators, and guarantors of legitimacy principles

The above-described expansion of international legitimacy principles has gone hand in hand with changes in the dominant actors that are involved in defining what counts as 'good order'. In this sense, changing notions of legitimate authority also led to the expansion of authorities beyond the state, whose very existence came to be legitimated on the grounds of changing notions of legitimate statehood. IOs thus became the producers, disseminators, and guarantors of changing notions of legitimate authority (Clark 2005: 176; Sandholtz & Stiles 2008: 319). This is particularly true for regional organizations, which, despite great differences, have over the last decades developed a broad array of political norms that condition membership and prescribe a particular vision of good political order among their member states (Pevehouse 2005; McMahon & Baker 2006; Börzel & van Hüllen 2015). IOs therefore increasingly serve as 'sites for the negotiation and formulation of universal categories and practices of rule' (Neumann & Sending 2010: 136). As will be elaborated in this section, these categories and practices of rule provide the texture, the normative webbing, upon which IOs increasingly base their claims to authority. The expansion of international legitimacy principles thus also shaped the very *form* of the international. The analytical task is hence to inquire and delineate in better terms what this new form of the international amounts to and how it affects the changing relationships between states, societies, the individual, and the international.

In his account of the history of 'international legitimacy', Wight (1972) described how both the League of Nations and the UN were crucial arenas for the definition of principles of legitimate authority. The Charters of both organizations laid the grounds for interpreting under what conditions membership in the international society of states was rightfully granted, although actual political practice often diverged from prescriptive texts. Inis Claude (1966: 370) likewise observed that 'a highly significant part of the political role of the United Nations' was their role in 'collective legitimization' (i.e. the creation of an arena and audience for governments' claims to legitimacy).

Since then, IOs have not only become an arena for state elites' own claims to legitimacy, but the state itself has become an object of IO policies: either directly through setting standards and benchmarks for membership, or indirectly through reorganizing social, political, and economic relations by way of IO policies. International conflict resolution and the rebuilding of states after violent conflict, for instance, became a large area of IO activity and a field of expertise for IO professionals (Sending 2015). Gender mainstreaming, healthcare, and child protection were turned into missions of international social policy; election observation, anti-corruption campaigns, human rights monitoring, and capacity-building for civil servants became fields in which IOs are today involved in reorganizing state–society relations (for overviews, see Avant et al. 2010; Harman & Williams 2013).

For a long time, IR scholars conceived of IOs as merely the result of states' interests. The power of IOs was the consequence of delegation by states, as there was no higher authority than that of the state (Mearsheimer 1995; Hurd 2014: 7). With a more recent interest in IR scholarship in the nature and consequences of international authority, this perspective has changed considerably (see generally Hooghe et al. 2017; Zürn 2018; Daase & Deitelhoff 2019). Yet even before that, Michael Barnett and Martha Finnemore (2004) famously challenged the long-held IR premise and redefined IOs not as the mere reflection of states' interests and delegated authority, but as autonomous actors on their own terms. IOs, the two argued, have to be understood as what they are, namely bureaucracies, which grants them a particular authority over constituting social reality (Barnett & Finnemore 2004: 9). The power of IOs, as with all bureaucracies, lies in their guidance by and production of impersonal rules, which confer upon them the image of neutral and impartial guardians of the public good (Barnett & Finnemore 2004: 3). Impersonal rules not only regulate or prescribe, but rather constitute social reality: 'IOs, through their rules, create new categories of actors, form new interests for actors, define new shared international tasks, and disseminate new models of social organization around the globe' (Barnett & Finnemore 2004: 3). Fifteen years before, Nicholas Onuf and Frank Klink (1989: 158) already noted that the international realm is made up of different kinds of rules – instructions, directions, and commitments – which are all constitutive of social reality. These rules produce different kinds of authority, understood as figurations of sub- and superordination. The capacity of rule-making thus provides a heuristic inroad into understanding the 'ruled character' of the international realm and with it the emergence and character of authority beyond the state (Onuf & Klink 1989: 169).

Barnett and Finnemore (2004) thus introduced a new way to conceive of the power relationship between IOs and states. The innovation was that power was not only understood as power to regulate and command, but also as a power to constitute and produce social reality: to determine the conditions of possibility for agency, problems, and objects of (international) governance. This power derives from IOs' capacity to define problems and responsibilities and to transform information into knowledge, and from their being perceived as representing universal moral principles that counter self-interested states (Barnett & Finnemore 2004: 29). In all this, 'IOs define problems for actors (by classifying them as such), specify which actors have responsibility for solving those problems, and use their authority to identify the right or appropriate kind of solution for the particular problem under consideration' (Barnett & Finnemore 2004: 34).

Moreover, by depicting IOs as bureaucracies, Barnett and Finnemore also highlighted the pathologies that come with bureaucratic rule. A crucial determinant of such pathologies is that rule-making is reflexive and expansive: IOs tend to create more rules and thus expand their missions (Barnett & Finnemore 2004: 163). Driven by the desire to solve an ever-expanding array of problems, bureaucracies' tendencies to compartmentalization, specialization, and routines more often than not turn out to be counterproductive (Barnett & Finnemore 2004: 38). With this, the two authors not only laid the foundation for a more nuanced understanding of the kinds and locales of authorities that were emerging beyond the state, but also showed how this was indeed part of an expansive process that was ambiguous in its consequences. In contrast to the liberal hope that IOs represent an alternative to state particularism, Barnett and Finnemore warned that IOs' expansion may lead to mission creep, forms of domination, and an 'undemocratic liberalism' that expands on claims of advancing the global good, but does so on an unaccountable and undemocratic basis (Barnett & Finnemore 2004: 172).

However, because Barnett and Finnemore (2004: viii) focused on demonstrating the ontological autonomy of IOs, they conceived of IOs in contradistinction to the state. Like states, they were a priori existing entities with interests, defined by their nature as bureaucracies. The power of IOs was their capacity to shape the behaviour of states, either by ensuring compliance or by reshaping their interests. In this understanding, IO authority derives from their autonomy vis-à-vis the state, and it is exercised *over* states. IOs, though far from replacing states, were nevertheless imagined as state-like units.

In their critique of this account of IO authority, Iver B. Neumann and Ole Jacob Sending (2010) argue that the authority of IOs derives from their function as sources of definitions of what states *are*, rather than being measured relative to their member states. Here, the power of IOs lies in their role as producers and implementers of standards for statehood and in how this constitutes both the state and international authority at the same time. On the one hand, IOs serve as locales for the definition of global standards and benchmarks of 'good statehood'. On the other hand, IOs have developed the instruments and practices to actually reconfigure states, for instance through international state- and peacebuilding interventions, through security sector reform, or by reforming economies after violent conflicts.[7]

A similar understanding of the power of IOs also underpins Anne Orford's (2011) work on the UN as an international executive authority and on the dissemination of principles of legitimate authority. Here, the UN's power does not stem from providing prescriptive rules to member states. Rather, it is based on the gradual institutionalization and normalization of practices and purposes within the organization. In contrast to Barnett and Finnemore's account, in Orford's work the power the UN exercises is not exercised over member states through the definition of rules or the dissemination of knowledge, but is exercised over *others* (here, the Congolese, the East Timorese, etc.) through constituting the state and defining its overall purpose (Orford 2011: 201; see also Sending 2015: 130). In sum, Neumann and Sending (2010) and Orford (2011) underline that in order to grasp the power of IOs, the analytical gaze has to shift to much more subtle and fine-grained ways in which IO norms and practices serve to define new purposes and ends, change relationships, and recreate authorities, including their own (see also Merlingen & Ostrauskaite 2005; Merlingen 2011; Zanotti 2011; Sending 2015).

Both accounts thus move beyond describing IOs as mere makers of norms and constructors of social reality by shifting the focus towards the rationalities and relationships that constitute and sediment the growing authority of IOs. Like Barnett and Finnemore (2004), Neumann and Sending (2010) too stress that the formulation and dissemination of knowledge and norms results in an increasing institutionalization and sedimentation of IO authority. Yet by defining the purpose of statehood, IOs do not authoritatively change states' interests, but rather produce statehood in the first place. IOs and states are therefore not tied together in a zero-sum power relationship, but rather in one of mutual constitution. In this sense, the task for empirical research is to 'grasp how states are conceptualized within IOs if we are to understand the specific rationality by which IOs seek to govern and act on states' (Neumann & Sending 2010: 149).

Both Neumann and Sending's (2010) and Orford's (2011) works draw on a conception of power as developed by French philosopher Michel Foucault (see also Merlingen 2003). In this part of his work, Foucault was interested in how power relations work and are reproduced not by prescription, submission, or the use of force, but by a form of power that 'structure[s] the possible field of action of others' (Foucault 1982: 790). In order to understand the workings of power, Foucault turned the analytical gaze away from the capacity of actors to act upon another's will – which has been the predominant understanding of power (Guzzini 2005) – and towards the conditions of possibility that render this acting upon others possible (Walters 2012: 11). For Foucault, these conditions are to be found in the knowledge regimes, the purposes and ideals, as well as corresponding techniques and practices that render subjectification possible and hence constitute a particular relationship of power, be it between women and men, parents and children, or 'ruler' and 'subjects'. Moreover, in his reconstruction of the emergence of the European state, Foucault described the latter by pointing to the various sites in which a particular knowledge–practice complex was enacted, gradually centralized, and expanded, and which in turn led to the sedimentation and normalization of both relationships of power and the institutions and locales in which these were inscribed (Foucault 2004; Walters 2012: Chapter 1).[8]

With this in mind, IOs can be conceived of as sites of particular knowledge–practice complexes defining how states should be governed. They are producers and disseminators of particular knowledge regimes, purposes, and ends (e.g. through collectively defined standards, benchmarks) and engage in concrete practices that are rationalized on the ground of such regimes (e.g. third-party mediation, international state-building efforts, international sanctions). Such knowledge regimes and their enactment in practice, in turn, contribute to altering or sedimenting relationships of power. Analytically, the aim of such a perspective is to investigate the underlying rationalities that sustain and the power relations that result from these knowledge–practice complexes (see also Merlingen 2003; Malmvig 2014). Thus, unlike in Barnett and Finnemore's account, the power of IOs is not defined in terms of their capacity to *act upon states*: to prescribe, define, or even manipulate states' interests.

Rather, the power of IOs stems from the fact that their purpose and expansive roles are based on the idea and the definition of the purpose of the state. So, what such a perspective calls for is not scrutiny of power shifts in the relationship between IOs and states, but a deeper understanding of how the formulation and enactment of international norms and expansive IO missions weave together and redefine the relationships between IOs, states, and the societies they are deemed to represent. Such a perspective is more open to grasping the nuanced changes in relationships that emerge from the expansive roles and engagements of IOs in creating and reorganizing states that apparently do not (yet) meet the collectively set standards (see also Hameiri 2010). Consequently, the analytical gaze is turned towards analysing the underlying rationalities that change and sustain relationships of power and that legitimate particular sets of practices. Also, more emphasis is placed on the empirical reconstruction of small-scale, allegedly mundane practices that turn such rationalities into effects (Merlingen 2003; Walters 2012: Chapter 2).

In this sense, Orford's (2011) book, for instance, renders visible how the UN – through defining abstract benchmarks for statehood – normalizes a particular form of domestic political organization and thereby shapes the possibilities for political articulation in existing states. Indeed, historically and for the majority of the world's population, the existence of the international system of states has always had this effect: 'populations found themselves governed both by modern states of their own and by the overarching system of states within which their own states had been incorporated' (Hindess 2005: 408–409). As argued above, for many scholars in African studies, this has long been the point of departure for describing political dynamics in African states. However, they have so far largely ignored the critical role played by IOs in this regard, particularly by African regional organizations. In turn, a crucial addendum to the critical constructivist perspectives in IR, as discussed in the preceding section of this chapter, is to consider the international not merely as a set of relationships between states, but rather as an emerging web of power relations between a variety of agents. IOs, including regional ones, play an important role therein, as they increasingly serve as 'sites for the negotiation and formulation of universal categories and practices of rule' (Neumann & Sending 2010: 136). Looking from this vantage point at the evolution of the idea and resulting practices of outlawing coups and re-establishing constitutional order in African states therefore allows scrutiny of how both the very idea and the concrete practices of 'undoing' coups contribute to reordering the state, societies, and the international, as well as giving more prominence to the role of African regional organizations as sources, agents, and products of such processes of reordering.

Intervention as transboundary formation: spaces of politics and power

The previous two sections established a theoretical vantage point that relates changing international norms of legitimate authority to the constitution of orders both within and beyond the state and explained the specific role occupied by IOs in this process. But how to describe the moments in which we can actually observe and analyse such order formation? Put differently, how to conceive of the processes, the agents, and their interactions that make orders? I propose the term 'intervention' in order to describe a transnational space of interaction between a variety of agents, interests, and rationalities that contributes to the sedimentation and reconfiguration of orders and that serves in the following as a theoretical vantage point to analyse the ordering effects of the AU's anti-coup norm. For this purpose, I will draw on both historical sociology and works on the sociology of intervention as debated in peace and conflict research.

IR scholars have long conceived of interventions in terms of their ordering effects, yet mainly with regard to the system level and as an exception or challenge to the international order of sovereign states (see Bull 1984; Reus-Smit 2013). George Lawson and Luca Tardelli (2013: 1237–1238) questioned this focus from the perspective of historical sociology by noting that interventions have always fulfilled a simultaneous function of order maintenance and transformation both internationally and within the territorialized 'units' subject to intervention. From this perspective, interventions are 'historically contingent social practices' employed to coercively mediate 'tensions between territorial and transnational forces' (MacMillan 2013: 1044).[9] Reus-Smit likewise suggested freeing the concept of intervention from its 'sovereignty frame' (Reus-Smit 2013: 1058) and conceiving of interventions as constitutive instances of 'systematic configurations of political authority' (Reus-Smit 2013: 1062). Seen from this angle, the international and the 'domestic', however constituted, appear as 'interpenetrated and mutually constituted' orders, as 'overlapping and intersecting sociospatial networks of power' (Hobson, quoted in MacMillan 2013: 1043). A historical sociology of intervention thus allows taking into focus the connections between international ideational and material structures and the concrete reconfigurations of order in 'domestic' units, however constituted. Yet while providing a valuable understanding of intervention as transnational interaction with ordering effects, the above-described (re)conceptions of intervention still repeat much of

IR's structural bias and entail little instruction on how to analyse the actual *processes* and *practices* of intervention.

Understanding interventions as social space and practice

Such a process- and practice-based understanding of interventions can be found in a strand of critical state- and peacebuilding research that analyses the sociology of interventions on a more micro level (see generally Autesserre 2014b). Here, interventions are defined as social spaces of interaction between international, national, and local actors, different interests and legitimacies. This perspective emerged from a critique of both the ontology of contemporary interventions – primarily the so-called liberal peace as the normative-political underpinning of interventions – and what Roger Mac Ginty (2011: 4) called our own 'antennae' – that is, dominant ways to look at, record, and see interventions (for an overview, see Richmond & Mac Ginty 2015).

Scholars in this tradition thus conceptualized interventions as arenas in which a multiplicity of actors engage in negotiating an intervention's purpose and effects (Hagmann & Péclard 2010).[10] To take one work as an example: John Heathershaw (2009) analyses how in post-conflict Tajikistan, peace and legitimate order are the ambiguous result of a complex negotiation involving international norms and agents, local elites, and subordinates, as well as dominant local political cultures. What emerges from these interactions is neither the successful realization of international peacebuilding scripts nor their mere failure. Rather, peace and legitimate order in Tajikistan, as elsewhere, are the work of 'contending discourses and practices of peace' made and remade through interactions between internationals, elites, and what he calls subordinates (Heathershaw 2009: 1). In this strand of research, interventions are thus studied in terms of the politics and power struggles they engender between a variety of actors (i.e. their 'messiness') (Curtis 2012: 3). Such an understanding of interventions as social practices and a space of interaction thus allows rethinking: (1) the effects and outcomes of interventions; and (2) their primary agents.

With regard to the effects and outcomes, the concepts of 'hybridity' and 'friction' gained currency in describing what emerges from these interactions, neither in terms of success/failure nor as the mere effect of external stimuli, but as what these effects are in and of themselves (see Mac Ginty 2011; Millar et al. 2013; Björkdahl et al. 2016). What this perspective particularly renders visible is that international interventions often come with illiberal and unintended consequences: the reproduction of state violence and authoritarian governance systems

(Heathershaw 2009: 174), the empowerment of sectarian and violent actors through their integration into peacebuilding efforts (Veit 2010: 234; Mac Ginty 2011: 203; Zanotti 2011: 124), the creation of 'subjects' rather than 'citizens' (Veit 2010: 17), or the diffusion of governmental responsibilities that leads to a decrease in accountability (Andersen 2012: 146). In short, ambiguous outcomes have become a common observation in this strand of literature, where such outcomes are not considered failures, but part of what interventions produce.

In parallel to the description of their hybrid consequences, a second issue, an intervention's primary agents, came more into focus. This particularly refers to so-called 'local' agency in terms of which intervention scholars increasingly studied how local actors resist and reappropriate international demands for reform, and thus divert the initial aims and purposes of interventions for their own purposes (see, for instance, Mac Ginty 2011; Richmond & Mitchell 2011; Björkdahl & Höglund 2013; Millar et al. 2013). This emphasis on local agency and the frictions that result from it stems from the observation that interventions are not solely what interveners do (Mac Ginty 2011: 2).

However, as a consequence, accounts of 'resistance' and 'frictions' sometimes tend to provide only a caricature of international interveners, and thus harbour the danger of a priori rationalizing and exaggerating 'local' agency (see also Chandler 2013; Björkdahl et al. 2016). Moreover, the ideational sources of contemporary interventions are often assumed to be 'Western', thus implicitly turning the local arena of interventions into a struggle of 'Western' versus 'non-Western' ideals, discourses, and agents (Richmond & Mitchell 2011; Kühn 2012: 399; for a critique, see Sabaratnam 2013). In fact, international norms and policy scripts are often taken as monolithic instructions rather than as in themselves hybrid and contradictory texts. This undermines the interactive and relational character of interventions, which the authors otherwise stress and which would require a similar focus and fine-grained analysis of international agency in interventions. As shown in Heathershaw's above-cited study, international interveners are not simply implementing what headquarters mandate(d) them to do. Instead, those sent to intervention arenas are torn between a formal commitment to an idealized mandate and its rather technical implementation, because what they face in reality on the ground is not an 'empty shell' (Lemay-Hébert 2011).[11] Heathershaw (2009: 57) thus concluded that the role of international interveners is 'not that of a third party, nor that of a powerful and relatively homogeneous agent, but that of a dispersed range of actors, each under the influence of discourses beyond their individual control'.

But in order to grasp this 'dispersed range of actors', the analytical gaze also has to go beyond the 'local' as a site of intervention. Alex Veit and Klaus Schlichte (2012: 168), for instance, suggested studying intervening organizations as 'coupled arenas' (i.e. different power figurations at different levels of an organization that shape the knowledge and practices with which interventions are ultimately carried out). Different offices of an organization – such as the headquarters and field offices – but also different sections within a bureaucracy often function according to different rationalities and purposes. They nevertheless all interact with and affect the 'localized' intervention (see also Zanotti 2011: ix; Williams 2018). As concluded by Alex Veit (2010: 256) in his work on intervention as indirect rule in Ituri, we still know fairly little about 'how the international community on the ground is interlinked and interdependent with forces in other arenas'.

In a nutshell, the turn in state- and peacebuilding research to the 'local' may have actually confined rather than broadened the analytical gaze by reifying the distinction between the 'local' and the 'external' (see also Chandler 2013: 32). A focus on local agency and resistance harbours the danger of caricaturing both the underpinning norms and the international agents in contemporary intervention efforts and of spatially localizing interventions that are in fact a very transnational situation. Against this background, I will suggest an understanding of interventions as a transboundary formation in order to do justice to both the relational/social and the transnational character of interventions, in which a variety of actors interact in order to define what kind of order is to emerge, and how.

Post-coup interventions as transboundary formation

In order to analyse post-coup interventions, I conceive of these situations as what Robert Latham et al. (2001) described by the term 'transboundary formation'. Transboundary formations 'link global, regional, national, and local forces through structures, networks, and discourses (…) [and they] play a major role in creating, transforming, and destroying forms of order and authority' (Latham et al. 2001: 5).

The idea of transboundary formations explicitly breaks with prevalent analytical boundaries between 'the global', 'the national', and 'the local', and offers a perspective that cuts across such allegedly distinct social spaces.[12] According to the critique of Latham et al. (2001: 6), this division is often based on an essentialized understanding of social space as neatly separated and located at different 'levels' (*the* global, *the* regional, *the* local). Moreover, the 'local' is either conceived of as subject to global stimuli (international norms, structural adjustment programmes, global capitalism, etc.) or as the theatre of their failure. Instead, Ronald Kassimir and Robert Latham (2001: 269) argued that the concept of transboundary formations attempts to offer 'a more rigorous theorizing of globalization and at the same time a more sophisticated analysis of what constitutes local order and authority'. Such a perspective requires a more thorough engagement with the 'structures and relations that emerge through the intersection of social phenomena', which means that the effects of these engagements are neither the mere result of an external intentionality nor described in binary terms of success/failure (Latham et al. 2001: 6). Such a thorough engagement with the intersections of social phenomena should expose 'the rich kernels of specific junctures joining diverse structures, actors, ideas, practices, and institutions with varying ranges in a common social and political frame' (Latham et al. 2001: 6). Reactions to coups in Africa, I argue, create such a frame, and it is the aim of this book to describe one instance of such 'rich kernels' and their consequences for the reconfiguration of orders.

Thus, an intervention is not the practice of a particular actor, but rather a social space, a moment of collision and interaction of a variety of forces and logics. I will therefore speak of post-coup engagements as intervention, not to define what the AU, SADC, or UN *do*, but to describe the social space of transnational interaction that is opened at the moment of the AU PSC's demand for a 'speedy return to constitutional order' (OAU 2000a: 3). This, as will be elaborated below, is both a space of *politics* – the struggle over the rules of the game – and one of *power*, in which the 'possible field of action' (Foucault 1982: 790) is structured for a variety of actors and in which orders are (re)created, legitimated, and contested.

The conception of interventions as transboundary formations thus seeks to combine the more systemic perspective of historical sociology and the practice-oriented critical sociology of intervention by merging but also refocusing them through a transboundary perspective. What, then, does it mean to think of interventions as transboundary formations and as sites of both politics and power? I summarize my answer in four steps.

First, interventions are sites of politics (i.e. the struggle over competing attempts to define what the 'problem' is that ought to be resolved). If politics is about conflict, then interventions open an arena to define the *scope* of conflict (Schattschneider 1960: 7), to delineate the 'appropriate and legitimate range of controversy' (Shapiro 1981: 210). In this struggle, it will be decided which issues, which problems, and which conflicts are included in or excluded from the 'political universe' (Schattschneider 1960: 62). International diplomats, bureaucrats in headquarters, local elites, party officials, civil society actors, traditional authorities, and church leaders, mediators, and peacebuilding experts

NORMS, INTERVENTION, AND THE MAKING OF ORDERS

all engage in defining the terms of the intervention (Curtis 2012: 3). Like policies and any other object of government, the objects, subjects, and purposes of interventions are neither given nor inevitable. They are negotiated and the outcome of a struggle between competing problem constructions. This is a consequence of the fact that interventions are by definition limited: where to draw the boundary is thus both contested and momentous (Latham 2001: 81).

One important aspect of these interactions is that they do not necessarily take place in a single locality. Rather, interventions span a web of interaction between actors that are often *not* located in the same physical terrain. The intervention is a web that connects these otherwise distant places, different rationalities and values, different purposes (Behrends et al. 2014: 15; Williams 2018). All these actors thus contribute norms, discourses, justifications, and sometimes even tangible values to the interactions and shape the 'possible field of action' (Foucault 1982: 790), and hence the scope of possibility and the consequences of the intervention.

Second, interventions are sites of interaction and emergence rather than the attempted (and at times failed) imposition of pre-written scripts upon passively receiving societies. They are, however, also more than merely clashes between 'external' and 'local' rationalities and interests (Björkdahl et al. 2016: 9). Interventions may be conceived of as sites of subjectification (i.e. the creation or becoming of agencies): they define international hierarchies, divisions of labour between different interveners, and institutional realms of action; they require negotiators of peace agreements and trustworthy military to secure elections; they constitute citizens who vote for post-conflict governments, party officials who represent the 'popular will', experts who accompany reconciliation efforts, culprits and victims who make reasonable efforts for 'national reconciliation'. An intervention is thus not the mere clash of a priori defined interests, but rather the site at which interests and identities are constituted and redefined. The power of interventions thus lies in their role of opening possibilities for new subjectivities and power relations to emerge. In line with Michel Foucault's above-described account of power, these processes of subjectification are both enabling and constraining at the same time: they empower and they subjugate. They open possibilities but at the same time set limits. They offer freedoms but tie them to responsibilities (Foucault 1982; Walters 2012). Moreover, not all actors are equally able to participate in the contest over delineating the scope of conflict. It will therefore be a matter of empirical inquiry to understand better how and by what means international interventions offer opportunities and who is able to seize them.

Third, I therefore conceive of interventions in terms of their constituting, ordering effects. Orders are 'what is produced when groups and institutions attempt to establish reproducible boundaries to what they do in the world, involving specific people and places, social relations and practices, and mechanisms and methods (…)' (Latham et al. 2001: 8–9). Interventions contribute to the redefinition of authorities, relationships, and hierarchies through the establishment of reproducible boundaries. They open possibilities, and these possibilities are neither a priori benign nor malign. The analytical gaze is thus shifted away from questions of success and failure – outcomes measured according to predefined standards or the analyst's own normative expectations – towards understanding what it is that emerges from interventions (Björkdahl et al. 2016). This includes scrutinizing not only what interventions invent, but also what they sustain (see also Richmond & Mac Ginty 2015: 7). As evident from the interactive and relational approach to interventions, these ordering consequences are not confined to the locality of intervention. Rather, the link between 'global, regional, national, and local forces through structures, networks, and discourses' that make up a transboundary formation may have effects on *all* those involved, including those at distant places (Latham et al. 2001: 5; Ambrosetti & Buchet de Neuilly 2009; Heathershaw 2009: 174).

Fourth, the above-described subjectification and the ordering functions of interventions are always grounded in particular rationalities that render certain practices meaningful and that shape to a large extent what is possible in these engagements. It is hence a task for empirical inquiry to excavate these underlying rationalities that delineate the scope of politics. These can, for instance, be found in the definition where and with whom negotiations ought to take place, in how boundaries between the official and the non-official are set, and in how the inclusion of some actors rather than others is justified. In short, in order to understand the effects of post-coup engagements, it is not sufficient to describe the reorganization of relationships, to name the winners and the losers. Rather, what is necessary is to understand the underlying rationalities that make these particular reconfigurations possible and legitimate in the first place.

Translating these four arguments into a concrete analytical practice, Chapter 4 will look into the interactions between a variety of protagonists of the post-coup intervention in Madagascar and their struggles to define the scope of recognized conflict. Chapter 5 analyses the rationalities and logics underpinning the post-coup intervention. Chapter 6 finally reconstructs how the transboundary formation of post-coup intervention in Madagascar contributed to the reconfiguration of orders in and beyond the country in question by defining new and sedimenting old power relations through responsibilities and hierarchies.

2
Crafting an African anti-coup manual

> Ten or so years ago we did not address, as the OAU, issues that had to do with coups d'état as such. We merely regretted that they had occurred. But now we want to address them and address them as vigorously as we can (...). It may take us some time, but that is our position.
>
> Robert Mugabe, *33rd OAU Summit in Harare,*
> *2 June 1997* (quoted in Reuters 1997)

The above quote from Zimbabwe's then President Robert Mugabe, serving as Chairman of the OAU at that time, is one of the early public statements in which an African head of state explicitly demands that coups should be outlawed and that 'we' should 'address them as vigorously as we can' (Reuters 1997). This demand exemplifies an ideational shift by which questions of legitimate authority and order in African states were turned into a collective concern and one for its continental organization. This chapter traces how coups in Africa have become framed as a problem that needs to be outlawed and how the reasons given for this have evolved over time. One concern in this is to render visible the struggles and dynamics behind the idea to outlaw coups. These struggles took place within the OAU/AU, driven by the organization's bureaucracy, member state representatives, experts, and a number of international and African non-governmental actors. Much of the reconstructed processes took place behind closed doors. The reconstruction is therefore mainly based on reports retrieved from the AU's archives, communications from civil society organizations, and media articles, as well as interpretations offered in the secondary literature. These sources were supplemented by interviews with AU officials and experts who participated in these processes.

This chapter makes two contributions. First, it shows that the ideational history to outlaw coups in Africa can neither be interpreted as a collective embracement of 'democracy' (Leininger 2014) nor does it constitute a mere veil to promote governments' hidden and devious interests (Omorogbe 2011). Rather, it is an incremental, contested expansion of the scope of ideas that define 'good' political order and their legalization (i.e. enshrinement into continental law). This process only evolved against obvious resistance. It required both negotiation and craftsmanship. The chapter therefore reveals what actually evolved *despite* resistance. This was a particularly legalistic and prescriptive approach to the problem of coups, which followed the rationale of writing – as much as possible – an unambiguous and politics-free manual of what to regard as and how to react to coups. Whereas for some this is the particular strength of the AU's anti-coup regime (Tieku 2009: 84; Legler & Tieku 2010: 467), I point out several pitfalls and pathologies in such an approach.

Second, the chapter reveals how the idea to outlaw coups was intimately tied to a process of authorization (i.e. attributing a particular responsibility to the AU). Unconstitutional changes of government were increasingly turned into a *mission* whose successful accomplishment was important for the legitimacy and perceived relevance of the organization. This mission, it will be argued, increasingly shaped the way unconstitutional changes of government were approached. It thereby also subverted a deeper engagement with the more general dilemmas and contradictions involved in the idea to prescribe and defend continental standards of legitimate authority.

The chapter is divided into five sections. The first section briefly reflects how even before the adoption of the Lomé Declaration, coups figured on the OAU's agenda and served as background for formulating new roles for the continental organization. The second and third sections reconstruct the preparation of the two main legal documents: the 2000 Lomé Declaration and the 2007 African Charter on Democracy, Elections and Governance. The fourth section traces how a renewed wave of unconstitutional changes of government since 2008 sustained the demand for reforming the continental approach to coups. This demand increasingly focused on strengthening the AU to show 'zero tolerance' (AU Assembly 2010a). The fifth section concludes the chapter.

Early experiments: from anti-imperialism to 'the people'

The development of the continental anti-coup regime is often said to originate in the 1997 summit of the OAU in Harare and the decision of the OAU Council of Ministers 'to assist the people of Sierra Leone to restore constitutional order' following the ouster of President Ahmad Tejan Kabbah (OAU Council of Ministers 1997; Souaré 2009: 4, 149; Tieku 2009: 78; Omorogbe 2011: 127). This section sets the emergence of the continental anti-coup norm in a broader historical perspective in order to show that there is indeed a history of condemning and dealing with coups d'état in Africa that preceded this summit event. This is crucial in order to render visible the broader institutional transformations the continental outlawing of coups implied.

Between 1960 and 1990, coups d'état were the most prevalent means of regime change in Africa. According to Patrick McGowan (2003: 363–364), 66 successful coups and 71 failed coup attempts were staged in this period. At the end of 1990, Botswana, Cape Verde, and Mauritius were the only African countries that had been independent for more than 25 years and never experienced a coup d'état (McGowan 2003: 345; Decalo 1990). As an intergovernmental organization, the OAU functioned on the basis of sovereignty and mutual recognition among its member states. As a consequence, coups inevitably affected the organization, as they sparked conflicts as to whose claims of representation should be considered legitimate (Kufuor 2002: 370). It was hence not in spite of, but because of, the OAU's stated purpose of defending the sovereignty of its member states that the prevalence of coups had repercussions on the organization.[1] What is more, coups in fact created a moment to question, renegotiate, or reconfirm the fundamental principles that undergirded the continental organization (see also Welch 1975).[2]

However, as argued by Kofi Oteng Kufuor (2002: 370), the OAU's recognition policy 'depended on the interplay of legal, social, and political factors' rather than a prescriptive norm. It was characterized by 'illegality, inconsistency, and a lack of transparency' (Kufuor 2002: 389). There were two main principles that served as justification to withdraw recognition from putschists: anti-mercenarism and anti-imperialism, two foundational norms enshrined in the OAU Charter (OAU 1963: Art. II (d); OAU 1977). This was, for instance, the case following Kwame Nkrumah's ouster in 1966 as well as the overthrow of Milton Obote's government by Idi Amin in 1971 (see Welch 1975; Kufuor 2002: 372–379).[3] Yet in light of a lacking mandate to deal with coups, the OAU's role was altogether dependent on the positions of dominant member states, even though, as, for instance, in the case of Idi Amin's coup, the OAU Secretariat was not entirely silent on that matter.

With the beginning of the 1990s, fears of regional instability and concerns about overt infringements of fundamental rights gradually became part of the discourse on African coups. One reason was that despite the spread of multiparty democracy across Africa, the number of coups in the decade between 1990 and 2001 remained unabatedly high: 50 out of 188 coup attempts between 1958 and 2001 alone took place within this period, though only 13 of them were successful, less than in earlier times (McGowan 2003: 348).

A crucial driver behind a more constructive continental engagement with coups was then OAU Secretary-General Salim Ahmed Salim, who held that the challenge of the day was 'to work for the upliftment of the lot of our people' and that the OAU should become more actively involved in solving conflicts within African states (Novicki 1992; Witt 2019). Thus, even before the 1997 Harare summit, the OAU Secretariat publicly condemned unconstitutional changes of government and involved itself in ad hoc mediation missions to establish constitutional order in the countries concerned. This happened in at least the following cases: Burundi (1993), Lesotho (1994), the Comoros (1995), São Tomé and Príncipe (1995), Burundi (1996), and Niger (1996).[4] Against this background, the OAU's immediate reaction to the 1993 military coup in Burundi, in which President Melchior Ndadaye was killed, can be seen as the first example of what became a rather experimental approach to coups (van Walraven 1996: 312). A day after the coup, OAU Secretary-General Salim announced:

> The verdict of the people so eloquently demonstrated in the country's presidential and legislative elections has been arbitrarily flouted by a military take-over. At a time when Africa is undergoing the process of democratisation and political renewal, it is unacceptable that the will of the people expressed through the ballot should fall victim to the power of the gun. What has happened in Burundi constitutes a serious blow to the process of democratisation not only in the country, but also in Africa as a whole. (Quoted in Reuters 1993)

In line with this statement, Salim's immediate condemnation of all ensuing coups clearly linked the rejection of unconstitutional changes of governments with the right of 'the people' to choose their own government, the uncompromised rule of law, and the necessity to find non-violent solutions to societal grievances. In relation to the coup in São Tomé and Príncipe, for example, he stressed that 'this is an era of dialogue and democracy. Whatever grievances there were (...) should be addressed through dialogue and not force' (Reuters 1995). Similarly, following the 1996 coup in Burundi, the OAU Assistant Secretary-General Pascal Gayama announced:

> The OAU is quite clear, quite firm that coups d'état are no longer on, that we no longer accept coups d'état, and that problems must be settled through existing constitutional mechanisms and by following the procedures for the peaceful settlement of conflict situations. (Quoted in Reuters 1996a)

The rule of law, people's right to choose their government in elections, and the non-violent resolution of conflicts thus became dominant tropes for rejecting coups. In addition, fear of regional instability and refugee flows added a strong incentive for OAU member states, particularly those neighbouring the country concerned, to support the OAU Secretary-General's condemnations. In sum, narratives of popular sovereignty and the rule of law thus merged with concerns for regional security.

Moreover, Salim Ahmed Salim's statements also constructed an African collective responsibility to react to coups. Their increasing number was said to be a 'serious blow to the process of democratization in Africa as a whole' (Reuters 1993), 'a matter of concern for the whole of Africa' (BBC 1993), and 'contrary to the will of the people (...), Africa and the international community' (AFP 1996). This construction of an African responsibility not only legitimated an African agency; it also authoritatively declared the existence of an African consensus around the illegitimacy of coups. This is mirrored in statements such as 'Africa is saying that it is now an age of the ballot and not the bullet' (BBC 1993) or 'any attempt to take power through illegal means will not be accepted by Africa' (Reuters 1996b).

These early condemnations show that even before the 1997 Harare summit and absent any formal mandate, the OAU Secretariat had already sought to establish itself as an active judge on what counts as good political order in African states. Also, the Secretariat's reactions were not confined to public statements: in the majority of the cases, diplomatic missions were dispatched in order to engage the coup plotters. These missions were usually led by Salim Ahmed Salim himself. Only in a few cases did he send other envoys to lead the missions, often diplomatic representatives of OAU member states in Addis Ababa.[5] The means by which coup plotters were engaged, however, varied from case to case. This underlines that the Secretariat was concerned about the particularities of each situation, recognizing that coup instances were often part of more general contests over legitimacy and authority in the country concerned.

Whenever the OAU Secretariat pronounced itself against coups, this clearly went beyond the principles of anti-mercenarism and anti-imperialism dominant in the first three decades. In the early 1990s, the ideal of people's right to choose their own government was turned into a collective, African concern. This increasingly justified the OAU's role as judge and as guardian of 'good' order within its member states. However, the ad hoc character of the Secretariat's interventions had so far made it possible to circumvent a general debate on the normative underpinnings of this new role. In the ensuing years, the various attempts to more concretely define and legalize the OAU's mandate to 'undo' unconstitutional changes of government forcefully demanded such an engagement.

Writing an anti-coup manual

Even the initiatives to craft a continental anti-coup regime in fact preceded the 1997 Harare summit. Following the 1995 coup in the Comoros, the OAU Central Organ decided to set up a subcommittee on unconstitutional changes of government. This was mandated to 'prepare a blueprint for future action by the OAU' (OAU Secretariat 1999: 2). The subcommittee was composed of representatives of five OAU member states (Egypt, Gabon, Kenya, Lesotho, and Senegal) and met three times between 1995 and 1996. It decided that in reaction to future coups, the OAU Secretary-General should act on behalf of the organization according to 'predetermined and agreed criteria and guidelines' (OAU Secretariat 1999: 2).[6] The aim was to develop a prescriptive text – a manual – on how to react to unconstitutional changes of government, a guide that would do away with the hitherto ad hoc and inconsistent practices.

In June 1996, the subcommittee presented the outcome of its deliberations to the OAU Central Organ. Here, the question of how to define unconstitutional changes of government sparked lengthy debates. The subcommittee originally proposed five scenarios: (1) military coups d'état; (2) the refusal by an incumbent government to relinquish power to a winning party after free and fair elections; (3) the refusal of a government to call for general elections; (4) government by decrees; and (5) mercenary intervention to replace a democratically elected government (OAU 2000d: 2). When the Central Organ debated these propositions, it 'requested that the list of changes hitherto considered unconstitutional be extended to include electoral frauds and palace coups' (OAU 2000d: 4). It was also noted that 'rule by decree (...) was not necessarily unconstitutional (...)' (OAU 2000d: 4). The Organ members also observed that 'the cancellation of an election in so far as such a decision aims to forestall the rise to power by a group that rejects democratic principles' should not be a priori considered unconstitutional (OAU 2000d: 4). This shows that what counts as an unconstitutional change of government was contested from the very beginning.

In its submission to the 64th session of the Council of Ministers in July 1996, the subcommittee stated that its mandate should be redefined so as to relate to 'all undemocratic changes' because members 'felt that the original designation (...) that all constitutions were democratic (...) was far from being the case' (OAU 2000d: 4). This may point to the fact that the members of the subcommittee wanted to make a clearer distinction between the democratic quality of a given constitutional order and its legal validity. A sustainable continental anti-coup doctrine would have to defend and promote *democratic* constitutions, not constitutions per se.

However, the Council of Ministers neither took a decision on the Central Organ's request nor on the subcommittee's recommendations quoted above. While these debates already reflect the contestedness of this endeavour, they also mirror the plurality of propositions as to what counts as an unconstitutional change of government. The subcommittee already anticipated that this would be contested by raising doubts about the 'extent to which the final recommendations and [the] subsequent decision on this matter would be binding on Member States' (OAU 2000d: 3). It therefore suggested to 'sensitise' member states and to strengthen the Central Organ's position in reaction to coups (OAU 2000d: 3; OAU Secretariat 2000: 3).

New momentum was injected into the debate in 1999 when the Council of Ministers, at its 70th ordinary session in Algiers, repeated its concern over the resurgence of coups. The ministers mandated the Central Organ to revitalize the subcommittee in order to finalize the work on an OAU reaction mechanism (OAU Council of Ministers 1999). Likewise, the OAU Assembly decided that 'Member States whose Governments came to power through unconstitutional means after the Harare Summit, should restore constitutional legality before the next Summit' (OAU Assembly 1999: 24). The Assembly also mandated the Secretary-General to 'be actively seized of developments in those countries and to assist in programmes intended to return such countries to constitutional and democratic governments' (OAU Assembly 1999: 24).

This decision was nevertheless contested. Some, among them Nigeria's President Olusegun Obasanjo and Zambia's President Frederick Chiluba, in fact opted for a stronger anti-coup decision, one that would have rejected retrospective recognition of *all* governments that had come to power unconstitutionally (*Africa Confidential* 1999: 1). Chiluba openly criticized the 'heads of state who cling to power for too long' (APN 1999) and called for 'condemnation of heads of state that (...) refuse political turn taking' (PANA 2000). He also demanded the immediate exclusion of the three governments of the Comoros, Guinea-Bissau, and Niger that had come to power unconstitutionally after the Harare summit. Contrary to that, South Africa's President Thabo Mbeki suggested 'working with them to return them to democratic society' (APN 1999). Chiluba's open attack against fellow African governments also showed that the debate had already moved beyond a mere focus on military coups d'état. Like the initial propositions from the subcommittee, his criticism raised the issue of the legitimacy of existing regimes and asserted that incumbents too can be a threat to the 'good' order.

Following the mandate from the Algiers summit, the subcommittee met once again in Addis Ababa in order to continue its work on a draft framework. This time, it was composed of delegations from Ethiopia, Gabon, Lesotho, Libya, and Nigeria (OAU 2000b: 8–9). At the 2000 summit in Lomé, the OAU Assembly discussed the draft framework prepared by the subcommittee (OAU 2000c). On this basis, the Assembly finally adopted the Declaration on the Framework for an OAU Response to Unconstitutional Changes of Government, which for the first time enshrined the continental anti-coup regime in a legal text. The Declaration opens with a paragraph on common values and principles for democratic governance, reflecting 'the view that there is need to provide a solid underpinning to the OAU's agenda of promoting democracy and democratic institutions in Africa' (OAU 2000a: 2). These common values and principles range from the adoption of a democratic constitution to the separation of powers and the independence of the judiciary, the promotion of political pluralism and respect for the role of the opposition, organization of free and regular elections, and the constitutional recognition and promotion of fundamental (human) rights. However, instead of a clear enforcement mechanism to guarantee member states' adherence to these principles, the Declaration only stated that '[o]ur Organization should therefore support all efforts aimed at promoting adherence to these principles' (OAU 2000a: 2).

With regard to what counts as an unconstitutional change of government, the Lomé Declaration proposed four scenarios: (1) a 'military coup d'etat against a democratically elected Government'; (2) 'intervention by mercenaries to replace a democratically elected Government'; (3) 'replacement of democratically elected Governments by armed dissident groups and rebel movements'; and (4) 'the refusal of an incumbent government to relinquish power to the winning party after free, fair and regular elections' (OAU 2000a: 3).

As an anti-coup manual, the Declaration entailed a clear reaction mechanism, deemed to guarantee the demanded 'predetermined and agreed criteria and guidelines' (OAU Secretariat 1999: 2). Instead of the previous ad hoc and open-ended reactions, the Declaration now prescribed that an unconstitutional change of government should automatically lead to a condemnation by the OAU Secretary-General urging 'the speedy return to constitutional order' (OAU 2000a: 3). While the country concerned would be automatically suspended from the OAU, the coup plotters were to be engaged in order to re-establish constitutional order within six months:

> At the expiration of the six months suspension period, a range of limited and targeted sanctions against the regime that stubbornly refuses to restore constitutional order should be instituted [potentially including] visa denials for the perpetrators of an unconstitutional change, restrictions of government-to-government contacts, trade restrictions, etc. (OAU 2000a: 4)

The Declaration thus prescribed an automated, non-military reaction that was altogether geared towards minimalizing its submission to political considerations (see also Tieku 2009: 84). This was the first instance in which 'undoing' coups in Africa was turned into a matter of clear, automated, legal procedure.

While the general structure of the Declaration was copied from the subcommittee's draft, the definition of what counts as an unconstitutional change of government was shortened. The following five scenarios entailed in the draft are missing in the adopted Declaration: (1) 'the refusal by a government to organise elections at the end of its term in office'; (2) 'manipulations of the constitution aimed at preventing a democratic change'; (3) 'any form of election rigging and electoral malpractice, duly confirmed by the OAU or ascertained by an independent and credible body established for that purpose'; (4) 'systematic and persistent violations of the common values and principles'; and (5) 'any other form of unconstitutional change as may be defined by the OAU policy organs' (OAU 2000c: 1–2).[7]

The Lomé Declaration thus represents a compromise. This compromise is reflected in the contradiction that, on the one hand, it notes that violations of democratic principles are a threat to peace and security and a source for further coups, while, on the other hand, the scenarios considered as unconstitutional changes of government only refer to the *acquisition of power*, but not to the *conduct of governance* (see also Ikome 2007: 33; Souaré 2009: 11; Dersso 2017: 657). Issues such as election rigging or manipulations of the constitution were explicitly not considered infringements of 'good' order. Moreover, two additions from the initial draft were not adopted: (1) that a 'systematic and persistent violation' of the common values and principles should be sanctioned; and (2) the option for the OAU to add further scenarios to the definition of an unconstitutional change of government (OAU 2000c: 3).

Altogether, the deletions thus refer to a different understanding of the problem of unconstitutional changes of government (see Table 2.1 on p. 68): those situations that were ultimately *not* recognized as an unconstitutional change of government take issue with the practices of incumbent regimes. Their point of reference is the citizen as a bearer of defendable rights vis-à-vis their government. More than a mere right to elections, these rights include the protection against manipulative governance practices such as the cancellation or rigging of elections, government by decrees, and other violations of the democratic principles set out in the Declaration. By contrast, those rules that *did* become part of the compromise guarantee a particular form of government. Their point of reference is not the rights of citizens, but procedural correctness. The recognition of democratic elections as the only legitimate avenue to access state power means that governmental rule is indeed conditioned. What this protects is not incumbents (Sturman 2008: 105), but an orderly established government legitimated by elections. In this imaginary, the rules that regulate access to state power are simply assumed to guarantee a similar rule-governed conduct of governance in the future.

Although the wording of the Lomé Declaration was finalized at the level of the OAU's intergovernmental institutions, the OAU Secretariat overall played a crucial role in pushing the agenda for legally enshrining the anti-coup manual: through the preparation of meetings, informal negotiations, and the drafting of background documents (see also Tieku 2009). In reality, however, the Secretariat's room for manoeuvre was also limited. In fact, the OAU Secretariat's initial agenda was much more encompassing than what was adopted later on. This is, for instance, reflected in Salim Ahmed Salim's recommendations submitted with the draft Lomé Declaration. Here, he reminded member states that:

> Given the importance of democracy and good governance, and their impact on peace, security and development, there is a compelling need for the OAU to address in a pro-active manner, issues relating to good governance, respect for human rights, democratization, corruption and the allocation of resources (...) (OAU 2000c: 6)

This request for the (O)AU 'to address in a pro-active manner' issues of good governance and democracy became the backbone for continued efforts to write the 'good' order into continental law and to authorize the continental organization to serve as its custodian.

The Charter project: contesting and expanding the manual

Three years after the adoption of the Lomé Declaration, coups were not at all a thing of the past. After unconstitutional changes of government in Côte d'Ivoire (2002), Madagascar (2002), the Central African Republic (2003), Guinea-Bissau (2003), and São Tomé and Príncipe (2003), the Central Organ at its last meeting demanded 'concrete proposals aimed at strengthening the effectiveness of the Declaration' (AU 2003: 2). For an enhanced future anti-coup regime, the Central Organ also demanded a clear prohibition as to 'any participation (...) of the perpetrators of coups d'Etat (...) in elections organized to restore constitutional order' (AU 2003: 3). Such participation had in fact taken place in several of the above situations and threatened to create a precedent in which the continental anti-coup doctrine would help putschists to *ex post facto* auto-legitimize their actions.

In the meantime, the AU had officially succeeded the OAU. With this, the Central Organ's attention to unconstitutional changes of government became integrated into a new normative and institutional framework. Altogether, this placed more emphasis on conflict prevention, democratization, and the protection of human rights, and thus assigned new responsibilities to the continental organization (OAU 2000e; AU 2002). With the establishment of the AU, the organization's anti-coup norm was also elevated to a legally binding commitment. Article 30 of the Constitutive Act stipulates: 'Governments which shall come to power through unconstitutional means shall not be allowed to participate in the activities of the Union' (OAU 2000e: Art. 30). The PSC, which henceforth came to replace the Central Organ as the central decision-making body in the area of peace and security, was mandated to 'institute sanctions whenever an unconstitutional change of Government takes place' (AU 2002: Art. 7(1g)).

It nevertheless took until 2005, following a coup in Mauritania, for the rewriting of the anti-coup manual to gain momentum. At that time, Jean Ping, then Chairperson of the AU Commission, criticized in a report to the Assembly that the Lomé Declaration was silent as to the undemocratic behaviour and human rights violations of incumbent governments, which impede 'all possible democratic change' (AU Commission 2005: 10). Ping therefore called on the AU to revise the Declaration accordingly (AU Commission 2005: 11). An independent expert study was commissioned to review the Organ's and Ping's suggestions (AU 2005c). However, for some time, no tangible reactions followed.

What happened instead was a merger of these calls for reforming the Lomé Declaration with a more comprehensive undertaking: to formulate an African Charter on Democracy. This was yet another sign that the debate on unconstitutional changes of government had increasingly moved away from a strict focus on (military) coups d'état towards a more comprehensive definition of continental standards for legitimate order.

The idea of an African Charter on Democracy evolved from decade-long lobbying by the OAU Secretariat, which in 2002 had, inter alia, resulted in the adoption of the OAU/AU Declaration on the Principles Governing Democratic Elections in Africa, in which elections were defined as 'the basis of the authority of any representative government' (AU Assembly 2002: Para. I; see also Matlosa 2008: 4). More importantly, though, the OAU Secretariat was given the mandate 'to be fully engaged in the strengthening of the democratization process, particularly by observing and monitoring elections in our Member States' (AU Assembly 2002: Para. IV). The AU Commission, which had replaced the OAU Secretariat, embraced this mandate to proactively support the democratization of member states. In a first step, this mandate was linked up with an initiative by several South African non-governmental organizations (NGOs) aimed at boosting the democratization and good governance agenda on the continent (see also Tieku 2009: 79). At an international conference held in Durban in April 2003, jointly organized by the AU Commission, the Independent Electoral Commission of South Africa, and the African Association of Electoral Authorities, more than 400 participants discussed ways and means to strengthen democratic governance in Africa as well as the AU's potential contributions (AU Commission 2003: Annex I). The AU Commission used this forum to present a Draft Declaration on Democracy, Elections and Governance in Africa (AU Commission 2003: 12). From the very beginning, the Commission portrayed the Charter project as being solely about a summary of commitments OAU/AU member states had already made so far in this area. The novelty and change that emanated from the document was hence strategically played down (see also Matlosa 2008: 6–7).

As follow-up to the debates at the conference, the AU Commission convened a meeting of government experts in order to discuss its own 'draft document on Democracy and Governance' (AU Executive Council 2003: 1). What followed between 2003 and 2007 was a play of meetings, Executive Council decisions, and again meetings that addressed both the demand to strengthen the Lomé Declaration and the AU's role in democracy promotion more generally (see also Matlosa 2008: 10). In light of the continuing prevalence of coups, the search for a stronger response mechanism increasingly concentrated on the effectiveness of the AU's legal framework to *prevent* coups and to deter future coup plotters. However, the ubiquitous narrative of prevention was not based on a consensus, neither as to what prevention implied nor that prevention meant bolstering AU instruments to promote democracy and human rights. Hence, despite the unanimously repeated need to review the Lomé Declaration, it was not at all agreed that this meant furnishing the AU with a more intrusive mandate to actively *promote* democratic governance within its member states (AU 2006a: 4–6).

Two documents structured the ensuing meetings: first, a proposal for an African Charter on Democracy, Elections and Governance drafted by Dr Khabele Matlosa, then expert at the Electoral Institute for Sustainable Democracy in Africa (EISA), South Africa, on behalf of the AU Commission; and second, the above-mentioned independent expert study on the reform of the Lomé Declaration (AU 2005c).[8]

The independent expert study came up with three main observations. First, due to 'an abnormal situation with regard to democratic standards created by bad governance, dictatorship, and human rights violations among others', there continue to be situations in which 'national interests prevail over regional public standards' (AU 2005c: 8). This observation calmed the desire to legalize reactions to unconstitutional changes of government even further and pointed to a potential friction between generalized continental principles and domestic specificities of legitimate order. This potential friction has been discussed, for instance, by Francis Ikome (2007: 14) in the 'good coup' scenario, where coups receive widespread legitimacy among the population because they 'are seen as generally acting in the public interest' (see also AU Commission 2005: 10). Second, the study laments that the AU has often opted for the 'mild approach' towards coups, which, according to the report, reveals 'the ineffectiveness of the deterrent effect intended' (AU 2005c: 8). Third, it finds a lack of commitment from member states to implement AU decisions on coups, extending at times even to full support for coup plotters. It also notes that 'in some cases, the positions adopted at subregional level prove to be contrary to those of the continental organization, [leading to] (...) a problem of the credibility of the said organization and its decisions (...)' (AU 2005c: 8–9).

The study therefore makes three fairly modest suggestions on how to amend the existing policy framework: first, to introduce an AU monitoring mechanism on good governance and democracy that is mandatory for all AU member states; second, the elaboration of a sanctions mechanism in order to 'establish a real power relationship with the perpetrators of coups d'état' (AU 2005c: 9); and third, to turn the Lomé Declaration into a legally binding document (AU 2005c: 9). These three suggestions thus largely glossed over the contradictions pointed to in the observations at the beginning of the study: the potential friction between regional principles and domestic struggles for legitimacy, as well as the likely conflicts in interpretation, approach, and proposed solutions between the AU, its member states, and other regional organizations. The study thus effectively depoliticized the search for a better continental manual against coups and underlined the hitherto dominant legalistic and technocratic approach to 'undoing' coups.

Still under the overall banner of prevention, two reform approaches were discussed over the following years. The first one addressed the question of how and to what extent to strengthen the AU's legal and policy instruments in order to deter future coup plotters – in other words, how to make the AU's reactions more compelling. The second one focused on finding ways to define and monitor continental governance standards and thus to prevent coups in the long run. This approach aimed at granting the AU a more prominent role in promoting governance in its member states and thereby enhancing the quality of existing political orders.

In relation to the first approach, an early agreement evolved with regard to the need to strengthen the AU's sanctions regime and for perpetrators to be barred from participating in transitional elections (AU 2006b: 6–7). Without further debate, both aspects were later included in the African Charter on Democracy, Elections and Governance (AU 2007: Art. 25(4) and 25(6–7)). With this decision, the manual on how to react to coups was further refined, now leaving less room for manoeuvre to negotiate with coup plotters. It equipped the AU with new punitive measures in the form of sanctions against putschists and against member states that cooperate with putschists, as well as the possibility to try perpetrators of unconstitutional changes of government 'before the competent court of the Union' (AU 2007: Art. 25(5)).

The second approach was more contested. The proposition to establish a mandatory AU monitoring mechanism and to strengthen the AU's early warning system sparked fierce controversies. The idea of an obligatory monitoring mechanism was immediately rejected because 'the notion of national policy control was the prerogative of states' and monitoring duties were already done by national parliaments, the PSC, or the African Peer Review Mechanism (APRM) (AU 2006b: 5). The suggestion to set up an early warning system that would put more emphasis on situations 'of a breakdown of social dialogue', for instance, was similarly contested and finally rejected with reference to already existing provisions in the PSC Protocol (AU 2006b: 6). Both issues were excluded from the ensuing meetings.

The only continental governance standard that remained on the agenda of the deliberations was the suggestion to outlaw constitutional manipulations aimed at prolonging incumbents' stay in power. As mentioned above, this had already been debated during the preparations of the Lomé Declaration, and it was explicitly taken up again in the Draft Charter on Democracy, Elections and Governance (see also AU 2005a: 5).[9] Yet the issue remained as contested as before.

The 2006 ministerial meeting on the Charter project, for instance, ended with the observation that for some, 'the constitutions of states already provided for constitutional amendments and it would be superfluous to mention it [constitutional amendment] among the measures aimed at strengthening the Lomé Declaration' (AU 2006f: 5). The contentions became clearer at the second ministerial meeting, on which the report notes:

> Some delegations were against maintaining this phrase on grounds that such a prolongation depended on the expression of democracy, in accordance with the constitutional rules and procedures in force. (...) Other delegations insisted on the need to maintain this phrase, basing their argument on the fact that it was essential to ensure democratic alternation and thus prevent any attempt to remain indefinitely in power through revision of constitutions and relevant legal instruments by the incumbent government, contrary to the spirit and letter of constitutional provisions. (AU 2006c: 5)

This latter group held that:

> (...) Article 28 [now 25] of the Charter is one of the most important articles. The question at stake is not the issue of revising the constitution with the aim of improving the performance of the State. (...) [W]hat is at stake is the manipulation of the constitution by some regimes in order to remain in power. Paragraph 5 would put an end to violations of the constitutions and to 'legal coups d'état'. (AU 2006e: 20)

In response, the first group of delegations argued that 'the failure to adhere strictly to the procedure for amending constitutions was not a violation of the constitution' (AU 2006e: 19).

Since 'the question of the revision of constitutions as a ploy to stay in power had dissenting opinions' (AU 2006a: 2), the ministerial meeting referred the issue to the Executive Council.[10] The Executive Council, in turn, requested the Commission to 'review the legal form of the Draft Charter including the content of Article 25 (5) in the light of comments and observations made on that article' and to resubmit it for final approval to the coming summit (AU Executive Council 2006: 1). The Charter text ultimately adopted stipulates that '[a]ny amendment or revision of the constitution or legal instruments, which is an infringement on the principles of democratic change of government', is an unconstitutional change of government (AU 2007: Art. 23(5)).

The contestations during the preparation of this paragraph are evidence of resistance to the formulation of clearer continental legitimacy principles. One participant in the meetings even described the negotiations as 'war'.[11] Sovereignty and national jurisdiction were repeatedly invoked against a more intrusive AU monitoring or in order to defend particularities in national constitutions. The final wording of the article on constitutional manipulations hence lacks a clear reference to undemocratic intentions and malpractices by incumbent governments. While Sekai Saungweme (2007: 3) fears that the vague wording of this provision may invite 'manipulative, corrupt governments (…) [to] easily circumvent it', others point to the fact that it is exactly this vagueness which creates an opportunity to capture a variety of 'democratic backsliding' practices in one provision (McMahon 2007: 3; Glen 2012: 139). Irrespective of what the actual consequences of this particular wording are, overall the debates reconstructed above underline the contested character of the Charter project that stood in contrast to the otherwise unanimous rhetorical reference to democracy and the rule of law as principles of a 'good' order.

The Charter nevertheless enlarged the set of issues recognized as unconstitutional changes of government and for the first time wrote them into a legally binding text.[12] Previously rejected ideas thereby also re-entered the debates. With the outlawing of constitutional manipulations, incumbent governments themselves were for the first time marked as culprits (see also Ikome 2007: 47). Law was increasingly recognized as political and hence did not alone suffice to define 'good' order. With respect to the underlying norms, the debate overall strengthened the reference to people's rights to choose their own governments, thus clearly going beyond a purely legalistic understanding of unconstitutional changes of government – that is, as infringements of the legal order or the rights of incumbent regimes (see Table 2.1).

However, some of the propositions debated in preparatory meetings were later entirely abandoned. One such example is the concern raised in the above-mentioned expert study, which had pointed to a possible friction between a legalistic approach to unconstitutional changes of government and the observation that in some cases a coup might be the only avenue for change, and in fact welcomed by the people. While the meeting of independent experts of November 2005 recognized this as a 'complex question of legitimacy and legality', it nevertheless concluded that:

> politics should [at] all times be conducted through a constitutional order and rule of law. Legitimacy of regimes has to be measured [at] all times in tandem with the broader agenda of democratisation and constitutionalism. Thus, legitimacy should not be considered in isolation from the quest for democracy, political stability and peace. We need to avoid and discourage take-over of power by unconstitutional and violent means, if we are to inculcate a culture of democracy and peace (...) (AU 2005a: 4)

The ensuing ministerial meeting finally closed the debate by stating that 'there was no such thing as a good coup d'Etat. A coup d'Etat was a coup d'Etat. What was important was to address the root causes of such changes' (AU 2006f: 5).

Another concern that was raised during the 2005 meeting of independent experts also vanished in the course of the debate: the observation that the Lomé Declaration was silent in relation to 'a culture of impunity in cases of human rights abuses' (AU 2005a: 5). It was recommended that 'firm action and effective sanctions should be meted out against perpetrators of massive human rights abuses and the culture of impunity expunged from Africa's political tradition' (AU 2005a: 5). Impunity remained an issue during the meetings, but with a different connotation: it came up again once the status and fate of 'former heads of state' were debated. Here, the initial call for criminal investigation into human rights violations was transformed into an effort to incentivize heads of state to relinquish power once defeated in elections or once they had reached the allowed number of terms of office (AU 2006b: 6; AU 2006f: 4–5). The meaning and relevance of impunity had thus been turned upside down: from a right of victims to a political instrument for co-optation.

A glance at the participants in these debates once again underlines the dominant role played by the organization's bureaucracy. The AU Commission thus followed the path of its predecessor through the preparation of reports and summaries as well as through the organization of the preparatory meetings. This at least sustained a discussion, although it did not necessarily affect the outcomes of the deliberations in a substantial way. This time, the level of representation of member states at the ministerial meetings was also high and increased over the course of time. This reflects that member states – albeit not pushing the process – indeed considered the debates on continental governance standards as relevant, if only to prevent a more consequential and intrusive continental regime. Moreover, the exchanges were also attended by other international and regional organizations such as the UN Economic Commission for Africa (UNECA), the International Organisation of La Francophonie (OIF), the New Partnership for Africa's Development (NEPAD) Secretariat, NGOs such as International IDEA, the Open Society Institute, and EISA, as well as representatives from various donors. Despite an increasing presence of member states, the meetings were dominated by experts and bureaucrats as opposed to diplomats, with an unconventionally broad participation by non-state and international actors (see also Tieku 2009: 76).

'Zero tolerance': strengthening the manual, strengthening the AU

Despite the years of preparation and discussion, ratification of the Charter proceeded at a slow pace. One year after its adoption, not a single AU member state had ratified it. It was only on 15 February 2012 that the Charter finally entered into force after the required number of 15 member states had deposited their ratifications. The list of first signatories and those who have still neither signed nor ratified the Charter does not indicate a link between ratifications and regime types, with the continent's 'democrats' pitted against 'the others' (Engel 2019).[13] Nevertheless, the reluctance of member states to sign the document reflects that the Charter project was not necessarily the expression of a collective embracement of democracy as a shared normative principle (see also Kane 2008: 55; Matlosa 2008: 9).

Yet since the adoption of the Charter in January 2007, unconstitutional changes of government and constitutional crises did not abate. The overthrows of governments in Guinea (2008), Mauritania (2008), and Madagascar (2009) in fact proved the opposite and gave new impetus to the AU's 'concern' about a 'resurgence of the scourge of coups' (AU Assembly 2009b: 1). In January 2009, the AU Assembly therefore mandated the Chairperson to submit a report on recommendations relating to 'the implementation of appropriate preventive measures against unconstitutional changes of government as well as the enhancement of efficiency and capacity building in early warning, good offices and mediation (...)' (AU Assembly 2009b: 1). Moreover, one year later, the Assembly proclaimed a policy of 'zero tolerance' aimed at 'strengthening the capacity of the African Union to manage such situations' (AU Assembly 2010a).

The Chairperson's preliminary report submitted in June 2009 defined the terms and structure of the ensuing debates. Reminiscent of earlier debates, these were organized along three propositions: first, to enhance AU instruments in order to deter future coup plotters; second, to invest more in the structural prevention of coups; and third, to address the question of international and regional coordination in reactions to coups (see AU Commission 2009: 15–18; AU Commission 2010: 5–11).

With regard to more effectively deterring coup plotters, the Assembly reiterated in 2010:

> the need for Member States to uphold the rule of law and abide by their own Constitutions, especially with regard to constitutional reforms, bearing in mind that failure to respect these provisions could lead to situations of tension which, in turn, could trigger political crisis.[14] (AU Assembly 2010a: 3)

Thus, for the first time, the Assembly discussed constitutional manipulations – although euphemistically termed 'constitutional reforms' – under the heading of unconstitutional changes of government. It also decided that perpetrators of coups shall not be allowed to participate in elections, that they should face 'punitive economic sanctions', and that member states supporting coup plotters shall also face sanctions (AU Assembly 2010a). The decision hence deliberately repeated the provisions of the African Charter on Democracy, Elections and Governance, which thereby became legally binding even though the Charter had not yet entered into force. In the same vein, a special retreat of the PSC was held in Ezulwini, Swaziland, which proposed strengthening the AU sanction regime, including the establishment of a PSC Committee on Sanctions (AU PSC 2009c). Moreover, knowledge of developments on the ground was identified as an important means to sharpen the AU's reactions, and a number of suggestions were made on how to improve this knowledge (AU PSC 2009c: 5; AU Commission 2010: 9; see also Engel 2012a: 77). For the AU Commission, these were all measures to ensure clear, coherent, and uncompromising reactions, which would help deter potential coup plotters in the future (AU Commission 2009: 15).

Concerning the second proposition, the Assembly followed the Chairperson's suggestions on strengthening AU instruments to structurally prevent coups through democratization and good governance. It was noted that while the AU has hitherto adopted numerous declarations and decisions, ratification and implementation have been slow at best. In order to 'truly consolidate the values of democracy and good governance in our continent' (AU Commission 2009: 16), adherence to the already adopted declarations and decisions was indispensable (see also AU Assembly 2010a; AU Assembly 2013a). At the same time, the Assembly decided in 2010 that the PSC should 'examine regularly progress made in the democratisation processes, on the basis of a report prepared by an independent Rapporteur' (AU Assembly 2010a). In their final declaration of the 2011 summit on 'shared values', the AU Assembly declared:

> We call on the AUC and other Organs to establish African ownership over Shared Values by way of wider communication and information sharing, through direct support to Member States, by ensuring the strengthening of institutions and by way of putting in place measures to ensure that success is monitored and that there is ongoing review of progress in the implementation of adopted Shared Values instruments. (AU Assembly 2011: 3)

Today, this mandate to 'ensure that success is monitored' is part of the so-called African Governance Architecture (AGA), through which the AU Commission seeks to set up regular, consultative mechanisms to monitor the governance of its member states (Wachira 2014: 13–14; Wiebusch et al. 2019: 25–26).

The increasing attention to structural prevention gained even more currency in the wake of the so-called Arab Spring. In its decisions on the situations in Egypt and Libya, the PSC, for instance repeatedly recognized 'the aspirations (…) for democracy, political reform, justice, peace and security, as well as for socio-economic development (…)' (AU PSC 2011b; AU PSC 2011c; AU PSC 2011d). The momentum of the uprisings overall shifted greater attention to the so-called structural causes of the crises and people's (legitimate) aspirations for better lives (see also AU PSC 2011a; AU Panel of the Wise 2012). Until the second time the government in Egypt was toppled in 2013, the events in Northern Africa were thus deliberately *not* interpreted as unconstitutional changes of government, but as 'consistent with the relevant instruments of the AU and the continent's commitment to promote democratization, good governance and respect for human rights' (AU PSC 2011c: 1). This was later on repeated when the AU PSC reacted to the 2014 'popular uprising' in Burkina Faso that ended Blaise Compaoré's 27 years in power (AU PSC 2014d). In all these situations, the identified problem was no longer the unlawful acquisition of power, but the overt and more general negation of the 'right of the people to peacefully express their will against oppressive systems' (AU Assembly

2013b: 6). Once again, this served to underline the importance of the AU in defining and monitoring continental legitimacy principles in its member states.

With regard to the third proposition, international and regional coordination, the AU Commission started a consultation process with other African so-called Regional Economic Communities (RECs), the AU's Economic, Social and Cultural Council, the Pan-African Parliament (PAP), 'other relevant organs and institutions', and international partners (AU Commission 2010: 4). This took place against the rationale that 'AU's action on unconstitutional changes must, to be effective, have the full support of the Regional Mechanisms for conflict prevention, management and resolution and of AU's international community partners' (AU Commission 2009: 17). As a result, since then the Assembly repeatedly stressed the 'primacy of the Union's responsibility in the promotion of peace, security and stability in the continent' (AU Assembly 2010a; AU Assembly 2013b). Regarding the RECs, the Assembly reiterated that:

> whenever the AU takes a decision on an unconstitutional change of Government, it must do so in close consultation with the Regional Mechanisms (...) [which] must conform with the decision thus taken and, in particular, refrain from admitting States suspended from participating in the AU activities. (AU Assembly 2010a)

This again underlines that the dominant, mechanistic approach to 'undoing' unconstitutional changes of government had largely prevailed and continued to define how arising practical challenges were dealt with. The above-described imposed coordination between the AU and RECs is but one example of this approach. It completed a trend by which the mission to prevent unconstitutional changes of government had turned almost any challenge into a search for 'more effective' reactions (AU Commission 2010: 3).

In sum, the debate on how to address unconstitutional changes of government remained dynamic, which was not least reflected in the reoccurrence of themes such as stricter mechanisms to monitor the compliance of member states with continental standards and a growing recognition of the contested legitimacy of existing political orders. Over time, the themes and issues discussed under the heading of 'unconstitutional changes of government' thus gradually expanded. However, this expansion should not be taken as a well-founded normative consensus. Rather, this last phase once again highlighted that efforts to legalize the AU's approach to legitimate order in its member states clearly faced resistance.

Last but not least, one can also observe a shift in the focus of the debate. Together with the unabated stress on deterrence and prevention, the call for 'strengthening' the AU's responses has become a powerful metanarrative. With this, the problem of unconstitutional changes of government increasingly became a matter of preventing future coups through legal prescriptions and continental monitoring mechanisms: in both cases, 'strengthening the AU' (i.e. endowing the organization with ever-more or more intrusive roles) seemed to be *the* inevitable solution.

Expansion and claims of the African anti-coup manual

While initially a concern only when 'imperial' forces or mercenaries were involved, since the mid-1990s coups in African states were increasingly debated both as a threat to regional stability and as an infringement of people's right to choose their own government (Murray 2004: 74). The history of the idea to outlaw coups in Africa therefore reflects a gradual expansion of what is considered as legitimate order and, as a consequence, of what is debated, and why, as 'bad' under the label of 'unconstitutional changes of government'. This expansion is most evidently reflected in the enlargement of the legal definition of 'unconstitutional changes of government' itself: with the inclusion of constitutional manipulations in the African Charter on Democracy, Elections and Governance, the hitherto dominant focus on illegal *acquisitions* of power shifted towards an – albeit limited – concern with the *practices* of incumbents (Wiebusch et al 2019: 20).[15] Moreover, this general enlargement of what counts as a good political order is also reflected in a growing attention to 'root causes' and the 'structural prevention' of future coups, although these issues were not considered with the same legal consequences. Table 2.1 summarizes five distinct problem constructions that occurred in the debates reconstructed in this chapter. As this chapter demonstrated, the dominant problem constructions increasingly revolved around the idea that unconstitutional changes of government are an infringement of people's right to choose their own government. Neither the mere stability of regimes nor their legality alone qualifies as good (enough) political order. References to stability and an assumed a priori quality of legal order do remain important, but they are woven together with the idea that legitimacy can only be established through elections.

Apart from the reconstructed gradual expansion, this chapter also demonstrated the growing legalization of continental legitimacy principles.

The history of the African anti-coup regime thus reflects an expansive collective effort to find better answers to the question of legitimate order through law, driven by the desire to make unconstitutional changes of government a matter of the past. This is evidenced by collective attempts to define (and expand) the situations considered unconstitutional changes of government, the legal measures taken against perpetrators of coups, and the institutional capacities to take consequential action in response to such situations.[16] However, contrary to this narrative of a gradual expansion and legalization over time, this process was contested. The anti-coup manual is therefore the result of both negotiation and craftsmanship, a process in which several ideas have also effectively been silenced and excluded.

Silences and exclusions

The above reconstruction revealed a divide between those issues that entered the legal definition of unconstitutional change of government (i.e. extreme deviances from the 'good order' requiring correction) and those that were debated as more general problems of political order. There was, in this sense, a clear hierarchy of problems. While the search for better strategies to prevent future coups increasingly focused on the quality and conduct of governance, the legal definition of 'unconstitutional changes of government' still largely concentrated on protecting a particular form of government, established through (democratic) elections (see Table 2.1). Alternative propositions that had been raised, for instance, during the preparation of the Lomé Declaration challenged the way this line was drawn – referring to the fairness of electoral processes, violations of human rights, and the impunity of incumbents. As mentioned above, these questions have also increasingly been debated in the context of the so-called Arab Spring and the PSC's search for an adequate response to what has been termed 'popular uprisings'. In its 2011 review of the state of peace and security in Africa, the PSC observed, for instance, that 'neglect of the political and socio-economic needs of the population, in particular the youth, by Governments, create[s] conditions favorable to the outbreak of crises and conflicts' (AU PSC 2011a: 1). It therefore argued that:

> strengthening of democratic culture and institutions, respect for human rights, upholding of the rule of law and respect for people-centred constitutions (...) [are] means for preventing conflicts and enhancing the people's participation in fostering solutions to the prevailing problems. (AU PSC 2011a: 1)

Table 2.1 – Ideal-typical problematizations of infringements of legitimate order

	Coups infringement to...	Possible solution
Anti-imperialism	Independence/sovereignty	Collective defence
Stability	Regional security	Military intervention
Legality	The rule of law	Constitutional order
Form of government	People's right to choose their government/to rule-governed access to state power	Elections
Exercise of governance	People's right to just and inclusive forms of government	Monitoring of democratic and human rights standards

Source: Author's compilation.

In a similar vein, the African Commission on Human and Peoples' Rights (ACHPR) as well as the PAP, for instance, repeatedly diagnosed an 'ever growing gap between the governments and the governed' (PAP 2013: 2), manifested in much broader and more constant violations of fundamental rights (ACHPR 2010; ACHPR 2012). Such understandings of infringements of the good order would not only demand other forms of intervention; more importantly, they also challenge many assumptions underlying existing forms of intervention, for instance regarding the extent to which people can effectively exercise their rights as citizens in elections under given political and economic circumstances (see Peterson 1990; Aidoo 1993).

All these problematizations of the exercise of governance, however, were marginalized over the course of the debates. With the sole exception of constitutional manipulations, the practices of incumbents, the relationship between governors and governed, or questions pertaining to the justice of existing orders were *not* problematized in a similarly consequential way. They were nevertheless turned into future mandates: for the AU to monitor progress and for member states to 'work towards a better fulfilment and effective follow up on the commitments made' (AU Commission 2009: 16).

The expansive mission

The expansive problematization of coups also expanded the role and responsibilities of the AU to address what was identified as a collective problem in more and more intrusive ways. While this intrusiveness has been and remains contested, the role of the AU increasingly moved away from a merely reactive one, with the AU becoming responsible for *preventing* coups. Prevention therefore increasingly served as a metanarrative to expand the responsibilities of the AU. As noted by Stef Vandeginste (2013: 23), with the adoption of the Lomé Declaration, the continental organization had shifted from being a mere registrar to being a judge. Taking the full history into account, these metaphors may be extended: in addition to being the judge, the AU's role has become that of a police force (stressing its responsibility to directly intervene or to apply deterring sanctions) and, increasingly so, that of a social worker (mandated to monitor and counsel member states) on how to realize the 'good order'. In line with this, the responsibilities of the AU Commission in particular expanded and received a new potential for agency, particularly through tasks such as monitoring and knowledge creation (see also Engel 2013; Wiebusch et al. 2019: 26).

As this chapter has shown, over time the discourse on how to reform the AU's policy on unconstitutional changes of government was more and more confined to 'strengthening' the AU's responses, referring to both the organization's capacity to deter coup plotters and to its role as a guardian of the quality of governance in its member states. Unconstitutional changes of government increasingly became a mission in which the AU's 'effectiveness' has been turned into an end in itself. At the same time, any identified challenge served as a background to formulate new mandates and new responsibilities. All attempts to 'strengthen' the AU's responses thus followed the same logic: expanding the scope of continental legal and policy prescriptions and the institutional mechanisms to implement such laws and policies. Clearer, stricter, more comprehensive rules, whether binding law or mere policy frameworks, seem to have been *the* inevitable solution. This had indeed been the starting point of the debate: the Lomé Declaration was a collective effort to legalize and regularize the continent's approach to questions of legitimacy and authority in African states (OAU Secretariat 1999: 2; Tieku 2009: 84) – and it has continued to be the dominant approach to unconstitutional changes of government since.

A more recent example in this line is the above-mentioned debate about how to interpret and what lessons to take from the popular uprisings in Northern Africa, the 2013 coup in Egypt, and situations such as that in Burkina Faso in 2014 and the Sudan in 2019. As noted by then AU Commissioner for Peace and Security Ramtane Lamamra in 2011:

the uprisings in North Africa exposed a dangerous vacuum in the arsenal of AU instruments that needs to be urgently filled by putting in place appropriate response mechanisms that will enable the continental body to timely respond to such phenomena with the required robustness and effectiveness. (Quoted in Dersso 2019: 115)

The PSC, for its part, recognized that 'the flexibility and inconsistency in the interpretation and application of the relevant instruments created a credibility problem for the AU' (AU PSC 2014c: 2). It therefore suggested that all existing provisions on unconstitutional changes of government should be 'consolidated into a single document' and that this 'consolidated AU framework' should also include 'the appropriate refinement of the definition of unconstitutional changes of government, in light of the evolving challenges facing the continent, notably those related to popular uprisings against oppressive systems (...)' (AU PSC 2014b: 31; AU PSC 2014c: 3).

The challenge to differentiate between (legitimate) uprisings and (illegitimate) infringements of the good order – a question that had come up at several points in the course of the debates reconstructed above – was hence once again to be addressed through legal precision and turned into the starting point for yet another, *better* manual (AU Commission 2014a: 5; Dersso 2019).

What, then, might go missing in this expanding mission? First, the seemingly unanimous acceptance and automatic answer of 'strengthening' the AU conceal that member states, RECs, and other international actors constantly challenge this proclaimed authority. Member states in particular are important here as more intrusive continental rules may in fact further alienate rather than integrate them into the AU's project. Second, and more importantly, the expanding mission also means that there is little room for substantive engagement with the normative and practical dilemmas and tensions that come with this self-ascribed role as judge of questions of legitimate order. Questions pertaining to the processes of detecting, formulating, and defending common values, as well as what exactly needs to be changed in order to build more just and sustainable orders, have remained largely unanswered in the reconstructed search to 'strengthen' the AU (Cowell 2011: 759). Moreover, there is little reflection about the normative assumptions that underpin the prescribed reactions to unconstitutional changes of government and about the representational claims that justify the AU as embodying African 'shared values'. Neither the justifications for particular purposes nor the adequacy of the envisaged solutions are subjected to critical (self-) reflection if questions of legitimacy are immediately and somewhat automatically turned into legal missions.

Mugabe's announcement held true. Probably unlike he had foreseen in 1997, the continental organization came to address coups 'as vigorously as we can', both in practice as well as in the formulation of ever-more legal prescriptions and policy instruments to turn this vision into reality (Reuters 1997). The result of this was an expanding notion of the problem of unconstitutional changes of government and corresponding mandates for the AU to take care of them. It was an evolving legal mission to outlaw and 'undo' unconstitutional changes of government. This process is remarkable, and it underlines a continued belief in the necessity to eradicate arbitrariness in the internal order of states and ad hoc reactions to such situations. This, however, does not overcome the very politics inherent in the idea of legalizing the question of legitimacy and imposing answers to it through a continental organization.

3
What 'crise malgache'?

On 17 March 2009, after weeks of anti-government protests, the President of Madagascar, Marc Ravalomanana, signed *ordonnance 2009-001*, with which he handed over power to a military directorate led by Vice-Admiral Hyppolite Ramaroson. This took place under the eyes of the special envoys of the UN and the AU as well as the US ambassador to Madagascar at the time (Ralambomahay 2011: 37). The ordinance called for the military to: (1) organize national consultations about a constitutional reform; (2) prepare a revision of the national electoral code; (3) prepare new legislation on the status of political parties; and (4) organize elections within 24 months (République de Madagascar 2009a). Shortly afterwards, when international mediators presented the ordinance to the opposition, this meeting was stormed by a group of soldiers led by General Noël Rakotonandrasana. Rakotonandrasana was a key figure in a mutiny that had broken out ten days earlier at CAPSAT military camp, just outside of Antananarivo.[1] There, mutineers denounced the violence used by Ravalomanana's Presidential Guard to quell the anti-government protests happening in Antananarivo. They also criticized the presence of mercenaries on the island that Ravalomanana had allegedly recruited (*Midi Madagasikara* 2009b). Recruiting predominantly from lower ranks, the mutiny also pointed to more deep-seated conflicts over roles, ranks, and inequalities within the Malagasy army (Ramasy 2012: 79). In the afternoon of 17 March 2009, the military arrested the appointed head of the military directorate and compelled power to be handed over to a High Authority of the Transition (*Haute autorité de la transition*, HAT) headed by Andry Rajoelina (*L'Express de Madagascar* 2009d; République de Madagascar 2009b).

Andry Rajoelina had been mayor of Antananarivo until he was sacked by Ravalomanana a month before. This was a reaction to Rajoelina's rise as the public face of anti-government protests in Antananarivo. Since January 2009, these protests had brought several tens of thousands of Tananariviens to the streets and to the historical *Place du 13 mai*. On 31 January, Rajoelina demanded Ravalomanana's resignation and declared himself president as head of the HAT. He described himself as 'porte-parole des aspirations populaires', the spokesperson for people's aspirations, and thereby claimed his role in the transitional government being demanded (*L'Express de Madagascar* 2009e). Orange

T-shirts and banners became the symbols of the protest, linking the anti-Ravalomanana movement to the so-called Orange Revolution in Ukraine, which in 2004 effectively enforced a regime change (Galibert 2009a: 142).

Three public scandals in late 2008 accelerated the popular mobilization against Ravalomanana and thereby set the terms for Rajoelina's claim to power and political renewal (Ralambomahay 2011: 17; Ratsimbaharison 2017: Chapter 4). First, in November 2008, a public scandal erupted over the purchase of a second presidential airplane for an estimated 60 million USD. At a moment when the socio-economic situation of many Malagasies in fact declined rather than improved, the so-called *Air Force One II* scandal symbolized to many the irresponsibility and greed that became so characteristic of the country's political elite and Ravalomanana's rule (Marcus 2008). Alleged acts of corruption and unclear financial management in the context of the purchase of the plane finally also led important donors – among them the IMF, the World Bank, and the EU – to temporarily suspend the transfer of aid money (Marcus 2016: 196).

Second, in November 2008, the *Financial Times* reported about a land deal between the Malagasy government and the South Korean company Daewoo Logistics in which more than 1.3 million hectares – more than half of Madagascar's arable land – were leased for 99 years. Daewoo wanted to use the land for agricultural production and biofuels, whose main target was the export market. In Madagascar, this fueled public outrage. The land deal not only provoked an unprecedented international mobilization; it also sparked Malagasy protest against foreign land acquisition on the island and the altogether legally and financially nebulous handling of the deal (Gingembre 2010; Marcus 2016: 197).

Third, on 13 December 2008, at a time when public pressure on Ravalomanana had already reached a certain level, Rajoelina's radio station VIVA aired an interview with former President Didier Ratsiraka. Ravalomanana subsequently ordered the closure of VIVA radio, arguing that it threatened public order. An attack on freedom of speech and a sign of Ravalomanana's increasingly authoritarian and executive policies to quell rising discontent, the closing down of VIVA became a triggering event in the mobilization of the anti-Ravalomanana protests (*Madagascar Tribune* 2008; Ratsimbaharison 2017: 57). Soon afterwards, thousands of Tananariviens gathered in support of Rajoelina, marking the starting point of mass demonstrations that followed over the ensuing weeks. It did not take long to turn Rajoelina's initial, personal demand to reopen VIVA radio into more general, societal demands for press freedom, democracy, and the resignation of Ravalomanana.

The anti-Ravalomanana protests had been largely peaceful until the end of January 2009, when they took a violent turn. On 26 and 27 January, hundreds of protestors – mainly urban youth – stormed, looted, and pillaged supermarkets and small businesses around the inner city of Antananarivo. The main scenes of violence were the *quartiers* Behoririka and Analakely, where most of the shops are owned by Chinese, Indians, and Malagasies of foreign descent (Galibert 2009a: 143; Vivier 2010: 64–67). At the same time, many of Ravalomanana's firms – among them his radio station and the wholesaler Magro – were attacked and partly destroyed. The violence against private property also spread to the countryside, which had hitherto been less affected by the protests (Galibert 2009a: 144). Altogether, an estimated 100 people died, mainly as victims of lootings. Yet violence also came in the form of state repression. On 7 February, Ravalomanana's Presidential Guard opened fire on a protest march towards the presidential palace in Ambohitsorohitra. More than 30 people died, while hundreds were injured (Amnesty International 2010: 9). This violent crackdown on demonstrations marked a turning point in the build-up to 17 March 2009, as it split the political and military elite and imbued the protests with both caution and further determination behind the claim that Ravalomanana's rule had exceeded its time.

The events of March 2009, which became known as 'la crise malgache', the Malagasy crisis, were only one among several moments of crisis in the island's history. In fact, there is hardly anything said or written about the history of Madagascar that does not use the term 'crisis'. The 'cyclical crises', referring to recurring moments of political turmoil, have become the master narrative that structures and rationalizes Madagascar's past and present (see Ralambomahay 2011; Razafindrakoto et al. 2014a; Razafindrakoto et al. 2018; Razafindrakoto et al. 2020). This narrative has served scholars and diplomats to explain Madagascar's lag in development, and it provides many Malagasies with a rationale for their everyday lives (Jütersonke & Kartas 2010: 14). The AU and other international actors who came to be involved in re-establishing constitutional order in Madagascar after Ravalomanana's ouster also used the term 'Malagasy crisis' to describe what was going on. Yet unlike numerous academics before, they did so without an explicit definition of what 'crisis' really meant.

The aim of this chapter is to consider crisis neither as inevitable nor as interruption, but as evidence of more long-term struggles for the resources and technologies of political and social organization, and thus also the general 'rules of the game' (see also Allen 1995; Razafindrakoto et al. 2014b). Seen from this vantage point, the political history of Madagascar and its 'cyclical crises' can be read as a history of contested legitimacies. In fact, unless understood as chronic, crisis may therefore not be an adequate heuristic to conceive of this history, as the momentous character of crises logically contradicts seeing political events in their structural context and *longue durée* (Marcus 2016: 12; see generally Vigh 2008).

For the sake of contextualising the events of March 2009, briefly revisiting the preceding three moments of crisis is in order. At the surface, the moments in Madagascar's history later identified as crises all culminated in changes of the head of state. In 1972, the first president, Philibert Tsiranana, was forced out of power after months of student protests and a rising disappointment about the yet to be fulfilled social and economic promises of independence. Preceding peasant protests mainly in the south of the island were violently suppressed (Randrianja & Ellis 2009: 187). As argued by Solofo Randrianja and Stephen Ellis (2009: 185), in 1972 'a whole society was in search of a new mode of existence, amounting to perhaps the most profound crisis in Madagascar's history'. Despite mobilization in both urban and rural parts of the country, the historical opening of the political space soon faded as power was transferred to a military directorate led by General Ramanantsoa (Randrianja & Ellis 2009: 193; Sellström 2015: 85). In 1975, after infighting within the military, Ramanantsoa handed over power to Colonel Richard Ratsimandrava. Within less than a week, Ratsimandrava was assassinated. The young navy general Didier Ratsiraka took over the presidency and set Madagascar on a path to socialism and integration into the global non-alignment movement (Raison 2007; Lavrard-Meyer 2015: 170).

Starting in 1991, it was again a popular movement – led by the *Forces Vives* (Living Forces) and the Malagasy churches – that brought Ratsiraka's reign to an end. This started a transitional period that culminated in Madagascar's first democratic elections in 1993, won by Albert Zafy. The democratic opening was, however, short-lived. The fragmentation of the party system, an economic downturn, and high levels of corruption, as well as enduring rivalries between the president and the parliament, soon became characteristic of Madagascar's first democratic experiment (Randrianja & Ellis 2009: 204; Jütersonke & Kartas 2010: 47). In 1996, President Zafy was impeached by the *Assemblée nationale* (Allen 2003). In a climate of disillusionment over the failed democratic experiment, Didier Ratsiraka returned to power, this time through elections held in December 1996.

In late 2001, the results of the first round of presidential elections sparked yet another crisis. President Ratsiraka and the then mayor of

Antananarivo, Marc Ravalomanana, both claimed victory. In early 2002, Ravalomanana declared himself president and refused to run for a second round. The confrontation turned violent and brought the country to the brink of civil war. In one of its earliest responses to unconstitutional changes of government, the OAU/AU organized several rounds of negotiations between the two protagonists in Dakar (OAU Secretariat 2002; Cornwell 2003). Yet Ravalomanana created facts and was soon recognized by the former colonial power France, Madagascar's main bilateral donors, and finally also the AU. The only partly resolved crisis of 2001/2002 not only created a lasting memory of (failed) regional involvement in the resolution of political crises on the island; it also produced clear losers who were not willing to accept this as their destiny for long (Lavrard-Meyer 2015).

As will become evident in the course of this chapter, what became known as 'la crise malgache' in 2009 stemmed from and integrates into this long-term history of contested legitimacies in Madagascar. Despite their differences, all the moments described above had several characteristics in common. First, they all involved a combination of popular mobilization and intra-elite struggles over the fruits of both the postcolonial state and its economy (Razafindrakoto et al. 2014b; Marcus 2016: 41). Second, they all led to a change in the incumbents of state power, the dominant ideology, and the mode of accumulation, even though the deeper social figuration of Malagasy society remained fairly intact (Razafindrakoto et al. 2014b: 25). Despite rhetorical revolutions, there was little profound social change (Véron 2010: 122; Marcus 2016). The changes in power were nevertheless also accompanied by a shift in the political discourse that served to legitimate a novel political project: socialism, liberal democracy, market economy, equality. Third, Raymond Ranjeva (2012: 279) notes that despite these changing emblems, claims of democratization and of a humanization of politics abound at all times. At all moments, the 'people' played a significant role both in creating an initial momentum for change and in a general narrative of legitimation. Each crisis thus also entailed an important moment of popular agency, which was, however, soon reduced to a rhetorical emblem rather than marking a real shift in power. Fourth, contrary to the experiences elsewhere in Africa, the moments of rupture were accompanied by only sporadic physical violence. The use of violence against protestors, however, often marked the end point of an incumbent's popular legitimacy, reflecting and giving rise to the prevalent self-image of Malagasy society as particularly peaceful and non-violent (Véron 2010: 122; Rabemananoro 2014).

Despite their popular moments, the past two crises in particular also resemble each other in the role of what Didier Galibert (2011: 414) termed 'providential man'. As the chosen leader of the protest movement, the 'providential man' transported a sacred image of the precolonial monarchy into postcolonial struggles over the state. As a consequence, both crises ended up centralizing the demands for change in the hands of a few 'chosen ones' (Véron 2010: 123; Razafindrakoto 2014b: 46).

At the same time, one also observes an increasingly dominant internationalization in the way the crises were handled, in the norms that governed the format and content of the search for solutions, and in the protagonists that were involved therein. Since the early nineteenth century and the international recognition of the Kingdom of Madagascar under Radama I, political order in Madagascar has always been the product of a negotiation between competing Malagasy elites struggling over the appropriation of international norms, discourses, and resources. And yet over the course of time, what changed were not only the norms governing international life. Rather, the very imprint of the international has become much more direct and synchronous with political events unfolding on the island (Randrianja & Ellis 2009: 13).

2009: whose 'crise malgache'?

How to narrate the build-up of what came to be known as the 2009 Malagasy crisis? This book is built on the premise that which kinds of conflict we identify with a given 'crisis' also shapes which kinds of measures are deemed relevant and legitimate for its resolution. Rather than identifying 'the causes' of conflict that led to Ravalomanana's ouster, the remainder of this chapter offers a reading of multiple and overlapping interpretations of what constituted 'la crise' in early 2009. This will ultimately serve as a heuristic foil with which the approaches that international and regional actors such as the AU chose to address 'la crise malgache' can be interpreted and assessed.

The events of early 2009 are usually narrated following three broad – yet not mutually exclusive – interpretative schemes. First, the crisis is depicted as a personal conflict that pitted two men – President Ravalomanana and the mayor of Antananarivo, Rajoelina – against each other. In such a reading, the conflict is located at the individual level, nourished by personal ambitions for power and economic influence (Pellerin 2009a). This follows a widespread narrative in which Malagasy politics is, as summarized by Oliver Jütersonke and Moncef Kartas (2010: 13), depicted as a 'complex brew' and 'Byzantine-like' elite struggle beyond rationalization. Second, the events of March 2009 are interpreted as a popular revolt or people's revolution, as a sign of Malagasies' thirst for democratic emancipation (Gingembre 2010; Jackson 2013: 237). Critics, in turn, hold that compared to previous times, the 2009 protests mobilized far fewer people and only a small fraction of the capital's population (Andrianarimanana 2012: 180; Rabemananoro 2014: 67). They also argue that many of those protesting in favour of Rajoelina had actually been paid (Jütersonke & Kartas 2010: 42). Moreover, the same mobilizing force can be attributed to the incumbent government in whose support 30,000 people rallied in the capital's Mahamasina Municipal Stadium at the beginning of February 2009 (Pellerin 2009b). Who then represented 'the people' in early 2009 is the subject of controversial debate, which, as will become evident later in this book, also divided the various international actors that came to assist in the resolution of 'la crise malgache'. Apart from these empirical objections, such a reading also carries the danger of reflecting the hopes and desires of the analysts much more than an understanding of the ambiguous play between dependencies and spaces of articulation that constitute political subjectification in most of today's postcolonial contexts (Abu-Lughod 1990). Moreover, interpreting protest too hastily as democratic often means failing to interrogate what people are actually protesting *for*. This may lead to a simplification and essentialization of protest. It therefore also comes at the expense of turning a blind eye to other, non-democratic ways to express opposition and discontent that might capture far better how people (in this case, Malagasies) reacted to the political order in place (Randrianja 2012b: 256–257). Third, the events of March 2009 are often narrated by identifying short-term and long-term causes that explain the complex network of overlapping conflicts, protagonists, and alliances that had forced Ravalomanana out of power (Ralambomahay 2011; Randrianja 2012a; Ratsimbaharison 2017). Such a perspective points out that below the surface of the events chronicled above, there was a much more gradual erosion of the political, economic, societal, and moral fabric and similarly diminishing channels for the expression and negotiation of conflicts.

I will largely follow this latter narrative, although in a slightly different way. The point to make here is not merely a temporal distinction between different *causes* of conflict, those of a short-term and those of a long-term kind. Rather, I aim to make visible that from the very beginning, there was a *multiplicity of conflicts*, where 'multiple' refers to both numbers and kinds. This multiplicity of conflicts gave expression to very different readings of what the problems really are and thus different suggestions as to how to resolve them. Moreover, it meant that those who became protagonists in the anti-Ravalomanana protests came from different social and political backgrounds and disposed of very different means to organize and articulate their grievances. Beyond those who became heard and seen, others may have remained publicly largely unnoticed. Such an approach to narrating the conditions upon which the 2009 crisis developed seeks to evade the objectifying, rationalizing, and linear character the analysis of a conflict's so-called root causes can take (Woodward 2007: 155). It also seeks to acknowledge the politics involved in conflict analyses per se and the implications and solutions a particular analysis renders possible (Heathershaw 2009: 21; Bliesemann de Guevara 2014).

Rather than telling a teleological story that ends in the fall of Ravalomanana, this chapter maps issues that came to be increasingly politicized and thus *subject to conflict*, and it identifies different actors behind these issues. The aim is hence not to provide an explanation for why Ravalomanana was ousted, but to offer a 'lateral cut' through Malagasy society on the eve of 17 March 2009, which maps different conflicts, different protagonists, and their different means of articulation. The issues and protagonists that emerged over the months preceding March 2009 therefore somewhat contradict the image of clear sides and a conflict of who against whom. Rather, they draw a picture of overlapping conflicts that emerged and existed in parallel and which may have demanded contradictory solutions. Finally, such an analysis also points to those conflictual issues that did not reach the level of public or international attention. In this sense, the chapter also illustrates how these different protagonists and overlapping readings of what constituted the problem around 2009 disposed of very different resources and potentials to make their cause resonate with the course of the crisis and the slowly evolving international attention to it. The different protagonists hence ended up having very different imprints on what came to be known and addressed as 'la crise malgache' once it became subject to regional intervention.

Mobilization beyond institutions

The mobilization against Ravalomanana's government in 2009 rested on a loosely organized 'coalition of circumstances' (Pellerin 2009a: 164). Many of those actively articulating themselves and organizing against the established order had either become victims during Ravalomanana's presidency or were opportunists in search of something better. In this sense, the coalition of circumstances has also been described as the 'coalition des mécontents' (d'Ersu 2009: 454), the coalition of the discontent, whose uniting force was their loosely defined opposition to the existing regime in place.

Contrary to the narrative of a personal conflict between Ravalomanana and Rajoelina, the latter only emerged as the public face of the protest a few months before Ravalomanana agreed to go into exile. In 2007, under the name of *Tanora malaGasy Vonona* (TGV) – the young determined Malagasies – Rajoelina had successfully rallied a broad movement of mainly urban youth, who formed the backbone for his election as mayor of Antananarivo in December 2007. The abbreviation TGV, in its reference to the French high-speed train, merged determination, strength against resistance, rapid ascendancy, and a general search for modernization (*L'Express de Madagascar* 2007). Remarkably, the symbolism as well as the personal motivation behind Rajoelina's rise as the public face of the protests seemed to mirror Ravalomanana's rise in 2001 (Pellerin 2009a: 153). Like Ravalomanana had been, Rajoelina was welcomed as a figure of political renovation, as a symbol of the youth and of renewal (Gingembre 2010: 187). With his 34 years of age, he captured the hopes of the younger generation particularly that with his political ascendancy, the political class in general would undergo renovation. Like Ravalomanana in 2001, Rajoelina neither had a political party background nor did he promote a particular ideology (Ralambomahay 2011: 33), and thus he broke with everything characterizing the established and institutionalized political order. Indeed, reminiscent of Ravalomanana in 2001, his public speeches and campaign slogans entailed a purposeful apolitical message. As a former DJ and organizer of the annually held and very popular Life music events in Antananarivo, Rajoelina's political events too merged politics and entertainment, social grievances and pop culture (Galibert 2009a). Finally, like Ravalomanana, Rajoelina also had personal business interests to defend: with his firm INJET, he became the organizer of several public music and entertainment events and entered into billboard marketing and digital print, two economic domains connected to the digital change that had reached at least Madagascar's capital (Galibert 2009a: 140–141; Sellström 2015: 103). Moreover, in May 2007, he bought a radio station and a TV station that were merged under his VIVA media group. With the latter, Rajoelina was a direct competitor to Ravalomanana's Malagasy Broadcasting System (MBS). Rajoelina's decision to run as mayor of Antananarivo coincided with increasingly harsh legal and administrative measures undertaken by the incumbent regime to limit the expansion of his firms. In 2003, for instance, the then mayor of Antananarivo, Patrick Ramiaramanana, had barred Rajoelina from installing INJET billboards in Antananarivo, the main market for digital print products. Once in office, Rajoelina immediately reversed this decision (Pellerin 2009a: 164). These executive interventions in order to limit economic competition did not cease with Rajoelina's election as mayor of Antananarivo. The final closedown of his TV station VIVA in December 2008 was therefore only the last and by far economically least painful event in a series of repressions against Rajoelina's growing business interests.

Long before the rise of Rajoelina as the public face of the protests, however, other forces had started to articulate and organize themselves. These mainly drew from members of the political and economic elite whose social and economic outlook had increasingly become constrained under Ravalomanana's rule. Many of them had previously been linked to the former Presidents Zafy and Ratsiraka. Their activism was also mobilized on the basis of previous political experiences and a history of conflictive relations with the protagonists of the regime in place. Almost immediately after the temporal resolution of the post-electoral crisis of 2001/2002, for instance, a loose group started to agitate for a more profound reorganization of the political landscape, particularly demanding a process of national reconciliation. To this end, a group around Albert Zafy established the so-called Committee for National Reconciliation (*Comité pour la réconciliation nationale*, CRN), which became a forum for political dialogue and exchange in Antananarivo as well as a platform to organize political reunions in other parts of the country (CRN 2003; Vivier 2010: 22). The explicit *national* agenda of the CRN's work was an important critique of the established practice of seeing Antananarivo as the island's sole political centre and the centralizing forces that marked the last phase of Ravalomanana's presidency (Imbiki 2014: 29; Marcus 2016).[2]

With the CRN, a loose network of other groups and organizations emerged with whom the members of the CRN sought to push for political, economic, and social reforms. Under the header of the Three National Forces (*Trois forces nationales*, 3FN), the CRN held regular exchanges with a group of party representatives and members of parliament: the Solidarity of Parliamentarians for the Defence of Democracy and National Unity (*Solidarité des parlementaires pour la défense de la démocratie et de l'unité nationale*, SPDUN) and the Rally of National Forces (*Rassemblement des forces nationales*, RFN). All these meetings, however, increased rather than settled the divergences among the groups mobilizing against Ravalomanana's government (see, for instance, 3FN 2005).[3]

Over the course of Ravalomanana's presidency, similar other groups emerged or continued their work in Antananarivo. One of them was the

National Economic and Social Council (*Conseil national économique et social*, CONECS). At its tenth anniversary in 2008, the group adopted a manifesto in which it formulated its demands for political reform:

> Every man for himself seems to be the rule that condemns us. Our development projects are beyond our national competencies and the citizens assist as simple spectators in such programs to develop our economy. Our homeland should not be only a reservoir of raw materials and cheap labour, and worse, a dump of imported products. Its citizens must be stakeholders and actors in any scheme to promote our economy by liberalizing opportunities and initiatives and by putting an end to any inclination for oligopoly. (Author's translation; CONECS 2008)

Another group was the Club for Development and Ethics (*Club développement et éthique*, CDE), a 'cercle de réflexion' (Pellerin 2009a: 157) organized by Serge Zafimahova, a former counsellor of Albert Zafy. These groups mainly drew on renowned figures of the capital's small political and economic elite and often served as fora for exchange and the formulation of political alternatives. Reflecting the merger of the political and economic spheres that increased over the course of Ravalomanana's presidency (see further below), the majority of these individuals also held explicit business interests. Business associations and interest groups thus integrated into these ascending organisms of political opposition.

Towards the end of 2008, a loose alliance of these groups sought to organize a national dialogue – *États généraux* – with the aim of 'normalizing the proper functioning of democracy, the institutions of the republic, the decentralization and healthy economic competition' [author's translation] (SeFaFi 2014h: 254). Among the organizers were not only the above-mentioned CONECS and CDE, but also the Federation of Professional Mining Associations (*Fédération des associations professionnelles de mines*, FEDMINES) and the National Federation of Malagasy Engineering Organizations (*Fédération nationale des organisations d'ingénieurs Malagasy*, FNOIM), both corporate associations. They were also joined by the civil society organization National Election Observation Committee (*Komitim-pirenena Manara-masony Fifidianana*, KMF/CNOE) as well as the Observatory of Public Life in Madagascar (*Sehatra Fanaraha-maso ny Fiainam-pirenena*, SeFaFi), both established civil society groups supported through international donor funds. For several reasons, the envisaged *États généraux* had to be postponed, initially to mid-January 2009, and were then overtaken by the events of March 2009.[4]

In sum, the antecedents of the anti-Ravalomanana movement indeed drew on a group of established and experienced – mainly male – figures of the political and economic elite (Pellerin 2009a; Razafindrakoto et al. 2014b: 44). As will be explicated further below, for many of them, political and economic questions were inseparable. Others drew their motivation from unresolved issues of the 2001/2002 crisis, such as the question of national reconciliation. Strikingly, most of them were organized in associations and clubs, and thus outside of – but with linkages to – political parties and the official institutions of the state. This was a reaction to and a reflection of a more general trend towards devaluation of (public) institutions during Ravalomanana's presidency.

Monopolization and depoliticization under Ravalomanana

The intra-elite opposition towards the regime of Ravalomanana has to be understood against the background of an economic and political order that over the course of Ravalomanana's time in office became increasingly restrictive. In the economic realm, Ravalomanana's firm Tiko developed into a business conglomerate absorbing almost all possibilities for private sector development in Madagascar. Having started initially solely in the area of dairy products, the evolving conglomerate soon also comprised the media (with MBS), the building industry (with Alma and the so-called Malagasy Construction Company, *Compagnie de construction malagasy*, CCM), the aviation sector (with Tiko Air), the publishing and paper industry (with Blueprint), and the petroleum sector (with Tiko Petroleum) (Pellerin 2009a: 154; Marcus 2010a: 121). While the liberalization policies introduced during Ravalomanana's first presidential term had supported a steady growth of the Malagasy economy, this also markedly benefited his own economic interests. Tiko's profits had quadrupled since 2002, and Ravalomanana became Africa's fourth-richest head of state (ICG 2010b: 16). On the one hand, the economic opening thus introduced a phase of overall prosperity: for the first time in Madagascar's history, the economy grew more than the population. On the other hand, it soon became clear that the benefits were distributed highly unequally (Randrianja 2012b: 254; Ratsimbaharison 2017).

The president not only benefited from the general macroeconomic liberalization policies, but also from direct legal interventions that worked in favour of the former's economic interests. In 2006, for instance, Ravalomanana's wholesale firm Magro received a tax holiday on rice imports after Madagascar had been hit hard by a general rice shortage. At the same time, competing private importers had to pay the full tax and so became uncompetitive (Marcus 2010a: 121). One year before, Tiko benefited from a tax cut on crude oil – which Tiko refined – while the import of refined oil remained heavily taxed

(Marcus 2010a: 123). Another example is that of the Kobama facility, a flour mill that competed with a newly set-up Tiko flour mill. Initially a lease from the government, the Kobama contract was not renewed once Tiko had set up its mill, ultimately pushing Kobama off the market (Marcus 2010a: 121). In short, a number of business actors were increasingly kept away from the fruits of the liberalized economy.

In addition, Ravalomanana increasingly used the legislative and administrative power of the state for economic purposes, primarily in order to restrict economic competition. This system of merging the liberal economy with the institutions of the state was best reflected in the Independent Anti-Corruption Office (*Bureau indépendant anti-corruption*, BIANCO) that Ravalomanana established in 2003. While pushed by public, international, and also personal concerns for Madagascar's rising level of corruption (Bachelard 2014: 77), the monitoring system remained institutionally dependent on the president and was therefore soon criticized for not being able to fulfil its initially envisaged purpose (Marcus 2008). By December 2008, 'opposition leaders accused it of becoming a political police force and there was a movement within the administration itself towards auditing BIANCO' (Marcus 2008).

With these developments, it was not only the general level of competition and indeed liberalism that eroded, but also the institutionalization and official face of the economy more generally. In this sense, trade unions as well as business groups increasingly lost their corporate power as representatives of and channels for the dissemination and organization of societal interests and for the articulation and resolution of conflicts. In turn, Ravalomanana's firms served as chains that merged the economic and political realms, and thereby increasingly blurred the boundaries between the public and the private. This became evident, for instance, in the links between Tiko and Ravalomanana's I Love Madagascar (*Tiako I Madagasikara*, TIM) party. Already in his political ascendancy, Tiko had played an important role. Over the course of his presidency, this became even more pronounced. On the one hand, Tiko and Magro served as primary pools for recruiting political and administrative personnel for the state as well as Ravalomanana's personal circle of allies (*Jeune Afrique* 2003; Sellström 2015: 101). On the other hand, as a political party, TIM itself turned into a structure for individual economic opportunities rather than a transmission belt to channel societal grievances and interests into the political process (Marcus & Ratsimbaharison 2005: 507–508).

In the political realm too, the space for and institutionalization of competing interests became increasingly diminished. In 2007, a new constitution increased the level of centralization of power in the hands of the executive and thus completed a trend towards presidentialism that had marked Madagascar's post-independence political history (Marcus 2016: 52). On the one hand, similar to the constitutional reform of 1998, the president was granted ever more exceptional powers. On the other hand, the role of the legislative was decisively reduced. While from 2003 to 2006 the legislative had only submitted eight law proposals and 37 amendments – contrasting 218 proposals and 316 amendments coming from the executive – the new constitution rendered the parliament 'all the more inactive, with no law proposal or even amendments coming from the legislative during the 2007–2009 period' (Jütersonke & Kartas 2010: 49). The constitution thus only legally cemented a trend that had already turned the parliament away from being a forum for dialogue, the representation of competing societal interests, and the articulation of political alternatives. During the 2006 legislative elections, Ravalomanana's TIM party won 105 of the 127 seats and henceforth became the unchallenged force in parliament.

The anger over TIM's monopolization of the political space was channelled in the demands of a group of party officials and members of parliament to reform the legislation for political parties and enhance the status of the opposition in parliament (Rabanirinirarison & Raveloson 2011: 6). So far, inclusion into the political process was subject to functional rather than democratic concerns. In late 2007, Ravalomanana, for instance, organized a so-called presidential dialogue that took place as part of the preparation of the national development strategy, the Madagascar Action Plan (MAP). The dialogue, however, excluded most opposition parties. Coined a 'presidential monologue', the effort mainly served to co-opt members of the opposition rather than to renegotiate the substance and beneficiaries of Madagascar's development (*Madagascar Tribune* 2007; Pellerin 2009a: 156).

In late 2008, Ravalomanana reacted to the opposition's demands by seeking to reform the legislation for political parties. As summarized by Richard Marcus (2008), the approach was technocratic and 'the lack of ensuing debate made it clear that the implementation of party reform would be contentious and the president would be accused of advocating a new law that would make it more difficult and expensive to register parties'. The new legislation, which was adopted in parliament without much debate in January 2009, in fact limited political competition by banning independent candidates from running in elections (Rabanirinirarison & Raveloson 2011: 7). As with the presidential dialogue before, the reform proposal thus fomented rather than appeased the increasingly overt opposition against Ravalomanana (Galibert 2009a: 142).

Since 2004, Ravalomanana had also engaged in the reorganization of the Malagasy state. These efforts were, inter alia, supported by the World Bank and took place within the framework of anti-corruption measures and efforts to strengthen local governance. Taking back decentralization policies undertaken by his predecessor Ratsiraka, Ravalomanana's administrative reform substituted the six provinces with 22 regions, each headed by a *chef de région*. However, the *chefs de région* were appointed by the president and directly answerable to the newly created Ministry of Decentralization rather than the local population (Marcus 2010a: 123). In turn, the *communes* – the second-lowest level of administration – were vested with increased responsibilities but lacked adequate fiscal instruments. This created a dual system that merged official decentralization with a concentration of control in the presidency (Marcus 2010a: 123–124). It thus replicated a pattern in the organization of the Malagasy state in which decentralization paradoxically meant the administrative strengthening of the centre, but at the expense of the capacity of the polity to actually 'shape and strengthen the social fabric and initiate progress' (Jütersonke & Kartas 2010: 44). As Marcus (2010a: 123–124) observed, 'less than 3 percent of revenues make it to the local level'.

In late 2007, Ravalomanana introduced a further moment of centralization and de-democratization of the local political life: the *chefs de fokontany* – the local government representatives at the lowest administrative level – were no longer nominated by the elected mayors, but from now on by the appointed *chefs de district*. This further squeezed their power, but more so threatened the legitimacy of the last and lowest government representatives, who were torn between local demands and administrative and fiscal constraints. Moreover, this reorganization became decisive for the administration of elections, in which the *chefs de fokontany* played an important role. As observed by Didier Galibert (2009a: 148):

> In contrast to the demands of civic NGOs for the promulgation of an electoral code establishing independent commissions to set up electoral lists, the power in place entrusts this task to small notables, most of them illiterate, who are officially paid by the state and who will be able to shield, if necessary, the wishes of the mayors. (Author's translation)

In their functions for the organization of elections, the *chefs de fokontany* – administratively appointed and often inadequately equipped – had an important influence on the (de)legitimation of the entire democratic process. Apart from strengthening the administrative at the expense of the democratic face of the state, these reforms fomented conflicts in many rural parts of Madagascar. This became visible, for instance, during election times and in struggles over the financial allocations from Antananarivo.[5] For a long time, however, these conflicts remained local, without repercussions at the political centre in Antananarivo. Throughout 2007 and 2008, SeFaFi, the civil society organization introduced above, repeatedly dedicated their regular communiqués to this issue, which underlines that the reform of the local governance system was in fact seen to have profound consequences for the more general organization and nature of the polity. The SeFaFi communiqués underscored that this reorganization was not just an administrative question, but that it had effectively eroded the quality of local governance. For the majority of Madagascar's population, the reforms had a tangible impact on everyday democracy (see SeFaFi 2014a; SeFaFi 2014b; SeFaFi 2014c; SeFaFi 2014d).

Altogether, the reform of the polity was in line with a more general logic that defined Ravalomanana's approach to governance: in 2003, he explained that leading a country is like leading a business firm (*Jeune Afrique* 2003), which underscored his managerial approach to politics and the state (Sellström 2015: 101). This mirrored a more general and increasingly overt marketization of social relations and a trend towards evading debates about political ends (Jackson 2013: 207). Ravalomanana's neoliberal approach supported empowerment, growth, and indeed socio-economic development, but this took place within an executive and technocratic framework that excluded any engagement with alternatives, inequalities, ambiguous consequences, or competing ends.[6]

In the polity as a corporate enterprise, transparency, for instance, became a central concern in Ravalomanana's work towards good or better governance. Participation, in turn, was almost completely wiped off the good governance agenda (Bachelard 2014: 74). Characteristic of this was the above-mentioned fact that opposition parties and local governments were invited to join forces in the implementation of the MAP, but that this took place without recognition of what interests and grievances they were understood to represent (Marcus 2007). At the same time, Jennifer Jackson (2013: 216) argues that the discourse of transparency itself became a powerful tool to stigmatize other political projects as non-modern and nourished 'a culture of secrecy and concealment'.

The very logic of governance under Ravalomanana thus indeed contributed to a much deeper transformation of relationships and roles within the polity. As observed by Randrianja (2012b: 263), the corporate logic of governance meant that politicians were increasingly turned into entrepreneurs and that elections became an economic battlefield in which participation was both conditioned upon and for the sake of securing economic gains. As a consequence, institutions increasingly lost their public function (i.e. their objective to serve the public good). That the MAP – the developmental social contract – was adopted more or less without public debate, but with profound input from international experts, is a case in point (Randrianja 2012b: 270).

An urban coalition of circumstance

The above-mentioned organizations that were formed in opposition to Ravalomanana's presidency drew on individuals whose position within the Malagasy economic and political elite had increasingly become compromised. André Ramaroson, President of CONECS, for instance, was CEO of a soap works whose land the Malagasy state expropriated in order to build a pipeline for the Canadian mining company Sherritt (Pellerin 2009a: 156). Edgard Razafindrahavy, owner of *L'Express de Madagascar* as well as the above-mentioned flour mill Kobama, became one of Rajoelina's early supporters (Marcus 2010a: 121). Others, such as Roland Ratsiraka and Jean-Eugène Voninahitsy, were not only affected in their personal economic activities, but had also come in contact with the state's judicial power. Political exclusion too became a crucial individual experience and incentive for mobilization, as shown, for instance, by Jean Lahiniriko, the former speaker of the *Assemblée nationale*, whom the pro-Ravalomanana faction ousted in 2006 (Vivier 2010: 19–20).

Opposition against Ravalomanana's presidency thus mobilized political newcomers and established figures alike, who followed different strategies to integrate into the emerging movement. Some, such as Jean Lahiniriko, Norbert Ratsirahonana, and Roland Ratsiraka, used their newly established political parties as vehicles to integrate into the broad anti-Ravalomanana movement. Others were established figures of Madagascar's postcolonial political scene or children or grandchildren of such figures, such as Monja Roindefo, Ny Hasina Andriamanjato, Pierre Tsiranana, or Madeleine Ramaholimihaso, then coordinator of SeFaFi (Pellerin 2009a: 165; see generally Galibert 2009b: 422–443). Not all of these figures remained overt supporters of Rajoelina, nor did all later join the HAT government. The majority, however, continued to play a role in one way or another during the transitional period that came to follow the events of March 2009. Paradoxically, at least some of these figures had initially been strong supporters of Ravalomanana at the beginning of the 2000s and only later turned against him.

Apart from the excluded political and economic elite, the forces that came to articulate themselves against Ravalomanana increasingly mobilized from two important institutions: the army and the Catholic Church. This further underlined the alliance's network character and the observation that the uniting bond was the shared victimization under Ravalomanana rather than an explicit and shared political programme.

For parts of the army, Ravalomanana's presidency became problematic when he introduced an internationally supported Security Sector Reform (SSR) in late 2007. The rationale for such a reform came from the observation that the violent turn of the post-electoral crisis of 2001/2002 had revealed once more the need to define the exact role and function of the military within the order of the state and to altogether depoliticize the security forces (Ramasy 2012: 83). During the post-electoral crisis of 2001/2002, Ravalomanana was mainly supported by reservists and the gendarmerie. After the latter's successful claim to power, this group increasingly expected rewards. In turn, a significant number of generals felt Ravalomanana's promotion policy discriminated against established rules of hierarchy and respect for age. In addition, the imprisonment of a number of military officers loyal to Ratsiraka nourished anti-Ravalomanana tendencies within the army (Ramasy 2012: 84). The SSR programme of 2007 thus raised hopes for better positions particularly among lower parts of the army. The reforms also threatened the established order between the military, the gendarmerie, and the police by introducing more profound changes to the organization of the Malagasy security apparatus. Beyond the material cuts or threats to individual positions, the way the SSR was drafted completely deprived the army of any active role in formulating the requirements, concerns, and conflicts that were at stake (Jütersonke & Kartas 2010: 68).

Ravalomanana's decision in late 2007 to appoint a general as prime minister was therefore also an attempt to ameliorate the government's links to the security forces – though in vain. As evidenced by the abovementioned CAPSAT mutiny, the anti-Ravalomanana protests drew on active support from parts of the army and the declared neutrality of others. The HAT government therefore initially counted seven militaries among its members (Ramasy 2012: 89). As soon as power was handed over to Rajoelina, he introduced a series of new institutions that enhanced the security forces' overall standing and access to the state. Rajoelina also introduced several economic advantages and increased the military's salary (Ramasy 2012: 91).

The Catholic Church, in turn, had increasingly come in conflict with Ravalomanana over the protection of the Church's role as moral authority and pillar of Malagasy society. Since 2000, Ravalomanana served as lay vice-president of the Protestant Church of Jesus Christ (*Fiangonan'i*

Jesoa Kristy eto Madagasikara, FJKM). On the one hand, this meant that Christian morality and extracts from the Bible became an integral part of his political discourse (Randrianja 2003: 314; Galibert 2009b: 139; Jackson 2013). On the other hand, he introduced a series of measures that compromised the freedom and role of faith-based institutions as authorities beyond the state and as important locales of societal organization. In this sense, the 2007 constitution, for instance, erased the clause guaranteeing Madagascar's laic state order, while the introduction of English as a third official language threatened educational institutions affiliated to the Catholic Church, in which Malagasy was the main language of instruction. The Catholic Church thus vehemently protested against both aspects (Marcus 2010a: 126). In a similar vein, the Catholic Church – later joined by the mushrooming evangelical churches (New Protestant Church in Madagascar, FPVM) – became increasingly critical of the subtle merger between the FJKM and the institutions of the Malagasy state (Urfer 2009; Gingembre 2011). Moreover, the different churches also became directly targeted by restrictive state policies: the radio station of the Catholic Church, Radio Don Bosco, for instance, was threatened by Ravalomanana's MBS consortium, and several popular programmes were subsequently banned (Galibert 2009a: 148). The repressions also targeted individual figures of the Catholic Church such as the French Jesuit Sylvain Urfer, a member of SeFaFi and open critic of Ravalomanana, who was expelled in May 2007 (Urfer 2009).

Finally, as evident from both the rise of Rajoelina as well as the acts of violence committed during the first weeks of anti-Ravalomanana protest, the urban youth as well as the population from the so-called *bas quartiers*, the poorer parts of Antananarivo, contribute an important key to understanding the different and overlapping conflicts that merged over the last months of Ravalomanana's rule.

While the economy enjoyed a steady overall growth, inflation also rose dramatically. In September 2008, SeFaFi issued a communiqué on the increase in the cost of living, thereby merely publicizing a situation that had long turned the lives of many Malagasies working in the informal sector or under minimal wages into a daily struggle. Between 2007 and 2008, the price for basic foodstuffs had risen by 52 per cent. This also affected the price for rice, the main staple consumed by Malagasies: for 1 kg of rice, one had to work, on average, three hours in 2008, while in 2001 two hours had sufficed. Those working in the informal economy or under minimal wages spent, on average, more than half of their income on alimentation. The rising prices therefore meant further cuts on health, education, or other activities to participate in public life (SeFaFi 2014g). The protestors gathering daily around the *Place du 13 mai* thus largely came from this stratum of Malagasy society.

As mentioned at the beginning of this chapter, the role of this group remains contested, often downplayed and depoliticized (see, for instance, Véron 2010: 123; Andrianarimanana 2012). Allegations of large sums of money that were paid to those gathering in the inner city abound. As recorded by Jütersonke and Kartas (2010: 42), Malagasies often hold clear images as to what and how much it requires to mobilize the poor to the streets: 'Stirring up fears and prejudices is not a major challenge, and gathering a crowd of 15,000 would cost less than 115,000 (excl. transportation)'. In this sense, the observation that the protestors of the *Place du 13 mai* have all been paid serves to depoliticize and delegitimize the reasons that had brought them to accept both, the payment and the protest, in the first place. Irrespective of what they fought for or were motivated by, their role should not be underestimated since – at the very least – they formed a crucial component of the public visibility of 'la crise malgache' in 2009.

Altogether, the protagonists of the anti-regime forces and their themes thus indeed resemble a 'coalition of circumstance' (Pellerin 2009a: 164) that organized itself against the shrinking political and economic space. In the economic realm, this mobilized both the cadres of the old oligarchic economy as well as small entrepreneurs who, despite an official policy of market liberalization, were prevented from harvesting the promised fruits. In the political realm too, the constitutional reform had legalized a trend towards presidentialism and executive authority, while the dominance of Ravalomanana's TIM party and the parallel further disintegration of the Malagasy party system had turned institutionalized political debate and the representation of diverging political interests into a theatre with neither roots in the larger society nor political substance. For the elite, neither established institutions of the state nor political parties bore a realistic opportunity to ameliorate one's individual socio-economic position. In a similar vein, the reform of the army as well as the conflict with the Catholic and evangelical churches erupted because of an increasingly intrusive and centralizing executive that threatened both individual careers as well as the identity and role of the very institutions per se. In this sense, rather than a fight over theological or security doctrines, the emerging conflicts were about the defence of fundamental roles and positions within a societal and political order that became increasingly threatening (Gingembre 2011: 59).

Altogether, the events of March 2009 thus erupted within a context of a *multiplicity* of conflicts that had been building up for much longer. Rather than merely a feud between Rajoelina and Ravalomanana, there was a history of exclusion and grievances, but also organization and articulation against the government of Ravalomanana.

However, it would also be wrong to see the 'coalition of circumstance' as merely an elite formation. On the one hand, the popular symbolism attributed to and the language employed by Rajoelina are evidence of a much more fundamental political and economic crisis and the existence of conflictive lines within Malagasy society that go beyond the threat of eroding individual privileges. On the other hand, the demonstrations in Antananarivo and the outbreak of violence across the island epitomize conflicts that remain unaccounted for if one only looks at the political elite. In this sense, it is not important to verify whether people had gathered in Antananarivo for *genuine* political reasons or as an expression of their free political will. Rather, the ease with which mobilization was made possible as well as the targets of violence are in themselves a meaningful demonstration of the contradictions that formed the complex web of conflicts present on the eve of 17 March 2009.[7]

As argued by Jütersonke and Kartas (2010: 43), 'discontentment within the underprivileged rural and urban populations is a constant feature of Malagasy society and provides a large reservoir to stage social unrests'. However, it is also necessary to consider this anonymous mass of the underprivileged on their own terms, not merely as a dangerous reservoir for mobilization (see also Razafindrakoto et al. 2014b: 47). The remainder of this section will therefore allude to some economic and political conflicts that resulted from the above-described broader transformations during Ravalomanana's presidency. Their repercussions in the discourse of protest and anti-regime criticism in Antananarivo came late and only in a mediated and somewhat distorted form. Against this background, the trends towards exclusion and monopolization discussed above have an even more profound magnitude if the analytical gaze is moved beyond the political and economic elite and away from those forces that were able to organize and politically articulate themselves.

Looking beyond the metropolitan scene

With regard to the economic realm, it is telling that two of the scandals of late 2008 were not only seen as a moral transgression, but also exposed an economic system that had led to an increasing level of social inequality. Moreover, rather than simply distributing gains unequally or excluding others from the benefits, for parts of Malagasy society, the economy had in fact become a threat to the very sources of subsistence. Particularly in rural Madagascar, economic dispossession did not mean a loss of privileges or a comparative disadvantage, but an actual erosion of fundamental livelihoods. The public outrage that followed the Daewoo deal thus denounced not only a system of personal self-enrichment and corruption; it also transported a conflict over land, rights, and resources to Antananarivo that had hitherto not reached the political discourse at the centre, but had been a daily lived reality in other parts of the country. The scandalization of the Daewoo deal clearly benefited from the relentless efforts of national trade unions and environmental organizations to make this a public concern. In doing so, they also counted on international NGOs such as Friends of the Earth and the London-based Panos, who lent their technical and financial support and opened access to an international public (Friends of the Earth 2007; Pellerin 2009a: 161). For years, the two organizations had been monitoring and publicly contesting the rising private investments in fertile land and the extraction of mineral resources (see, for instance, Harbison 2007).

Since 2003, the national trade union FISEMA (General Confederation of Malagasy Workers' Unions, *Confédération générale des syndicats des travailleurs de Madagascar*) had lobbied for workers' rights, consultation measures, educational programmes, economic linkages to local business, and stricter environmental protection measures around the new investment sites. In June 2007, FISEMA, for instance, noted that it was time for the population to know for what purpose and with what economic return the Malagasy state invests 35 million USD into infrastructure projects for the benefit of an ilmenite mine in the south of the island, run by QIT Madagascar Minerals (QMM), a joint venture between Rio Tinto and the Malagasy government. The union criticized the rising inflation, the influx of foreign as opposed to local workers, and the attempts to whitewash the negative consequences of QMM's investment through the declaration of and financial support for environmental protection zones that further increased the local population's pressure to find fertile land (Harbison 2007; Randrianasolo & Ravoavy 2007). Moreover, the group denounced that 'suspicion and lack of sincere social dialogue are sources of controversy and conflict. Informing people does not at all mean a "public consultation" as long as meetings are just one more way to impose Rio Tinto proposals' [author's translation] (Randrianasolo & Ravoavy 2007).

Dialogues about the means and benefits of development were demanded that benefited not only the current, but also future, generations. The conflicts over access, benefits, and meaning of Madagascar's land and natural resources also found reflection in the communiqués of SeFaFi. On the one hand, the group demanded a more thorough focus on participation, fair sharing of the economic benefits, and a transparent treatment of the contracts and commitments by the Malagasy state. While Madagascar had joined the Extractive Industries Transparency

Initiative (EITI) in February 2008, little progress was seen as a result of this accession. As repeatedly stressed, the crucial problem remained the secrecy with which deals were made as well as the overall lack of knowledge the local population had about the negotiation of contracts, the consequences they came with, and their rights to defend themselves (SeFaFi 2014e; SeFaFi 2014f).

On the other hand, the conflicts over land and resources in rural Madagascar also hinted at a more fundamental problem of agricultural development and the economic subsistence of the majority of Madagascar's 80 per cent rural population. In this sense, SeFaFi communiqués point to larger societal transformations stemming from an increasing marketization of the rural economy and warn of its potential impacts on escalating social conflict. Denouncing the evolving private agribusiness that had turned agricultural production into a large-scale economic endeavour through 'ranching', land consolidation, and private legal claims, SeFaFi (2014i: 245) warned, 'to marginalise the Malagasy farming community would be suicidal for society as a whole, as this would lead to a faster and more massive rural exodus' [author's translation].

Over the month of November 2008, these testimonies and controversies found their way into the political debate in Antananarivo. Rajoelina immediately condemned the 'big companies that amass national riches' (Pellerin 2009a: 161). On 14 February, he announced that:

> Negotiations with investors coming to Madagascar, like QMM, Dynatec, Sherritt, do not even have an impact on the Malagasy people. They think Madagascar belongs to them, and they can do what they want here. The contracts are made in secret and unfortunately do not reach the Malagasy people. (Author's translation; quoted in Pellerin 2009a: 161)

It is, however, noteworthy that never before late 2008 had a single land deal or international investment in the extractive industry provoked a similar level of protest and public attention (Gingembre 2010: 191). Their consequences for rural livelihoods, however, had been present and felt for a long time.

Marginalization was not only an issue in the economic realm. In the last years of Ravalomanana's presidency, politics too was marked by an increasing depoliticization and deinstitutionalization of political representation (see generally Marcus 2016: Chapters 3 and 7). This was reflected in the above-mentioned reform of the system of local governance and the eroding role of political parties within the *Assemblée nationale*. Both had profound consequences for the representation and institutionalization of societal interests. As discussed above, the reform of the local governance system in particular had replaced elected officials with appointed ones. This increased the conflict between elected local representatives, on the one hand (those disposing of popular legitimacy and therefore addressees of popular demands and expectations), and those appointed by the state, on the other (who substituted popular legitimacy with administrative and financial power).

This system was a perfect realization of the 'État administratif' (Galibert 2009a: 148) as well as Ravalomanana's ideal of a polity organized as private business (*Jeune Afrique* 2003). As analysed by Lauren Hinthorne (2011), the crisis that had unfolded in many parts outside of Antananarivo was therefore not one of competing political blocs, but a more fundamental crisis of confidence in the very structures and protagonists of the existing political order (see also Marcus 2016: 15). In her analysis of 'perceptual lenses' among citizens of the Antsinanana region in northern Madagascar, Hinthorne (2011: 548) found that the most prevalent understanding of 'democracy' was that of 'freedom of speech', which her respondents considered to be increasingly threatened. More importantly, however, the respondents showed a general electoral fatigue and depicted voting as an obligation, a tiresome routine. They regularly mentioned that electoral rigging and intransparency had become a normalcy in the political process. All these practices were associated with the ruling party per se, so that even a change of government was not seen as offering a viable solution. Protest – even though perceived as illegal – was said to be the much more adequate avenue for the expression of political interests (Hinthorne 2011: 548–549). Altogether, for this group of respondents, 'the political sphere prior to 2009 was dominated by an authoritarian regime that limited free speech, suppressed supporters of the opposition, and undermined fair electoral procedures. In short, there was no democracy to preserve' (Hinthorne 2011: 552).

In this sense, Hinthorne (2011: 543) argues, 'the perspectives offered by people (...) suggest alternate interpretations for why events in the spring of 2009 unfolded as they did'. Although referring to concrete political interventions under the regime of Ravalomanana and more recent experiences with democratic elections, the argument made here is that the crisis is not a crisis of a particular political regime or government, nor a matter of the legitimacy of the president or his party (see also Razafindrakoto et al. 2009: 10). Rather, what is in crisis is the legitimacy and authority of the political order more generally, which has not only failed to deliver expected services and rewards, but which has practically reneged on any meaningful *engagement* with the social, economic, and moral reality that shaped many people's daily lives. The reform of the local governance structure and the preparation of the 2008 MAP, based on international expert knowledge rather than consultation and dialogue among those to whose benefit it was meant to be, illustrate how the practices and structures to institutionalize dialogue and deliberation had increasingly lost in substance, if they had not been dismantled altogether (Jütersonke & Kartas 2010: 45).

The more profound crisis of the political order is also evidenced in public opinion surveys conducted during the 2008 wave of Afrobarometer. While 27 per cent of the respondents believed that it does not matter what *kind* of government is in power, 28 per cent were in fact unable to identify any preferred type of government (Afrobarometer 2008: 3). Some 41 per cent of the respondents answered being 'not at all satisfied/ not very satisfied' with the way democracy works in Madagascar, while only 16 per cent were 'very satisfied/satisfied', a sharp decrease from 26 per cent in 2005 (Afrobarometer 2008: 12). In a similar vein, there was an increase in the perception of corruption, which, particularly with regard to the parliament and other institutions of or individuals employed by the central state, corresponded with an overall decrease in trust in the political system (Razafindrakoto et al. 2009: 2; Marcus 2016: 58). More emblematically, however, 41 per cent of the respondents – compared to 32 per cent in 2005 – said they simply do not know how satisfied they are with the 'way democracy works' (Afrobarometer 2008: 12). This mirrors the 45 per cent who responded that they did not know what democracy actually is. In Hinthorne's ethnography, the second most prevalent understanding of 'democracy' was that of a 'big question mark' (Hinthorne 2011: 546).

Although ethnographic research and Afrobarometer polls share limits with regard to representativeness, their results point to the same important phenomenon. Beyond the visible and audible signs of 'la crise malgache' in Antananarivo, one could also register a profound alienation from the official and public political system altogether. While democratic institutions and ritualized elections remained in place, the lived realities of many Malagasies obviously contradicted this image of a good order in place. With this, the identities as citizens too became a hollow shell, not demanded and reclaimed, but questioned and even rejected altogether. One major problem was thus not only the decreasing availability of and access to the deliberative and representative institutions of the state, but also the widely felt irrelevance of and general scepticism towards this system more generally.

Crisis of institutions, crisis of identities

This chapter mapped out multiple issues of conflict and numerous protagonists that merged in a 'coalition of circumstances' (Pellerin 2009a: 164) against Ravalomanana's presidency. As observed by Galibert (2009a), compared to previous crises in Madagascar's history, the events of early 2009 were marked by a hitherto unknown transgression of social rules. This mainly revealed itself in the destructive violence against private property and its likewise violent repression. This reflected the profound alienation mainly of the urban youth from the existing social and moral order (Véron 2010: 126). Moreover, one also observes a more general deinstitutionalization both with regard to the character of the political system in place and with respect to the nature of the forces organizing against Ravalomanana, which either took place outside of institutions or, if within institutions such as the military and the churches, contributed to their internal splintering. The established institutions such as the parliament and political parties, in turn, had increasingly been subverted as sites for the articulation of political alternatives. While in its activism against the established order, the political and economic elite still formed associations – as the examples of CONECS, CDE, and CRN discussed above illustrate – this also meant that opposition became increasingly privatized and itself more volatile. It was turned away from the established institutions for political debate and the articulation of interests. All this together not only underlined the eroded state of the established political system; it also meant that as a political activity, opposition became even more dependent on individual resources, previous experiences, and access to (international) networks.

The preceding discussion sought to capture these different forms of opposition by explicitly moving beyond elite activism and the ideas and criticisms directly articulated against Ravalomanana's presidency. By widening the focus on the multiplicity of conflicts that came together in the build-up to Ravalomanana's ouster, the chapter underscored that the crisis of 2009 was more than simply the clash of interests between two political opponents. First, it was preceded by a history of opposition activism from parts of the elite who increasingly saw their political and economic opportunities restricted. In their activism, economic and political interests often merged, as did the associations and discussion groups that served as fora for political deliberations.

Second, the chapter also showed that the mobilization of the urban poor and particularly the younger generation took place against the background of a more general erosion of livelihoods and an increasing social inequality that translated into tangible hopes for a more profound political renewal (Gingembre 2011). This, in turn, became an important ingredient of the language and symbolism of the anti-Ravalomanana protests. Rather than seeing urban protestors as a passive reservoir and an instrument for elite manipulation (Véron 2010), it is therefore important to reveal the discursive grounds upon which mobilization becomes possible in the first place. Moreover, the chapter also stressed the importance of moving beyond the visible, audible, and organized protest as expression of 'people's' concerns. Beyond these overt symbolic and practical acts of discontent, the preceding section therefore alluded to areas of conflict that found much less reflection in the events in Antananarivo. Outside the political centre, the increasing marketization of land and natural resources had turned rural areas into spaces of economic growth, but this happened at the expense of local livelihoods and environmental sustainability (Sellström 2015: 121). Moreover, the managerial and technocratic approach to governance under Ravalomanana had contributed to an erosion of the quality of local governance and an overall de-democratization of the local space. Both developments together are reflected in a growing alienation of many Malagasies, particularly in the rural areas, from official politics. With this, the preceding discussion also pointed to an important societal divide along urban and rural lines as well as with regard to the potentials to articulate and institutionalize diverging interests and conflicts (see also Jütersonke & Kartas 2010: 70). The short excursion beyond the political theatre of Antananarivo surely only captured a small glimpse of the manifold ways in which Ravalomanana's presidency impacted rural Madagascar. It nevertheless pointed to immense asymmetries with regard to the means of articulation, which were already noted in relation to the urban elite, and to the trend towards privatizing and deinstitutionalizing political opposition. Together with the observed merger between the economic and political realms, these differences will provide an important background to assess the *scope* of conflict that was recognized in the international crisis management, which came to address 'la crise malgache' in reaction to the events of March 2009.

4
The intervention scenario

The Lomé Declaration's ideal of a 'speedy return to constitutional order' (OAU 2000a: 3) did not materialize easily in the case of Madagascar. To the contrary, almost five years of post-coup intervention are proof of a complex and contested figuration of actors and interactions that shaped what it meant to restore constitutional order in this particular case. This chapter offers an empirical reading of what post-coup interventions are. It explores the protagonists in the 'intervention scenario', their properties, relationships, and interactions that all shaped how 'la crise malgache' was ultimately approached. The term 'intervention scenario' denotes a social field that is, as elaborated in Chapter 1, created by and during an intervention in which a variety of national, regional, and international actors struggle to shape the content and course of the intervention and what it eventually brings about (see Figure 4.1). It is a contested field in which a variety of actors and a multiplicity of conflicts among them overlap. Altogether, the chapter shows that Madagascar was neither experiencing the almost mechanistic imposition of an external policy framework – as the authors of the Lomé Declaration may have envisaged – nor did it undergo neutral and merely assisting third-party mediation. The description of the intervention scenario instead renders visible the multiple sites and sources of conflict that defined how the variety of actors were able to approach 'la crise malgache' and shape its resolution. Many of these conflicts were actually created and nourished by the intervention and the interactions within the intervention scenario itself, and some of the sites were far away and disconnected from what was happening on the island. As a consequence, what became possible sometimes depended on considerations entirely disconnected from what was officially at stake – resolving 'la crise malgache' – because it responded to different rationalities and interests. The following sections zoom in on three different types of protagonists of the intervention scenario: the Malagasy negotiating parties, the various international actors, and the mediation teams.

The four mouvances

When the Malagasy military handed over power to Andry Rajoelina in March 2009, the AU PSC, along with other international and regional actors, swiftly condemned this as an unconstitutional change of government and demanded the rapid restoration of constitutional order (AU PSC 2009b). In order to meet this demand, it was decided to organize internationally mediated negotiations among the so-called 'four mouvances', comprising the two protagonists Rajoelina and Ravalomanana as well as the two former Presidents Albert Zafy and Didier Ratsiraka. This section shows that the four mouvances were in fact a product of the intervention, and analyses how they became shaped by and themselves shaped the intervention scenario.

Though the decision to negotiate in this particular format is retrospectively almost consensually criticized among diplomats and scholars alike, at the time there existed at least three reasons for doing so. First, it was noted that the events of March 2009 were in fact a prolongation of the post-electoral crisis of 2001/2002. Anger and resentment prevailed among the then pro-Ratsiraka camp. The 2009 crisis could therefore only be resolved if the hitherto neglected aspects of the previous crisis were finally addressed. As reflected in Chapter 3, the composition of the anti-Ravalomanana movement supported this interpretation. As a consequence, moving beyond the mere focus on Rajoelina and Ravalomanana as protagonists of the crisis appeared only logical (Ralambomahay 2011: 41).

Second, the inclusion of Zafy and Ratsiraka was said to lend the mediation process greater popular legitimacy. This was also supported by the fact that both Zafy and Ratsiraka are of *côtier* origin. Because questions of representation, access to resources, and political inclusion in Madagascar are often interpreted as conflicts between *merina* – the population of the highlands that has hitherto dominated the economy and politics on the island – and *côtiers*, the representation of alleged *côtier* voices at the negotiating table was only logical (Jütersonke & Kartas 2010: 12; Imbiki 2014). Their inclusion promised a much more encompassing and nationwide support for the international mediation.

Third, in bringing in Zafy and Ratsiraka, the two were imagined as playing a 'buffer' role as facilitators between Ravalomanana and Rajoelina. Zafy in particular was expected to function as a potential mediator between the two rivals, based on his role during the democratic transition of the early 1990s and the assumption that he lacked an immediate personal political ambition.[1] This attributed role meant that the two additional negotiators were not supposed to bring in their *own* political demands. In fact, their predefined role was rather to facilitate an internationally prescribed course of the mediation.

Thus, while several reasons suggested broadening the negotiations, whom to include was a matter of controversy. In fact, UN special envoy Tiébilé Dramé initially envisaged a much broader negotiation format, which additionally included other party leaders. He also proposed to open the negotiations to representatives from civil society, the private sector, the churches, and the military.[2] This resembled the format initially proposed by Zafy, which comprised political mouvances, including his own CRN, the opposition parties in parliament, Rajoelina, Ravalomanana, and Ratsiraka, as well as the security forces and representatives from the six provinces (Mouvance Zafy 2009c). In any case, the concentration on these four parties was neither inevitable nor without alternatives.

The making (up) of negotiating parties

Upon creation, the primary *raison d'être* of the four mouvances was to participate in the envisaged international negotiations. In fact, they were all established because of the internationally requested need to *negotiate* Madagascar's post-coup order. For instance, one of the initial members of the mouvance Ravalomanana explained the establishment of his mouvance in the following words:

> At first, we were just a small group of people. The party leaders. And then we reached out to others, other associations. We said, 'If you support Ravalomanana, come with us'. The mouvance was invented by the African Union. That's why, that's how we became the mouvance Ravalomanana. We, at first, we did not present ourselves as 'the mouvance Ravalomanana'. (Author's translation)[3]

In order to recruit members, secure internal coherence, and gain popular support, the mouvances of Ratsiraka and Ravalomanana drew on the structures of their respective parties, Association for the Rebirth of Madagascar (*Andry sy Rihana Enti-Manavotra an'i Madagasikara*, AREMA) and I Love Madagascar (*Tiako I Madagasikara*, TIM). However, both mouvances also included leaders from other, smaller political parties, as highlighted in the above quote (Rabanirinirarison & Raveloson 2011: 6). They too therefore reflected a certain degree of ad hoc formation, mainly attracting members of the already established political elite. In the end, both mouvances kept the character of a spontaneous assemblage of allies, united in support of an individual leader.

The network and organizational structures from which the mouvances of Zafy and Rajoelina drew were broader, looser, and a lot more spontaneous. The mouvance Zafy was mainly composed of individuals who had been loyal to Zafy's CRN, discussed in the previous chapter. They included members of AREMA, the Rally of Political Forces (*Hery Politika Mitambatra*, HPM) – a political party set up in March 2009 – smaller political parties, and civic associations.[4] Though also drawing on the established political elite and hence benefiting from a certain experience in political organization, Zafy's mouvance is often described as a 'conglomerate' that was difficult to bring in line politically.[5]

Rajoelina's mouvance, in contrast, formed itself based on members of the 'coalition of circumstance' against Ravalomanana as well as a fairly loose alliance of forces and individuals who had supported his ascendancy as mayor of Antananarivo under the banner of his party TGV (Pellerin 2009a: 163).[6]

As explicated in the previous chapter, the anti-Ravalomanana movement drew to a large extent on those parts of the Malagasy elite that had been gradually excluded from access to political and economic resources. In a similar vein, the HAT, in whose name Rajoelina came to negotiate, formed a rather mixed amalgam of political figures, some of whom had joined the anti-Ravalomanana camp only days after the latter filed his resignation. Matthieu Pellerin (2009b) noted that compared to the anti-Ravalomanana movement, the HAT did not include what he calls historical opposition figures. Instead, Rajoelina's strategy to 'surround himself with personalities that are not likely to overtake him' [author's translation] (Pellerin 2009b) meant that historical opposition figures were replaced, for instance, by army officials. From all the mouvances, Rajoelina's thus drew least on already established networks and structures of political organization, and was hence prone to much more fierce internal power struggles and conflicts that erupted as a result of the opportunities provided by the negotiations (see also ICG 2010b: 12; Ratsimbaharison 2017: 39).[7] Altogether, Rajoelina's mouvance, and to some extent Zafy's mouvance, suffered most from such internal divisions and a lack of leadership, despite the fact that both Zafy and Rajoelina ultimately played the role of authoritative executives during the negotiations.[8] As described by one interviewee, within the mouvance Zafy, 'everyone wants to take the caliph's place' [author's translation].[9] With regard to the mouvance Rajoelina, another interviewee observed during the negotiations in Maputo:

> The problem was Mr. Rajoelina, who was under the influence of the members of his mouvance. When we met in the format of just the four, he accepted, but when we reunited in plenary he renounced the concessions he had made. This is how he differed from Mr. Ratsiraka or Mr. Ravalomanana: when they decided, the other members of their mouvances followed. For him [Rajoelina] it was the opposite. He was under the influence of the members of his mouvance. (Author's translation)[10]

A case in point are the negotiations at Hotel Carlton in Antananarivo in June 2009. The focus of these negotiations was to reach an amnesty arrangement. Yet determining the scope and substance of such an arrangement created a division within Rajoelina's own delegation (Mouvance Zafy 2009b). This was one of the reasons why the negotiations ultimately failed.

Despite their different roots within existing party structures, all mouvances retained a high degree of personalization and focus on their respective leaders. Both the internal organization and the selection of the actual negotiating teams, for instance, were highly dependent on the choices and strategies of the individual head of the mouvance rather than a matter of extensive internal debates. As one representative of the mouvance Zafy pointed out:

> The mouvance Zafy, that's Zafy. The mouvance Ratsiraka, that's Ratsiraka. The mouvance Ravalomanana, that's Ravalomanana. Maybe the mouvance Andry [Rajoelina] had others to speak, different ideas (...). The mouvance Zafy, that's Zafy. You count nothing in that mouvance. And even when we debated, it was Zafy who debated. (Author's translation)[11]

In a similar vein, one of the members of the mouvance Ravalomanana recalls having observed Ratsiraka during the negotiations in Maputo: 'There was only him who spoke (...) there was only him who thought (...). They were all there, the other members, but they said nothing. It was Ratsiraka who spoke on his own (...)' [author's translation].[12] This concentration on the *chefs de file* was in fact not only reflected in the mouvances' internal organization, but also in the substantive contributions they brought to the negotiating table.

Interests and strategies

With regard to their respective positions at the negotiating table, the four mouvances were distinguished by their leaders' rivalries or alliances rather than by broader political visions. This is not to say that the mouvances did not have particular themes that shaped their respective contributions to the negotiations (Ratsimbaharison 2017: 112). However, it underlines how limited the scope of the negotiations was altogether.

For instance, in line with the background of his mouvance, Albert Zafy contributed his proposals for a comprehensive process of national reconciliation. For his mouvance, this remained the constant theme throughout the entire negotiation process (Mouvance Zafy 2009a; Mouvance Zafy 2009d). Ratsiraka, in turn, stressed the importance of a revision of the constitution, including measures for decentralization (Lavrard-Meyer 2015: 597). Moreover, for Ratsiraka, amnesty was an important, personal issue to negotiate as he and other AREMA members still faced legal proceedings in Madagascar as a consequence of the 2001/2002 post-electoral crisis. As he lived in exile in Paris, a comprehensive amnesty provision was the only condition upon which Ratsiraka would have been able to return freely to Madagascar. During the first rounds of negotiations in Antananarivo, Ratsiraka's insistence on the term 'annulment' of legal proceedings rather than 'amnesty' – which leaves open the question of guilt – was one of the reasons for the stalemate the negotiations reached (AU 2009; see also Lavrard-Meyer 2015: 556).[13] The mouvance Ravalomanana focused their negotiating strategy almost exclusively on the question of the latter's return and on compensation for the destruction of his personal fortune during the pillaging in early 2009.[14] As in Ratsiraka's case, 'blanket amnesty' and the release of those imprisoned since the HAT had taken power also took much of the mouvance's attention. Rajoelina, in turn, concentrated on two issues he brought to the negotiating table: first, on being recognized as President of the Transition; and second, on preventing Ravalomanana from returning to Madagascar. As for Rajoelina, these two issues were the conditions upon which the promised renewal of Madagascar's political and economic order were to be realized; no further substantive issues had to be negotiated. This is, for instance, illustrated in Rejoelina's communiqués about the negotiations in Maputo (HAT 2009b; HAT 2009c; HAT 2009d; HAT 2009e) that reflect his limited interest in more substantive negotiations and his fixation on excluding Ravalomanana from the political arena. On 6 August, for instance, he announced that SADC mediator Chissano recognized him as president of the HAT and that according to the documents under negotiation, Ravalomanana was nothing but 'a simple citizen' [author's translation] (HAT 2009b: 1).

These examples underline that while the mouvances' respective positions added individual issues and foci to the negotiations, they all mainly reflected the individual interests of their respective leaders rather than tangible programmes for the political, social, or economic (re)organization of post-March 2009 Madagascar. As a consequence, none of the mouvances were really interested in making compromises and conceding to the respective other sides. Though to a different degree, all four mouvances thus negotiated with an exclusive, confrontational strategy that made a negotiated resolution largely elusive. What is more, the mouvances' internal organization and their positioning vis-à-vis key political questions of the crisis and its resolution replicated the personalist, in parts paternalistic, and often ad hoc pattern characteristic for the post-independence Malagasy party system (see Marcus & Ratsimbaharison 2005). Despite their novelty and artificiality as political formations, these structural continuities are evident. While this observation may not be surprising, it is crucial for understanding the course of the negotiations and the high levels of rivalry and conflict that soon emerged both between but also within the mouvances. It also provides reason to question the extent to which the negotiations' protagonists could be expected to bring about change and to work for undoing coups in the long term.

The limited value the four parties attributed to the negotiations also becomes evident in the various practices the four mouvances employed to contribute to and shape the course of the negotiations. While the mouvances of Ratsiraka and Rajoelina prepared for individual, closed-door negotiations, Zafy's mouvance worked with written proposals distributed ahead of the respective rounds among the other mouvances and the mediators. None of the other mouvances explicated their position in such a comprehensive form.[15] This strategy of 'paper communication' with the other mouvances and the mediation team was also upheld after the failure of the Accords of Maputo and Addis Ababa in summer/fall 2009, despite the fact that – in the eyes of the authors – the reactions to these proposals had been largely disappointing.[16]

Ravalomanana, in turn, made extensive use of his diplomatic contacts as well as international legal support, and thus sought to influence the course of the negotiations rather away from the official table.[17] This was accompanied by an extensive 'letter diplomacy' to the mediators as well as SADC and AU decision-makers. The mouvance Ravalomanana also published written communiqués (in English) following the official negotiations. These were disseminated online to a wider public, inter alia, via the website of TIM as well as through email distribution lists to the diplomatic community.[18]

Rajoelina – in his capacity as President of the Transition – used a similar strategy to gain authority over the interpretation of the respective rounds of negotiations: communiqués, written in French and Malagasy, and published both online and in the Malagasy press. In contrast to those from the mouvance Ravalomanana, however, these communiqués targeted a national rather than international audience. In order to communicate with his Malagasy support group, Ravalomanana also used the weekly reunions of his supporters at one of the branches of Magro, Ravalomanana's wholesale firm in Antananarivo. Through video messages from South Africa, Ravalomanana regularly addressed his supporters and informed them about strategic questions. These different strategies to shape how the course of the negotiations was publicly and internationally interpreted thus also entail a crucial commonality: they all speak of a rather limited focus on what was going on at the negotiating table itself, the official and formal site where Madagascar's post-March 2009 order was supposed to be negotiated. Rather, both Rajoelina and Ravalomanana heavily invested in gaining support from beyond the table in order to further diminish the need to make compromises. These various practices thus replicate the above-observed limited substantive meaning the four mouvances were willing to attribute to negotiating Madagascar's post-2009 order in any more profound way.

Unequal resources: international networks, knowledge, and money

The four mouvances were also shaped by unequal access to various kinds of resources. Three of them were particularly important: access to international networks; human resources, including professional knowledge and diplomatic experience; and financial and other material resources. These (unequally distributed) resources shaped how the four mouvances were able to enact their prescribed role as negotiating party.

First, the four mouvances held different positions of access towards the mediation team and the various international actors, who promised crucial symbolic or material backing for their respective positions. One issue relevant in this regard was locality. Particularly at the time when negotiations still took place in Antananarivo, the mediation team was much more focused on the parties present on the ground. Ravalomanana – still in exile in South Africa – was officially represented through the spokesperson of his mouvance. This, however, became more difficult over the course of the mediation. For the mediation team, it became increasingly unclear who really represented the mouvance (Chissano 2011a: 15).[19] Locality therefore became a potential source of tension between the mouvances and the mediators. It also encouraged Ravalomanana to adopt a particular set of strategies to keep up international attention to his cause. Cases in point are the above-mentioned focus on the international diplomatic community as well as a number of his erratic, ad hoc decisions, such as the spontaneous but effectively stage-managed attempts to fly back to Madagascar in February 2011 and January 2012 (IOL News 2011).[20]

Ratsiraka and Zafy both benefited from pre-existing contacts to Chissano as well as their shared identity as former heads of state. During his time in office, Ratsiraka had supported the Mozambique Liberation Front (*Frente de Libertação de Moçambique*, FRELIMO),

THE INTERVENTION SCENARIO   107

of which Chissano was a founding member (Raison 2007). Zafy and Chissano, in turn, met several times in the context of conferences organized by the National Democratic Institute (NDI). These were meant to facilitate contacts between African heads of state who had left power voluntarily or through democratic elections in order to turn them into role models for incumbent presidents. Chissano and Zafy thus shared this particular identity.[21] To what extent these links actually facilitated the interactions admittedly remains difficult to assess. However, my interviews provide evidence that they certainly raised expectations that were soon to be disappointed by a much more complex, non-linear course of the mediation, which ultimately depended on more than an ideational fraternity and pre-existing contacts with the mediator.[22]

With regard to international contacts, Ravalomanana was probably positioned best. The US embassy in Antananarivo, for instance, regularly held exchanges with his representatives on the ground and lobbied for the release of those in prison. Ravalomanana also made use of his wide network of international diplomatic contacts.[23] Access to such networks was something Ravalomanana shared with Ratsiraka. Ratsiraka not only counted on a wide network of support within influential political and diplomatic circles in France; he was also frequently visited by the various mediators (Lavrard-Meyer 2015: 557).[24]

Ravalomanana, in turn, although not always officially invited, sought to be present at the meetings of the AU PSC in Addis Ababa as well as those of the SADC troika and summit, either in person or through an appointed delegate (Mouvance Ravalomanana 2011c; Mouvance Ravalomanana 2012). This presence at summit meetings turned out to be decisive. Especially for the SADC meetings, Ravalomanana's constant lobbying shaped SADC heads of state's initial interpretation of the situation on the ground and supported their principled stand with regard to his return.[25] As recalled by one interviewee:

> The big problem with SADC is that those who came here may have had a certain idea about the situation. But they were not the ones to decide last. And since it was not them who ultimately decided, but rather the heads of state, these heads of state remained in their own pattern [of thinking] (...). It must be said that at the beginning, the lobbying of Mr. Ravalomanana was extremely rewarding. He had been lobbying very hard and so he had managed to persuade those at the level of SADC that his return was necessary and so on and so forth. (Author's translation)[26]

Moreover, Ravalomanana's lobbying also meant that, at least retrospectively, the other mouvances considered the international outside of Madagascar – especially SADC and the AU – as already 'occupied'. Discussing the imbalance with regard to international diplomatic contacts, one of Rajoelina's close advisors argued that the lack of a diplomatic strategy was the major error of his mouvance from early on.[27] That SADC member states effectively prevented Rajoelina from addressing the UN General Assembly in September 2009 underlined this instructively (UN News 2009). While the *de facto* government may have benefited from the network of Malagasy embassies around the globe – also in Addis Ababa and Pretoria – there was no explicit or strategic placement of individuals that would have allowed the embassies to be used as diplomatic channels (*Midi Madagasikara* 2010). In addition, as in the case of the Malagasy embassy in Addis Ababa, the flux in allegiances during the transition also meant that the diplomatic staff on post too was often caught between the different political camps, and thus a rather unreliable international point of contact.[28]

The HAT nevertheless made use of the embassy in Addis Ababa in order to convey messages to the AU and the local diplomatic community (HAT 2009a). In a similar vein, Rajoelina's visits to Libya and Senegal, as well as to the newly emerging financial donors such as China and Saudi Arabia, underlined that the HAT government was not at all isolated from international networks (ICG 2010b: 10). In this sense, it also benefited from the fact that every time Rajoelina left the country, rumours abounded as to whether his journey amounted at least to an informal recognition of the HAT as the legitimate government of Madagascar. This was particularly relevant every time Rajoelina visited France. In March 2011, for instance, French government officials had to confirm publicly that Rajoelina's visit to Paris, including a meeting with the French Minister for Cooperation and the General Secretary of the Presidency, was in fact 'private' (*Midi Madagasikara* 2009a; *L'Express* 2011; Sellström 2015: 111).[29]

Second, the mouvances also disposed of different human resources. The composition of the negotiating teams is evidence of different individual capacities, know-how, and professional or diplomatic expertise that came together in their ranks. The concrete negotiating teams selected to represent each mouvance at the negotiations in Maputo and Addis Ababa hence differed tremendously in terms of quantity as well as character. While officially only delegations of seven – in addition to the four protagonists – were allowed to participate during the negotiations, Rajoelina's mouvance was represented by more than the officially sanctioned number of participants.[30] Although excluded

THE INTERVENTION SCENARIO   109

from the negotiating table, these additional supporters were nevertheless present in the corridors. They were hence perceived as additional backing for his negotiating strategy because they could easily assist with research, quickly provide requested additional information, and deliberate further strategies.[31] However, many interviewees acknowledged that the internal incoherence of Rajoelina's mouvance may have outweighed this perceived advantage.

The composition of the negotiating teams also reflected differences with respect to the professional knowledge and the cultural capital that each mouvance was able to build upon. In this sense, the mouvances differed dramatically in terms of their members' experiences in diplomacy and international negotiations. The huge gap in this regard already becomes visible between the four *chefs de file*, from the diplomatically experienced and rhetorically versed Ratsiraka to the internationally hitherto unknown and diplomatically inexperienced Rajoelina. Rajoelina's lack of diplomatic experience is often said to have resulted in a high degree of disrespect towards international interlocutors and an unpredictability that constantly subverted the conduct of the mediation (Lavrard-Meyer 2015: 561).[32] The mediators may have interpreted this as a general weakness and considered Rajoelina as a diplomatically inexperienced 'boy', the former DJ, not counting for much in the formalized and ritualized diplomatic world.[33] In the end, however, this may have been a fatal misinterpretation: unpredictability and subversion at the table indeed proved to be highly successful (Ratsimbaharison 2017: 40; see generally Pearlman 2008). Also, Rajoelina was often represented by one of Madagascar's most experienced diplomats: Norbert Ratsirahonana, a former jurist of the High Constitutional Court, former president *ad interim* following the parliamentary impeachment against Albert Zafy, and one of the leading figures in Ravalomanana's negotiating team during the post-election crisis of 2001/2002. Ratsirahonana shared this experience in negotiating Madagascar's previous crisis with other protagonists of the post-2009 negotiations: Ratsiraka himself, Manandafy Rakotoniringa (an active member of Ravalomanana's negotiating team since the negotiations in Maputo), and Pierrot Rajaonarivelo (now an ally of the mouvance Zafy).

Not only diplomatic experience, but also the professional backgrounds of the delegates, distinguished the four mouvances and consequently shaped their respective potentials at the negotiating table. Given its general legalistic reading of the crisis, Ravalomanana's negotiating team largely drew on judicial expertise, both Malagasy and international.[34] The international jurists whom Ravalomanana regularly consulted, and who themselves negotiated on his behalf, also included the internationally renowned South African lawyer Brian Currin, who had been involved in international mediation in Rwanda, Sri Lanka, Northern Ireland, and the Basque Country. Retrospectively, members of the mouvance Ravalomanana interpret this focus on jurists as a major shortcoming in the negotiating strategy because it constrained the mouvance to adapt to the often quickly changing, informal, and highly political circumstances on the ground.[35]

Apart from differences in diplomatic and professional experience, language proficiency, particularly in English, became a crucial condition for participating in the mediation process. While the negotiations were initially mainly conducted in French, English language skills became much more important once negotiations were officially conducted under SADC leadership. None of my interviewees mentioned that language was a matter of difference between the four negotiating teams. And yet, when asked further, they all seemed to have worked with low levels of command. The mouvance Zafy, for instance, more or less entirely relied on one former English teacher in their ranks.[36] The English language communiqués of the mouvance Ravalomanana too are evidence of a lack of language proficiency (see, for instance, Mouvance Ravalomanana 2012). At the same time, several interviewees raised the importance of language as such, pointing to the difficulties *all* negotiating parties encountered (cf. Lavrard-Meyer 2015: 565). Rather than marking a difference between the four negotiating teams, language was thus a barrier between the mediation team, on the one hand, and almost all Malagasy protagonists, on the other (see also the section on the mediation team(s) on p. 128).[37]

Third, the four mouvances had unequal access to financial resources. For instance, Ravalomanana's recruitment of international jurists, the additional flight diplomacy within his own mouvance, and his international lobby trips required considerable financial means. Rajoelina's mouvance, in turn, benefited from the privileged position as the *de facto* government. As with the financing of the transitional period in general, rumours abound but little is known with certainty. However, many of the participants observed that Rajoelina's much larger delegations sent to Maputo and Addis Ababa, for instance, also produced high costs that had to be covered by someone.[38] Ratsiraka, in turn, was financially supported by the French government, which also covered for his entire participation in the negotiations in Maputo and Addis Ababa (France Diplomatie 2010; Châtaigner 2014: 121).

Out of all interviewees, members of the mouvance Zafy stressed the issue of financial means most. They deplored the necessity of having negotiations outside of Madagascar, as this raised costs and made technical preparation and the logistics of negotiations much more difficult.[39] While acknowledging that at least the minimal requirements for the negotiations in Maputo and Addis Ababa had been provided for by SADC, one interviewee observed:

> So every time we went there, it really was a problem for the mouvance Zafy. Because everyone had to pay for their own participation. There were no structures for that. And when we arrived there, we did not have much money to get around, to lobby or to do anything. So people had to stay there and attend the official meetings, while everything should happen in the corridors, on the phone (...) [author's translation][40]

This quote underlines the significance of resources of various kinds in order to participate in negotiations. It also highlights the obvious gap that existed between the ideal and requirements of international negotiations, on the one hand, and the actual roles exercised by the four mouvances, on the other.

Summary

In summary, this section has argued that the four mouvances were a product of the intervention. Their very formation stemmed from the idea that a negotiated solution to the Malagasy crisis should be the result of 'a productive and successful dialogue (...) with the key stakeholders in Madagascar' (SADC 2009d: 3). As a consequence, the parties that came to negotiate were heavily dominated by their respective leaders and internally split, as membership in the mouvance promised access to the fruits that were divided at the negotiating table. As a result, none of the mouvances were really willing to make concessions or to compromise at the negotiating table. Altogether, the mouvances' contributions to the negotiations were thus limited, focusing on the respective leaders' personal interests rather than any substantive programme for how to reorder Madagascar after the events of March 2009. Despite differences, the mouvances hence reified the personalization and instrumentalization characteristic for the party system and formal political organization in Madagascar (Marcus & Ratsimbaharison 2005). Altogether, the intervention made up negotiators but did not produce coherent and legitimate political actors that were willing and capable to engage in any meaningful way in reimagining and negotiating Madagascar's future.

Moreover, resources (i.e. international contacts, knowledge, and financial means) were distributed unequally among the four mouvances. On the one hand, this meant that differences between the four mouvances were levelled out, so that none of the mouvances were able to entirely dominate the negotiations. On the other hand, the distribution and at times shared lack of necessary resources also explains the parties' partly destructive behaviour at the table. The demand for a 'productive and successful dialogue' hence not only invented the mouvances (SADC 2009d: 3). It also required the various mediators to continuously discipline and guide the negotiating parties so that actual negotiations could take place as prescribed in the mediators' respective mandates.

Thus, although officially formed to be negotiators, the mouvances' internal organization, strategic orientations, and resources altogether suggest a rather limited willingness and capacity to actually negotiate in the ideally envisaged manner. Despite their differences, they all heavily deviated both from the ideal image of a coherent, interest-driven negotiating party and from the claims to legitimacy and representation that had justified this approach in the first place. Nevertheless, apart from upholding the image of an international mediation, for their members the mouvances still served as opportunities, and in this sense certainly fulfilled a purpose – albeit not the officially attributed one.

The international interveners

The events of March 2009 focused hitherto unprecedented international attention on Madagascar. Altogether, four different types of international actors became active in returning Madagascar to constitutional order: African regional organizations (AU, COI, COMESA, SADC), other international organizations (EU, UN, World Bank), cultural organizations (OIF), and bilateral partners (see Figure 4.1). In one way or another, they all became part of the intervention scenario. This section shows the diverging mandates that shaped how and by what means the various internationals approached 'la crise malgache' and thereby also created conflicts among them. Apart from different mandates, preceding encounters with Madagascar and the public perceptions and expectations these created also shaped the various internationals' scope of action in the intervention scenario. Finally, this section also 'unpacks' some of the international protagonists, tracing the various sites and actors that defined the respective organizations' approach towards 'la crise malgache'. This shows that the intervention in fact took place at distant, often disconnected sites, which affected how knowledge about the situation in Madagascar was transferred and on what grounds decisions were taken. The intervention scenario thus stretches both horizontally – pulling together Malagasy ex-presidents, party members, resident diplomats, and special envoys – as well as

Figure 4.1 – The intervention scenario

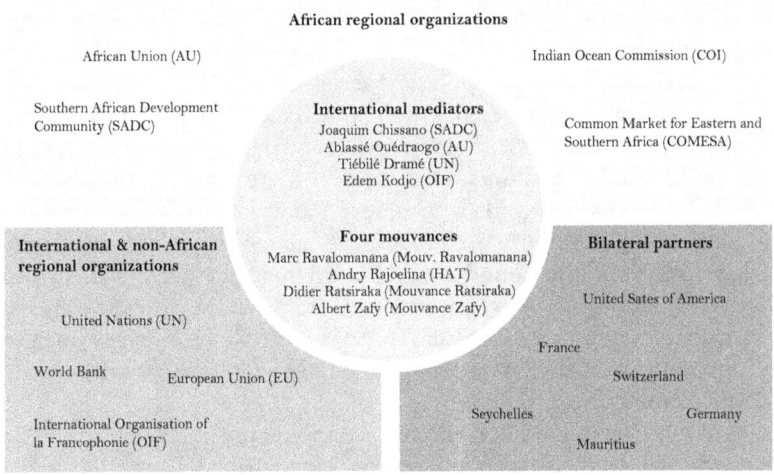

Source: Author's figure.

vertically – linking various actors and agencies that were physically far away from what happened at the official negotiating table.

Entering the intervention scenario: different mandates and interests

The variety of international actors that came to shape the course of events in Madagascar entered the intervention scenario on quite different grounds. Not all of them justified their involvement in returning Madagascar to constitutional order on the basis of a clearly spelled-out and official mandate, and even those with an official mandate differed in what that mandate prescribed.

The AU's entry into the intervention scenario was based on the principles enshrined in the 2000 Lomé Declaration, the Constitutive Act of the AU, and the Protocol Relating to the Establishment of the Peace and Security Council (see Chapter 2). On 20 March 2009, the PSC decided to suspend Madagascar from the organization and demanded the restoration of constitutional order (AU PSC 2009b).[41] With its normative framework, the AU's position initially favoured a mediation process. The PSC thus immediately urged 'the Malagasy parties to uphold the spirit of dialogue and compromise in order to find, as soon as possible, a peaceful and consensual solution to the crisis' with the help of the mediators (AU PSC 2009a: 1). Three days later, the PSC reiterated that the Chairperson of the Commission shall 'work closely with SADC and AU partners (...) to contribute to the rapid restoration of constitutional order, and to take all the initiatives he deems necessary to this effect' (AU PSC 2009b: 1). The AU's focus on a mediated solution was also evidenced by the deployment of Ablassé Ouédraogo as the organization's special envoy. Officially, however, this mediation was restricted. On the one hand, the Lomé Declaration prescribed a certain time pressure by setting deadlines for the application of targeted sanctions and the use of more coercive instruments. On the other hand, the AU's normative framework not only forced the organization to condemn the situation as coup, but – at least from early 2010 onwards – also bound the AU to prohibit 'the perpetrators of an unconstitutional change of government' from running as candidates in transitional elections (AU Assembly 2010a: 2). While officially open to negotiations, the AU thus entered the intervention scenario with clearly defined boundaries.

SADC entered the intervention scenario on more vague terms. The organization's official mandate derived from Article 11 (2b, ii) of the Protocol on Politics, Defence and Security (SADC 2001). On 19 March 2009, the SADC Organ condemned the takeover of power by the HAT and suspended Madagascar from the organization, calling for using 'all relevant resources available to restore order in Madagascar' (SADC 2009c: 1).[42] However, the SADC Protocol neither prescribes a particular mode of intervention nor does it set deadlines or other conditions for how the intervention ought to be conducted. Moreover, SADC's initial role in the intervention scenario was profoundly shaped by the decision of the extraordinary summit of heads of state and government of 30 March 2009, which demanded the 'unconditional reinstatement of President Ravalomanana' and suggested to 'consider other options to restore constitutional order' (SADC 2009b; SADC 2009c). In the eyes of many of the Malagasy protagonists, this decision underlined SADC's pro-Ravalomanana stand and thus compromised the organization's claims to be a neutral or impartial mediator. The communiqué's wording was interpreted as referring to the SADC standby brigade and thus evoked the fear that SADC troops could invade the island (*Madagascar Tribune* 2009b). This nourished a deep-rooted suspicion against SADC, which continued to dominate the public narrative about and the image of the organization. In the words of one of the SADC representatives frequently flying to Madagascar at that time, this translates into the simple observation: 'They just didn't like us'.[43]

For the OIF, the involvement in re-establishing constitutional order in Madagascar was a logical consequence of the organization's mandate to promote democracy as formulated, inter alia, in the 2000 Bamako

Declaration (OIF 2000). Following the events of March 2009, the OIF therefore suspended Madagascar and offered to support the eventual transition process, especially the organization of elections (OIF 2009). The dispatching of Edem Kodjo as special envoy of the Secretary-General signalled that the OIF also actively supported a mediated solution to the Malagasy crisis. Compared to that of the AU, however, the OIF's policy framework was less rigid and prescriptive.

Although COMESA did not appoint a special envoy, the organization's entry into the intervention scenario nevertheless took place on a similar basis. While the organization's legal provisions vaguely define a political mandate in support of democratization and structural conflict prevention, there is no definitive prescription as to how to react to unconstitutional changes of government. In June 2009, the COMESA Summit threatened to examine all options available in order to return Madagascar to constitutional order, 'including the possibility of military intervention' (Afrik-News 2009). Hence, from the very beginning, COMESA's position within the intervention scenario was defined by a rather limited scope of possible action.

The UN officially entered the intervention scenario with the arrival of UN Under-Secretary-General Haile Menkerios and his inclusion in the intra-Malagasy search for a negotiated solution preceding the events of March 2009. On 4 March 2009, Menkerios was substituted by Tiébilé Dramé, the former Minister of Foreign Affairs of Mali, who had been appointed as UN senior political advisor, assisted by two UN experts (see next section). In contrast to the AU, SADC, and OIF, the UN does not have a particular legal script guiding the organization's reactions to unconstitutional changes of government (Call 2012: 1). Madagascar also never featured on the agenda of the UN Security Council. From a UN perspective, Madagascar was not a matter of global security concern. The developments in Madagascar were therefore monitored and handled by the UN Department of Political Affairs (UN DPA). Yet unlike the AU, SADC, and OIF, the UN already disposed of an institutional infrastructure on the ground, even though, as will be elaborated below, this did not make it easier for the UN to immediately respond to the unfolding crisis.

For the EU, the transfer of power from Ravalomanana to the HAT was an infringement of the principles set out in the Cotonou Agreement that regulates the EU's relationship with countries of Africa, the Caribbean, and the Pacific region (ACP countries). As a consequence, the EU immediately suspended all budgetary aid and opened so-called Article 96 consultations.[44] Hence, unlike any other international actor, the EU had its own parallel mechanism to set benchmarks for Madagascar's return to constitutional order.

In contrast to these regional and international organizations, the bilateral partners that came to be involved in re-establishing constitutional order in Madagascar merely did so as a result of their interrupted diplomatic relations. This meant that they were neither limited by specific legal provisions nor were they bound by any predefined mode of intervention. Compared to other African countries, Madagascar receives only a small amount of development aid. In 2012, Madagascar's share in total aid to the African continent amounted to 0.9 per cent (OECD 2015: 8). This situation is also reflected by the small number of diplomatic representations in Antananarivo. In March 2009, only China, Egypt, France, Germany, India, Indonesia, Japan, Libya, Mauritius, Morocco, Norway, Russia, South Africa, Switzerland, the US, and the Vatican had embassies in Antananarivo.

Those bilateral partners with substantial development cooperation and embassies in Antananarivo handled the consequences of the political crisis quite differently. While Germany, Japan, Norway, Switzerland, and the US suspended their regular development cooperation, the French government explicitly decided not to do so (France Diplomatie 2009j). Other bilateral partners such as China also continued their regular development cooperation with Madagascar (Pellerin 2011: 16). Out of all international interveners, the US retained the most principled position (see US Government 2010). This was often perceived as being per se siding with Ravalomanana, although in reality the US policy was much more nuanced (Cawthra 2010: 18; Dewar et al. 2013: 14).

Since France is the former colonial power, its approach to 'la crise malgache' was without doubt the most crucial one. Apart from not suspending its development aid, France also retained some personnel in the Malagasy army in the context of a cooperation programme with the Malagasy security forces.[45] The initial French position right after the transfer of power to the HAT was much more accommodating towards the HAT than that of any other international actor. However, Paris also sent diverging messages. While then President Nicolas Sarkozy used the term 'coup d'état' right from the beginning (France Diplomatie 2009h; France Diplomatie 2009k), the Ministry of Foreign Affairs and Minister Bernard Kouchner stressed that although outside of the constitution, the situation amounted to a 'revolution' or was at least a 'popular coup d'état' (France Diplomatie 2009a; France Diplomatie 2009g; France Diplomatie 2009i).[46] In fact, even before the official transfer of power, French diplomacy supported the idea of a negotiated solution to the evolving stand-off between Rajoelina and Ravalomanana. After the transfer of power, this quickly became a demand for a 'transition', including the rapid organization of elections, so that 'democracy can express itself as quickly as possible' [author's translation] (France Diplomatie 2009b; France Diplomatie 2009c; France Diplomatie 2009l). Although ambiguous, the French position was thus, from the very beginning, less conditional and principled, but clearly geared towards elections organized by an independent electoral commission as well as monitored by international election observers (France Diplomatie 2009d; France Diplomatie 2009e).

In contrast to international and regional organizations, bilateral partners' different approaches to formal recognition thus altogether meant that at least some of them were allowed to maintain official relations with the HAT government. Switzerland, for instance, by following a policy of recognizing states, not governments, was able to retain contacts to the HAT government throughout the five years of transition.[47] To a certain extent, the bilateral partners were thus much more flexible as to how to react to the unfolding (diplomatic) crisis. In turn, however, this also meant that they threatened to subvert the official international consensus that Madagascar's return to constitutional order should be accompanied by an African-led mediation process.

Known and unknown interveners

Many of the international actors involved in re-establishing constitutional order in Madagascar in fact had previous encounters with and presences in the country that shaped their respective relationships with the Malagasy protagonists, and thus their chances to influence the course of the intervention. It also affected how the respective internationals' involvement in resolving 'la crise malgache' was perceived by the wider public. For reasons of space, I will limit this discussion to three examples.

First, the AU entered the intervention scenario based on the collective memory of its role during the post-electoral crisis of 2001/2002, in which the organization first upheld its anti-coup principles and pressured the parties to negotiate but eventually gave in and accepted the fait accompli (Cornwell 2003; see also Chapter 3). This meant that in the eyes of some of the negotiating parties, the AU first of all had to repair its credibility. For those who had supported Ravalomanana in 2001, the AU's then legalistic approach had not proven that the organization was siding with the people. For those on the side of Ratsiraka, however, the AU's final renouncement to implement the negotiated agreements was a matter of strong disappointment. For both sides, the AU was an unreliable organization (Rajaonah 2002). For the AU, in turn, the renewed crisis was proof that the solutions of 2001/2002 had utterly failed and that a more principled position may in the end also lead to more sustainable results (see also OAU Secretariat 2002). The need to repair an image hence not only mattered vis-à-vis the various Malagasy actors, but also with regard to the organization's general credibility in its efforts to 'undo' and ultimately prevent unconstitutional changes of government.

Second, unlike the AU, SADC had not been involved in the 2001/2002 post-electoral stand-off. Indeed, SADC's relationship to Madagascar was fairly novel: until March 2009, no major SADC event had ever happened in Antananarivo, and not a single Malagasy had worked at the Secretariat in Gaborone. Madagascar had joined SADC only in 2005, as part of Ravalomanana's general policy of diversifying the island's economic and political alliances within the region (Oosthuizen 2006: 134–136). As observed by Anne Hammerstad (2005: 2), this decision had raised 'questions and eyebrows', as it suggested a clear departure from Madagascar's hitherto francophone international orientation. It was, however, understandable given Ravalomanana's economic reform programme since 2001, the prospects of closer regional integration, and Ravalomanana's experience of 2001/2002 on 'what happens if you do not have regional allies' (Hammerstad 2005: 3). For both SADC member states and the Malagasy political elite, economic considerations were therefore the primary motivation behind Madagascar's integration into SADC.

As a consequence, this meant that both sides to this novel relationship only disposed of a minimum of knowledge about the respective other. As recalled by a member of the Malagasy diplomatic corps, it was the SADC Desk at the Foreign Ministry who had to explain to the HAT government the reasons, legal basis, and procedural aspects of SADC's involvement after the events of March 2009.[48] This not only reflected the diplomatic inexperience of the members of the HAT (see preceding section); it also reflected a much deeper and more consequential lack of knowledge about the regional and continental institutions that shaped the international encounters over the coming years. When SADC issued its decision to suspend Madagascar, for instance, Rajoelina immediately announced that Madagascar was no longer a member of SADC (FES 2009: 16).

Given these overall limitations in knowledge and mutual understanding, SADC's initial siding with the pro-Ravalomanana camp was even more consequential. As underscored in the testimony by one of the SADC envoys quoted above, this meant that all those sent to Antananarivo with the aim of engaging the Malagasy parties were first of all forced to repair a broken image and to regain credibility and trust among the Malagasy protagonists.[49] This was particularly vital for SADC's relationship with all those who had played key roles in the anti-Ravalomanana movement, but also for SADC's links to other international actors. To the former, SADC had to prove its neutrality and impartiality; to the latter, SADC had to show its interest in mediation and a transition programme beyond the demand for Ravalomanana's return.[50]

SADC's role within the intervention scenario did evolve and eventually took a clear turn with the appointment of Joaquim Chissano as mediator in June 2009. The difficulties tied to defining SADC's position within the intervention scenario, however, remained. The turn towards a more moderate position in favour of an inclusive and consensually negotiated solution was a heavy disappointment especially for the mouvance Ravalomanana. As, for instance, reflected in Chissano's reports, their constant lobbying for SADC to return to its initially principled, pro-Ravalomanana position rendered the mediation difficult. Rather than being a mere convener of negotiations, SADC and Chissano in particular consequently had to manage, reject, and often disappoint a variety of often contradictory expectations (Chissano 2011b: 6–8).[51]

Third, as the former colonial power, France entered the intervention scenario with the most overt history of previous encounters. France remains Madagascar's most important bilateral partner and therefore also played a crucial role in the course of the post-2009 events. There are an estimated 25,000 French nationals in Madagascar and more than 700 French companies. In the French self-image, Madagascar is France's neighbour – geographically apt because of its proximity to the French overseas department La Réunion – and hence of national interest per se (France Diplomatie 2010). The embassy is France's eighth-biggest in the world, which primarily reflects Madagascar's economic relevance for France (Rakotomalala 2012: 214). In Madagascar, suspicion towards French neocolonial influence is widespread. Yet at the same time, France is often referred to as *reny Malala*, the dear mother, denoting the exceptional and indeed ambiguous position the former colonial power still holds in the political imaginary of Madagascar (Rajaonah 2002: 158–159; Rakotomalala 2012: 214). In this sense, it comes as no surprise that despite this ambiguous relationship to the former colonial power, Rajoelina and Ravalomanana both repeatedly insisted that their respective positions were supported by France (ICG 2010b: 7).

From the very beginning, however, France was perceived as taking a pro-Rajoelina stance. In the Malagasy public and to some extent the international diplomatic community, rumours abounded that France even orchestrated Ravalomanana's reversal (Châtaigner 2014; Rakotomalala 2014).[52] Several factors nourished this perception. During Ravalomanana's last years in office, the relationship with France had clearly deteriorated. Ravalomanana, often described as a 'francophobe', diversified Madagascar's bilateral relations, enshrined English as a third language into the constitution of 2007, and challenged the interests of many established French firms with the expansion of his own business. All this clearly went against the idea of a privileged French role in Madagascar's international orientation. In mid-2008, the French ambassador Gildas Le Lidec left his post early after Ravalomanana had several times refused to grant him an audience (*Le Monde* 2008). In January 2009, the French *Chargée d'affaires* had offered Rajoelina refuge, reacting to the latter's claim that his life was threatened. At the same time, the newly appointed French ambassador Jean-Marc Châtaigner was the first member of the diplomatic corps to visit Rajoelina on 19 March 2009, just two days after the official transfer of power to the HAT.

This particular relationship as the former colonial power, overt interests, and this public perception clearly shaped France's role in the intervention scenario. On the one hand, the less rigid positioning vis-à-vis the HAT government opened avenues to inner circles of the HAT that most of the other internationals had either consciously cut or never established. While officially not recognizing the *de facto* government, the French ambassador nevertheless regularly met high-ranking HAT figures. In early April 2009, then US ambassador Niels Marquardt observed:

> The new French ambassador and DCM [deputy chief of mission] are engaged in many direct ways with a government which France does not (yet) recognize (...) and to which he is not yet formally accredited. He called formally on Prime Minister Roindefo on Friday, generating much press attention and the appearance of normal relations, and met today with 'FM' [foreign minister] Andriamanjato. Apparently he is not operating under any restriction vis-à-vis contact with the HAT.[53]

On the other hand, the widespread suspicion and perception that France was playing a double game – too yielding towards the HAT – also forced French diplomacy to repeatedly affirm their support for the ongoing mediation activities and that African actors should be playing the lead role therein. Then French Foreign Minister Bernard Kouchner continuously stressed that the French policy in early 2009 was in line with the ongoing efforts, notably the initial mediation under the auspices of the Malagasy churches and the work of the AU and UN special envoys (France Diplomatie 2009b; France Diplomatie 2009c). He particularly stressed the French support for African leadership and underlined that the French policy towards Madagascar is always integrated into multilateral arrangements, particularly the OIF and the COI (see also France Diplomatie 2009f: 4-5). Irrespective of whether these announcements matched the actual conduct of French diplomacy, the apparent need to justify France's role in Madagascar in relation to African actors and the ongoing mediation efforts underscores the significance of mutual perception and positioning vis-à-vis the other international actors in the intervention scenario. Apart from official mandates and established alliances, meta-norms such as multilateralism and an African primacy in deciding African issues thus also shaped the scope of possible action in the intervention scenario (see next section).

Looking inside: organizational disconnects

How the various international actors engaged 'la crise malgache' was also shaped by the way they organized their respective involvement in Madagascar. A closer look into the various actors, institutions, and locales that came to shape their respective policies towards 'la crise' underscores that most of the organizations were marked by a network of different actors and sites. At the same time, this 'look inside' also highlights that crucial international actors conducted their involvement in Madagascar mainly from afar, disconnected from the actual developments on the ground. Again, for reasons of space, the discussion is limited to the AU, SADC, and the UN, for they had the most relevant impact on the form of Madagascar's return to constitutional order.

The AU's policy frameworks mandate a variety of actors to become involved in re-establishing constitutional order following an unconstitutional change of government in a given country. AU policies towards Madagascar were therefore formulated and implemented at different locales. The AU Assembly (the highest decision-making organ), for instance, once took a decision directly pertaining to Madagascar (AU Assembly 2010c) and regularly mentioned Madagascar in its periodic review of PSC activities on the situation of peace and security on the continent (AU Assembly 2009a; AU Assembly 2010b; AU Assembly 2013a). All decisions, however, merely reiterated the preceding PSC decisions; they did not add any substantive change. The actual decision-making power with regard to the AU's policies on Madagascar was therefore left to the PSC. The PSC convened altogether 19 times over the course of five years.[54] It decided on the application of individual targeted sanctions as well as on the lifting of Madagascar's suspension (see, for instance, AU PSC 2010a; AU PSC 2013a).

In addition, the AU Commission played an important role in preparing reports and formulating – and indeed executing – decisions of the PSC. On the one hand, Jean Ping, until 2012 Chairperson of the

AU Commission, became directly involved as a mediator in early 2010. Similarly, AU Commissioner for Peace and Security Ramtane Lamamra led the mission to Antananarivo in the summer of 2013 in order to convince the so-called 'illegal candidates' to withdraw their candidacies (see Chapter 5). On the other hand, the more general work of monitoring the situation in Madagascar, drafting reports, and accompanying missions to Antananarivo was done by the AU Commission's Peace and Security Department. Here, over the course of time, two senior staff members covered the Madagascar file among other issues on their respective portfolios.[55] Once elections became more likely, the Commissioner for Political Affairs was also invited to attend and brief meetings of the PSC (see, for instance, AU PSC 2013c; AU PSC 2013d).

There were several ways in which the AU sought to bridge the distance between Addis Ababa (the centre of decision-making) and Antananarivo (the site of the actual intervention): through the appointment of a special envoy as well as through ad hoc visits to Antananarivo by the Chairperson of the Commission and the Commissioner for Peace and Security. Moreover, the PSC meetings were regularly briefed by SADC mediator Chissano, by representatives from any of the other international organizations or bilateral partners involved (for instance, SADC and OIF), and by the protagonists themselves (AU PSC 2013b). While reflecting the increasing international coordination in reactions to unconstitutional changes of government, the briefing practices of the PSC also highlight that the direct flow of information from Antananarivo to Addis Ababa was rather limited. The members of the PSC heavily depended on indirect channels, either through AU missions or through diplomatic services of other international organizations and bilateral partners. The AU Chairperson only submitted three reports to the PSC over the entire course of the intervention: the first in February 2010 and two more in 2013. In contrast to many other conflict scenarios on the continent, the three reports are minimal in both quantity and substance if they were meant to actually inform and guide a decision-making process.

Only since early 2013 was the AU permanently represented on the ground through the SADC-AU liaison office. The office initially comprised two senior staff with professional backgrounds in post-conflict reconstruction and elections who were, upon the arrival of the head of the office in early 2014, directly answerable to the Commissioner. While mediator Chissano and several PSC meetings had indeed demanded that a local presence be set up much earlier (Chissano 2010; AU PSC 2011e), this obviously proved to be more cumbersome than expected. As will be elaborated in Chapter 5, the internal organization of the liaison office eventually also compromised its potential to contribute to the ongoing transitional process.

As in the case of the AU, SADC's roles and policies too were interpreted and shaped by a number of actors. The overall decision-making function remained with the summit of heads of state and government. The summit holds an annual ordinary meeting at which questions relating to peace and security in the region are discussed among any of the other issue areas relevant to regional integration in Southern Africa. Between 2009 and 2014, the summit took decisions relating to Madagascar at five ordinary as well as ten extraordinary summits. At the same time, the summits also covered the ongoing conflicts and political crises in Zimbabwe, Lesotho, and DR Congo, although the latter two only a few times.

The second locale of decision-making was the troika of the SADC Organ, which convened altogether six ordinary and two extraordinary meetings dedicated, inter alia, to Madagascar. Unlike the SADC summit, however, the annual rotation of the troika chair meant that the actual composition of the troika was constantly changing, and with it the priorities, interests, experiences, and individuals representing SADC. This became visible in SADC's initial reaction to the situation in Madagascar, which was clearly shaped by then troika chair Swaziland's priorities. In June 2009, the then South African ambassador to Madagascar, for instance, mentioned to his US interlocutor that in order to change SADC's position, the 'first task was to neutralize King Mswati'.[56] This dependency on individual member states, however, is a structural phenomenon, and thus continued to shape SADC's role even after Swaziland passed on the troika chair to Mozambique in the summer of 2009. As observed by one interviewee, even the two succeeding chairs – Mozambique and Zambia – had their own urgent issues: the first prioritized Lesotho and Zimbabwe on SADC's peace and security agenda, while the coincidence of Zambia's 2011 elections diverted attention away from the latter's regional engagements.[57] As with the AU, debates and divisions within SADC's decision-making bodies are difficult to reconstruct. However, SADC's initial decision in defence of Ravalomanana was not without internal discontents. As argued by Laurie Nathan (2012: 94), as with previous conflicts in the region, the crisis in Madagascar split SADC member states into one camp favouring military solutions and regime security and another camp in favour of mediation, democratization, and human security. Changing from a militarist pro-Ravalomanana position towards one of leading an international mediation thus required a decisive internal mediation effort. This was particularly driven by South Africa.[58]

Unlike the meetings of the PSC, SADC summit and troika meetings were not attended by invitees, such as representatives from any of the other international or Malagasy actors involved in returning Madagascar to constitutional order. The only exception was Marc Ravalomanana, who regularly attended SADC meetings, though not always officially invited.[59] Information on the developments on the ground thus mainly came from Chissano himself, the SADC Secretariat, or member states' own diplomatic networks.

Apart from the decision-making organs, the SADC Secretariat as well as the Directorate of the SADC Organ were in charge of the implementation of summit decisions, preparation and planning of the missions to Antananarivo, and maintaining a communicational channel to the team of mediator Chissano. Mirroring the picture of the administrative structure of the AU, initially only one senior staff member at the Organ Directorate was, inter alia, in charge of the Madagascar file.[60] Where possible, he joined mediator Chissano's missions to Madagascar. Later, he stayed for two months in Antananarivo in order to prepare the establishment of the liaison office until it was finally staffed.[61]

As with the AU, the inauguration of the SADC-AU liaison office in 2012 thus meant a permanent SADC representation in Madagascar for the first time. Unlike the AU side, SADC dispatched seconded diplomatic personnel of the troika members to serve in rotating format in the liaison office. The establishment of the liaison office was bitterly contested among SADC member states, which also contributed to the long delay between the decision to establish it and the actual deployment of permanent staff (see also Chapter 5).

As noted above, the UN's initial mediation efforts were organized through the UN DPA. On the ground, however, the UN was already represented by the resident coordinator of the UN Development Programme (UNDP). As coordinator of all UN operational activities in the area of development, the resident coordinator was also the official representative of the entire UN system. The local presence of the UN DPA now questioned this hitherto uncontested role of representing the UN and brought to the fore an internal conflict as to who was mandating, defining, and conducting the political lines of the UN's engagement in Madagascar. As a consequence, the now two UN representatives were more often in competition with and disconnected from each other rather than supporting each other's work. As will be elaborated below, this, for instance, affected the resources made available to UN special advisor Tiébilé Dramé. In the end, the much more advanced capacities, financial means, and network of professionals the UN disposes of, particularly if compared to the AU and SADC, were not utilized effectively.[62]

The ICG-M: persisting promise of coordination

In order to 'better coordinate the efforts of the international community' (ICG-M 2009: 1), the AU on 30 April 2009 decided to set up an International Contact Group on Madagascar (ICG-M).

The composition of the group followed the pattern of contact groups previously established by the AU: chaired by the AU, it comprised the UN and EU, SADC, COMESA, COI, and OIF, the respective chairs of the AU Assembly and PSC, and permanent as well as African members of the UN Security Council. Later, so-called 'partners of Madagascar', initially only Germany and Japan, also participated in the meetings. Over the course of time, the group grew significantly.

At the inaugurational meeting, the ICG-M members defined that the return to constitutional order should be realized through a transition leading to free and fair elections under the participation of all relevant Malagasy actors, including Ravalomanana. They decided to 'continue working together under the auspices of the AU and in support of its efforts to promote an early settlement of the crisis and a return to constitutional order in Madagascar' (ICG-M 2009: 2). Compared to other international contact groups (ICGs) set up after unconstitutional changes of government in Africa, this mandate was defined in fairly vague terms (Witt 2012b: 226).

The ICG-M met altogether nine times between 2009 and 2014, mainly in Addis Ababa. Only twice did the group hold its meetings in Antananarivo. The choice of venue had two crucial consequences for the work and perception of the ICG-M. First, it defined who represented the respective members of the ICG-M, thus favouring diplomats resident in Addis Ababa over those more familiar with the situation in Madagascar. Second, the context in which the meetings took place also shaped the overall atmosphere of the exchanges. This imprint of the venue is, for instance, reflected in a cabled report from the US embassy in Antananarivo, describing the third ICG-M meeting exceptionally held in Antananarivo:

> Although pro-HAT groups had threatened to block the mediators' arrival at the airport following SADC's recent move to stop HAT leader Rajoelina from speaking at the UNGA [UN General Assembly], security was ensured by the HAT, which even went so far as to break up a small gathering of peaceful protesters outside the meeting venue on Oct 6 by firing tear gas to disperse the approximately 100 people. The local nature of the event significantly altered the dynamic compared to the previous ICG-M's [sic] held in Addis. Discussions were heated and not particularly diplomatic.[63]

The ICG-M's general disconnect from the developments in Madagascar meant that it depended on indirect knowledge about the situation on the ground. With only a few exceptions, those representing ICG-M members at meetings in Addis Ababa had never personally been to Antananarivo.[64] The group therefore received regular briefings from the various special envoys, from the mediator, or from representatives of the group's member organizations and governments. In fact, according to interviews, the ICG-M's main value for its members remained that of a forum to receive and exchange information.[65]

Similar to the workings of ICGs in other conflict scenarios, a local chapter was set up in order to follow up developments on the ground, establish lines of communication to the parties, consult other relevant Malagasy actors, and coordinate the overall international reactions. The local chapter of the ICG-M met much more regularly, but it was also less strict and formal in its composition. It therefore did not substantively distract from the otherwise normal diplomatic coordination practices in politically turbulent times. Furthermore, there was no formal agreement as to whether and how the local ICG-M was to channel information and recommendations back to the diplomatic level in Addis Ababa.[66]

From the outset, the work of the ICG-M was shaped by profound divergences among its members. Resulting from the different mandates, as explained above, it was contested who ultimately led international efforts to restore constitutional order in Madagascar. This unsurprisingly compromised the work of the ICG-M and its capacity to act as guardian of the rapid restoration of constitutional order. As a result, the first of its meetings was shaped by fierce controversies in which several participants repeatedly asked the plenary what was actually the overall purpose of the ICG-M.[67]

Moreover, once SADC had appointed Chissano as mediator, there was a general confusion with regard to the position he was to take vis-à-vis the ICG-M. As observed by one participant, a number of ICG-M members preferred to consider themselves as mediators, and hence came in conflict with Chissano's and SADC's own leadership claims. Their reading was that negotiations should take place in the context of ICG-M meetings. By contrast, Chissano and SADC's reading was that the ICG-M should serve as a support structure while negotiations were a matter of closed-door interactions between the four mouvances and the Joint Mediation Team (see next section).[68] Much therefore points to more general power struggles within the ICG-M that were more relevant than substantive differences. Such differences, however, also became evident, for instance in diverging approaches to the application of sanctions, the suspension of development aid, or the schedule and conditions set for transitional elections (see ICG-M 2010; ICG-M 2011).

Among the ICG-M members, these divergences were frankly debated. At the fourth meeting in January 2010, for instance, the ICG-M was split as to how to deal with Rajoelina's decision to (temporarily) withdraw from the mediation. This, however, did not lead to a significant shift in the role, position, or composition of the group. The US ambassador to the AU observed that despite hardened divisions, actual decisions were ultimately postponed. He therefore concluded that '[i]n all likelihood, the ICG will reconvene on the margins of the AU Summit within the next month in order to grapple once again with the question of restoring democratic rule in Madagascar'.[69]

As a consequence of its internal conflicts, the ICG-M's communiqués were often poorly drafted and vague in wording, hardly reflected the actual developments on the ground, and entailed contradictory statements and decisions that were never followed up.[70]

Over the course of time, the ICG-M therefore altogether lost its importance as a unifying forum for the various international actors involved in re-establishing constitutional order in Madagascar. Between 18 February 2010 and 26 June 2013, the ICG-M held only one meeting (on 8 December 2011). Here, the ICG-M noticed that closer cooperation on a political and technical level was important, and so the group decided to meet at least every three months, preferably in Antananarivo (ICG-M 2011). Like preceding decisions, this one too was not followed up. In sum, the ICG-M was a reflection of the internationals' diverging approaches to 'la crise malgache' and the competition among those involved in resolving the crisis. However, the ICG-M also demonstrates the persistence of the idea of international coordination as a meta-norm for the international governance of political crises. While the ICG-M was actively subverting its initial *raison d'être*, coordination never seemed to have lost its appeal.

Summary

This section has shown that the various international actors involved in resolving 'la crise malgache' did so based on their own mandates and interests that defined what and how they approached the situation on the ground. None of them disposed of sufficient material and immaterial resources to claim and exercise uncontested leadership. There was also no clear hierarchy among them. Crucially, none of them had been invited by the Malagasy parties to resolve 'la crise'. Moreover, (collective) memories of previous encounters in Madagascar shaped how each of them related to the Malagasy 'stakeholders' charged to negotiate

Madagascar's post-March 2009 order and how they were perceived by the wider public. This altogether affected how and to what extent the various internationals were able to shape the course of the intervention. While keeping up the ideal of an internationally coordinated effort to return Madagascar to constitutional order, the ICG-M nourished rather than eradicated differences and conflicts among the various internationals involved in this effort.

By looking beyond individual policy frameworks and the official rounds of negotiation, the section also highlighted that international intervening actors themselves are composed of different arenas. For most of them, the decision-making process was disconnected and locally distant from the representation on the ground. This had crucial consequences for the kinds of knowledge that informed their decision-making processes: there was little direct exchange between the situation in Antananarivo and the actual sites of decision-making. In fact, it often remained utterly unclear how knowledge was being transmitted from one place to another. This has been particularly highlighted with regard to the AU and SADC, whose decision-making bodies decisively shaped the course of the intervention.

The mediation team(s)

Like those selected to negotiate Madagascar's post-March 2009 order, the individuals sent to realize the various international actors' mandates to engage 'la crise malgache' also had a crucial impact on the intervention scenario. Their individual capacities, professional backgrounds, personal links of amity and animosity, and questions of identity and political convictions shaped to what extent and how they were able to influence what was to evolve from the intervention. In line with a growing recognition in the literature that the strategies, knowledges, and relationships of a mediator have an important impact on the course and outcomes of a mediation process (Svensson & Wallensteen 2010; Maundi et al. 2006), this section zooms in on the work and practices of those sent to represent the various international organizations on the ground. Against this background, this section highlights how the above-described diverging mandates and interests of the various internationals also played out at the personal level: as competition between different mediators. None of the four envoys was able to impose himself as the uncontested mediator. Even Chissano's appointment as official lead mediator continued to be questioned and contested. Moreover, this section points to an important source of friction hitherto often unaddressed: a general disconnect between the various mediators, on the one hand, and the Malagasy negotiators, on the other. This became manifest in language barriers and in an overall limited recognition granted to the cultural and contextual features that were crucial for understanding what was at stake in post-March 2009 Madagascar. Irrespective of competitions and frictions between the various mediators and their respective mandating organizations, the mediation as such thus remained inherently disconnected from what was happening at and beyond the negotiating table.

Competition and rivalry

As a consequence of the internationalization of the Malagasy crisis, parallel and contradictory mandates were given to initially three, then four, different mediators. In the order of appointment, these were Tiébilé Dramé (UN), Ablassé Ouédraogo (AU), Edem Kodjo (OIF), and Joaquim Chissano (SADC).[71] Tiébilé Dramé was Foreign Minister of Mali following the fall of Moussa Traoré in 1991 and since then candidate in several presidential elections. He is one of Mali's nationally and internationally most renowned political figures. Apart from his national political career, he served as UN official and human rights expert in Burundi and Haiti. Ablassé Ouédraogo, an economist by training, also served as Foreign Minister of Burkina Faso from 1994 until 1999. Internationally, he worked for UNDP, the World Trade Organization (WTO), and the African Development Bank (AfDB). Edem Kodjo was OAU Secretary-General from 1978 until 1983 and again from 1994 to 1996, and was Prime Minister of Togo from 2005 until 2006. Thus, all three were internationally experienced diplomats from francophone West African countries with a varying but altogether rather limited track record in direct and protracted mediation. Their experience lay in diplomacy but not necessarily in conflict resolution. In this sense, their appointment fits into the general pattern of appointing diplomats rather than professional mediators in resolving African conflicts (Khadiagala 2011). By contrast, Joaquim Chissano, who served as President of Mozambique between 1986 and 2005, was a founding member of FRELIMO, negotiator of the peace agreements that led to Mozambique's independence in 1974 and the termination of civil war in 1992, and UN-appointed special envoy in various African conflicts, inter alia, in South Sudan, Guinea-Bissau, and Northern Uganda. Chissano's appointment seems to fit into the overall pattern of what Gilbert Khadiagala (2011: 32) calls the 'recycling' of mediators and special envoys, which particularly affects a few former African heads of state. Both commonalities and differences in their backgrounds came to shape the different mediators' respective roles in the intervention scenario.

Reflecting the differences in their respective mandating organizations' general approaches to 'la crise malgache' (see previous section), the different mediators worked in competition with each other from the very beginning. Since mid-March 2009 and continuing after Chissano's appointment in June 2009, the four officially formed a so-called Joint Mediation Team (Gavigan 2010; Lanz & Gasser 2013). Although 'at the operational level coordination worked relatively well' (Lanz & Gasser 2013: 12), they continued to pursue diverging strategies vis-à-vis the Malagasy negotiating parties. As until June 2009 the mediation was mainly driven by Dramé and Ouédraogo, competition also mainly took place between these two. For instance, the two mediators consulted different Malagasy parties, gave contradictory press statements, and altogether pretended to work in an institutional and political vacuum. As already discussed in the first section of this chapter, the question of whom to include in the mediation process is a good case in point, which publicly revealed the otherwise more subtle competition between Ouédraogo and Dramé. As reported in a cable from the US embassy:

> There was clear tension visible between Ouedraogo and Drame as they took turns describing their separate efforts over recent days to bring the Malagasy parties together. Ouedraogo seemed to describe a process intended to bring only the TIM and HAT together, and Ouedraogo said both parties are prepared to meet and work together (albeit initially only secretly). For his part, Drame described a much broader process, and a far greater range of political actors who need to be included. Drame reported progress in getting five or six different political parties engaged (including TIM), noting also that he had met in Paris on April 1 with former president Ratsiraka to obtain his – and Arema political party – buy-in; other participants would be civil society, private sector, the churches, and the military.[72]

The US diplomat thus concluded that:

> The UN and AU special envoys are leading separate but – so far – poorly coordinated efforts to bring the various Malagasy processes into some harmony; this disconnect, due primarily to free-lancing on the AU Envoy's part, is an increasing source of concern both to the Malagasy and to partners.[73]

What is more, coordination attempts among the various internationals in Antananarivo were boycotted by the respective other mediator.[74] Once the first rounds of negotiation in Antananarivo had reached a stalemate, Dramé and Ouédraogo also gave diverging opinions as to whether suspending the mediation or continuing to push the parties to agree to transitional elections was the better strategy.[75] At the same time, Ouédraogo's presence at the *Assises nationales* of early April 2009, a national conference organised by the HAT, nourished rumours as to whether this was a sign of his proximity to the HAT (Dalichau & Raveloson 2009: 2).[76]

Three aspects in particular explain why it turned out to be so difficult to ultimately define the relationship and hierarchy among the different mediators. First, the individual claims behind the competing mediation efforts only reflected that none of the mandating organizations were able to claim uncontested leadership. Dramé, for instance, based his claims for leadership on the UN's superiority and professionalism in managing conflicts globally. Ouédraogo, in turn, argued that Madagascar needs an 'African'-led mediation, thus per se discrediting any potential UN leadership.[77] Second, neither age nor status resolved competing leadership claims. Age, for instance, was not a sufficient criterion: this would have placed Edem Kodjo in the lead, who was, however, from the least powerful organization. Dramé's claims to UN superiority, in turn, were compromised by the fact that he was only appointed as UN senior advisor and *not* as special envoy of the Secretary-General.[78] This clearly lowered his standing vis-à-vis the other envoys (Call 2012: 20). Third, the relationships among the mediators remained unresolved because all three drew upon different individual capacities and resources, as well as different levels of preparation and backing from their respective mandating organizations. This impacted the way the mediators built up contacts to the various Malagasy parties. As a consequence, none of them were ultimately able to claim uncontested leadership of the process.

Although Dramé's classification as UN senior advisor and not special envoy also meant less resources, he still drew on the most comprehensive and elaborate diplomatic and technical apparatus. However, the internal divisions within the 'two UNs' on the ground, explained in the previous section, meant that the organization's overall institutional and technical support structure remained underutilized. Dramé's missions were therefore conducted rather disconnected from the wider UN support system. He was usually accompanied by two senior UN experts who, notwithstanding their professional expertise, did not have any previous relationship to Madagascar. Dramé therefore had to build from scratch his network of contacts into both the diplomatic community of Antananarivo and the Malagasy political elite.[79]

This was different for Ouédraogo, whose marriage to a Malagasy is often cited as a crucial advantage over any of the other mediators. Ouédraogo therefore disposed of knowledge about Malagasy political culture and history, as well as links into the political elite.[80] It was also Ouédraogo who worked with Malagasy facilitators, whom he consulted in order to establish further contacts, for translation works as well as for advice on strategic questions. Having observed all three mediators in action, Ouédraogo's consultant summarises that Ouédraogo '(…) was the only one who understood the Malagasy mentality, who knew that when a Malagasy says "yes" it may not be "yes" but "no" (…)' [author's translation].[81]

While Ouédraogo's pre-knowledge as well as already established personal contacts soon raised the criticism that he was partial and following personal interests, the quote underlines the importance of 'cultural knowledge' and context sensitivity on the part of those sent to realize international mandates to resolve crises on the ground (see further below). And yet in practice, such skills were granted only limited strategic relevance. At the same time, the AU's minimal technical support structure and the more prescriptive policy framework compromised this advantageous position. For instance, Ouédraogo was less often present in Antananarivo. Also, in contrast to the UN, the AU's more confrontational stance towards the HAT regime limited the mediators' actual room for manoeuvre (Nathan 2013: 12). However, to judge from Ouédraogo's various encounters during the first weeks of the mediation – including his presence at the *Assises nationales* – the real restrictive consequence of the AU's policy framework seems to have lain in the time pressure Addis Ababa was imposing for the 'rapid restoration of constitutional order' (AU PSC 2009b: 1), not in the AU's necessarily confrontational stance vis-à-vis the power in place (*L'Express de Madagascar* 2009a).

Language barriers, prejudices, and legitimacy

Despite these differences, the four mediators shared at least two things. First, they all worked on a short-term basis with limited to no permanent structures in Antananarivo. While the frequencies and durations of their respective sojourns in Madagascar varied, this meant that the mediation was sequenced to particular times, *ex post facto* designated as times of 'progress', and that the more continuous, permanent exchange with the parties remained indirect at best. This added to the general time pressure imposed on the negotiations, which had already been reflected in the announced calendars, schedules, and deadlines on the day of the official transfer of power (AU PSC 2009b; ICG-M 2009). It also meant that trust and relationships had to be built on a very short-term, ad hoc basis and that the mediators invested little in finding their *own* reading of the situation, based on their *own* observations and encounters on the ground. In this sense, the strategies of the four mediators in fact did not differ as dramatically as their staged competition might suggest. Whom to consult and where to look for information seem to have followed a rather default pattern. Even though there were differences in strategies and approaches, these did not amount to distinguishable models of mediation, neither in terms of process nor of substance.[82] As argued by Ouédraogo's consultant, one of the reasons for this was a lack of appreciation for the specificity of the case of Madagascar:

> They wanted to copy mediation techniques in Madagascar that they do in West Africa, East Africa, Burundi, etc. But it was not the same here. (...) It was a bit like that, the flaw in the mediation. They led the mediation as a mediation. (...) I think they really had a problem of preparation. (...) The mediators arrived immediately, without mastering the whole environment, the whole culture, the Malagasy reasoning (...). And beyond all that: the problem of language. (Author's translation)[83]

According to this account, the mediators shared an overall novelty to and ignorance of the more subtle contextual features shaping the conduct and dynamics that unfolded at the negotiating table. As stressed in the above quote, language was an important entry point to these contextual and cultural aspects of the mediation, which remained inaccessible to the mediators. Although both mediators and negotiating parties were francophone, none of the mediators spoke Malagasy sufficiently. At one instance in May 2009, Ouédraogo's consultant was asked to speak to the four parties in Malagasy. He recalls that:

> (...) so I was asked to discuss in Malagasy with the different mouvances and then to take stock with the mediators. (...) There were misunderstandings on some terms. And while discussing in Malagasy we managed to unblock some points. (...) It was on terms acceptable to everyone. In Malagasy it was acceptable for everyone. After that we had to find the French terms (...) to translate this state of mind. And in fact the advantage was when I discussed in Malagasy, in the presence of the four international mediators, the debates were more open, more direct. Because with the international mediators they were much more reserved, they dared not really say what they meant. (...) This type of

meeting in Malagasy (...) it allowed to really know the state of mind of each other. And that was so essential. Because the difficulty is that the mediators believed that we reached an agreement, but it was not yet that. (Author's translation)[84]

This quote reflects well that the choice of language was not only necessary for precision and agreement in wordings and terminology. The choice of language in fact profoundly shaped the social interactions at the table. In short, language defined the roles and identities of, as well as hierarchies between, those sitting around the table. Hence, the fact that the mediation was conducted in French (and later in English) did have a profound alienating effect.

A second point all mediators had in common was their African origin. This activated deep-seated, sometimes racist prejudices against 'Africans' prevalent in Madagascar (Nativel & Rajaonah 2007: 13). At several instances, anti-African tropes served as additional grounds to delegitimize the internationals' presence (Ralambomahay 2011: 90; Sellström 2015: 61). In addition, the open competition among the mediators – not concealed from the Malagasy public – contradicted the image of a mediator as *ray aman-dreny* (Rajaonah 2002: 168). In Malagasy political culture, *ray aman-dreny*, often translated as 'father-mother at once', denotes a political figure with a legitimate claim to authority, which comes with a responsibility to care for the well-being of the *zanaka*, the children (Wallner 2012: 188). Even in the postcolonial Malagasy state, relationships between state officials and ordinary citizens are often described in terms of such parent–children relationships (Jütersonke & Kartas 2010: 35–37; Fremigacci 2014: 131). What at least the public in Madagascar's capital was to observe in the first weeks following the transfer of power was hence anything but fulfilling the image of a competent and trustworthy caretaker for the interests and well-being of society as a whole, the essence of a *ray aman-dreny*.[85]

Chissano's appointment: contested leadership

The appointment of Chissano did not manifestly change the strained encounters among the various internationals, on the one hand, and between them and the Malagasy parties, on the other. Chissano's role continued to be questioned from within SADC and by other international actors involved in re-establishing constitutional order in Madagascar. Among the Malagasy parties, however, Chissano seemed to receive more support.

Chissano's status as a former head of state gave him a role different from those of the other mediators.[86] This, first of all, meant that he addressed the four protagonists as a former head of state, and thus equal to them. By this, Rajoelina in particular was granted the level of recognition he personally considered appropriate and which satisfied his self-understanding as the legitimate President of the Transition.[87]

More than his standing as a former head of state, it was his personal history as a key FRELIMO figure that shaped how he engaged the negotiating parties. Having himself been a member of a party to peace negotiations brought Chissano into the position of using this experience and talking in his addresses to the Malagasy negotiating parties about the possibility and potentials of peacemaking from a personal point of view. Also, his previous involvement as a mediator in South Sudan, Guinea-Bissau, and the Great Lakes region allowed him to draw on strategic knowledge on how to deal with parties reluctant to negotiate. Further, he was able to point the Malagasy parties to the fact that peacemaking had been possible in situations that were marked by much higher levels of destruction and violence. For instance, several participants to the negotiations recalled Chissano's repeated appeals to take into account that the peace processes of Mozambique and the Sudan show that parties were able to compromise despite the fact that they had been involved in killing each other's families.[88] And yet Chissano's comparisons to situations that were 'much worse' also had a flip side: while they spoke of his rich experience, it also meant taking something away from the seriousness with which the Malagasy parties negotiated. He therefore constantly played with the danger of further alienating the parties from the negotiation process.[89]

Moreover, the above-mentioned prejudices towards 'Africans' meant that for the Malagasy parties, negotiators from Juba or Kinshasa were not necessarily an evident reference for self-identification. Indeed, given that in public discourse the Rwandan *genoçidaires* are often used as the embodiment for anti-African sentiments (Nativel & Rajaonah 2007: 13–15), comparisons of this kind may ultimately have had an ambiguous effect on Chissano's position vis-à-vis the Malagasy parties.

Chissano did not work alone. Although officially the SADC Secretariat was in charge of technically and financially supporting the mediation process, in reality he relied on his own support structure from within the Mozambican Ministry of Foreign Affairs as well as the Joaquim Chissano Foundation.[90] Chissano therefore worked with a team of three, who usually also accompanied his visits to Madagascar: Leonardo Simão, former Foreign Minister of Mozambique; Chissano's long-time assistant Nuño Tomasz; and John Tesha, a Tanzanian national.

What applied to the three other mediators, however, also applied to Chissano and his team: their African descent was not unproblematic for the encounters with the Malagasy protagonists. In fact, the Malagasy term *Masombika* – in the nineteenth century depicting slaves brought to Madagascar from the African mainland – has since remained an anti-African trope, used simultaneously to defame continental Africans and to discriminate against coastal Malagasies based on their supposed slavery descent (Nativel & Rajaonah 2007: 11; Sellström 2015: 56). The fact that there was a time when both the mediation team and the SADC Secretary-General were all Mozambicans once again gave rise to these tropes.[91]

While the mediation team drew on accumulated experiences in diplomacy and mediation, they were relatively novel to the concrete social and political dynamics on the ground. The team's preparation for the mediation task thus mainly relied on previous experiences as well as a general sense of familiarity with the rules of diplomatic conduct.[92] At the same time, although fluent in French, Chissano's mediation team faced the same linguistic barriers when it came to the Malagasy language as all previous mediators did. At least on the part of the SADC Secretariat, there was an explicit decision *not* to work with Malagasy consultants.[93] The mediation team initially also did not expand its contacts beyond those who had already been identified in the first weeks of March 2009 as relevant to resolving the Malagasy crisis (Chissano 2010; Chissano 2011a; Chissano 2011b).[94]

Despite Chissano's potentially better position towards the Malagasy parties, he only received ambiguous support from both SADC and other ICG-M members. In fact, Chissano's first meeting with the ICG-M in Addis Ababa revealed two opposing visions of how the group ought to relate to Chissano and the ongoing mediation efforts.[95] At the same time, the PSC's own description of the negotiations in Maputo in August 2009, for instance, suggests a certain ambiguity as to the exact role attributed to Chissano, claiming that the process took place 'under the auspices of the AU' (AU PSC 2009e).[96] This ambiguous support for Chissano's role as lead mediator in fact continued after the Maputo negotiations. Before the negotiations in Addis Ababa in November 2009, AU special envoy Ouédraogo repeatedly stated in front of the press as well as Antananarivo's diplomatic community that Rajoelina's role as President of the Transition was confirmed – an interpretation of the Maputo Accords that entirely contradicted the position of the mouvance Ravalomanana and thus threatened their continued participation in the mediation process (*L'Express de Madagascar* 2009b; *L'Express de Madagascar* 2009c). At the same time, after the Addis Ababa meeting, UN advisor Dramé immediately flew back to Antananarivo and tried to reopen negotiations with the parties in order to settle the outstanding issue of finding a consensus prime minister. This too called Chissano's

THE INTERVENTION SCENARIO 137

leadership into question. It moreover undermined the claimed superiority of African institutions in finding a way out of the crisis in Madagascar. AU Commission Chairperson Jean Ping hence wrote to UN Secretary-General Ban Ki-moon allegedly demanding that the latter end Dramé's mandate.[97] Dramé was called back to New York, held a debriefing with the UN DPA, and never returned to Madagascar (UN DPA 2011: 5).

The parallel and competing mediation from Dramé was, however, not only a matter of the latter's personal ambitions. It was also rendered possible because in contrast to Chissano, he disposed of two crucial resources: time and money. On the one hand, Chissano had to leave the meeting in Addis Ababa for personal reasons, despite the still ongoing negotiations.[98] Here, in particular, Chissano's personal schedule actually invited others to engage in parallel activities and thus subverted his role as lead mediator.[99] On the other hand, the financial endowment of his mediation was uncertain throughout. In some cases, this hindered Chissano to serve as a flexible and prompt messenger between the ICG-M and the Malagasy parties, for the required financial means first had to be raised from ICG-M members.[100] In other cases, the financial burden was left to the Mozambican government or the mediators themselves.[101] Altogether, how the mediation was actually financed remains, despite great effort, unknown to the author. Yet what is clear is that SADC member states only reluctantly supported the mediation.[102] For instance, the SADC budget did not allocate a clear item to Chissano's mediation, a conscious decision taken by the SADC summit, which feared otherwise outstretching the Organ's financial capacities.[103]

Apart from contestations from within the Joint Mediation Team and SADC's ambiguous support, Chissano's role was also continuously questioned by the members of the ICG-M. For instance, the failure of the Maputo and Addis Ababa agreements was also used to question Chissano's overall competence as a mediator.[104] That the AU decided in November 2009 to set up an alternative follow-up mechanism to trace the implementation of the Maputo and Addis Ababa Accords is a further case in point (AU PSC 2009d).

There are, however, also signs that Chissano himself became increasingly frustrated with his role, caught between unclear international and Malagasy interests, especially the alleged French support for Rajoelina. In January 2010, the US *Chargé d'affaires* in Maputo, for instance, reported from a meeting with Chissano:

> Chissano was visibly frustrated by France's position in support of TGV [Rajoelina]. He said French expatriates in Madagascar have established a direct link to President Sarkozy and convinced him that the best course for French interests is to support TGV. Chissano explained that

as long as TGV was confident of French support, he would continue to be inflexible towards the other three movements and continue pushing for non-inclusive elections. The French are attempting to persuade the international community that TGV's proposed elections will be representative of the 'voice of the people', a claim which Chissano said he, SADC and the AU rejected.[105]

As a consequence, Chissano's growing frustration created space for others to develop their own ad hoc mediation profile. This opportunity was first taken by the then Chairperson of the AU Commission, Jean Ping, and later on by a joint South African/French initiative, in which Chissano played the role of a supernumerary: present but only to complete the picture (HAT 2010; see also Chapter 5).

Although Chissano remained the official SADC mediator until the end, he increasingly left the mediation to his above-mentioned team, composed of Leonardo Simão, Nuño Tomasz, and John Tesha. From November 2010 onwards and throughout the preparation of the SADC roadmap, it was these three men who became the official faces of the international mediation efforts. They undertook visits to Madagascar, liaised with the SADC Secretariat, convened meetings with the parties in Antananarivo, and became their principal addressees (see Chapter 5). Chissano remained in charge of the negotiations with Ravalomanana, whom he met at least two times in Johannesburg between February and April 2011 (Chissano 2011a).

Officially, Chissano's withdrawal is explained as being a reaction to the change among the Malagasy protagonists. While hitherto the negotiation process took place among three former and one *de facto* heads of state, the SADC roadmap was prepared with the participation of a much wider array of actors (see Chapter 5). The 'downgrade' in the mediator's official status thus only reflected this change in the composition and status of the Malagasy negotiators. Unofficially, however, many observers, as well as the participants in the negotiations themselves, also attribute the withdrawal to Chissano's growing fatigue with a mediation in which neither his role, nor his mandate, nor his political line were ever clearly defined.[106]

Summary

By zooming in on the individual level, this section has shown that each of the four mediators entered the intervention scenario on the basis of different mandates, institutional support, personal backgrounds, and links to the Malagasy parties. From the very beginning, the four mediators were in competition with each other, despite officially forming a

Joint Mediation Team. But they also encountered difficulties accessing and establishing relationships of trust with the Malagasy negotiating parties. This was highlighted with regard to language barriers, the prevalence of anti-African tropes, and a lack of (appreciation for) contextual knowledge. Thus, this section underlines the importance of understanding post-coup interventions *also* as encounters between individuals. Although this micro-level account reflects the same struggles and multiple arenas identified in the previous section, it also offers a better grasp of the role and limits of (individual) agency therein. This goes missing if post-coup interventions are merely seen from the perspective of competing organizations, irreconcilable mandates, and clashing a priori interests. In this sense, and despite differences in their respective personal experiences in peacemaking, institutional capacities, and individual traits, all mediators seem to have shared a remarkable degree of disconnection from the dynamics on the ground. This was most evident with regard to the level and methods of preparation, the limited interactions outside of the official framework, the short time frames allotted to official visits in Antananarivo, and as a consequence the rather exceptional physical presence on the ground.

The politics of unconstitutional changes of government

On 20 March 2009, the AU PSC requested 'the Chairperson of the Commission to work closely with SADC and all AU partners, notably the United Nations (...), the European Union and the International Organisation of la Francophonie, to contribute to the rapid restoration of constitutional order' (AU PSC 2009b: 1) in Madagascar. In contradiction to the hopes of the PSC, this chapter analysed the 'messy actualities' that international efforts to 'undo' coups face in practice. In doing so, I described post-March 2009 Madagascar as a social field in which numerous actors struggle to define the rules of the game and thereby shape what was ultimately addressed as 'la crise malgache', and how it was addressed. The multiple actors and conflicts that constituted the intervention scenario created a social field that was neither fully regulated, nor did it merely realize a predefined purpose. These 'messy actualities' demonstrate that post-March 2009 Madagascar was neither experiencing the mere implementation of an external policy framework, based on international coordination, nor a neutral third-party mediation assisting Malagasy parties in conflict. And they explain why the PSC's aim of a 'rapid restoration of constitutional order' turned out to be so elusive.

First, from the outset, the various international interveners followed diverging lines as to how to interpret and approach the situation in Madagascar. Neither the deployment of special envoys nor the establishment of the ICG-M ironed out these divergences. In fact, in many ways, the ICG-M rather exacerbated international competition: it provided a playing field and new incentives for claims to authority and leadership. These struggles over authority and leadership became visible, inter alia, in the competing efforts by the four mediators and in the ambiguous international support lent to SADC mediator Chissano.

Second, the chapter pointed out that for a variety of international actors, engaging the Malagasy negotiating parties turned out to be rather difficult. In some instances, this was due to particular positions taken, such as SADC's initial threat to 'consider other options to restore constitutional normalcy' (SADC 2009b: 3). In turn, France's alleged pro-Rajoelina position raised similar fears among the mouvance Ravalomanana, which was henceforth alert to any sign of a French imprint on the negotiation process. Also, the interactions between the mediators and the Malagasy negotiating parties underlined a more general conflict in which the legitimacy of external intervention was questioned as such. This was nourished by the fact that little relevance was attributed to local presence and cultural or contextual sensitivity – at least in practice – which raised the barriers and potential misunderstandings between the mediation team(s) and the negotiating parties.

Third, the four mouvances that were established to negotiate Madagascar's post-March 2009 order in fact heavily deviated from the ideal of committed and legitimate parties in a mediation process. Though SADC in June 2009 appealed to 'the Malagasy parties to fully cooperate with the SADC coordinated political dialogue aimed at restoring constitutional order' (SADC 2009a: 3), the reality on the ground looked quite different. As they were established only for the purpose of this process, the mouvances used the negotiations to make ever-more claims based on their respective leaders' personal interests. This came at the expense of both compromise among them and more substantive engagements with how to reorder Madagascar after March 2009. In the words of Ratsiraka, 'nous nous chamaillions comme des gosses' – the four parties instead 'quarrelled like boys' (Lavrard-Meyer 2015: 561).

Altogether, these multiple sites and sources of conflict heavily compromised the officially propagated image of a machine-like, automated international intervention based on coordination and cooperation among the internationals and compromise among the Malagasy protagonists (AU PSC 2009b; SADC 2009a). The point to make here, however, is not merely that the initial demand for a rapid return to constitutional order was constrained by the contestedness of the issue at hand and the multiplicity of actors involved. Re-establishing constitutional order in Madagascar was not only difficult because of the 'crowded field' (Lanz & Gasser 2013), a consequence of the sheer number of international actors. Nor was it merely complicated by diverging international norms (Nathan 2013) or competition and diverging interests among international interveners (Rakotomalala 2012; Châtaigner 2014). Rather, the in-depth description of the intervention scenario rendered visible that to a large extent, it was the intervention itself that produced new conflicts. In other words, the intervention was not only a site of, but itself *constitutive* of, conflicts. It provided the opportunities, incentives, and terms for many of the above-described claims to power, leadership, and legitimacy, which then nourished the multiple arenas of conflict that shaped the intervention scenario.

This constitutiveness of the intervention implies that international coordination alone can never be a recipe to turn post-coup interventions into *less* contested endeavours. First, a mere focus on enhancing international coordination ignores that what is at stake is not only finding the right formula for a division of labour or pooling together comparative advantages. Rather, if the conflicts are conflicts about power, leadership, and legitimacy, then coordination is not the solution, but itself a source of conflict. Second, treating international coordination as a panacea brackets the Malagasy protagonists, agencies, and dynamics, as well as the way they shaped and interacted with the various international forces. In fact, what this chapter underlined was the significance and indeed complexity of the *local* social figuration of Madagascar to which international interveners were forced to relate. Their difficulties in doing so may have been exacerbated by the above-described physical disconnect from Madagascar and the general ignorance of many interveners towards the contextual and cultural aspects of the intervention scenario. But in no meaningful way can this figuration be considered mere context.

5
The logic of intervention

As argued in Chapter 1, understanding how interventions contribute to the constitution and transformation of orders requires scrutinizing the particular logics upon which they operate. Interventions are not only social fields; they also express a particular rationality that structures 'the possible field of action' (Foucault 1982: 790). This rationality constructs certain issues as the intervention's objects and thus defines the problem at hand. By this, it also constitutes subjects – that is, it attributes roles and responsibilities for the resolution of the problem, and thereby defines the identities for a variety of actors. This chapter therefore interrogates the dominant logic with which 'la crise malgache' was addressed in the official and unofficial negotiations and how this evolved over time: about what, with, and for whom the 'rapid restoration of constitutional order' (AU PSC 2009b: 1) was sought to be realized. This analysis demonstrates a gradual shrinking of the scope of politics, of issues and problems recognized as crucial for resolving 'la crise malgache'. This was reflected in a transitional process dominated by the executive in which organizing transitional elections became an end in itself and a synonym for ending the crisis. Despite being driven by the ideals of 'inclusivity' and 'consensus', inclusion in the transitional programme rested on arbitrary grounds.

This logic did not fall from the sky. Rather, it was made possible by a particular set of practices by which the numerous internationals approached Madagascar's return to constitutional order as well as corresponding appropriations on the part of certain Malagasy actors, both of which will be explained in this chapter. Far from being an external imposition, Madagascar's post-coup reordering was therefore indeed a *transnational* endeavour (see Chapter 6).

Reordering what? Transition as executive politics

From the very first efforts to resolve 'la crise' by means of mediation – in February and March 2009 still led by the Malagasy churches – there was a strong tendency to address the crisis as a problem of access to and division of power among Madagascar's political elite. Direct negotiations among the identified protagonists, power-sharing arrangements, and transitional elections were treated as instruments of conflict resolution as if there was no alternative. Thus, the consecutive rounds of negotiations in Antananarivo and various African capitals produced a series of at times recycled texts that all revolved around an altogether limited range of questions. While the inclusion of Ratsiraka and Zafy broadened the scope of issues treated at the negotiating table, it did not change the overall restrictions of the debate on questions of the division of posts and access to power. During the negotiations, the bones of contention were consequently not defining abstract aims and objectives of the transition, but rather the concrete composition of the envisaged transitional institutions, eligibility to run in presidential elections, and the scope of the debated amnesty arrangements (Mouvance Zafy 2009a). The texts of the various agreements from Maputo to Addis Ababa demonstrate this concentration on issues of intra-elite power-sharing and access to the institutions of the state. However, as this section shows with the example of the politico-institutional order envisaged in the accords for the transitional period and with the notion of reconciliation, over the course of time the scope of the recognized problems and conflicts became even more restricted.

The presidential polity

The various agreements that were negotiated and signed between 2009 and 2011, despite their overall focus on politico-institutional arrangements among the island's elite, also envisaged different kinds of politico-institutional order, at least in degrees. They differ with regard to the meaning and functions they attribute to the institutions to be established and in the importance they attach to each of them. While the accords of Maputo and Addis Ababa, for instance, foresaw popular consultations to determine the transitional programme and an internationally monitored constitutional process, all this was abandoned later on in the SADC roadmap. Instead, the roadmap strengthened first of all the role of the president. In its imagination of the Malagasy polity, the roadmap replicated the 2010 Malagasy constitution, for which Rajoelina had organised a referendum in November 2010 against the will of the AU and SADC (*Madagascar Tribune* 2010a). According to Richard Marcus (2016: 48), this constitution epitomizes Madagascar's trend towards an 'untamed presidency'.

Article 3 of the roadmap defined that 'Mr Andry Rajoelina shall be the President of the Transition. In this capacity, he shall exercise the functions of Head of State' (SADC 2011a: Art. 3). The presidentialism that this article introduced became evident in a wide range of powers with which the roadmap equipped the President of the Transition: to nominate the consensus prime minister and to appoint the members of the transitional government, the additional members of the transitional congress, the high transitional council, and the national independent electoral commission. The roadmap explicated that such appointments should be based on the:

> fair and equitable distribution of positions, whilst adhering to criteria of political affiliation, gender representation, regional balance and balanced sharing among the Malagasy political stakeholders who are signatories to the Roadmap so as to ensure the smooth running of the Transition. (SADC 2011a: Art. 6)

Yet the roadmap mentioned neither measures to assess adherence to these principles nor sanctions in case of non-adherence. The transitional government was mandated to administer 'the day-to-day affairs of the country' and create 'the necessary conditions for credible, fair and transparent elections (...)' (SADC 2011a: Art. 8). The transitional parliament 'shall oversee the work of the Transitional Government. It shall also ratify the orders passed during the Transition, especially those pertaining to the electoral process, and propose and adopt relevant legislation' (SADC 2011a: Art. 9). Neither the government nor the legislative were envisaged as an effective counterforce, as checks and balances to the president. As observed by Toavina Ralambomahay (2012), this set-up heavily diverged from the democratic ideal of a separation of powers, while it legalized a kind of executive polity that surpassed the executive character of any of Madagascar's preceding constitutions (see also CNOSC 2011: 16).

Apart from endowing the president with excessive powers, this politico-institutional structure reflects that the transition was reduced to an executive process geared towards the organization of elections. The government is a mere implementing organ while the legislative is reduced to producing the scripts, here legal texts, that render this process possible. In line with this, the roadmap also excluded every option to diverge from the path to elections it had prescribed: 'No Malagasy political stakeholder, whether a party or not to this Roadmap, shall arrogate the right to veto the implementation of this Roadmap during the transitional period' (SADC 2011a: Art. 23; see also SeFaFi 2014n: 352). Moreover, Article 31 shielded the institutional arrangement of the transition against any attempted reversal: 'There shall be no impediment or removal procedure against the President of the Transition, no motion of no-confidence against the Transitional Government and no action to dissolve the Transitional Parliament during the Transition' (SADC 2011a: Art. 31).[1] The roadmap's presidentialism was thus based on a severely restricted space for contestation and for the legitimate formulation of alternative paths to resolve 'la crise'.

The presidentialism of the SADC roadmap was criticized by the three mouvances in particular, who feared becoming excluded from a transitional process that increasingly played out according to Rajoelina's rules. In a letter to SADC envoy Simão, the delegation of Zafy, for instance, noted that:

> your 'Roadmap' is fundamentally moving away from the spirit of the Maputo Accords and the Addis Ababa Addition Act by installing Mr Andry Nirina Rajoelina, author of an unconstitutional change of Government, as 'super-President' endowed with more powers and prerogatives than a democratically elected President of the Republic and that the concept of consensuality is, in this 'Roadmap', emptied of all its meaning. (Author's translation; Mouvance Zafy 2011c)

However, in their criticisms, the role of the President of the Transition and his wide-ranging powers were never raised independently of the fact that it was Rajoelina who was given that position. For the other mouvances, criticizing the presidentialism of the roadmap was identical to questioning Rajoelina's legitimacy as beneficiary of that provision. In other words, what was contested was the content of Article 3 more than the outlook of a presidential polity per se.

The three mouvances thus criticized that the SADC roadmap only served to legitimate Rajoelina's unilaterally organized transition, but this was tied in turn to their own claims to a more relevant role in the transition. The mouvance Zafy, for instance, observed that the roadmap:

> seems to gratify Mr. Rajoelina with too important powers and prerogatives, exceeding those of an elected President of the Republic (...). This gratification is, apparently, based on the fact that he has the power, the strength and the money, and that, as such, he must be preeminent to the other mouvances! (...) For the most part, [the roadmap] does not take into account the important points of the proposals of the mouvances other than that of Rajoelina (...). (...) the proposals of the Mouvance Zafy are not taken into account. (Author's translation; Mouvance Zafy 2011b: 1)

In the same vein, the delegation of Ravalomanana rejected the 'exorbitant powers given to the future President of the Transition for the discretionary choice of the members of the different institutions' [author's translation] (Mouvance Ravalomanana 2011a: 3). This, however, was preceded by the demand for a more equitable treatment of the 'two main protagonist mouvances' [author's translation] (Mouvance Ravalomanana 2011a: 1). In this sense, the criticism also repeated the overall orientation of the mouvances, as analysed in Chapter 4, by which questions of political order were always merged with those of individual political fates. This merger, in turn, also meant that a more general critique of the established presidentialism – as a kind of polity to resolve 'la crise' – was not to be found among the negotiating parties.

Reconciliation: whose rights?

The depoliticization of what was considered relevant to resolve 'la crise malgache' is also reflected in the way the SADC roadmap treated the question of reconciliation. In contrast to the previous accords, the roadmap treated the issue of reconciliation mainly as a matter of mutual assurance between the two rival camps of Rajoelina and Ravalomanana. Reconciliation thus became synonymous with 'confidence-building' measures for the two rival camps. The amnesty arrangements, the status of former heads of state, the guarantee for Ravalomanana's return, and several articles demanding the compliance of all Malagasy actors with the transitional programme of the roadmap were all mentioned under the heading of 'confidence-building measures and national reconciliation' (SADC 2011a: Part III). Reconciliation thereby gained a functional character as a precondition for the smooth organization of transitional elections. The roadmap therefore mandated the executive to adopt 'security and confidence-building measures in order to create a serene and peaceful environment by terminating the ongoing legal proceedings against members of the opposition', as well as to 'undertake to protect and promote human rights in Madagascar' (SADC 2011a: Art. 16 and 17).

This framing of reconciliation contrasts with others in which reconciliation is a comprehensive process of renegotiating fundamental relationships within Malagasy society. During the initial negotiations held in Antananarivo and those in Maputo and Addis Ababa, this had been demanded by the mouvance Zafy, in line with the work of Zafy's CRN, as described in Chapter 3. As also stipulated in the accords of Maputo and Addis Ababa, this reading interprets the events of March 2009 within a history of societal contradictions and unresolved tensions emanating from past political crises, particularly the post-electoral crisis of 2001/2002 (Mouvance Zafy 2009c). In this context, the purpose of the transition was to 'implement the process of national reconciliation to alleviate individual and collective injuries left by history' [author's translation] (République de Madagascar 2009c: Preamble). While this also referred to individual injustices experienced by Ravalomanana's political and economic opponents, the project of national reconciliation moved beyond that. Here, the role of a national process of reconciliation was not merely an intra-elite mutual assurance, but a demand to recognize and address long-nourished societal cleavages that have recurrently been a reason for mass mobilization and politicization in times of crisis (Zafimahova 2009; see also Galibert 2009b: 394; Rakoto & Urfer 2014). Zafy's programme for national reconciliation, for instance, particularly stressed divisions within Malagasy society along regional lines, with regard to access to resources, stigmatizations on the grounds of religion and ethnicity, and 'the appropriation, concentration and confiscation, by a minority oligarchy, of power, property and knowledge (...)' [author's translation] (CRN 2003; Mouvance Zafy 2010a). In this understanding, reconciliation is a process that is in itself a search for defining sources of tension, experienced injustices, and exclusion, and it constructively seeks to build something new. Its main purpose is to render visible and to renew.

As a consequence, the institutional structure proposed for the CRN rather resembled that of a forum – an architecture of different institutions and phases – whose purpose was to initiate consultation processes in which hitherto unaddressed sources of tension would become articulated. The role of the proposed institutions was therefore neither to execute nor to punish, but to amplify voices and testimonies hitherto struggling to receive recognition in the public debate and to constructively formulate alternatives (Mouvance Zafy 2009c; Mouvance Zafy 2009d).[2]

In a similar vein, the *Assises nationales*, which were organized in early April 2009 by the HAT in order to formulate a transitional programme, as well as the communiqués by various civil society organizations and 'reflection circles' during the anti-Ravalomanana protests, repeated this more comprehensive reading of the need for reconciliation. They particularly stressed that national reconciliation required a moral reorientation and cleansing that addresses all of Madagascar's society, but particularly the political elite (Various 2009; SeFaFi 20140; see also Zafimahova 2009). Another series of regional consultations organized in June 2010 by the Coalition of Civil Society Organizations (*Coalition des organisations de la société civile*, COSC) on behalf of the HAT came to similar conclusions. The participants identified the 'return to Malagasy moral and socio-cultural value', the 'society without tensions', and 'sustainable development' [author's translation] (COSC 2010: 16) as objectives of reconciliation. More importantly, however, they identified respect for law and society, professionalization of political parties, neutrality, and bottom-up political processes as preconditions for effective reconciliation (COSC 2010: 17–18). They also set clear boundaries for what should *not* be included in amnesty arrangements: 'misappropriation of money and public property', 'destruction of wealth and national heritage', 'sale of ancestral lands', and 'cattle theft' [author's translation] (COSC 2010: 18). These reflections hence underline, on the one hand, the breadth of accounts of what constitutes national reconciliation, what would be required to reconcile. On the other hand, it also became evident that making these different testimonies heard could precisely be the purpose of reconciliation. Moreover, in line with the 'lateral cut' through Madagascar's society in early 2009, as described in Chapter 3, the above-mentioned alternative accounts of reconciliation stressed two issues in particular: a high degree of suspicion towards the island's political elite as well as the link between questions of national reconciliation, economic development, and justice (COSC 2010: 24). None of this is reflected in the SADC roadmap.

The roadmap nevertheless also envisaged the establishment of a Malagasy Reconciliation Council (*Filankevitry ny Fampihavanana Malagasy*, FFM) in order to 'begin healing past individual and collective wounds and lay down a sound foundation for the future of Madagascar' (SADC 2011a: Art. 25). Moreover, the FFM was mandated to compensate assignees and victims of the 'political events that took place between 2002 and the signature date' through a National Solidarity Fund (*Fonds national de solidarité*, FNS) (SADC 2011a: Art. 27). In contrast to the previous accords, however, the roadmap itself was entirely silent with regard to questions of historical or underlying (in)justices or societal conflicts that would make such a process of national reconciliation necessary in the first place. In this sense, it lacked a narrative that would recognize particular conflicts as such and therefore explicate the function and importance of reconciliation as an instrument of conflict resolution. The nebulous wording with which the roadmap defined the mandate of the compensatory scheme underlines this observation. It stipulated that the FFM should be 'facilitated by the international community' and mandated the transitional parliament, an institution otherwise not given any political significance, to further define the FFM's exact role (SADC 2011a: Art. 25).

In a letter to mediator Chissano and the members of the SADC troika of June 2011, Zafy had proposed an alternative formulation of the roadmap's paragraph on the FFM. In his proposition, the FFM's role was to:

> dispel the misunderstandings and distrust associated with the past, be they historical, political, social and economic, so that we may then build together, in a climate of peace, an equitable future of social justice and fair, harmonious regional and national development. (Mouvance Zafy 2011d)

Its main purpose was therefore:

> recommending and supervising the implementation of all the measures designed to rehabilitate the past, including the amnesty and individual or group reparations, in order to strengthen national concord. To do this, it organises consultations that are representative and may go as far as proposals to revise or draw up basic legislation and regulations relating to re-founding the Republic. (Mouvance Zafy 2011d)

This proposition shows that not only had there been a more comprehensive understanding of what reconciliation implies; there were also attempts to concretize the mandate and function of the FFM and thus the form in which reconciliation is institutionalized (see also SeFaFi 2014m: 342). None of this, however, was recognized in the final version of the roadmap.

Altogether, in contrast to the institution envisaged in either Zafy's initial proposal or in the previous accords, the role of the FFM was reduced to dispensing compensations and moral observation of the transitional process, without actually delineating the morality this should be based on. It was a bureaucratic institution rather than a process or forum whose purpose, as envisaged in the initial propositions, was that of a constructive search.

The change in meaning and scope of reconciliation was also reflected in the way human rights were treated during the negotiations, which mirrored the elite-focused understanding of reconciliation as a confidence-building measure. There was an overt imbalance between the recognition of the rights and dignity of the protagonists and victims of past crises, on the one hand, and widespread, ongoing human rights violations, on the other. While the amnesty arrangements for former heads of state, their status and individual benefits, and the fate of political prisoners during Ravalomanana's incumbency were all extensively debated during the various rounds of negotiations, there was a marked silence with respect to the recognition of other violations and other subjects of human rights. This introduced a hierarchy of rights, or 'justice à deux vitesses', a 'justice at two speeds' (SeFaFi 2014k: 285), that favoured the rights of those who directly participated in or who were supporters of those present in the negotiations. It also introduced a hierarchy in time, recognizing infringements of rights prior to March 2009 but silencing those violations that either endured or directly stemmed from the actions of the transitional government itself (Amnesty International 2010: 12; Amnesty International 2011). This especially applied to questions of land, access to resources, and physical security, particularly in rural Madagascar (see also Chapter 6).

The time of no politics

The roadmap's politico-institutional order as well as overall shifts in the understanding of reconciliation and human rights reveal a trend towards minimalizing and depoliticizing the issues and conflicts that were recognized as relevant to resolve 'la crise malgache'. The final text of the roadmap gave expression to a vision of the transition as an executive process geared towards the organization of transitional elections.

This trend towards minimalizing the objects of intervention was finally also reflected in increasingly limited attention and significance being granted to debating the content of the roadmap itself.[3] In this sense, it is not surprising that the roadmap, as a document, did not change dramatically, despite more than eight months of 'negotiation'.[4] Where they existed, proposals made by those who later signed the roadmap were registered but rarely reflected in the text (see final section of this chapter). In addition to the criticism of the roadmap's presidentialism elaborated above, these proposals, for instance, demanded a more thorough engagement with different kinds of constitutions and their respective consequences for the overall organization of the Malagasy polity, a federal reform that addresses the relationship between the political centre in Antananarivo and the state provinces, and a more detailed reflection about the *Comité de pilotage*, an international/national joint mechanism to supervise the implementation of the roadmap (Mouvance Ravalomanana 2011a; Mouvance Zafy 2011b; see also Kotzé 2013a). All these propositions were elaborated in individual consultations, but without reopening the debate or reformulating the roadmap as such.

If the previous accords had recognized an albeit limited space for politics, this became increasingly restricted over the course of the negotiations and was ultimately channelled into the question of how and who is to organize transitional elections. In this sense, the provision of Article 8 of the roadmap, stipulating that the transitional government shall 'refrain from making new long-term commitments' and instead concentrate on organizing elections, reflected an artificial division of time in 'pre-' and 'post-election time', where the first was imagined as a pause in politics (SADC 2011a: Art. 8). The presidential polity and the difference between reconciliation as a functional confidence-building measure, on the one hand, and an albeit vaguely defined search, on the other, both epitomize this imagined transitional period of no politics.

The transition as a time of no politics meant that even after the signing of the roadmap, the only bone of contention was how to realize the demand for an 'inclusive, consensual and neutral' transition (SADC 2010c: 2). Rather than opening a debate on the representativeness or modus operandi of the transitional institutions, however, this demand mainly referred to two questions: whether or not Rajoelina was allowed to participate in transitional elections, and whether, when, and under what conditions Ravalomanana would be allowed to return. Politics thus remained a matter of personal fates. Representativeness and inclusion in the transitional process became a question of (individual) access rather than one of political substance.

Following the signing of the roadmap, SADC's initial demand for Ravalomanana's return and the inclusion of his mouvance in the transitional institutions became more and more compromised. With this, the last officially recognized politics of the negotiation process also vanished. In the end, SADC even endorsed the so-called 'ni-ni' (neither-nor) solution, by which neither Ravalomanana nor Rajoelina should stand in transitional elections. This ultimately reflected the pragmatism that had come to prevail. In the words of a high-ranking SADC official, SADC had to 'sacrifice Ravalomanana' for returning Madagascar to constitutional order.[5]

Apart from Ravalomanana's return and the question of who was eligible to run for the presidency, the roadmap's insistence on a 'fair and equitable distribution of positions' (SADC 2011a: Art. 6) altogether lost its significance over the course of time. Ravalomanana and Zafy addressed several letters to SADC in order to complain about the composition of the transitional institutions and the lack of inclusivity and compromise therein. In November 2011, the two, for instance, noted that only 12 out of 35 cabinet posts were filled by non-partisans to Rajoelina, and that in these appointments the president had entirely circumvented the prime minister. The two called upon SADC to 'consider and resolve our complaint (...) by ordering that the Executive arm of Government is reconstituted' (Mouvance Ravalomanana 2011b: 13).[6]

Yet like the questions of eligibility to run in elections and Ravalomanana's return, the composition and representativeness of the transitional institutions too was increasingly treated as a matter of no politics. While several AU and SADC decisions ritually referred to the need to 'scrupulously implement the commitments made' (AU PSC 2011e: 1), observing that 'some provisions of the Roadmap are still not implemented' (AU PSC 2013a: 2), these observations rarely translated into concrete practices. In May 2013, the PSC summarized that:

> some provisions of the Roadmap have not been implemented, while others have been implemented only partially. These relate in particular to the neutral, inclusive and consensual nature of the Transition process, confidence-building and national reconciliation, including respect for fundamental freedoms, the granting of amnesty and unconditional return to the country of all political exiles, as well as

support by the international community to the implementation of the Roadmap. (AU PSC 2013e: 9; see also AU Commission 2013a; AU PSC 2013b)

As will be explicated in the final part of this chapter, this quote illustrates that AU decision-makers were clearly aware of the above-described depoliticization of what returning Madagascar to constitutional order meant. In fact, the depoliticization was also sustained by a particular mode of engagement with which the variety of international actors executed their roles in this process. The shrinking scope of recognized politics was by no means a reflection of the depoliticized *nature* of the transition. Rather, it reflected the increasingly limited scope of conflict internationally recognized as relevant to resolve 'la crise malgache'.

Reordering with whom, for whom? Faking inclusivity

From early on, the AU and SADC declared that only an 'inclusive, consensual and neutral' transition (SADC 2010c: 2) would be accepted as returning Madagascar to constitutional order. This section demonstrates that also with regard to the subjects (i.e. those actors deemed relevant as protagonists of the negotiations and the transitional period), one can observe a crucial depoliticization over time. For this purpose, I distinguish between two kinds of subjects: *protagonists* (i.e. those considered relevant as direct participants in the negotiations) and *supporters* (i.e. actors who were given advisory or observatory roles). This in fact followed the dominant rationale in contemporary third-party peacemaking practices, where those who are here called supporters are increasingly seen as relevant for the legitimacy and sustainability of otherwise elite-focused power-sharing deals (Paffenholz 2014; Zanker 2018). In addition, the negotiations also constructed a series of future roles. Such roles were, for instance, formulated in mandates given to the wider Malagasy public, the media, or civil society organizations to fulfil certain functions during the transition. Or they were attributed to international actors: as guarantors of the agreements, arbitrators in situations of conflict, or financiers for the transitional elections. The politics of the logic that defined relevant subjects of the intervention hence lies in the definition of who counts as a protagonist, who is a mere supporter, and who has no role to play at all.

As argued in Chapter 4, the four mouvances, the protagonists at the table, were in fact a product of the intervention. They were spontaneously formed as negotiating parties rather than political actors in their own right. Their internal make-up, societal legitimacy, and willingness and competences to negotiate were heavily compromised. For this reason, the decision to work in the format of four mouvances was repeatedly questioned. UN special advisor Dramé, for instance, tried at several points in time to set up a fifth mouvance, led by former foreign minister Pierrot Rajaonarivelo (Mouvance Zafy 2009a).[7] Also, there were attempts to open the negotiations to direct participation from civil society actors (Mouvance Zafy 2009f). The mediators did, however, also work with a number of supporters who were regularly consulted during their visits to Antananarivo: the Malagasy Council of Christian Churches (*Fiombonan'ny Fiangonana Kristianina eto Madagasikara*, FFKM), civil society organizations such as KMF/CNOE or SeFaFi, individuals active in the anti-Ravalomanana protest, party leaders, and the security forces (Chissano 2010: 24). Moreover, in late August 2009, the mediators organised a public event in Antananarivo at which more than 50 organisations and groupings signed the Charter of Adherence to the Maputo Agreements (*Madagascar Tribune* 2009a). This too reflected the mediators' search for a broader societal backing for the transitional process. The agreements of Maputo and Addis Ababa also clearly assigned future roles: the envisaged popular consultations, the constitutional referendum, and the transitional elections, for instance, demanded an active citizenry to participate in the formulation of the transitional programme. In a similar way, the agreements mandated the international interveners to serve as experts to evaluate the conditions for transparent and fair elections and to serve as guarantors of the agreements (République de Madagascar 2009d: Art. 20–21). This apparently clear distinction between protagonists, on the one hand, and supporters, on the other, as well as the future roles assigned to 'the people' and international guarantors, profoundly changed during the preparation of the SADC roadmap.

Internal reorganization: the 'new inclusivity'

In May 2010, Rajoelina announced the dissolution of his mouvance and the introduction of the 'principe parti', the party principle (HAT 2011). In an HAT memorandum, this reads as follows:

> The transitional regime has been and today still is facing a major problem: the recognition of the international community. (...) The international community wanted the crisis to be solved in a consensual way. Several attempts have been made in this direction but have failed, or have not been followed by implementation. (Author's translation; HAT 2011: 8)

Rajoelina's decision to dissolve his own mouvance answered to increasing pressure from within the HAT to end the crisis and its state of institutional and diplomatic exception (see ICG 2010b: 20). More importantly, however, it also served to realign Madagascar's political dynamics to an albeit vague international demand for a 'consensual, inclusive, neutral and transparent transition' (SADC 2010a: 3) without having to make major concessions, particularly not to Ravalomanana.

In the ensuing months, the HAT realized its own transitional programme: it set the date for transitional elections, launched a process of national consultations held in all 22 regions, and prepared a new constitution. All this took place on the basis of a new political accord, signed on 13 August 2010, between Rajoelina and more than 160 political parties and associations. Only around 15 of these political parties had existed before (Grund 2010: 4). The signatories confirmed Rajoelina as president and were in turn guaranteed a seat in the newly composed transitional institutions (République de Madagascar 2010b; ESCOPOL 2011: 38). The HAT memorandum reads:

> The new political agreement (...) builds on a 'new inclusivity' based on the identity of each political party. (...) It also took into account the proposals of the different entities involved in the resolution of the current crisis: the entire population, the elders, the economic actors, the army and the security forces, the power in place, etc. (Author's translation; HAT 2011: 22)

In contrast to the hitherto failed international mediation, the self-organized transition was called a solution 'malgacho-malgache' – that is, it claimed to fulfil the international demand for an 'inclusive' transition and 'that the ownership of the political dialogue in Madagascar must lie with the Malagasy people themselves' (SADC 2009a: 3; SeFaFi 2014j).

The 'new inclusivity' took place against the background of a new dynamism in Madagascar's political elite and created new opportunities especially for its metropolitan members. This particularly benefited an albeit heterogeneous group of politicians who had already been active during the anti-Ravalomanana movement but had since taken a more and more distanced approach to the HAT government. In early 2010, many of them had created new parties, which finally signed the above-mentioned political accord with Rajoelina (see also CNOSC 2011: 10–11).

In the first half of 2010, an important faction of this group established the so-called Space for Consultation of Political Organizations

THE LOGIC OF INTERVENTION   155

and Parties (*Espace de concertation des organisations et partis politiques*, ESCOPOL). ESCOPOL was an umbrella organization initially founded by nine political parties whose self-declared goal it was to 'succeed in implementing a solution to the crisis that does not generate a new crisis and is recognized by the international community' [author's translation] (ESCOPOL 2011: 2). Over the course of the ensuing months, the number of parties and associations joining ESCOPOL rose to more than 100 (ESCOPOL 2011: 40–41). ESCOPOL was consciously established against the so-called National Coordination of Civil Society Organizations (*Coordination nationale des organisations de la société civile*, CNOSC), a formation of three umbrella civil society organizations with the aim of organizing an internal Malagasy-led mediation process (CNOSC 2010a; CNOSC 2010b). As later argued by Rajoelina, the CNOSC was founded on the premise that because international mediation efforts had failed, a solution 'malgacho-malgache', a Malagasy solution, had become inevitable.[8] In light of the stalemate between the rivalling factions at the negotiating table, a civil society-led process promised a more impartial solution (CNOSC 2010a: 7; Trois Mouvances 2010). The organization also increasingly gained international support for this, including the promise of international funding (Chissano 2010: 31; SADC 2010b).[9] For the members of ESCOPOL, however, the role of civil society should have been confined to accompanying and supporting, but not to steering a political process – that is, in the typology suggested above, they should have been supporters, not protagonists. In their view, the *political* process, and therefore also the resolution of a *political* crisis, was left to what they termed the 'société politique', the political society (i.e. political parties) (ESCOPOL 2011: 4–5). With all these developments, the category of protagonists was defined entirely anew.

Being in or being out: opportunities and exclusions

The above developments forced the mediation team to approach the aim of an 'inclusive, neutral, and consensual' transition from a completely new angle. In August 2010, Chissano reported to the SADC summit that 'The announcement by Rajoelina that he is no longer a Chef de file undermines and makes the mediation process based on the four chef de file [*sic*] unworkable, unless a new Chef de file is appointed' (Chissano 2010: 13).

Given this situation, Chissano further noted that it was unclear '[h]ow those who unlawfully maintain power under the leadership of Mr. Rajoelina will be involved in the process of negotiations, so that they can ensure the implementation of the signed agreements' (Chissano 2010: 13). The solution was to integrate them into a new agreement.

Chissano therefore concluded that there is a 'necessity of broadening the participation to include other stakeholders beyond the Mouvances' and that a 'strategic adjustment in the mediation approach is needed' (Chissano 2010: 34). A White Paper by the French government and one prepared by the COI likewise concluded that the momentum required using the 'new inclusivity' to sign a new agreement and organize elections: 'the rapid end of the transition' [author's translation] (Ambassade de France 2010; COI 2010b) was in sight.

With these shifts, the official negotiating table became generally open to whoever wanted to participate. As a consequence, the SADC roadmap was promoted as a means to mobility, a personal opportunity, rather than a tool for conflict resolution.

This change in approach particularly affected the encounters with three of the former protagonists, who were now pressured to adapt to the new circumstances. In a letter sent to the three mouvances, Chissano's envoy, Leonardo Simão, noted that Rajoelina's decision to disband his mouvance and the emergence of new actors who 'demanded their right to play a role in efforts to find a solution to the crisis' had 'compelled [the mediation] to accept these new political actors' (Simão 2011). In a meeting with the three mouvances, Simão explained that the mediation is powerless in the face of Rajoelina. The only option was thus 'the practical formula, that is, elections for the Malagasy people and for the international community. We advise you: be practical' [author's translation] (Mouvance Zafy 2011a). As a consequence, Simão argued, the mediation had adopted a twofold strategy: on the one hand, seeking to convince and pressure the incumbent government to organize transitional elections, and on the other hand securing sufficient support from the rest of the Malagasy political elite (Mouvance Zafy 2011a). This new strategy did not mean an end to the three other mouvances. Rather, Simão affirmed that:

> within the mediation framework of negotiations, the Chefs de File de Mouvances do have a role to play, including the possibility of attending negotiating meetings. These meetings could be convened by the mediation in due course. For the time being, the mediation prefers a negotiation process mostly based on informal exchanges with members of the delegations of the Mouvances, political parties and groups, as well as other political stakeholders. (Simão 2011)

The SADC summit on 31 March 2011 therefore urged 'all political parties to cooperate and to support the work of the SADC mediation with the perspective of holding free, fair and credible elections' (SADC

2011b: 3). This pressure to cooperate with the mediation team and accept the changed situation on the ground was heavily felt by the members of the three remaining mouvances. They were faced with the option of either accepting an already set plan to end the transition or being left out.[10] In this sense, Ravalomanana complained to the SADC summit that his meeting with mediator Chissano in early March 2011 was not actually intended to consider any of his proposals:

> Contrary to what Mouvance Ravalomanana leaders in Madagascar were told by Minister Simao, President Chissano was not prepared to receive any further representations from Mouvance Ravalomanana. He advised President Ravalomanana that the process was closed and that if he did not initial the Roadmap that had been agreed to by other Malagasy Political Actors on 9 March 2011 Mouvance Ravalomanana would be excluded from the Transitional government. (Mouvance Ravalomanana 2011c: 17; see also Chissano 2011a: 12–15)

The roadmap was thus promoted as a last chance and its signing as a public confirmation of a commitment to end the transition. Under this rationale, the transition had become something to be overcome rather than a moment of reorganization or change. This also reinterpreted the purpose of the negotiations. Chissano's above quote defining the aim of the mediation as rallying support in order to 'ensure the implementation of the signed agreements' (Chissano 2010: 13) vividly illustrates this shift in meaning. This reinterpretation was largely confirmed by the above-discussed minimalization with regard to the actual substance of the negotiations.

However, the prospects of transitional elections also allowed a variety of Malagasy political actors to seize the momentum and to redefine their respective roles according to the internationally demanded transitional path to elections. As a result, a number of political figures who had initially been close to Rajoelina were now given the opportunity to emancipate themselves from Rajoelina and participate in an internationally endorsed transition. This was mainly the case for the members of ESCOPOL and other, smaller political parties set up during the summer of 2010. By showing their commitment to elections and an end of the transition, they promoted themselves as forces of progress against the HAT regime. As a consequence, the line that henceforth divided Madagascar's main political actors was between those in favour and those against elections, rather than a more complex division along competing interests and political projects. As observed by mediator Chissano in March 2011:

(...) the roadmap has garnered wide support from political parties, most of them having expressed their willingness to be part of it. It is true that many may have been motivated by the possibility of having their members integrated into the transitional institutions, but they argued that having the opportunity to participate in the process was a sufficient incentive. (Author's translation; Chissano 2011a: 15–16)

Chissano's report reflects a clear engagement with questions of legitimacy and representation, as well as with the ambiguous dynamics that came with selling the roadmap as an (individual) opportunity (Chissano 2011a: 7–10). He notes that the political landscape became increasingly fragmented and that the signatories were in fact split-offs from the mouvances, especially the one around Rajoelina (Chissano 2011a: 5). In the end, however, Chissano opts for the 'approche plus pragmatique', the most pragmatic approach (Chissano 2011a: 6), based on the observation that:

> In the political process malgacho-malgache [Rajoelina's unilateral transition], most parties and political groups have shown a strong willingness to participate in the process and to work together to resolve the crisis through democratic elections as quickly as possible. However, it must be said that the mouvances of Ravalomanana, Ratsiraka and Zafy did not show the same goodwill, invoking procedural reasons to justify their refusal to participate in the national conferences that took place (...). All these developments have created a new dynamic in the search for a solution to the crisis in Madagascar. The mediator is of the opinion that these developments reflect a reality on the ground and cannot be ignored. In a significant way, the mediation process seems to be in the final stretch. (Author's translation; Chissano 2011a: 2)

So, although the roadmap generally recognized *more* protagonists compared to the negotiations of 2009, their selection was arbitrary and altogether intransparent. In interviews, representatives of the international guarantors to the roadmap and many signatories themselves were unable to identify concrete reasons why this particular selection of signatory parties was made, apart from the fact that 'all sides' were represented.[11] What constituted and in fact separated these 'sides', however, remained rather unclear. As reflected in the reports quoted above, the mediators openly accepted this arbitrariness. In this sense, Chissano observed that the arbitrary selection of signatories was not any different from the previous rounds of negotiations: 'the mouvances themselves are not the product of a democratic process, but rather an artificial creation of the first Malagasy mediation' [author's translation] (Chissano 2011a: 5).

So, who were the protagonists in the end? Apart from the mouvances of Ravalomanana and Zafy, eight political parties ultimately signed the roadmap.[12] Five of them (ESCOPOL, UDR-C, MDM, AS, and HPM) were newly created during the transition – four alone in 2010 – and so most of them lacked any structure outside of Antananarivo. Three of them (ESCOPOL, HPM, and AS) were in fact arrangements that regrouped a number of smaller parties. The majority of these parties were led by individuals who had been key figures in the anti-Ravalomanana movement, albeit in very different ways. Some had been members of the HAT and later on formed their own groupings, such as Jean Lahiniriko of the UDR-C or Jean Eugène Vohinahitsy of the AS. Others, such as the former Prime Minister Monja Roindefo, whose faction of the MONIMA party also signed the roadmap, had broken with Rajoelina a lot earlier, but had nevertheless played an important role during the first year of the transition (see also Vivier 2010: 70). With Pierrot Rajaonarivelo, whom UN mediator Dramé had wanted to include in one of the four mouvances in 2009, Roindefo shared a certain familiarity with the international mediation. For all of them, one can note that while the structures recognized as parties were fairly novel, the key figures behind and within them in fact represented a remarkable continuity of those who were part of the 'coalition of circumstance' against Ravalomanana (Pellerin 2009a: 164), as described in Chapter 3.

Within many of these parties, the decision to sign the roadmap provoked fierce struggles over influence and representation. One of the founding members of ESCOPOL, for instance, depicted the time until the signing of the roadmap as a 'permanent coup', referring to the intra-party rivalries it had provoked.[13] In fact, even during the signing ceremony for the roadmap, some parties were represented by several members, all claiming a mandate to sign the final document in the name of the party.[14] As mentioned above, this was noted by mediator Chissano, who added that the mediation team in fact discouraged this tendency, although it remains unclear by what means and with what success this actually happened (Chissano 2011a: 10).[15]

Contrary to Chissano's observations, however, this 'pulverization' of the political camp – as Didier Galibert (2009b: 163) depicted this more general pattern characteristic of Madagascar's political elite – not only affected the newly established parties such as TGV, UDR-C, HPM, and ESCOPOL. The more established parties, particularly Ravalomanana's TIM and Ratsiraka's AREMA, also became arenas for struggles over influence and positions. For them, the opportunity to sign up to the transitional programme had meant that 'party' and 'mouvance' were henceforth two potentially separate entities. The initial merger between party structures and mouvances and their personalization thus gradually eroded. Over the course of the transition, TIM therefore increasingly lost its structural coherence and in parts turned against Ravalomanana (*Madagascar Tribune* 2010c; *Madagascar Tribune* 2010d). The AREMA party too split between supporters of Ratsiraka and those aligning with Pierrot Rajaonarivelo, who served as the party's secretary-general during Rastiraka's exile (*Madagascar Tribune* 2011e; *Madagascar Tribune* 2011f). In February 2011, Ratsiraka wrote a letter to the mediation team denouncing that those who had so far negotiated in the party's name were not legitimate representatives of the latter (Chissano 2011a: 12; Lavrard-Meyer 2015: 565). This 'pulverization', for instance, led to the absurd situation that during the signing ceremony, the mediators initially asked Rajaonarivelo to sign the roadmap twice: once in his capacity as leader of his own party, MDM, and another time as the representative for AREMA, which he, however, refused (*Madagascar Tribune* 2011h).[16]

Supporters and future guarantors

A similar arbitrariness can be seen in the choice of civil society organizations that were mandated to 'oversee the implementation of the Roadmap across the country' (SADC 2011a: Art. 28). In the typology suggested at the beginning of this section, they were supporters of the transition. While consulted by the mediators during several visits in Antananarivo, none of the organizations had consented to this role before the roadmap was signed. Two organizations tasked with monitoring the implementation of the roadmap – the FFKM and the CNOSC – thus immediately rejected playing this role (see also CNOSC 2011: 3).[17]

The roadmap's claims of greater inclusivity can also be questioned with regard to the role attributed to 'the people' as a subject of the transitional process. Their role was increasingly reduced to that of the electorate, while the space for both participation and dialogue gradually became limited. The roadmap was officially said to be a logical consequence of the various popular consultations that had been organized since March 2009: the *Assises nationales* of April 2009, the HAT-organized consultations of June 2010, and the constitutional referendum of November 2010. This, however, contradicted the fact that all of them had received strong international criticism as being political instruments of the HAT rather than democratic consultations warranting the label of inclusivity (see also Sellström 2015: 109). Moreover, neither the roadmap nor the transition itself reflected a substantial engagement with the results of these consultations and the manifold conflicts and contradictions they had identified (Mouvance Zafy 2011b; see also previous section).

In contrast to this only marginal role the roadmap assigned to 'the people', the reverse is true for international actors. In fact, at least 14 out of 44 paragraphs of the roadmap solely clarify the future roles and responsibilities of the various international interveners. The UN were to become involved in determining the electoral calendar and the electoral framework, and the 'international community' was to facilitate the Malagasy Reconciliation Council, to build the capacity of civil society to monitor elections and the transitional process, as well as to support the National Solidarity Fund (SADC 2011a: Art. 10, 13, 25–27). A resident SADC mediation office was envisaged to support the 'inter-Malagasy dialogue on the transition' that should be supported by a similar office of the UN (SADC 2011a: Art. 29). Madagascar's 'partners' were called upon to financially, logistically, and technically support the transitional institutions as well as the elections, and to monitor the latter (SADC 2011a: Art. 35–38). Finally, the roadmap stipulated that 'under the aegis of the SADC Mediation Team, supported by the United Nations, the international community shall be responsible for monitoring and overseeing the *international implementation* of this Roadmap in collaboration with relevant national and international stakeholders' [own emphasis] (SADC 2011a: Art. 39). The 'international community' also served as guarantor and arbiter in times of conflict: 'any dispute arising from the interpretation of this Roadmap shall be referred to the attention of the SADC Mediation for resolution' (SADC 2011a: Art. 32).

Summary

The preceding two sections have shown how the issues and agents deemed relevant for returning Madagascar to constitutional order were gradually reduced to the executive organization of elections. This was shown with regard to the high degree of presidentialism and executive politics contained in the imaginary of the transitional order, as well as with regard to the reductionist understanding of reconciliation. This trend altogether curtailed the scope of politics (i.e. the recognition of the play of clashing interests and ideas). The meaning of the transition, and with this the purpose of returning Madagascar to constitutional order, became increasingly void of any deeper substance. Transition became equated with the organization of elections. And elections were turned into an end in themselves. Altogether, little pointed to any change that was negotiated or even prepared during the transition. In fact, the SADC roadmap even explicitly prohibited any political activity that could have had long-term effects.

The international demands for an 'inclusive, consensual and neutral process of transition' (SADC 2010c: 2) were shallow yet powerful emblems for this process. While it attributed a certain representativeness to the negotiating parties, the arbitrary inclusion of 'stakeholders' at the same time subverted the idea that the negotiating parties were negotiating on someone else's behalf. The SADC roadmap thus to a large extent resembled a technical manual, a contract for guaranteeing the smooth organization of transitional elections. Its subtitle, 'Commitment by Malagasy Political Stakeholders', reflected the political sparseness of what was supposed to be the substantive and normative foundation for the transition. The term 'stakeholders' underscores how the transition's subjectivities had changed over the course of time: they had become contractors rather than political agents.

In turn, the text of the roadmap also reflects a growing importance of international actors as protagonists of this transition: in guaranteeing the overall implementation, in acting as arbiters in case of conflicts over interpretation, in financing and technically supporting the organization of elections, and in raising international funds for economic relief. The roadmap, in this sense, was not only a roadmap to end a political conflict among Malagasies; it was also a contract between the international interveners, on the one hand, and those willing to organize transitional elections, on the other (SADC 2011e).

Reordering how? Between pressure and evasion

The reasons behind the curtailing of the scope of issues and agents recognized as relevant for the resolution of 'la crise' lay not just in the complexity of the issues at hand or in the lack of conflict over them, nor was it due to lacking capacities on the part of the various international actors that came to 'assist' Madagascar's return to constitutional order. Rather, it was sustained by a particular mode of approaching 'la crise malgache', inscribed in the techniques and instruments used by the various international actors and reflected in their interactions with the Malagasy protagonists. As a consequence, this enabled the depoliticization of Madagascar's return to constitutional order, described above.

Three such modes are discussed in this section: a trend towards pressure and coercion, an evasion of responsibility, and the financial and technical realization of the demanded transition.

From mediation to negotiation: pressure and coercion

The first mode of engagement concerns a growing coerciveness in the way the various internationals reacted to political realities unfolding on the ground. In 2009, the initial rounds of negotiation largely followed the image of a third-party mediation in which the – albeit competing – mediators sought to facilitate an agreement among the four mouvances. In this sense, the engagements were in line with the imaginary whereby mediation is 'a form of assisted negotiation' (Bercovitch & Jackson 2001: 61). Negotiations are thus part of a mediation process, but they primarily take place between the parties to the conflict. In this imaginary, the mediator – the 'intermediary' – enters a dyadic relationship between two adversaries and transforms it into a triadic one (Wall 1981).

Since the failure of the Addis Ababa agreement, the actual engagements between the international mediators and the various Malagasy negotiating parties gradually departed from this ideal. In fact, the mediation team's focus shifted away from facilitating interactions between the Malagasy negotiating parties towards making them parties to an internationally set agreement. What had changed was both the nature and the purpose of the interactions between the Malagasy protagonists, on the one hand, and the various envoys seeking to realize the international demand for a 'rapid restoration of constitutional order', on the other (AU PSC 2009b: 1). In spring 2010, France and South Africa organized negotiations between Rajoelina and Ravalomanana in Pretoria that were a harbinger of this shift. The purpose of the meeting was to foster an agreement between the two, but the agreement was already there. The initiative thus envisaged neither dialogue at the table nor a constructive role for the other negotiating parties (AIM 2010; Châtaigner 2014: 122).[18] The preparation and implementation of the SADC roadmap ultimately reflected the full extent of this shift in international–Malagasy interactions that was marked by ad hoc, confrontational, and sometimes even openly coercive negotiations, and thus gradually diverged from the ideal of a mediation.

This shift meant that the mediators themselves increasingly acted as negotiators. As described above with regard to the signatories to the roadmap, the interactions between the Malagasy parties and the internationals increasingly followed the logic of discipline or perish, of being *in* or being *out* of the transition whose end point and purpose were already set. As noted in the previous section, during the preparation of the roadmap, many of the parties felt pressured to sign the document. Deadlines and time pressure increasingly shaped the way the mediation team interacted with the Malagasy parties. They also experienced that despite regular consultations whenever the mediation team visited Antananarivo, none of these led to substantial changes.[19] The testimonies of the three mouvances quoted above, as well as the exchanges that took place between them and the mediation team, illustrated this situation particularly well (see also Lavrard-Meyer 2015: 566). But even those parties more in favour of the proposed roadmap observed a rather confrontational mediation in which consultations played a role but rarely led to substantial change.[20]

One reflection of this mode of engagement was the overall changed format in which the interactions between the mediation team and the Malagasy parties took place. As observed by one participant:

> Every time he [Chissano] arrives here, he consults everyone. But there have never been direct dialogues between the parties. Never. But you enter the room, they collect your ideas (...). The eleven entities enter one by one. He collects their ideas. Afterwards: they do their own thing (...). And then they say, 'Here are the results of the consultations.' All consultations are only facades. It was already written. (Author's translation; see also Simão 2011)[21]

As explained by the mediators, this mode was a conscious decision to reach an agreement as quickly as possible (see previous section).

To be sure, shuttle diplomacy and individual consultations are an established and effective instrument of third-party mediation. They neither curtail substance per se nor do they inevitably undermine ownership of a mediation process. Rather, they usually serve as an instrument in order to create trust between the mediator and the parties, to obtain knowledge on the negotiating parties, or indeed to foster more precise changes in the latter's perceptions and attitudes. They often reduce uncertainty and create confidence in the process for all parties, including the mediation team (see, for instance, Wanis-St. John 2006). The point to make here instead is that the mediation efforts increasingly focused on securing adherence to an already written roadmap. The individual consultations were thus not meant to reopen a debate, to collect perspectives in order to structure the ensuing negotiations. Rather, they replaced negotiations. The individual, often ad hoc, and confrontational engagements meant that the table – as an image of the locale of negotiation, compromise, and resolution – was not a relevant site any more.

It is hence hardly surprising that several interviewees noted that although they signed the roadmap, they did not know what this actually implied.[22] One interviewee in particular lamented that there was no joint plenary reading of the text of the roadmap before it was signed.[23] This particularly refers to the *Note explicative*, which was added to the roadmap in order to clarify the conditions upon which Ravalomanana was allowed to return to Madagascar. It was secretly drafted only minutes before the official signing took place and involved only a few representatives of those designated as potential signatories.[24] As became clear over the following months, the addendum did not serve to explicate, but rather to confuse, the meaning of the roadmap. This is an apt illustration of the extent to which signing rather than agreeing was attributed a significance in itself.[25]

These ad hoc and confrontational negotiations also continued after the signing of the roadmap. They occurred every time the course of the transition threatened to deviate from the minimalist international demands for an 'inclusive, consensual and neutral' transition (SADC 2010c: 2). Throughout the implementation of the roadmap, the role of SADC and the other internationals was therefore largely confined to disciplining Malagasy political actors to comply with the transitional programme. These moments of negotiations were spontaneous engagements, resembling an international fire brigade rather than the continuous guarantor of the rightful implementation of the roadmap, the role the roadmap had – as elaborated above – officially assigned to international actors (SADC 2011a: Art. 32).

An example of such an ad hoc, coercive negotiation is the concerted effort to prevent Rajoelina from running in presidential elections. In May 2013, Rajoelina filed his candidacy for the upcoming presidential elections. This was in breach of the previously negotiated 'ni-ni' (neither-nor) solution that neither Rajoelina nor Ravalomanana would participate in elections. Also, it was an infringement of the African Charter on Democracy, Elections and Governance, which prohibits coup plotters from running in transitional elections (see Chapter 2). In order to raise the chances of convincing Rajoelina not to run, the mediation team demanded that Ravalomanana's wife, Lalao, and former President Ratsiraka also withdraw their candidacies. Both were found to infringe national law, which demanded that candidates in elections have to be resident in the country at least six months prior to registration (AU PSC 2013c). While this decision was officially (wrongly) justified with reference to the AU Charter, the rationale behind it was that neither 'side' should explicitly benefit from the internationally organized elections. The 'ni-ni' formula to which both parties had agreed epitomized this thinking.[26]

The Special Electoral Court (*Cour électorale spéciale*, CES), an institution set up under the roadmap, nevertheless accepted the candidacies of Rajoelina, Lalao Ravalomanana, and Ratsiraka. The PSC and the SADC summit immediately denounced the three candidates as 'illegitimate' and demanded that the Malagasy parties should 'demonstrate a sense of responsibility and place the interest of their country and the people above partisan considerations and personal ambitions' (AU PSC 2013c: 1). They should therefore withdraw 'for the sake of peace and stability in Madagascar' (SADC 2013a: 3; SADC 2013b; SADC 2013c). To this end, the ICG-M defined a seven-point plan and threatened to withdraw funds for the organization of elections and to apply targeted sanctions against family members of the transitional government (ICG-M 2013a). Moreover, the group providently rejected 'the outcome of any election results which would include the candidates' (SADC 2013a: 3). In the Malagasy press, this seven-point plan was dubbed the 'seven commandments' (*L'Express de Madagascar* 2013).

Apart from the withdrawal of the three candidates, the seven-point plan demanded that Rajoelina dissolve the existing CES 'in order to guarantee impartiality and neutrality as well as to increase representativeness and independence' [author's translation] (AU Commission 2013b: 1). In turn, the PSC promised to lift the targeted sanctions against 109 members of the HAT, which had been in place since March 2010 (AU Commission 2013b: 2). Moreover, upon implementation of the seven-point plan, international economic cooperation would be relaunched (AU Commission 2013b). The ICG-M promised that 'the restoration of constitutional order would enable Madagascar to benefit from an increased support through international cooperation' (ICG-M 2013a: 1; see also ICG-M 2011). With Rajoelina's decision to reshuffle the court, the 'illegitimate' candidacies were turned into 'illegal' candidacies (AU PSC 2013d: 1). The court, in turn, published a novel list of candidates, excluding the three contested ones (ARB 2013). A new date for presidential and legislative elections was set. The ICG-M congratulated Rajoelina 'for his commitment to re-launch the crisis exit process' and threatened all those who 'hinder the ongoing process' with additional targeted sanctions (ICG-M 2013b: 1).

This international fire brigade to rescue the transitional elections was contested from at least three sides. Ravalomanana sent several letters to SADC and AU decision-makers, arguing that the above decisions infringed his wife's civil and political rights to present herself as a candidate guaranteed under the UN International Covenant on Civil and Political Rights (Mouvance Ravalomanana 2013: 8). He pointed out that the Malagasy authorities had actually prevented her from returning to Madagascar. The question of legitimate candidacies should be left to the Malagasy electorate; anything else 'would threaten to erode (...) peace and stability' (Mouvance Ravalomanana 2013: 19). In a letter to then AU Chairperson Dlamini-Zuma, Mamy Rakotoarivelo, the head of the mouvance, wrote:

> I welcome and challenge the AU and SADC to focus their efforts on implementation of the Roadmap, as well as focusing on the fairness of the overall electoral process. We do not support just any election that is unfairly held and not representative of the aspirations of the Malagasy people, but we do support every election that is free, fair, credible, and transparent. (...) If you support the Malagasy people, listen to their voices and hear their aspirations. (Mouvance Ravalomanana 2013: 9)

The apparent international unanimity with which the seven-point plan was defended also had its discontents. The US government, for instance, opted for dropping the 'ni-ni' principle, although this was a minority opinion among the ICG-M members in Addis Ababa (*Indian Ocean Newsletter* 2013b).[27] A similar criticism came from former AU special envoy Ouédraogo, who criticized SADC for having become part of the problem and held that one should trust the Malagasy electorate's ability to choose their favourite president (RFI 2013). In the diplomatic community in Antananarivo, the legend is told that in a meeting of the local ICG-M, Russia's ambassador noted with cynicism that if the international community already decides on the candidates for an election, why not also decide on the winner altogether?[28]

In Antananarivo, the FFKM also used the stalemate in order to organize a long-planned national dialogue. The three weeks of dialogue that brought together more than 800 people across the island ended with the demand for 'another transition': to bury the SADC roadmap and the electoral calendar altogether (*Madagascar Tribune* 2013a). Both the PSC and the SADC summit entirely ignored this call. Only in late May 2013, the PSC reported to the AU Assembly that the FFKM's demands are 'of concern, as they clearly deviate from the path being followed in the process for ending the crisis in Madagascar' (AU PSC 2013e: 8). As a reaction, the ICG-M's seven-point plan later suggested the 'opening up of a perspective of national reconciliation' under the auspices of the FFKM (AU Commission 2013b), even though this effectively contradicted the roadmap, which had tasked another institution, namely the FFM, with the process of national reconciliation (SADC 2011a: Art. 26; see also further below).

In the end, the international ad hoc and confrontational approach ensured that elections were finally held. For many of the local diplomats, this set an example for successful international cooperation, quite contrary to the earlier phases of intervention in Madagascar.[29] However, this 'success' also exposed the limited substantive focus and the compromises that underpinned the international fire brigade approach. Moreover, it underlined how deeply international actors had themselves become part of the struggle to determine which course reordering post-March 2009 Madagascar ought to take.

Division of labour and evasion of responsibility

The second mode of engagement concerns the organization of the various international actors' engagement in resolving 'la crise malgache'. The moment the holding of transitional elections became a serious option to end the crisis, an international division of labour emerged that divided those in charge of 'technical' from those in charge of 'political' aspects of the transition. While the UN, OIF, and COI, for instance, increasingly focused on supporting the electoral process, the responsibility for the 'political' was officially left to SADC (*Madagascar Tribune* 2012b).[30] In Antananarivo, Addis Ababa, and New York, this move was justified by the principle of subsidiarity. In reality, however, this idea of subsidiarity and SADC leadership was constantly subverted in at least three ways: first, because it was unclear who actually represented SADC; second, because of SADC's general inaccessibility; and third, because of SADC's often outright refusal to exercise this role.

First, it was often unclear who actually represented SADC. The mediation team was only infrequently present on the ground and itself dependent on the SADC summit, the organization's central decision-making organ (see Chapter 4). This was particularly exposed during the preparation of the roadmap. In the first half of 2011, the mediation team and the SADC summit were split on the question of whether or not Ravalomanana should be guaranteed a return to Madagascar. While, as explicated in the previous section, Simão's rationale was to follow the 'formule pratique' (Mouvance Zafy 2011a) seeking an agreement among those generally willing to organize elections, the SADC summit in several instances insisted that the roadmap should guarantee Ravalomanana's return (SADC 2011b; SADC 2011d). It hence demanded the amendment of the already initialled roadmap (SADC 2011c), which meant that the signing of the document was postponed for several months. This 'diplomatie balbutiante',[31] the stuttering diplomacy, as it was dubbed by one interviewee, also became evident when SADC Executive Secretary Tomaz Salomão wrote a letter to the

Malagasy parties in order to explain the above-mentioned SADC decision (*Madagascar Tribune* 2011c). Yet the content was so vague that each party interpreted the letter in their respective interests, and so envoy Simão once again flew to Antananarivo to meet the parties directly and explain SADC's decision (*Madagascar Tribune* 2011d). Later on, the SADC mediation team acknowledged that Salomão had 'misinterpreted' the SADC summit decision (*Madagascar Tribune* 2011a). Yet who and what ultimately defined SADC's position remained unclear.

This incidence even provoked a (temporary) shift in the organization of SADC's mediation efforts. When South Africa's turn as chair of the SADC Organ troika started in the summer of 2011, the South African government decided to make the preparation of the roadmap an issue of national foreign policy (Nathan 2013: 15). South Africa's Deputy Minister of International Relations and Cooperation, Marius Fransman, was appointed to lead the mediation. He also officially chaired the signing of the roadmap and later negotiated the roadmap implementation plan (*Madagascar Tribune* 2011i; SADC 2011e). His relationship to the SADC mediation team, however, remained unclear. When South Africa's turn as chair of the SADC Organ troika ended, Simão and Chissano once again took on their roles as SADC's intermediaries in Madagascar.[32]

Similar to this South African intermezzo, the regular presences of other international negotiators, such as representatives of the AU or COI (see further below), whose relationship to SADC altogether remained unclear, made it even more complicated to determine who really represented SADC. In July and August 2013, for instance, AU Commissioner for Peace and Security Lamamra acted as the speaker of the ICG-M, accompanied by but with an altogether unclear relationship to both Chissano and SADC. In short, from the perspective of many Malagasies, SADC, as an organization, remained incomprehensible and contradictory. As responsibilities were unclear, accountability for the decisions taken (or not) was difficult to claim.

Second, SADC remained not only incomprehensible, but also *inaccessible*, once Malagasy parties sought to approach the organization in its capacity as arbiter in 'any dispute arising from the interpretation and implementation of [the] Roadmap' (SADC 2011a: Art. 32). This is true for Zafy and Ravalomanana's above-mentioned letters documenting and lamenting the disregard for and infringement of some of the principles of the roadmap.[33] SADC's inaccessibility was also noted by civil society activists and the security forces, who all tried to point out problems in the course of the transition.[34]

SADC's inaccessibility, however, had already preceded the signing of the roadmap. The above-mentioned disagreement between envoy

Simão and the SADC summit about the draft roadmap meant that many of the Malagasy protagonists had to wait in vain for a response on how to proceed. On 4 August 2011, the three heads of ESCOPOL, for instance, wrote to Chissano asking, 'could you please inform us about the evolution of its [the roadmap's] implementation and at what date and place it is planned to be signed? Otherwise, could you give us your opinion on the current situation?' [author's translation] (ESCOPOL 2011: 140). Chissano, in turn, explained a few days later that he had undertaken a series of diplomatic efforts in the region, in Addis Ababa, and in New York, finally proposing to the SADC Executive Secretary to prepare a signing ceremony in Antananarivo. However:

> To this day the Executive Secretary of SADC has not yet completed the consultations to find a date for the signing ceremony. So, we should wait for the outcome of these consultations to determine when the signing ceremony will take place. (Author's translation; ESCOPOL 2011: 142–143)

On 24 August, the three ESCOPOL leaders wrote to South Africa's President Zuma, demanding once again that the initialled roadmap should be signed without further delay:

> (...) it has been 29 months that the Malagasy nation desperately expects a resolution to a major crisis, which is dramatically affecting our economy and by consequence dangerously breaks down our social fabric, already vulnerable by growing problems of insecurity. (...) Also, if you allow, Excellency, Mr. President, we would like to express the urgency of (i) finalizing the Roadmap; (ii) setting up the Permanent Office of the Mediation in Antananarivo in order to keep the ICG-M informed of the evolution of its application; (iii) appealing to the international community, to the United Nations and to all the necessary entities, to support our people in this critical situation which is likely to worsen. (Author's translation; ESCOPOL 2011: 145)

A similar picture of demands for clarity, on the one hand, and responses of diffused responsibility, on the other, can be taken from the numerous exchanges between Ravalomanana, Zafy, and the mediation team that preceded the actual signing of the roadmap and which were explored in more detail in the preceding section.

SADC's local representation in Antananarivo epitomized this inaccessibility. Opening an office in Antananarivo had been subject to fierce debates both within SADC and the AU, but also between the two organizations. None of them wanted to submit to the other's leadership (EU Commission 2013: 76).[35] While mediator Chissano had repeatedly raised the importance of a local office in order to facilitate the negotiation process (Chissano 2010: 13; Chissano 2011a: 1), it took until early 2012 for the first SADC staff to arrive at the SADC-AU liaison office.[36]

However, it soon became clear that the office was meant neither to engage the Malagasy public nor to substantively support the transition. The SADC staff was composed of seconded national diplomats of the respective troika members, who in their majority did not speak French. As seconded diplomats, they were also experts neither on Madagascar nor on mediation and peacebuilding. With each change in the troika membership, their respective posts in Madagascar ended as well. The office was thus marked by a high degree of fluctuation.

In light of the still turbulent phase of the implementation of the roadmap, especially with regard to the unresolved question of Ravalomanana's return, SADC staff were often frightened to defend SADC positions publicly. Instead, they referred the parties either to the decisions of the SADC summit or to the mediation team.[37] Moreover, in contrast to the office's name, there was no official mandate to liaise with the AU staff next door. Both AU and SADC officers noted that there was in fact little interaction between them.[38] Altogether, the SADC staff were present, but without a clear purpose. They were explicitly *not* meant to proactively communicate and interact, neither with the AU nor with what SADC called the Malagasy 'stakeholders' (SADC 2011a).[39] As phrased by one interviewee, only the mediator was supposed to be the 'custodian of communication'.[40]

Third, as has become evident from the above, SADC was anything but in the position to actually enact this attributed political leadership. For most of the international diplomatic community in Antananarivo, it was clear that SADC neither had the capacities nor the willingness to perform according to its officially ascribed role. This is reflected in a prevalent, often paternalistic discourse on SADC and AU peacemaking among the (Western) international diplomatic staff.[41] In reality, many of the even small-scale practices, such as sustaining dialogue with the Malagasy protagonists, calling for meetings of the local chapter of the ICG-M, preparing the missions of the mediation team, or facilitating the work of international election observation missions, were hence secretly conducted by others, while officially the banner of SADC leadership was upheld.[42] Although this certainly sustained the transitional process, it also meant a constant practice of pretention and thus increased the detachment between those acting and those claiming to act.

This gap between the official claim to leadership and the actual practices was already evident during the preparation of the roadmap. While officially SADC envoy Simão and then South Africa's deputy foreign minister Fransman led the negotiations with the Malagasy parties, in practice they increasingly depended on support by diplomats from Mauritius, the Seychelles, and the COI (Chissano 2010: 17). The above-mentioned conflict between the SADC summit and the mediation team, as well as the latter's only sporadic presence in Antananarivo, had further complicated the interactions with the Malagasy parties, particularly with Rajoelina. In the days before the signing of the roadmap, several COI diplomats were bridge-builders between the SADC mediation team and those still hesitant to sign the amendments as demanded by the SADC summit, Rajoelina in particular (COI 2011; *Madagascar Tribune* 2011b). Two meetings between Rajoelina and Ravalomanana organized in the Seychelles in the summer of 2012, as well as the fact that the notion of the 'ni-ni' was actually a proposal from Mauritius, are further signs of the increasing diplomatic significance of Madagascar's island neighbours in defining the content and course of the transition (see Chapter 6).

Altogether, all three aspects – the confusion about who represents SADC, the general inaccessibility, and the refusal to enact the assigned role – translated into high hurdles and a general intransparency for all Malagasy actors seeking to access those officially supervising the transition.[43] The claimed SADC leadership over the political aspects of the transition was thus constantly denied by fluctuating chains of responsibility and by other actors who stepped in to fill the void that SADC's physical and conceptual absence had created. In other words, despite the ubiquitous narrative of subsidiarity and SADC leadership, SADC was not only evading its responsibility, but in many ways actively resisted exercising its attributed role. This became a felt reality for all those who sought to report gaps in the implementation of the roadmap that soon became apparent (see CNOSC 2011). In the end, this situation effectively served to depoliticize and close the realm of what was considered relevant to accomplish the restoration of constitutional order in Madagascar.

Materialization: staging elections

A third crucial way to approach 'la crise' was the materialization of the transition, referring to the technical, financial, and logistical support in order to implement what had been set out in the roadmap. As elaborated above, the roadmap was as much a definition of how to organize transitional elections as it was about assigning international roles and responsibilities during this process. In this sense, the implementation

THE LOGIC OF INTERVENTION

of the roadmap sparked an unprecedented international technical and logistical support machinery present and effective in Madagascar.

As a consequence, the majority of the internationals reformulated their official position vis-à-vis the transitional government in order to be able to financially support the transition.[44] With the signing of the roadmap, bureaucratic and legal hurdles that had hitherto prevented the conduct of normal diplomatic relations, including the transfer of development aid, were successively lowered. The international financial and logistical support for the elections was channelled through the UNDP under the Support Project for the Electoral Cycle 2012–2014 in Madagascar (*Projet d'appui au cycle électoral 2012–2014 à Madagascar*, PACEM). It established a so-called joint basket fund to which almost all donors and international agencies contributed a total of 26 million USD. The EU alone financed 68 per cent of the electoral budget, followed by the UNDP (15 per cent), Norway (4.5 per cent), the COI (4 per cent), and Switzerland (0.8 per cent). Only the US refrained from funding the electoral process, which expressed the latter's objection to Ravalomanana's exclusion.[45]

The material realization of the transition became a first payout of the promised return of international donor money. It was also used strategically in order to pressure Rajoelina to abide by the transitional roadmap. In the 2013 stand-off between the ICG-M and Rajoelina over the latter's candidacy, for instance, the ICG-M not only threatened not to recognize the election results. More importantly, it also held the leverage that without international financing, these elections could not have been organized (ICG-M 2011; *Indian Ocean Newsletter* 2012b; ICG-M 2013a).[46]

International financial and technical support thus ultimately realized the elections in a number of ways: capacity-building for the staff of the Independent National Electoral Commission for the Transition (*Commission électorale nationale indépendante pour la transition*, CENI-T), the establishment of an electronic registration centre for processing the election results, capacity-building for journalists and media outlets, training for national civil society election observers, gender promotion programmes, mediation and conflict prevention training for local decision-makers, voter education through TV and radio spots, cartoons and leaflets, and the printing of ballot papers. All this made up the international support for the electoral process (see generally UNDP 2013). An incredible number of 74,083 persons received professional training under the above-mentioned PACEM programme.[47]

Altogether, however, the education of voters in particular received less attention than elsewhere and was largely confined to explaining the single ballot paper, which was used for the first time in Madagascar's history.[48] As summarized by KMF/CNOE (2014: 8–9), the Malagasy civil society organization specialized in elections: 'While the electoral process received substantial funding, the component for citizen education did not enjoy the same privilege and suffered from a lack of financial and material resources. Feedback from voters indicates a lack of education and awareness' [author's translation]. In early 2013, only 20 per cent of the respondents to a survey said that they felt sufficiently informed about the elections (Liberty 32 2013: 4). SeFaFi already criticized in March 2013 that the CENI-T failed to adequately communicate key information in relation to the electoral process, particularly on voter registration and the role of the electorate. The group indicated that the CENI-T seemed to be more answerable to its international donors than to the Malagasy electorate, which others later noted as well (SeFaFi 2014l: 401).[49] SeFaFi (2014l: 404) hence concluded that:

> All this only reinforces in the minds of the population the idea that the people are at the service of politicians, who are proud to offer to the citizens what they have acquired or realized with public money. The concept of accountability, which politicians must uphold, should be emphasized: they are elected to serve the community, and citizens are entitled to demand accountability. (Author's translation)

In October 2013, a survey in six rural provinces concluded that only 22 per cent of the respondents knew the presidential candidates, while altogether 25 per cent had been informed about how to utilize the new ballot paper (*Madagascar Tribune* 2013c). The short time frame for preparing the elections is usually cited as the main cause (KMF/CNOE 2014: 8).

Apart from the technical and financial realization of the elections, international observation missions were crucial in establishing international legitimacy for the process. The number of international and national observers who came to monitor the 2013 elections reached a historical peak (EU EOM 2014: 7). More than 800 international and more than 10,000 national election observers registered to monitor the second round of presidential and legislative elections (EU EOM 2014: 31). Almost all international actors who had supported the post-coup negotiations in one way or another also sent their own or financially contributed to others' election observation missions.

Despite these signs of international coordination and an increasing professionalization around the organization of elections in Madagascar, the materialization of the transition also came with crucial costs. First, it meant that elections were organized on the basis of clear shortcomings in their democratic quality. Second, other aspects of the transitional agenda to which internationals had agreed to provide technical and financial support were postponed until after the elections.

The various reports by international and national election observers detailed the shortcomings of the electoral process: high numbers of unregistered voters and problems with the distribution of voter cards (Carter Center 2013: 7; Mahitsy Fijery 2013: 3); absence of a legal framework on the financing of electoral campaigns (Mahitsy Fijery 2013: 2; EU EOM 2014: 5); an overall unclear legal framework and a lack of oversight of the electoral process (Carter Center 2013: 10; EU EOM 2014: 45); incapacity of electoral officers to handle the electoral material (EU EOM 2014: 7); incoherent public communication of important information on the elections on the part of CENI-T (EU EOM 2014: 19); threats to the physical security of candidates campaigning in the south of the island (AU Commission 2014b: 11); overt disadvantages for female candidates and voters (AU Commission 2014b: 10; EU EOM 2014: 69); threats against media outlets (AU Commission 2014b: 11); and a disparity in terms of voter education between urban and rural areas (AU Commission 2014b: 9).

Three aspects of the electoral context had a compromising effect on the quality of elections. First, the prescribed neutrality of the power in place could be rightfully questioned. Despite the roadmap's prescription that all institutions of the transition had to remain neutral, Rajoelina officially campaigned along Hery Rajaonarimampianina, who had been nominated as his replacement following the ICG-M's seven-point plan, as explained above. In October 2013, he had also replaced ten *chefs de région* with former military personnel. Because the *chefs de région* hold responsibilities in the electoral process, this was widely interpreted as a move to secure electoral support for the pro-Rajoelina camp (Carter Center 2013: 10; Ramasy & Vallée 2014: 12). Although both actions were criticized by all other candidates, neither SADC nor the AU or the ICG-M publicly denounced this.

Second, because there was no clear legislative framework to regulate the financing of electoral campaigns, access to financial resources became a crucial factor shaping the electoral race (SeFaFi 2014l: 404). Altogether, it is estimated that the costs for individual campaigns ranged from 2 to 30 million USD (PACTE 2013: 8). The EU election observers concluded that 'the inequality of means and chances among the candidates in the presidential and legislative elections is flagrant (...)' [author's translation] (EU EOM 2014: 16). The mission further noted that out of 33 candidates in the presidential race, only eight had the means to campaign across the island's territory. Hery Rajaonarimampianina was said to head the list. All others following him had either been in official positions during the transition, were established businesspeople, and/or disposed of crucial external support from the Malagasy diaspora (EU EOM 2014: 16). The electoral race had therefore also contributed to a rise in illegal economic activities. As noted by the Environmental Investigation Agency:

> (…) sources indicate that rosewood smuggling has increased dramatically since the summer 2013. News reports linked the continued trade in 2013 to the election process, as candidates reportedly used proceeds from the illegal precious woods trade to fill their campaign coffers. In September 2013, transitional President Rajoelina attempted to push Parliament to approve a rapid sale of existing stocks, a large proportion of which would directly finance the military in advance of the planned elections. (EIA 2014: 2)

Several public scandals revealed the economization that underpinned the electoral process. In early October 2013, for instance, journalists revealed that former prime minister Camille Vital received 340 4×4 cars for his electoral campaign as a donation from 'a friend' (*Madagascar Tribune* 2013d).[50] That the electoral race had turned into an economic race was also underlined in the everyday encounters between the candidates and the electorate. In the survey from October 2013 cited above, 45 per cent of the respondents answered that they had received T-shirts, hats, or money (*Madagascar Tribune* 2013c). Even if the campaigning was confined to just one constituency, it often required paying for media outlets, support teams, and gifts to be handed out to potential voters. Particularly for younger candidates without established networks in the transitional institutions or big business, this posed tremendous challenges (see also Ralambomahay 2014).[51]

Third, the deficient electoral register, especially in the first round of presidential elections, meant that a 'significant number' of eligible voters were not on the list (Carter Center 2013: 7). In 2012, this had already been noted by the UN election assessment mission, which admittedly found itself in a dilemma between the 'urgency imperative' to speedily organize elections and the fact that the register was not yet in a state to ensure the conduct of 'credible, transparent elections that would not fuel a resumption of the cycle of post-election crises' (UN 2012: 4).[52] Some 143,408 voters were added to the list for the second round, a marginal addition (Carter Center 2013: 8; EU EOM 2014: 6).

Irrespective of the quality of the register, only 50.72 per cent of those registered went to cast their vote in the second round of presidential and legislative elections. Together with the deficient register, this underlines the altogether limited popular engagement in the electoral endeavour. Whether due to a lack of voter education campaigns and the short preparatory process (KMF/CNOE 2014: 8) or simply a sign of lacking interest, the high rate of involuntary and voluntary abstention from the electoral process, in either case, undermines the narrative of popular ownership of Madagascar's 2013 election (Carter Center 2013: 7).

Together, the unsanctioned infringements to the principle of neutrality, the lacking legal framework on how to finance electoral campaigns, and the deficient electoral register all point to the more structural shortcomings affecting the quality of the electoral process. Instead of favouring one side only, these factors certainly undermined the democratic quality of the *overall* process (Carter Center 2013: 1; KMF/CNOE 2014). They only added to the irregularities observed on election day, which were soon also acknowledged and handled by the CENI-T (*Madagascar Tribune* 2013b; Mahitsy Fijery 2013: 5–6; AU Commission 2014b: 8). In four constituencies, the voting had to be repeated (*Madagascar Tribune* 2014a). More than 600 complaints were filed with the electoral court (*L'Express de Madagascar* 2014).

While the camp of Jean-Louis Robinson – who had run on Ravalomanana's behalf – immediately claimed victory, their alternative vote count was not seen as sufficiently challenging the overall results.[53] Irregularities, a perceived injustice during the process, and the high rates of absentees, however, remain apt illustrations of the more structural shortcomings of the process at large. In retrospect, in early 2014, it thus seemed to be almost self-evident that 'nothing could have stopped' these elections from producing an internationally accepted result, as noted by several interviewees.[54]

The almost exclusive focus on the organization of elections also meant that several of the other roles and responsibilities assigned to the internationals in the roadmap did not receive similar technical and financial support. This particularly applied to the FFM, the institution set up in the roadmap to organize the process of national reconciliation (see first section in this chapter). In early 2014, none of the international guarantors of the roadmap had agreed to (financially) support the establishment of this institution.[55] In a similar vein, the FNS, the national fund to compensate victims of past violence, including the families of those killed in January 2009, had not yet been set up. Moreover, by inviting the FFKM to open up 'a perspective of national reconciliation' (AU Commission 2013b: 2), as stipulated in the ICG-M's seven-point plan, the international guarantors of the roadmap had actually legitimated an alternative institution that consequently came to contest the FFM's responsibility for Madagascar's reconciliation process (*Madagascar Tribune* 2015a).

In short, the materialization of the roadmap underlined that the various internationals were playing an active role in both realizing but also limiting the transitional process. The focus on elections and the time pressure behind them revealed both that politics remained curtailed and that the meaning of transition was clearly following international priorities.

Summary

The preceding section has shown that the gradual depoliticization of the transition and the focus on the executive organization of elections corresponded with a particular set of practices by which the variety of international actors addressed 'la crise malgache'. These practices altogether ensured the return to constitutional order, but at the same time limited the scope of what that meant. All this contradicts the officially upheld image of a process to merely 'accompany the Malagasy parties' (AU PSC 2011e: 2) in which 'the ownership of the political dialogue (…) must lie with the Malagasy themselves' (SADC 2009a: 3) so as to find a more legitimate order than the one that had led to the crisis in the first place. Rather, it reflects that the internationals themselves were part of, not mere judges to, the struggle over legitimacy and authority in post-March 2009 Madagascar.

At the same time, however, this active involvement was also constantly denied. The AU and SADC's more coercive engagements were justified by the 'national and permanent interest of Madagascar' (AU PSC 2011e: 2; AU PSC 2013c; SADC 2013a), while the numerous small-scale practices to materialize the transition were carried out in the name of subsidiarity and 'African leadership', even though practice proved the opposite. In the end, this denial evaded actual accountability for the decisions that inevitably came with this involvement and the consequences this had for what kind of post-March 2009 order was to be established.

Moreover, the inevitability of elections, the pressure to keep the transition 'as short as possible' (ICG-M 2010: 3), dealt with as 'a matter of urgency' (SADC 2011c: 2), in fact justified a variety of illiberal practices: coercive negotiations; the use of law for political ends; unclear and shifting responsibilities; inaccessibility of those who decided upon the course of the transition; and the acceptance of an electoral process that – even though not overtly rigged – nevertheless perpetuated structures that undermine the ideal of a fair and transparent process of citizens' political self-determination.

The rationale that justified these at times illiberal practices was that elections are an insufficient but inevitable step towards a better future. The AU election observers noted that the purpose of the elections was 'to provide the country with legitimate and credible institutions capable of boosting the country's development and improving the living conditions of the population (...)' [author's translation] (AU Commission 2014b: 3). As noted above, the ICG-M had formulated it more clearly: that only through elections Madagascar would be able to 'benefit from an increased support through international cooperation' (ICG-M 2013a: 1). The attraction of elections thus entailed an ambiguous power: elections served as a narrative to curtail politics and even to justify illiberal practices, while at the same time keeping up yet postponing the promise for a better future and the change to come. The election observers therefore also concluded that 'the prospects for a definitive way out of the crisis can be envisaged. However, these elections are not a panacea' [author's translation] (AU Commission 2014b: 15). From the preceding analysis, however, there is little evidence to see on what grounds the postponed promise will ultimately bear fruits.

6
Reproducing old, legitimating new orders

Madagascar's history has been marked by recurring moments of crisis in which legitimacies and authorities were contested and redefined. The events of March 2009 and the subsequent internationalized search for a solution to what came to be called 'la crise malgache' integrate into this trajectory. However, as has become evident, this time the course and the solutions offered to 'la crise' have been shaped by an unprecedented presence of the international – its norms, ideas, and agents – that affects how legitimate order is defined today. In particular, the preceding chapters have demonstrated the crucial imprint the African international left on crisis resolution in Madagascar. Unlike in 2001/2002, when the AU's anti-coup policy was still in its infancy, Madagascar was not subject to merely ad hoc and spontaneous missions of self-appointed heads of state mediators. Rather, between 2009 and 2014, the situation on the island was a regular concern for the AU PSC and other bodies set up in the meantime to resolve conflicts and promote democratic governance on the continent. Yet the AU was not acting alone. In fact, the presence and increasing significance of SADC, the COI, and even COMESA reflect that the African international had become crowded. Moreover, the UN, the EU, and Madagascar's bilateral partners, including France, now portrayed their own role in Madagascar in terms of supporting 'African solutions', even if actual practices contravened this claim. All this would not have become possible if African heads of state had not mandated themselves in 2000 to undo future coups.

As elaborated in Chapter 4, in practice this mandate brings with it more than problems of international coordination and the definition of hierarchies between the numerous international agents that seek to define the content and course of crisis and its resolution. In fact, the chapter explicitly argued against the interpretation of this as merely a 'crowded field' (Lanz & Gasser 2013). Unlike the AU's ideal of a 'speedy return to constitutional order' (OAU 2000a: 3) suggests, the international demand for a negotiated solution first of all requires local agents that comply with this ideal. The demand to re-establish constitutional order thus constitutes its own subjects and with this also conflicts. The numerous international actors are therefore not only faced with problems of coordination, but with the consequences of their own very presence in the intervention scenario. Their involvement crucially shapes the boundaries of what kind of (constitutional) order can be re-established and how.

At the same time, the expansion of international norms and practices and the undeniable international efforts that have been put in place for re-establishing constitutional order in Madagascar stand in contrast to the substance of what reordering Madagascar ultimately implied. Chapter 5 described a process of gradual depoliticization, a minimalization of the scope of conflict (i.e. what was recognized as politically relevant to end 'la crise') and thereby a reduction of how 'crisis' itself was defined. Instead of conflict resolution and dialogue among Malagasy parties, the negotiations and the subsequent transition increasingly focused on organizing elections and re-establishing a government that fulfils international standards for recognition. The transition was thus reduced to a technical process – a pause in politics – while the promises of a better future were postponed to a time after the elections. In fact, already the first rounds of negotiations in Antananarivo were opened by AU special envoy Ouédraogo declaring that the objective of the negotiations was to adopt a consensual charter in order to pave the way for elections (Mouvance Zafy 2009a). As recalled by one of the civil society facilitators in this process:

> It must be said that they [the mediators] did not have an objective. For them it was to arrive at elections. That was it. It was an obsession. And then later on it turned out that everybody's obsession was elections. As if elections were suddenly going to solve all the problems. (...) Everyone wants to come to elections. But how to get to elections? (...) What are the steps? What are the (...) prerequisites that must be met before reaching elections? And the elections would lead to what? [Author's translation][1]

So, the expansion in international attention and practices altogether did not translate into more elaborate approaches as to how to resolve 'la crise'. What went missing in all this was time and space for dialogue, a search for identifying problems and corresponding solutions. Yet despite, or in fact *because of*, its failure to instigate more fundamental change, the international post-coup intervention in fact did have tangible effects. The almost five years of efforts to return Madagascar to constitutional order indeed contributed to (re)ordering and sedimenting power relations both within the Malagasy polity as well as beyond. It is this effectiveness of the post-coup intervention that this chapter turns to.

Reordering Madagascar

In early 2014, in its decision to lift Madagascar's suspension from the AU, the PSC expressed 'its appreciation to the Malagasy people, as well as to all political actors and institutions of the country, for the smooth and peaceful conduct of the elections and the completion of the transition process' (AU PSC 2014a: 1). The PSC, however, also noted that the newly established government would have to 'work towards the promotion of national reconciliation, good governance and respect for human rights, in order to consolidate the important gains achieved' (AU PSC 2014a: 2).[2]

Against the background of the preceding chapters, it is hardly surprising that in early 2014, almost no one thought that Madagascar had undergone a fundamental change compared to the time before March 2009 (ICG 2014; Pellerin 2014a). To the contrary, the transition itself had produced a growing rate of poverty and social inequality, ecological destruction, and a rise in the perceived level of corruption. The World Bank (2013: 17–18) estimated that between 2008 and 2013, the number of Malagasies living on less than 2 USD a day rose by more than 10 per cent to 92 per cent of the population. In late 2010, the international jurist Raymond Ranjeva, one of Madagascar's most internationally renowned public figures, noted that instead of crisis, 'maladie', disease, was the more apt description, particularly of the social situation prevailing on the island (*Madagascar Tribune* 2010b). Moreover, the public attitudes towards the transitional institutions reflected a widespread suspicion vis-à-vis the state (Liberty 32 2013; Rajerison 2013: 2; Rakotomamonjy et al. 2014a). This applied, for instance, to the two legislative institutions of the transition: in early 2013, only 17 per cent of the Malagasy respondents to the Afrobarometer survey said they had confidence or partial confidence in the *Congrès de la Transition*, while only 16 per cent trusted the *Congrès Supérieur de la Transition*. More striking, however, was that more than 50 per cent of the respondents answered that they did not know anything about these institutions (Rakotomamonjy et al. 2014a: 8). Only 28 per cent had confidence or partial confidence in either opposition parties or the party of the president (Rakotomamonjy et al. 2014a: 8). Right before the elections, 88 per cent of the respondents to another survey answered that politicians only serve their personal interests (Liberty 32 2013: 3).

This points to more fundamental structures that have been replicated by the very logic with which 'la crise' was interpreted and approached. The international demand for a recognizable government coupled with principles of representation and inclusivity meant that what has been re-established was not merely constitutional order – the rule of law – but rather a particular ideal image, a myth of the liberal polity. This ideal assumes that politics takes place in official institutions and that the will of the people is represented and channelled through political parties. This ideal underpinned the various practices by which 'la crise malgache' was addressed, even though reality heavily deviated from this ideal: the selection of the mouvances justified by their representativeness, the principles of 'inclusivity' and 'consensus' upheld against all odds, the inclusion of parties irrespective of their societal backing, the focus on finding arrangements to share power in state institutions, and the pressure to end the transition through elections, executed on the basis of unfavourable conditions and through partly illiberal means, are cases in point.

As has been argued above, this logic provided opportunities for a variety of Malagasy actors to seize the momentum and indeed claim the 'ownership' that SADC's decision-makers wanted to see (SADC 2009d: 3). The narrative of a solution 'malgacho-malgache' provided a political alternative particularly to those members of the elite who had gradually broken ranks with Rajoelina. In 2011, the year in which the roadmap was signed, the number of registered parties rose to more than 300 (Rajerison 2013: 14). As said in Chapter 5, out of the 160 parties that signed up to Rajoelina's transitional programme, only 15 had existed before September 2010 (Grund 2010: 4). Similarly, five of the signatories to the roadmap were established only shortly before. In March 2011, the civil society organization CNOSC (2011: 10–11) reported that:

> about 85% of the parties declared to the Ministry of the Interior are only small groups with the practice of political mercenaries. Political parties, including small parties that have some verifiable activity, do not even count fifty – at the most. [Author's translation]

In a similar vein, Rindra Rabanirinirarison and Jean-Aimé Raveloson (2011: 8) observe that only around ten parties were not what the two authors call 'strategic parties', set up as personal vehicles to participate in the political contest. After this sudden explosion, the number of political parties remained undiminished: when transitional elections were held in 2013, there were still 173 registered parties (Sellström 2015: 56). Several interviewees by themselves noted that to them, it is unclear under what conditions the Ministry of Internal Affairs actually accepts party registrations (Rabanirinirarison & Raveloson 2011: 8).[3]

Moreover, in the course of the transition, the number of seats in the legislative institutions rose steadily from 160 before the crisis to 356 in November 2010 and 526 during the transition (Razafindrakoto et al. 2014b: 45; SeFaFi 2014n). The number of ministerial portfolios reflects a similar trajectory. Disputes over the distribution of posts were resolved by increasing their number. Not least, the attraction of the representative institutions of the state is also symbolized by the sheer number of 33 presidential candidates who stood for election in 2013, an unprecedented historical peak. What this shows is a steady expansion of the representative institutions of the state and a broadening of the agents that have come to contest inclusion therein.

The internationally promoted ideal of the liberal polity hence served all those who sought inclusion in the official institutions of the state and who were able to claim a role as representatives of something. In this sense, there was indeed a powerful imprint of the international intervention that has to be taken seriously in its own right and its effects. The international demand for a negotiated return to constitutional order not only invented the mouvances as negotiating parties, but also served as an incentive and legitimation for political parties and all those willing and able to appropriate this minimalist international demand. In general, this has mainly benefited an already well-established urban elite that were able to seize the momentum, create political parties, and reclaim their place in Madagascar's re-established polity.

As elaborated in Chapter 3, during Ravalomanana's presidency, the role of the legislative and of political parties in general had been increasingly curbed. His managerial approach to governance had effectively depoliticized the institutions of the state. It was argued that 'la crise' in early 2009 was therefore not merely a struggle between two rivals and their supporters. Rather, it amplified a more fundamental crisis of confidence in the official institutions of the state (Razafindrakoto et al. 2009; Hinthorne 2011). The international efforts to re-establish constitutional order in Madagascar in this sense contributed to a general reopening of the institutions of the state and a renewed appreciation of the idea that parties are transmitters of the popular will. The initially rather loose anti-Ravalomanana protest thus, at least in part, became more institutionalized as it integrated into the institutions of the transition.

As has become evident in the two preceding chapters, however, the ideal of the liberal polity was upheld based on a high degree of ignorance. The arbitrary selection of parties at the negotiating table and the incentives to create political parties in order to participate in the transitional process in fact rendered the idea of representation almost meaningless. Representation became a rhetorical emblem to support individual claims to authority, but more often than not this was accepted without scrutiny. This arbitrariness gives reason to doubt that the renewed appreciation of institutions also affected their quality, that the rhetorical and practical incentive to create and capture institutions also *institutionalized* politics – that is, rendered them less arbitrary, volatile, and more directed towards a public commitment (see also Marcus 2016: Chapter 8). In a similar vein, the almost 30 per cent of elected members of parliament who were running as 'independents' in the 2013 transitional elections shed doubts on the effective appreciation of political parties. In fact, while the official narrative kept up the ideals of political parties as transmitters of people's interests, surveys and perception monitors regularly pointed to decreasing public trust both in the institutions of the state and in political parties, which rather reflects a perpetuation of the 'crisis of confidence' discussed in Chapter 3 (Hinthorne 2011; Rajerison 2013: 2; Rakotomamonjy et al. 2014a). In a similar vein, the continuing 'transhumance' between political camps (Galibert 2009b: 419) and the shifting alliances among the political elite do not provide evidence for the assumption that the reopening of the struggles over the state and the renewed appreciation of parties had instigated any change in the underlying logic of elite politics in Madagascar (Jütersonke & Kartas 2010: 40).

In this sense, rather than channelling the political contest into public institutions, the particular way the transition was organized meant that institutions of the state had become the object, not the sites of political contest. Not the play of diverging programmes, but access to the state, drives the struggle over the rules of the game. The exclusive focus of the negotiations on questions of access to state institutions and the division of posts therefore nourished and legitimated an exclusive understanding of politics as a struggle over being in or being out. This not only upheld a zero-sum approach to politics that may stand in the way of compromise or consensus; it also limited the overall *meaning* and scope of politics to that of an intra-elite affair.

Shortly after the elections, another political stalemate was therefore on the horizon. The newly elected parliament was unable to decide on the meaning of Article 54 of the constitution, which stipulated that the prime minister should be selected from the parliamentary group that holds the majority of the seats. In the meantime, however, the newly elected President Rajaonarimampianina had broken ranks with his initial supporter Rajoelina, in whose place he had run in the presidential race. This happened against the background of international pressure to prevent a 'scénario russe' by which Rajoelina would have become prime minister (ICG 2014: 7).[4] With this, the lines between the different camps of the presidential race were suddenly blurred: weeks of secret negotiations and reshuffling of alliances were proof of the continued 'transhumance' among the Malagasy political elite (ICG 2014: 9–10). Although parliamentarians were not allowed to switch sides, many of those initially elected as members of Rajoelina's MAPAR party over the course of the years 2014 and 2015 became members of the newly formed party of the president. This episode therefore epitomized the perpetuated logic of the transition: the short-lived character of affiliations and alliances in search for political opportunities and the continued role of the international in incentivizing political contest in Madagascar. Moreover, the posterior and sporadic reinterpretation of positions and party affiliations ultimately also subverted the idea that it was the electorate that decided who has access to power. It is an irony of the situation that it was of all things the constitution, its Article 54 in particular, that set the stage for the continued rivalry over access to power and the state among the island's elite.

Crisis, however, not only prevailed in the dynamics between Madagascar's political elite. Mirroring the build-up to the events of March 2009, as described in Chapter 3, crisis also continued under the surface. Apart from the above-mentioned prevailing distrust in the institutions of the state, crisis became most evident in the economic realm: as the World Bank (2015: 12) concluded, '[a]bout a third of the population in Madagascar is deprived on multiple dimensions, including consumption, access to education, usage of electricity, and possession of basic household assets' (see also SeFaFi 2015b). Some 83 per cent of the respondents to the Afrobarometer survey in Madagascar therefore said that the economy, alimentation, and agricultural development should be the new government's priorities (Rakotomamonjy et al. 2014b: 8). In Antananarivo, rising insecurity on the streets and the ubiquitous corruption of the security forces were a growing concern in early 2014 (*Midi Madagasikara* 2014a). Enduring electricity cuts resulted in manifestations across the island that in some cases even turned violent (*Midi Madagasikara* 2014c). Across the island, students and university teachers had been on frequent strikes throughout, demanding better working conditions and the payment of their stipends. Often the protests were violently cracked down (*Midi Madagasikara* 2014b).

The transition's focus on the re-establishment of the institutions of the liberal polity only worked on the basis of two crucial exclusions (see generally Latham 2001: 81). First, it drew a line between Malagasy politics and the economy that negates how both have always been interlinked (Jütersonke & Kartas 2010: 17; Razafindrakoto et al. 2014b). The 'coalition of circumstance', as elaborated in Chapter 3, in fact demonstrated this in the individuals and their incentives to join the anti-Ravalomanana movement. In turn, the latter's declared understanding of government as management of a business had itself eroded the distinction between politics and the economy. Moreover, Chapter 5 showed how the 2013 electoral race was infused by unequal access to financial resources and how this in fact perpetuated illegal economic activities that had prevailed throughout the transition (ICG 2014: 17–18; see also *Indian Ocean Newsletter* 2013a). It is remarkable that investments into the nascent mining and natural resource industries – ilmenite, titanium, nickel, cobalt, and iron – rose considerably over the course of the transition. In fact, in 2013, they accounted for a large part of Madagascar's yet minimal economic growth (AfDB et al. 2013: 246). In 2010, some 35 per cent of Madagascar's surface area was sold to international firms in the extractive industries (Marcus 2010b). Apart from the extractive industries, foreign land acquisitions for agribusiness exploded during the transition, although mostly through small and medium-sized companies (Burnod et al. 2013: 362). Moreover, parallel to the ongoing post-coup negotiations, the EU renewed and gradually expanded its fishery agreement with Madagascar, which entered into force in 2013 (*Indian Ocean Newsletter* 2012a). In 2011, UN special rapporteur Olivier de Schutter had criticized that the negotiations were intransparent and warned of the detrimental effects on Madagascar's development:

> Madagascar currently receives financial compensation of just less than 1.7 million euros per year. This represents 125 euros per ton of tuna, while the price per tonne received by fishermen at the first landing point is more than 1,000 euros. [This] reflects the unequal relationship of the parties in the negotiation of fisheries agreements. (…)
> Madagascar cannot develop without being assured of fair treatment in fisheries agreements. (Author's translation; UN General Assembly 2011: 13)

These investments did not take place outside of, but in fact with – and sometimes against – the state. Not least, they raised questions as to what extent the official legal provisions have to be respected, who defines them, and who benefits from the investments (Burnod et al. 2013). In either case, they affected public goods as well as the livelihoods and opportunities, particularly of the rural population. The World Bank (2015: 1) therefore concluded in 2015, 'Madagascar has been depleting its natural resources to achieve economic growth'.

As in late 2008, the sites of foreign investment continued to be sites of contestation and protest: whether for the fair share of the extracted wealth, for employment, or for the protection of the ecological system (Panos 2009; TANY 2013). Apart from negating the political significance of these lived realities, excluding the economy from the official negotiating table also meant negating how these developments might affect the solutions that were finally offered to solve 'la crise malgache' – in other words, how constitutional order was re-established on the basis of deep-seated contradictions that have for a long time contributed to fuel the cycle of recurring Malagasy crises (see Razafindrakoto et al. 2020).

Second, the mere focus on the official institutions of the liberal polity also meant that the spatial divide between the urban and the rural – the idea that politics only takes place in the capital – was further perpetuated (Jütersonke & Kartas 2010: 70). On the one hand, it meant that overall little change was effected in the way the institutions of the state reached into the regions. Local elections, for instance, were postponed to July 2015 and hence left unelected officials in power for much longer than the official return to constitutional order. On the other hand, it also meant that the continuation of illiberal state practices, particularly the unaccountable use of violence, remained largely unnoticed. In the south of Madagascar, the increasingly lucrative trade with zebu had sparked an unprecedented rise and professionalization of cattle raids, so-called *dahalos*, in the course of the transition. Local administrations and security forces were shown to be involved in the *dahalo* business (Jütersonke 2011: 183; RFI 2014; Tarabey 2014). In response, local defence groups were set up, which have increased insecurity and led to a spiral of violence (Jütersonke 2011: 168). The anti-*dahalo* campaign Tandroka, launched under the transitional government in summer 2012, was widely criticized for its excessive use of violence against civilians. In late 2012, an investigation by Amnesty International demanded the establishment of an international inquiry (Amnesty International 2012). In view of the planned transitional elections, international diplomats in Antananarivo, however, explicitly decided not to support this demand, even though the concerns were widely shared (Tarabey 2014: 209; see also AU Commission 2013a: 4). Both extensive cattle raids and repressive reactions by the security forces have continued since (Pellerin 2014b: 18; SeFaFi 2015a).

Like the question of large-scale foreign investments, the security situation in the south and the ambiguous reactions to it affected the livelihoods of a significant part of Madagascar's population. Moreover – again, like the question of large-scale foreign investments – it was also a legal question, namely for whom law also means rights. For the rural population, the re-established polity is thus a present reality, but neither necessarily accessible nor necessarily liberal.

Against all signs of perpetuated crisis, there remains another long-term continuity: in late 2013, hopes that the new government would resolve the crisis were still high. Only a small proportion of 3 per cent of the respondents to the Afrobarometer survey considered it unlikely that the government will resolve Madagascar's 'principal problems' within five years (Rakotomamonjy et al. 2014b: 10). The belief in the potentials of 'l'homme providentiel' (Galibert 2011: 414), the providential man, has not been erased (see also COSC 2010; Liberty 32 2013: 4). In this sense, the postponed promise of the transition may have also added new momentum to the history of undiminished hope in salvation that characterizes Madagascar's post-independence polity (Galibert 2009b: 422).

In the years since, this hope has not faded. Unsurprisingly, in view of the preceding analysis, President Rajaonarimampianina's time in power was marked by a high degree of volatility and recurring signs of crisis: four prime ministers in five years, several cabinet reshuffles, an albeit failed impeachment by the national assembly, and public corruption scandals were all signs that behind the orderly, legal process to guide politics now back in place, reality was all the more turbulent. As a consequence, citizens' trust in the representative institutions of the state remained low (Afrobarometer 2018). After four years of constitutional order, high crime rates, a lack of infrastructure, and food insecurity were identified as citizens' most pressing concerns on which the government has altogether failed to deliver (Isbell 2018). In 2018, only two of altogether 36 candidates had the financial means and political alliances to challenge the sitting president in elections: Rajoelina and Ravalomanana, who had returned to Madagascar in late 2014. After a conflictual build-up to the elections, which brought several of the international protagonists back to Madagascar to mediate between the parties, Rajoelina ultimately won the elections. Like Rajaonarimampianina in 2013, he had campaigned under the slogan of 'emergence', vowing to quickly lift Madagascar on to a path to development (*Madagascar Tribune* 2019). Thus, neither the postponed promise of better times to come nor the providential man had disappeared over the four years that Madagascar was back to constitutional normalcy.

In sum, the prevailing signs of crisis in early 2014 were not surprising. Yet there is also little evidence to assume that the transition has laid the foundations for any future change to come. The keeping up of an ideal of the liberal polity, against all odds, and the shrinking of the scope and locus of politics provide little reason to assume that the 'rupture with the past', as then EU High Representative Catherine Ashton formulated it, was a realistic demand (EU 2014). Nor did the developments in the ensuing years. So, although the re-establishment of constitutional order in Madagascar did not instigate any fundamental change, it would nevertheless be wrong to assume that almost five years of international intervention occurred without effects. The retention of an ideal as well as the empowerment of all those able to seize its opportunities demand both analytical and normative recognition. Perpetuation itself is also an effect, because it relegitimizes what already exists and eliminates alternatives. In this sense, it is also important to look beyond the Malagasy polity so as to grasp the consequences of post-coup interventions and how they contribute to the reconfiguration of power relations, even outside of the concrete context of intervention.

Reordering the international

As described by a Malagasy journalist, the events of March 2009 indeed brought a veritable 'armada' of representatives of the international to Madagascar, who came to be involved in re-establishing constitutional order in the country (*Midi Madagasikara* 2009c). In this sense, the post-coup intervention also had consequences for the reconfiguration of order and power relationships beyond the Malagasy polity. In fact, it also added to 'thickening' the international and attributing it with new contours. There are at least two crucial paths through which the reordering of post-coup Madagascar also affected and reordered the international.

Fixing the postponed promise

The first path concerns the process by which 'la crise malgache' served the various international actors as a source for detecting new areas for future engagement in the country. In this sense, the international attention to 'la crise' had uncovered new issue areas identified as problematic, in which international actors later offered their expertise, capacity-building efforts, or financial assistance. The postponed promise of the transition therefore helped to create a series of tasks and urgencies that were – once an internationally recognized government was in place – turned into new projects of Malagasy–international cooperation. The ICG-M's repeated references to the windfall of development aid that would follow Madagascar's official return to constitutional order already pointed to this (ICG-M 2013a; ICG-M 2013b), and in many ways this has indeed come true (Marcus 2015). The more permanent international presence in Madagascar's continued 'transition', however, is more than merely the deepening of already established donor relationships. Rather, detecting new problems and future areas of engagement also established entirely new relationships.

South Africa, for instance, launched a support programme to the Malagasy government focusing on Rajaonarimampianina's envisaged process of national reconciliation. This was based on South Africa's own experience in national reconciliation after the end of apartheid (Fabricius 2015).[5] National reconciliation was also one of the priority areas for the AU liaison office, which continued its work in Madagascar even after the official return to constitutional order (see further below; see also Butedi 2018). Another postponed aspect of the transition that turned into a post-transition project was the reform of the Malagasy security sector. Upon request from the Malagasy government, a delegation consisting of representatives of different organizations visited Madagascar in the autumn of 2014 in order to 'identify the key requirements for reforming the security sector in Madagascar' (AU 2014a: 1). One of the organizations represented in this delegation was SADC, which had identified SSR as a potential area of future engagement in Madagascar. Military cooperation has always been a crucial component of regional cooperation in Southern Africa (Nathan 2012: 33). As explained by SADC officials, the shared identities of military personnel from across the region carry the promise that cooperation between national security forces may facilitate mutual understanding within the region at large.[6] As throughout the crisis the interactions between officials from the SADC region and their Malagasy counterparts had been complicated on exactly these grounds, the envisaged security cooperation was only logical. Moreover, it also fit SADC's general focus and expertise in the field of military cooperation and Madagascar's corresponding need for reform (Ramasy & Vallée 2014). For this purpose, even prior to the 2013 elections, SADC had already sent several technical missions to engage the Malagasy security forces on their role during the elections and to pre-negotiate the envisaged cooperation.[7]

All these efforts underline that the transition itself had created an expanded space of transnational engagement in Madagascar. In March 2014, the ICG-M decided to transform itself into the International Support Group for Madagascar (*Groupe international de soutien à Madagascar*, GIS-M) and to accompany the efforts of the new Malagasy government, 'notably in the area of socioeconomic development and governance in all its aspects' [author's translation] (ICG-M 2014: 3). This is a further case in point for how the post-coup intervention itself created new opportunities for transnational engagements and new areas for more permanent and subtle interventions.

The ICG-M's decision to enhance international coordination in support of Madagascar's post-transition development also underlines a more general trend that was observable over the course of the transition: an increasingly formal representation of the various international actors on the ground. The SADC-AU liaison office was only one among several diplomatic representations that were newly established to accompany the transitional process and which continued to exist afterwards. Likewise, the COI and OIF established permanent offices in Antananarivo in 2013 and 2015, respectively (RFI 2015).[8] Togo, Guinea, and Tanzania opened new embassies a year after the transitional elections (*Madagascar Tribune* 2015b). The UK, the Seychelles, and Turkey, among others, had already opened new embassies, or reopened embassies, during the transition. In 2016, both OIF and COMESA held their annual summits in Madagascar (*L'Express de Madagascar* 2015; RFI 2015). Even though this was first of all a symbolic act, it was another vivid demonstration of the increasing presence of the international in Madagascar and the island's growing integration into regional and global networks of diplomatic interaction. In this sense, the post-coup intervention not only created new problems for international fixes, but also expanded Madagascar's very traditional international diplomatic relations in an increasingly dense and regionalized world.

Laboratory and institutional expansion

The second path describes a process by which for several international actors, the involvement in re-establishing constitutional order in Madagascar became an opportunity to expand their respective issue areas and to incrementally develop new policy instruments and practices. The intervention was hence also a laboratory to experiment with the expansion of the scope of international authority and to establish new locales of power.

The best case in point were those organizations such as the COI or the OIF that had hitherto only limited experience with political engagements within their member states, and in response to crises in particular. For both organizations, the post-coup engagements in Madagascar translated into new practices and the acquisition of new expertise. It also created an opportunity to become recognized internationally and hence to redefine their relationships vis-à-vis other organizations in that field.

As mentioned in Chapter 5, in light of SADC's reluctance to enact its ascribed leadership, other actors came to fill that void. In the summer of 2012, it was the president of the Seychelles who sought, albeit in vain, to make Rajoelina and Ravalomanana agree on a 'ni-ni' (ARB 2012: 19345). During the preparation of the SADC roadmap too, diplomats from COI member states facilitated and translated between SADC officials and their Malagasy counterparts (*Madagascar Tribune* 2011i). This reflected an overall more strategic engagement on the part of the COI – driven by diplomats from Mauritius and the Seychelles and the organization's executive head – to become more actively involved in ending 'la crise malgache'.

All this was based on a background document, which COI Secretary-General Jean Claude de l'Estrac presented in November 2010 in order to delineate the COI's lines of engagement. The document set out a clear strategy to engage the ICG-M so as to use the momentum created by Rajoelina's unilateral transition in order to move to elections as soon as possible. For this purpose, the document concluded:

> For the COI, it is necessary to contribute to the preparation of the next meeting of the ICG-M and to make proposals that bring a regional added value in the new context of the crisis (...) and that help the positions of the international community, particularly the Southern African Development Community (SADC) to evolve. (Author's translation; COI 2010b: 1)

In June 2010, the COI Council of Ministers had already noted 'the economic and social impacts of the Malagasy institutional crisis on the population' and called for 'free, open and transparent presidential and legislative elections in Madagascar, as soon as possible, respecting international criteria in order to allow their support and recognition by the international community' [author's translation] (COI 2010a: 1). In order to claim a more proactive role in Madagascar, the COI clearly defined its own role in juxtaposition to that of SADC. The COI thus promoted the idea of an 'Indianocéanie' (COI 2012: 5), to which Madagascar belongs and which makes the organization a natural friend and partner to the Malagasy people. Mirroring SADC's stress on ownership and assistance to 'Malagasy stakeholders' (SADC 2011a), the COI too employed the image of 'helping' the Malagasy people to re-establish stability and economic prosperity:

> The Malagasies appreciated the support provided by the COI throughout the crisis, in strict respect of their sovereignty. We are a small, yet proximate organization, and our islands have forged strong ties with each other for 30 years. We therefore have a good understanding of the Malagasy situation, and we can offer sound advice (...) (Author's translation; COI 2012: 11)

In the words of a high-ranking COI diplomat, this reads:

> By participating fully in the efforts of the international community to find a solution to end the crisis, the COI has played since 2009, and

increasingly so, a constructive and dynamic role, acting as a relay of proximity and historical partner with the stakeholders in the Malagasy crisis. Our geographical and cultural proximity means that the COI's support in Madagascar is natural. (Author's translation; Morel 2014: 2)

This stress on cultural proximity and mutual understanding made the COI's help for Madagascar appear natural and inevitable. In this context, the COI built not only on its diplomatic and symbolic infrastructure, but also on the fact that it was the only organization that had upheld Madagascar's membership throughout the crisis. More than merely a matter of different legal provisions, this was a question of principle: it meant playing 'la carte de solidarité' (Morel 2014: 2), the solidarity card, which the COI explicitly defined as a counter-approach to the more confrontational stances of SADC and the AU (COI 2013a: 53).[9] In the ICG-M, for instance, COI representatives repeatedly lobbied against other members' policies towards Madagascar, especially on the question of aid withdrawal and economic sanctions.[10] That the two protagonists of this approach, Mauritius and the Seychelles, are in fact also members of SADC and the AU was seen as an asset rather than a contradiction or hindrance.[11]

The COI's greater involvement in defining what returning Madagascar to constitutional order meant was therefore not merely an instance of inter-organizational competition. Rather, it contributed to redefining the purpose and role of the COI more generally. While it was set up in 1982 as a body for promoting economic integration and trade, the crisis in Madagascar triggered the development of a more proactive political engagement. Offering expertise in mediation, financing the preparation of elections, voter education, or media training, and monitoring political developments – all these tasks performed by the COI in Madagascar were in fact new practices for the organization (COI 2012: 59). Yet for the COI, it was also clear that even though the crisis in Madagascar:

> has demonstrated the COI's legitimacy to intervene, (...) it also shows the necessity for the organization to put in place the instruments, mechanisms and financial means in order to reinforce its action in the area of prevention, mediation and conflict management. (Author's translation; COI 2010c: 16)

The crisis in Madagascar was thus not meant to be an exceptional adventure, but rather should pave the way for a more long-term strategic role in the area of mediation, election observation, and conflict prevention, even if this required additional resources. The COI annual report of 2014 thus concludes:

Prevention, mediation, participation in the resolution of regional crises and observation of electoral processes are at the heart of the COI's approach to peace, stability and democracy. In a decade, COI has emerged as a credible regional actor promoting stability, working in close collaboration with the international community, including the African Union. Its role of proximity and its capacity to propose solutions in line with the socio-political realities were recognized and welcomed, in particular in the framework of the resolution of the crisis in Madagascar and the international contact group. (Author's translation; COI 2014: 67)

The annual report's clear reference to a new role for the COI underlines the more general consequences that the post-coup intervention in Madagascar had for redefining the COI. In its first strategic development plan, adopted in 2013, the organization's first priority goal was therefore to 'contribute to the creation of a secure, stable and solidary Indian Oceanic space, notably by the consolidation of democracy, the rule of law and good governance' [author's translation] (COI 2013b: 4). Since then, the COI monitored elections in the Seychelles (2011, 2015, 2016), the Comoros (2011, 2016), and Madagascar (2013, 2018) and facilitated among the parties after election results had been contested. In order to further professionalize its election-monitoring functions, the COI also established a special reserve fund (COI 2012: 59).

In response to these developments, the EU launched a capacity-building programme for the period of 2016–2020 in order to support the COI in the areas of mediation, recognition of the COI as a regional mechanism under APSA, election observation, democracy promotion, and ocean governance (COI 2014: 69). On the more strategic side, in 2017, the COI further refined its tasks in the area of 'peace and stability' and, inter alia, identified conflict prevention, mediation, and electoral assistance as key areas for future engagement (COI 2018: 24). To this end, the organization has also teamed up with the UN, which will support these efforts financially and through capacity-building projects (COI 2018: 25). The long-term institutional effect of all these efforts is, of course, difficult to assess. Not least, the opening of a permanent office in Antananarivo and regular election-monitoring practices are cases in point that already now the COI's new role has become sedimented.

However, experimenting with and expanding into new areas of engagement and practice was not confined to the COI. For the OIF, for instance, returning Madagascar to constitutional order provided an opportunity to expand and professionalize the organization's expertise and practices in the area of election monitoring, legal advice for the electoral process, and civic education. For the OIF, the focus on elections is a way to strike a balance between the organization's increasingly political mandate, on the one hand, and its still limited financial and human capacities, on the other (see also Tavares & Bernadino 2011: 621).[12] Between 2011 and 2013, more than ten OIF missions evaluated progress and challenges in the organization of the elections, five of which alone took place between January and September 2011 (OIF 2011; OIF 2012). In October 2012, the OIF signed an agreement with the government of Madagascar, which defined the CENI-T, the CES, and the media as focus areas for OIF's technical cooperation with and financial support for the 2013 electoral process.

Expanding one's areas of engagement, however, was neither inevitable nor uncontested. For COMESA, an albeit passive member of the ICG-M, for instance, the post-coup intervention was not a laboratory to expand the organization's expertise and practices in the field of mediation, democratic governance, or electoral support in any way comparable to the COI and OIF. In other cases, the laboratory obviously provoked intra-organizational conflicts. For both SADC and the AU, for instance, the establishment of liaison offices in member states is still a novel policy practice. In both organizations, defining the exact role, composition, and long-term mandate of the liaison office in Antananarivo provoked fierce debates. As elaborated in Chapter 5, for SADC, this led to the office being organized in a minimalized and heavily member state-dependent way. Once the crisis was over, it was immediately closed down, although some member states had been in favour of a more long-term presence on the ground.[13] Experimentation was thus reduced to its very limit. While the above-mentioned planned cooperation in the area of SSR is a consequence of SADC's engagement in Madagascar, this was confined to an already established policy field. Like COMESA, SADC hence shows that neither expansion nor institutionalization is an inevitable feedback that post-coup interventions have on the constitution of international order.[14]

For the AU, the liaison office did turn into a laboratory, albeit a limited and contested one. While the PSC had expressed in early 2014 'the commitment of the AU and the SADC to continue to support the new Malagasy authorities and the other concerned stakeholders in the country in their efforts, including those relating to socio-economic recovery (...)' (AU PSC 2014a: 2), the exact role of the liaison office remained unclear. At the beginning, this required daily small-scale negotiations between the officers in Antananarivo and the AU Commission in Addis Ababa, in which the former were caught between personal ambitions to become more 'proactive' and 'visible' in support of Madagascar's post-transition development, on the one hand, and the ambiguous signals, bureaucratic hurdles, and lack of funds they received from Addis Ababa, on the other.[15] Reconciliation and SSR were nevertheless identified as key areas of the AU's future engagement in Madagascar (Butedi 2018: 108–109) and have since then led to regular activities (AU 2015; AU 2018). In March 2014, right after the return to constitutional order was officially attained, the AU special representative finally arrived to head the AU liaison office. In 2015, the PSC decided, in light of remaining challenges, to extend the mandate of the liaison office geographically so as to also 'monitor political and other developments in Madagascar and the Indian Ocean region' and assigned it with all tasks relevant to 'consolidat[ing] the process of reconciliation and stabilization of Madagascar' (AU PSC 2015: 1). With this, the office set out for a more permanent engagement and a novel chapter for the AU's nascent policy on post-conflict reconstruction and structural conflict prevention.

Altogether, after almost five years of post-coup intervention, the more revolutionary changes in fact took place outside of, though crucially connected to, the Malagasy polity. In Madagascar, the promise of institutions mainly contributed to relegitimizing an ideal of the liberal polity as an object of politics. For the international, in turn, the illusions and exclusions of this ideal provided the texture for expanding and sedimenting international solutions to address the obvious gap between ideal and reality. The two phenomena of order formation and sedimentation are therefore inevitably linked. The international is part of the reconstituted Malagasy polity, not only in how it emerged (i.e. the processes that led to its establishment), but also in what sustains it. In turn, the expansion of the international builds on the diagnosed deficiencies of the Malagasy polity and its integration into an expansive network of international and regional relations. Neither can be rendered intelligible without the other. Neither can claim its *raison d'être* without the other. The close reconstruction of the processes and effects of almost five years of post-coup intervention in Madagascar hence demonstrates that not only order-making as a process, but the emerging orders themselves, are transnational and therefore have to be understood proceeding from their intersections and mutual references.

7
Politics and power of post-coup interventions

International organizations as well as regional ones are increasingly concerned with the domestic governance of states. This has become evident in ever-expanding norms and benchmarks defined by international and regional organizations for what counts as 'good order' in states, as well as corresponding practices of intervention in cases where such orders are under threat. The emergence of the AU's anti-coup norm is emblematic of these broader changes in the fabric of the international and its effects on the constitution of order within existing states. As elaborated in Chapter 2, since the end of the Cold War, the internal make-up of African states has been gradually turned into a continental concern. Due to this development, the AU and other African regional organizations increasingly served as judges over questions of legitimate authority in African states. However, 25 successful coups between 1990 and 2012 showed that politics within African states had not yet become entirely institutionalized (Souaré 2014: 75; see generally Posner & Young 2007). The AU therefore formulated a 'zero tolerance' policy towards coups and became actively involved in re-establishing constitutional order in its member states in case such order has been interrupted (AU Assembly 2010a). Despite the empirical relevance of these interventions to re-establish constitutional order after coups, IR scholars and those interested in (African) regional governance in particular have so far not paid adequate attention to this phenomenon. In fact, when studying interventions, scholars still mainly concentrate on Western interveners or allegedly global organizations such as the UN. They hence neglect the practical but also analytical relevance non-Western, in this case particularly African, intervention practices can lend to our understanding of the constitution of order and the constitutive links between international and domestic politics. Those scholars studying the AU's role in 'undoing' coups, in turn, have provided competing interpretations as to whether the AU's anti-coup norm should be seen as a means to promote democracy (Afro-optimists) or rather as an instrument to serve incumbent governments and guarantee regime security (Afro-pessimists). Both perspectives, as I have argued throughout this book, are prevented by their normative and analytical restrictions to fully grasp the ambiguous consequences post-coup interventions can have for the reconfiguration of power relations. This book therefore set out to develop a novel reading of what post-coup interventions are, and to explore how and with what effects the 'undoing' of coups happens in practice, based on an in-depth case study of almost five years of post-coup intervention in Madagascar. There are five conclusions to be drawn from the case of Madagascar.

First, this book demonstrates that contrary to the dominant view in the literature and the AU's self-portrayal, the 'undoing' of coups is neither the mere top-down implementation of a given policy framework nor do these situations constitute a case of international mediation (i.e. impartial third-party assistance to parties in conflict) (Moore 2003: 15). The first perspective overestimates the AU's capacities to simply 'implement' its mandate to restore constitutional order and underestimates the amount of conflict this mandate itself creates. The second perspective, in turn, underestimates the resistance of those with and for whom constitutional order ought to be established and overestimates the extent to which post-coup interventions meet their consent. Moreover, it essentially negates to what extent the demand to return a country to constitutional order itself establishes conditions and expectations that invalidate the assumption that those mediating do so merely in assistance to parties in conflict.

Reactions to coups instead open up a complex field of interaction – a 'transboundary formation' (Latham et al. 2001: 5) – between international, regional, and national actors that all struggle over defining the rules of the game and with this the terms of what returning a country to constitutional order means. As has been shown, international actors, including the AU and SADC, are part of these struggles. They are neither able to simply carry out their mandates to 'facilitate the restoration of constitutional order' (OAU 2000a: 4), nor are they benign external mediators who merely 'assist' and 'accompany'. Conflicts exist not only among those local parties competing to define the post-coup order. Rather, the demand for a rapid return to constitutional order itself becomes a source of conflict because it entails a minimal yet crucial set of conditions on how to do so. On the one hand, to fulfil these conditions, allies are required: national actors and negotiating parties who meet the international demand for a rapid return to constitutional order. On the other hand, the conditional demand also means that international actors such as the AU and SADC set the terms of *how* the return to constitutional order ought to occur. This demonstrates international actors' own involvement in negotiating and defining the terms of post-coup interventions while at the same time underlining their constraints in actually 'undoing' coups. Neither policy implementation nor mediation is therefore an adequate perspective to grasp the politics and power inherent in these engagements. Both perspectives – policy implementation and mediation – might therefore serve more to tell us about the organizations' own efforts to make sense of their highly contradictory mandates than to provide adequate heuristic lenses for understanding the character of these engagements from an analytical point of view.

The first conclusion is thus that by re-establishing constitutional order, the AU, SADC, and other international actors neither merely implement policies nor are they mediating between parties in conflict. Rather, they become involved in a transnational arena and a struggle over defining the terms of legitimate order. They are part of, not bystanders to, this struggle, and they come with their *own* terms of what 'legitimate order' means.

Second, contrary to what the legal language in most of the AU's talk about unconstitutional changes suggests, returning a country to constitutional order is therefore not merely the re-establishment of legality. Rather, post-coup interventions are a case of transnational order-making that comes with crucial consequences for the reconfiguration and sedimentation of legitimacies and power relationships.

The case study on Madagascar showed that what has ultimately been re-established is the ideal image, the myth, of the liberal polity – a polity based on the ideal of political representation in the official institutions of the state in which the meaning of politics is reduced to an intra-elite struggle over access to the institutions of the state. This has been the focus of the almost five years of concerted international efforts to re-establish constitutional order on the island.

This had tangible consequences for a variety of mainly elite political actors that were able to seize the momentum and opportunities that this imaginary of order comes with. But it also meant reproducing subjectivities – the electorate, the 'people', the representative political party – whose empirical role heavily diverged from that implied in the ideal. Irrespective of this, the ideal image served to re-legitimate and reproduce the institutions of the liberal polity as object of politics, while at the same time upholding the myth of their representativeness and popular legitimacy. In this sense, constitutional order itself should be seen as part of an imaginary of political order that does more than merely re-establish law: it nourishes political expectations and it defines subjectivities and responsibilities that are neither given nor without alternative.

Moreover, the case study underlined that the various reactions to the crisis in Madagascar also contributed to reordering the international itself. On the one hand, 'la crise malgache' produced problems that justify new areas of international assistance and intervention, from national reconciliation to the reform of the security apparatus. This affected 'traditional' donors as well as new 'partners'. On the other hand, for various international organizations, the post-coup intervention served as laboratory to reach out into new realms and to define new areas of expertise and claimed authority, such as mediation, post-conflict reconstruction, or electoral assistance. The post-coup intervention in Madagascar thus also expanded the reach and depth of the international and contributed to a gradual change in its fabric.

In sum, this book underlined the importance of scrutinizing what post-coup interventions do beyond their asserted 'light' effect of merely re-establishing constitutional order and their alleged failure to bring (more) democracy or fundamental political change. The second conclusion is therefore that post-coup interventions are *effective*, in that they (re)configure power relations in and beyond the polity concerned. Such effects cannot be grasped in binary terms, such as democracy promotion or regime security, nor can they be reduced to those within the country concerned.

Third, negotiating Madagascar's return to constitutional order revealed the ambiguous power of international norms in providing the terms of these engagements. On the one hand, international norms of state sovereignty meant that from the very beginning, the purpose of returning Madagascar to constitutional order was the re-establishment of an internationally recognizable government. On the other hand, this demand today comes with at least a rhetorical commitment to popular legitimacy. Not *any* government, but one that is legitimated through inclusively and consensually organized elections, is the ultimate benchmark for international recognition.

The unrelenting international efforts to facilitate a negotiated solution to 'la crise malgache', the numerous agreements, the reconvened negotiating tables, and the AU's own description of its engagement as merely assisting third-party mediation vividly epitomize these ideals. Not least, the effective creation of negotiating parties in the so-called four mouvances – as described in Chapter 4 – embodies the international demand for an 'inclusive' and 'consensual' solution to 'la crise malgache' and demonstrates how much effort has been put into realizing this demand, against all odds. Both international sovereignty and the ideal of popular legitimacy thus set the terms, rationalities, and subjectivities for negotiating a post-coup order in Madagascar, and thereby left a powerful imprint on what this order ultimately looked like.

In practice, however, this narrative of consensus, inclusivity, and ownership had quite ambiguous consequences. It served to broaden participation in the transition, but this inclusion was built on a high degree of ignorance. The narrative of ownership in particular glossed over the role the international plays in ultimately deciding who 'the people' are and to what (limited) extent they actually are the masters of their political fate (see generally Chesterman 2004). As a consequence, over the course of time, all those questioning the predefined end point or demanding another course of the transition were delegitimated as working against the interests of the nation. With this, the overall meaning of the transition was increasingly depoliticized. The externally prescribed ownership thus disciplined the reach and breadth of politics, rather than creating space for a search for alternatives to the orders already in place.

This merger of state sovereignty and popular legitimacy is crucial to understanding both the potentials and the limits for change in the context of transnational efforts to re-establish constitutional order. These ambiguous consequences cannot be grasped if post-coup interventions are a priori seen as either 'democracy interventions' (Edozie & Gottschalk 2014: 117) or defence of regime security (Omorogbe 2011). The third conclusion is therefore that what post-coup interventions do is heavily shaped by international norms of both state sovereignty and democracy. It is this merger of norms that affected how 'la crise malgache' was approached and what its resolution ultimately implied.

Fourth, this book provides empirical evidence for the crucial role played by African actors in sustaining and shaping interventions to undo coups. Chapters 4 and 5 in particular demonstrated that the ubiquitous narrative of African leadership and subsidiarity serves a variety of other international actors such as France and the UN to make sense of their own place in and contribution to these endeavours. The AU's anti-coup norm is hence not only constitutive of AU practices, but also serves as an enabling factor for numerous other international actors. This also applies to SADC, whose less explicit mandate on how to react to unconstitutional changes of government was increasingly interpreted in terms of the AU's anti-coup policy (SADC 2013a). For other international actors, integration within the African peace and security architecture provides legitimacy but also sets limits (see also Gelot 2012: 137). Such limits became evident, for instance, with regard to the question of whether Rajoelina was allowed to participate in transitional elections, a question to which the French and US governments, for instance, initially had positions that ran against the African Charter on Democracy, Elections and Governance (Châtaigner 2014: 119). Moreover, as explicated in Chapter 4, the UN's initially more active role in negotiating with the four mouvances was scaled down to the very minimum because it contradicted the ideal of African leadership.

At the same time, however, taking a closer look at the actual practices of post-coup intervention reveals a much more ambiguous picture of African agency. The almost five years of negotiating post-coup order in Madagascar provide evidence for the power of the narrative of, but less so for the actual practice of, African leadership. This has been shown, for instance, with regard to the way the international intervention operated in Antananarivo, the distant and ad hoc engagements, and SADC's overall evasive approach to the crisis in Madagascar, as described in Chapter 5. In practice, this meant that several other actors – including the UN, France, and the COI – filled the void that resulted from the discrepancy between words and deeds. The fourth conclusion is thus that post-coup interventions demonstrate the growing empirical evidence of the African international in which claims to African agency serve to constitute roles and responsibilities for African *and* other actors (see also Brown & Harman 2013b: 10).

Fifth, almost five years of post-coup intervention in Madagascar have shown the ambiguous consequences that international efforts to re-establish constitutional order may have for the prospects for change and the search for more legitimate orders than those currently in place. Chapter 3 integrated the events of March 2009 into a broader perspective on multiple crises of legitimacy prevailing on the island at that time. Contrary to the Lomé Declaration's imaginary of a coup as mere deviance and disorder, what ultimately crystallizes in an unconstitutional change of government can therefore also be interpreted as amplifying deeper social and political grievances. The narrative of Chapter 3 was meant to stress the ambiguity and contradictions of these moments, which defy a dichotomous reading as either people's revolt or coup. As a multiplicity of crises, these moments are neither per se benign nor malign, but should be taken seriously as moments of political significance.

The preceding analysis shed a sense of doubt on the prospects for these political moments under the current ideational and institutional order. On the one hand, both the academic literature and international responses seem to favour a binary reading of these instants, squeezing them into categories of legitimate/illegitimate or democratic/non-democratic. The debates among the various interveners that came to interpret 'la crise malgache' and the AU's continuous attempts to box these situations as either/or through legal precision, as summarized in Chapter 2, are cases in point. Neither the multiplicity of legitimacies nor the longevity of social and material structures underpinning even moments of rupture and change can be adequately grasped with such a binary, momentary perspective.

On the other hand, the way 'la crise malgache' was ultimately resolved gave little reason to hope that what has been set up may indeed provide the basis for a 'rupture with the past', as then EU High Commissioner Catherine Ashton demanded in early 2014 (EU 2014). To the contrary, the depoliticization of the transition and the perpetuation of the myth of the institutions and protagonists of the liberal polity, against all odds, speak in favour neither of transformative change nor of the empowerment of forces that will be working in this direction in the future. The solutions that were offered to 'la crise' were thus overall fairly unimaginative, despite an undeniable institutionalization and professionalization that had taken place in the international since AU heads of state had decided in 2000 that coups are bad and should be a thing of the past.

The fifth conclusion is therefore that in efforts to undo coups, the search for alternatives is indeed limited: imagination has little room despite its vitality to peace (Lederach 2005; see also Mac Ginty 2011: 23). More often than not, the same institutions and practices are offered as solutions to problems that have not even been explicitly identified. Whether they will ever fulfil their promise remains to be seen.

Taken together, these five observations reflect both the politics and the power of post-coup interventions. They are contested endeavours that create rather than merely resolve conflicts. And they have tangible consequences for the creation, (re)legitimation, and institutionalization of power relations. All this is the effect of transnational interactions, which constitute orders both within and beyond the state concerned.

Madagascar in the bigger picture

The events of March 2009 in Madagascar were only one among 13 situations in Africa in which, since the establishment of the AU PSC in 2004, incumbent regimes were toppled by unconstitutional means. Since 2010, when the AU declared its 'zero tolerance' towards coups, eight cases alone were added to the list. Hence, Madagascar's case is not singular, and it therefore demands to be interpreted in light of a broader picture of post-coup interventions in Africa. This is what this section does, by arguing that not only was Madagascar's case not singular; the country's concrete experience too fits into a larger pattern. To be sure, this book's case study demonstrated in various instances that the specificity of each case matters. This became evident, for instance, in the emphasis placed on the need to understand the larger social and conflictual context in which unconstitutional changes of government take place (see Chapter 3). Moreover, I also showed what happens practically when this specificity is ignored – for instance, when a lack of appreciation for contextual knowledge or preceding (mis)perceptions fostered conflicts between AU and SADC envoys and those identified as local protagonists to resolve 'la crise malgache' (see Chapter 4). So, to show such a broader picture is not to argue that all these situations *are* similar, but to show that they are to a certain extent *treated* as similar. And because it is reasonable to assume that they are in fact *not* similar, it also makes sense to expect that interventions treating such cases as similar will still end up having *similar effects*. From this perspective, I argue that there is indeed evidence to assume that other post-coup interventions in Africa too are instances of a particular form of effective – if contested – transnational order-making.

Available overviews of AU reactions to unconstitutional changes of government emphasize patterns in the practices by which unconstitutional changes of government have been treated – for instance, with regard to regular diplomatic condemnations by the AU, the application of sanctions, the supply of mediation, or the establishment of international coordination mechanisms (Souaré 2009; Engel 2012a; Witt 2012a; Vandeginste 2013; Nathan 2017). In particular, such overviews often demonstrate deviations from the predefined script of the AU's policy frameworks. Moreover, they all point to the high degree of conflict resulting from competing international reactions to coups (Engel 2012a: 82; Witt 2013b). In contrast to this, the pattern I seek to identify here is not one confined to the (ir)regularity of international practices, but one about the character and, by consequence, the effects of post-coup interventions. In fact, this book's recurrent emphasis on the significance of local context for what it means to re-establish constitutional order, and what consequences this ultimately has, defies the assumption that underlies most of the existing literature that post-coup interventions *should* follow a generalizable script, by which local actors are merely reacting to outside stimuli, be they normative expectations or material pressure. The pattern in post-coup interventions in Africa I wish to highlight here rests on three dimensions.

First, a closer look at any of the recent cases of unconstitutional changes of government in Africa suggests that they are about much more than merely deposing incumbent governments. As in the case of Madagascar, the actual fall of a regime is often only the culmination of a multiplicity of crises, which has both a history and its own contradictions (see also Johnson & Thyne 2018). Vincent Bonnecase (2015: 153), for instance, offers an account of the 'heterogeneity of anger', as he calls it, which prevailed in Burkina Faso shortly before the so-called popular insurrection forced President Blaise Compaoré to flee to neighbouring Côte d'Ivoire in November 2014. He thereby underlines that what is otherwise often portrayed as a popular movement against Compaoré in fact brought together quite disparate forces with very different and diffuse perceptions of legitimacy, including about Compaoré's own reign (Bonnecase 2015: 167). These multiple, overlapping, and often contradictory legitimacies and forces have also been observed by others (for the case of Burkina Faso, see Frère & Englebert 2015: 301–303; for Mali, see Hagberg & Körling 2012: 8; Whitehouse 2013: 4; for Mauritania, see N'Diaye 2006: 425; for Guinea, see Barry 2009; Picard & Moudoud 2010: 56–57). The most recent case of the Sudan and the popular movement for democracy and freedom that led to the ouster of long-standing President Omar Hassan Al Bashir provides further evidence for this argument (Berridge 2020).

This more general pattern in the sociology of these situations underlines that they sit uncomfortably with the logic of the AU's anti-coup norm that sharply distinguishes between order and disorder, normalcy and exception. Also, they question the binary reading as either popular revolt or coup d'état, which underpins much of the literature and international responses to such situations. The AU's more recent efforts to develop a legal answer to the question of what counts as a legitimate popular uprising and what counts as an illegitimate coup is emblematic for these efforts to define legitimacy top-down and prospectively. As I showed in Chapter 2, such questions and their normative and practical dilemmas have been discussed throughout the evolution of the African anti-coup norm. What I want to suggest here instead, with the sociology of such situations, is to think of these situations as struggles between different legitimacies, which defies approaching them both intellectually and practically in a priori normative categories. Moreover, the empirically evident overlapping angers have crucial consequences for the local figurations that international actors, including the AU, will face 'on the ground', but also for the hopes and despairs that the international demand for 'inclusive and consensual transitions' and a return to constitutional order will raise locally.

Second, as summarized in Table 7.1, all 13 cases of unconstitutional changes of government to which the AU has reacted since 2004 included the organization of transitional elections. In most cases, these elections also served as a final benchmark to define the official return to constitutional order. In contrast, for instance, to the practice of the Organization of American States (OAS), the requirement of organizing elections means that the reinstallation of the ousted government is not at all the default option for 'undoing' coups in Africa (see, in comparison, Cooper & Legler 2005; Legler 2012). In fact, apart from

Table 7.1 – Cases of post-coup interventions by the African Union (2004–2019)

Case	Condemned/ suspended	'Inclusive' transition	Elections	Putschist victory	Duration (months)
Togo (2005)	X		X	X	3
Mauritania (2005)	X	X	X		20
Mauritania (2008)	X	X	X[1]	X	12
Guinea (2008)	X	X	X		24
Madagascar (2009)	X	X	X		58
Niger (2010)	X	X	X		14
Guinea-Bissau (2012)	X	X	X		26
Mali (2012)	X	X	X[1]		18
CAR (2013)	X	X	X		35
Egypt (2013)	X	X	X	X	11
Burkina Faso (2014)	X[2]	X	X[1]		14
The Gambia (2016/17)[3]	X		(X)		2
Sudan (2019)[4]	X	X	X[1]		

Source: Author's compilation based on primary documents and Nathan (2017).

[1] The country's suspension was lifted already before transitional elections were held.

[2] Only suspended from the AU after another coup d'état during the transitional period in September 2015.

[3] The case of The Gambia differed from the other cases in that it was the incumbent who did not accept his electoral defeat. The regional intervention was thus geared towards enforcing an existing electoral result.

[4] As of June 2020, the transition in Sudan is still ongoing.

those instances where putschists won the transitional elections (Togo, Mauritania in 2008, and Egypt), post-coup elections often resulted in a change of the governing party (Nathan 2017: 14–15). Table 7.1 further shows that, as in the case of Madagascar, this international demand for transitional elections also goes hand in hand with a demand for a negotiated and 'inclusive' transition. Power-sharing agreements are thus a standard tool in post-coup transitions to guarantee a comprehensive elite buy-in (Vandeginste 2013; Nathan 2017: 13–14). On average, it took a little less than 20 months to re-establish constitutional order. If the extraordinarily long Malagasy case is omitted, this is reduced to 16 months. The overview of Table 7.1 reflects what this book reconstructed more comprehensively for the case of Madagascar: a particular pattern in the imaginary of legitimate order that is promoted and actualized in these interventions, in their focus on representative institutions, intra-elite power-sharing, and elections as means to resolve political crises. As concluded above, this fairly restricted array of solutions offered to 'undo' coups reflects a merger of international sovereignty and popular legitimacy norms. While this imaginary may resemble what is generally termed the 'liberal peace', it is important that it is much more constricted than what is usually seen as the ideational models that define liberal peacebuilding interventions today (Campbell et al. 2011; Richmond & Mac Ginty 2015). For instance, it deliberately does *not* entail an economic component and it does *not* seek to induce long-term change. Thus, as shown in the case of Madagascar, this imaginary's particular character in fact stems exactly from its limits: its restrictive focus on re-establishing a government that comes to power through internationally sanctioned, 'inclusive' transitions and elections.[1]

Third, the international demand for a return to constitutional order and for the organization of transitional elections raises the question of who participates in this endeavour. In Madagascar, the artificial creation of the four mouvances as well as the explosive increase in the number of political parties highlighted how this international demand constitutes agents and impacts on dynamics within the political elite. Elsewhere too, participation in the demanded transition provoked fierce debates about representativeness and the fairness of the overall process (Witt 2012a: 25; Nathan 2017: 21–22). As has been described for Madagascar, other accounts also point to a similar pattern of elite reconfiguration shortly before or after the coup happens, which favours, again as in Madagascar, the urban, politically organized elite (N'Diaye 2006: 436–439; Chouli 2015: 330; Frère & Englebert 2015: 305–307). More often than not, this also means that rural populations and the forces *not* organized in formal political parties – which, as in Guinea, Burkina Faso, Egypt, and the Sudan, have played significant roles in the build-up to the respective crises – are gradually sidelined by the post-coup reconfigurations.

Against the background of these three observations, it is reasonable to assume that by promoting a particular, restrictive imaginary of political order, post-coup interventions are likely to leave a similar imprint on such open situations and struggles of competing legitimacies. What is more, international interveners elsewhere too are confronted with their own inclusion in these very struggles. Despite reference to ownership, they remain the ultimate arbiters of who counts as a legitimate agent for re-establishing constitutional order, whether they decide this willingly or just let things happen. Other experiences of post-coup interventions in Africa thus indeed confirm the interpretation of this phenomenon as an effective albeit ambiguous process of transnational reordering, triggered by the AU's decision to 'undo' coups in Africa. While it is attractive to see such a larger pattern, how exactly this process takes place, how it concretely affects power relations, and to what extent change is possible can only be established through close empirical reconstruction of each case, as this book demonstrates. However, this section may serve as sufficient proof that this would be an effort worth undertaking.

Implications

In order to understand what post-coup interventions are and what they do, this book drew on literature in the field of IR, peace and conflict research, and African studies alike. In turn, it may therefore also offer insights for a number of current concerns in these fields. I limit this discussion of the implications of this research to: (1) those for studying the AU and the APSA; and (2) those for (global) IR theory and its links to African studies.

Studying the AU and the APSA in practice

Since its establishment in 2002, the AU and the evolving APSA increasingly received academic attention (Engel & Porto 2010; Engel & Porto 2013; Engel & Porto 2014; Williams 2014; Tieku 2016). This book has underlined the importance of these developments for the reconfiguration of order on the African continent. It has shown how the AU and other regional organizations such as SADC emerged as locales to define legitimate order and demonstrated that this has powerful effects, not least on what kind of and whose orders prevail on the continent. For the growing body of literature on the APSA, this has several implications.

First, this research showed that in order to understand the power and ambiguous effects of the AU, it is both pertinent and worthwhile to move beyond the top-down 'view from Addis'. This also implies taking other methodological routes and studying more than policy documents and official statements. Chapter 2 underlined how important it is to understand policy*making* within the AU and to take a closer look at the more incremental ways in which change is negotiated and crafted (see also de Waal & Ibreck 2013). But these processes alone are not enough to understand the effects of AU decisions, declarations, and announcements. The case study on Madagascar revealed the powerful consequences of the AU's anti-coup norm, even though these consequences were neither the effect of what the AU *did*, nor did they fulfil the normative expectations on democratization and political change prevalent in the literature. Both academic research and the self-descriptions of the AU and RECs tend to omit such consequences of the APSA as seen 'on the ground' (see also Witt & Khadiagala 2018).[2] Tracing these consequences, of course, comes with its own difficulties: it requires a particular openness to surprise, access, time, money, and patience – not all of which are available in plenty and at all times in all stages of an academic career. This research is nevertheless a plea to engage more vigorously with these worlds, indeed in the plural, 'beyond Addis', and to bring their voices, experiences, and contradictions into an understanding of the role and significance of the AU, RECs, and the APSA more generally.

Second, this research underlined the importance of studying the AU and other RECs from different theoretical angles and demonstrated the value of a more explicit engagement with theory. In this regard, Chapter 1 used IR thinking on the power of IOs – their role as sites for the definition and dissemination of particular governmental knowledge regimes – as a background for interpreting the definition of continental standards of legitimate order not only as policies to defend and promote 'democracy', but as an expression of a more fundamental process of reorganizing the relationship between states, societies, and the international (Neumann & Sending 2010: 136; Orford 2011: 27). Chapter 2 highlighted how the evolution of the idea to outlaw coups was tied to the expanding responsibilization of the AU to master the unabated occurrence of coups. This process gradually institutionalized and centralized what OAU Secretary-General Salim Ahmed Salim had repeatedly stated: an African responsibility for the internal make-up of states. With this, the organization's radar increasingly moved towards the prevention of future coups, an expansive field of new roles and responsibilities. I used the metaphors of the police force and the social worker to describe how the AU's role and its relationship vis-à-vis states and societies have changed since. The case study on Madagascar ultimately showed how post-coup interventions too serve to expand the reach of the international, including that of African and other international organizations.

Rita Kiki Edozie and Keith Gottschalk (2014: xxix) also called for a more theory-informed and theory-informing perspective on the AU.

Their conclusion is to describe the AU as an evolving '"African" suprastate' (Edozie & Gottschalk 2014: 29). Taking Michel Foucault's thoughts on the emergence of the state and the currently ongoing governmentalization of the international as background – as described in Chapter 1 – one may concur with this observation. Without this, however, it seems to be a redescription of the AU's own self-image rather than a valuable heuristic for understanding the reconfigurations of authority and power that this implies and for taking a more critical stance towards their consequences. What a description of the AU as a 'suprastate' fundamentally misses is how the idea(l) of the state is itself an important ingredient to the AU's claims to power, and how, through practices such as reactions to coups, the state itself is both subverted and reconstituted. Understanding the consequences of the increasing sedimentation and institutionalization of power within the AU and other RECs thus requires seeing them integrated into, and not 'above', the logics of an international order of states (see next subsection).

Third, and resulting from this, the conclusions of this book lead to what Laura Zanotti (2011: 147) called an 'informed prudence' about the expectations formulated towards the AU's policies on unconstitutional changes of government. Here again, a different theoretical perspective was helpful: the 'transboundary formation' (Latham et al. 2001: 5) allowed the AU's practical integration to be seen within a network of at times competing and contradictory agencies, logics, and discourses that heavily constrained the organization's realm of action to 'implement' its mandate to undo coups. Informed prudence, however, is also in order with regard to the AU's more general approach to legalize issues that are inherently political. Chapter 2 discussed how the AU's efforts to define its role as guardian of the good order followed the logic of expanding and refining the organization's legal instruments. The experiences in Madagascar call into question the assumptions underpinning this effort: that it is possible to circumvent the politics and messiness of the situations at hand by an ever-clearer, mechanistic manual of how to react to such situations. The spread of internationally enshrined rights to popular legitimacy and democratic governance and corresponding responsibilities of IOs does not mean that it is always clear who the subject of these rights really is. The reconstructed process of negotiating and crafting the anti-coup norm as well as the post-coup negotiations in Madagascar at the very least show a remarkable gap between the discourse of popular sovereignty, participation, and ownership, on the one hand, and the exclusivity of politics in practice, on the other. Moreover, reducing reactions to unconstitutional changes of government to a mere legal question fails to take into account how the efforts to undo coups themselves promote a particular form of order, the liberal polity and its institutions, that is often at odds with the realities on the ground. Altogether, the call for more 'informed prudence' therefore means investing more in in-depth analyses to gain a more realistic picture of what African regional organizations can and should do in situations of multiple crises and contested legitimacies such as most unconstitutional changes of government. It also means that neither more capacities, nor more efficient international coordination, nor more refined legal scripts alone will provide adequate solutions to the problems of an inherently political undertaking.

Fourth, a key issue currently debated in the literature on the APSA and the AU is that of the relationship and coordination between the AU, RECs, and other international actors (Engel & Porto 2014: 136; Brosig 2015). The post-coup intervention in Madagascar was in this sense exemplary of overlapping mandates, unclear responsibilities, and fierce competition between all those involved in re-establishing constitutional order and of how this can derail the officially propagated image of an internationally coordinated effort (Cawthra 2010: 16; Lanz & Gasser 2013; Nathan 2013: 5; Witt 2013b). Much of this debate is informed by a search for how international coordination and division of labour could be made more efficient, where international coordination is ascribed an intrinsic value. This research underlined the flip side of both the discourse and current practices of international coordination. It showed the importance of the discourse of international coordination and African responsibility in an international division of labour *and* its constant subversion in practice (see, in particular, Chapter 5). Concretely, this has meant that the gap between the narrative and the actual practices contributed to evading responsibilities and accountability. The book therefore underlined the ambiguous effects of the discourse on African responsibility: it may at once hinder actual coordination and allow responsibility and accountability to be evaded.

Fifth, and tied to this, the case study on Madagascar also provides a more nuanced account of the professionalization of African regional organizations, and their peacemaking practices in particular (Engel 2012b: 260). As noted in Chapter 4, those sent to negotiate Madagascar's return to constitutional order widely followed the established pattern: former heads of state, thus diplomats rather than professional mediators (Khadiagala 2011: 31). Also, more often than not, they worked with minimal financial and logistical support. Moreover, both the AU and SADC conducted their engagements in Madagascar from afar and in an often ad hoc way. This also resulted in difficulties in gaining access to the parties and meant that knowledge about developments on the ground was often gathered indirectly, or not at all. The tedious process of setting up the respective components of the SADC-AU liaison office, their lack of mutual engagement, and unclear mandates of local liaison officers are further cases in point. Disconnect was a recurring theme in Chapters 4 and 5. There were, however, also crucial differences between the AU and SADC in how they organized their respective roles in post-March 2009 Madagascar that resulted from different normative provisions, resources, internal politics, and organizational cultures. So, this is explicitly *not* to invoke the image of unprofessionalism that indeed many of the interviewed international diplomats painted of both organizations. Rather, it highlights once more the limited resources and internal divisions under which African regional organizations operate, which more often than not leads to a much more ambiguous organization than self-descriptions (including narratives of 'African leadership') may suggest. This underlines that in order to understand how African regional organizations operate in practice, the specific internal complexities and organizational cultures of each organization have to be taken (more) seriously. But it also contradicts all efforts to professionalize African regional organizations through application of a public management blueprint.

Finally, this book identified an area of research hitherto largely ignored in the study of the APSA: the economic conditioning and effects of interventions by the AU/RECs. This involves scrutinizing how economic aspects shape and subvert African peacemaking efforts. In the case of Madagascar, economic questions were consistently excluded from the negotiations, despite having obviously shaped both the conflictive figurations prior to March 2009 and the course of the transition. As noted in Chapter 6, this exclusion may have crucial consequences for how just and legitimate Madagascar's post-coup order will be perceived in the future. In particular, more analytical attention must be paid to the extent to which post-coup interventions are shaped by or themselves deepen the integration of African states into the global economy (e.g. through growing extractive industries), and for whose benefit this takes place. The effectiveness of economic sanctions applied by African regional organizations also demands further exploration, including their potentially negative consequences of fostering illicit economic activities.

(Global) IR theory and African studies

In line with Amitav Acharya's (2014) call for 'globalizing' the study and theorizing of international politics, this book was an attempt to analyse contemporary developments on the African continent, and AU policies in particular, from a more theory-informed perspective. For this purpose, the book also sought to bridge IR and African studies. In the remainder of this section, I highlight three insights from this study that I consider relevant to broader theoretical and conceptual questions in the two disciplines.

First, for both IR and African studies, this research underlined the relevance of African actors in making and remaking order on the African continent. This is an important case and form of African agency to which neither discipline has so far paid sufficient attention (cf. Wodrig 2017). Order in Africa is still often seen as what externals do. In fact, in both intervention research and research on democratization processes, African regional organizations and their policies are still largely being ignored. And even recent calls to decentre the study of interventions have not yet led to an adequate recognition of African interveners and their effects (Schroeder 2018; Turner & Kühn 2019).[3]

In turn, the discussion on African agency has mainly focused on that which shapes *global* processes such as climate negotiations and trade partnerships or on African reactions to external structural constraints such as those revealed in relationships to donor countries (see, for instance, Bayart 2000; Brown & Harman 2013a; cf. Aning & Edu-Afful 2016). This research adds another perspective here: one that focuses on the emergence of an 'African international' – that is, a set of structured relations beyond the state based on the definition and sedimentation of governmental rationalities, and its order-constituting effects both within and beyond the state. The agency this implies is not the result of processes external to the continent, a mere reaction to or opportunity offered by the international system, although it remains intimately connected to and infused by global or extra-continental entanglements. This African international in fact allows particular agencies to emerge, which may in practice, as shown in this book, have multiple and ambiguous outcomes. This calls for a more nuanced analysis of what actually *constitutes* African agency today, under what conditions, and for whose benefit agency becomes effective (see also Beswick & Hammerstad 2013: 480). Thinking this through in terms of an African international helps to grasp more thoroughly both emerging agencies and the increasingly complex and diverse relationships among *different* African agencies involved in the making and remaking of (African) orders.

Second, the formation of the African international also holds implications for IR theory and investigations into 'the making of the international itself' (Dean 2010: 249; Walters 2012: 7). This research explored empirically how IOs such as the AU set and disseminate standards of legitimate authority and how this constitutes and institutionalizes international responsibilities. The case study on Madagascar provided an insightful example of the expansive nature of this endeavour, which reaches far beyond the AU. It showed how the practices of intervention provided the grounds for new roles and responsibilities for several international and regional organizations; the emergence of the COI as a political actor was but one illustration. The emerging African international and the definition and sedimentation of responsibilities and governmental practices in a number of regional organizations is therefore an invaluable source for theorizing the conditions for the making of the international and its changing contours.

These processes cannot be grasped merely in terms of international cooperation or inter-organizational relations. Rather, they require a different vocabulary to describe their conditions of possibility, forms, and implications. This study therefore feeds into a growing theoretical effort to go beyond the vocabulary of global governance for describing the make-up of and the transformations in the international order (Neumann & Sending 2010; Orford 2011; Sending 2015; Zürn 2018). Some of this literature has – like this book – taken a Foucauldian perspective in order to investigate how these transformations build upon and actualize changing relationships of power between multiple centres. If taken in Foucault's own sense of a 'toolbox' rather than a ready-made theory (Walters 2012: 103), this seems to be a path worth exploring further (see also Death 2013).

At a more general level, the insights generated here are therefore relevant for understanding how international norms weave together IOs, states, and societies. This constitutes and expands international authority, but also structures how governance *in* states takes place (Hameiri 2010; Orford 2011). A crucial observation in this regard is that both the conditions of possibility and the consequences of the expansive international are tied to the ideals (or problems) of governance and order in states. In this sense, the AU's anti-coup norm and the resulting intervention practices also underlined the persisting relevance of the state both as an imaginary *and* as an agent in international politics (see generally Migdal & Schlichte 2005). The re-establishment of constitutional order was about re-legitimating the liberal polity (i.e. the institutions of the state) as well as about regaining international sovereignty. The consequences of these processes, in turn, were a growing international presence to fix the remaining problems of the liberal polity and a deepening of Madagascar's international diplomatic contacts. The expansion of the international should therefore not merely be seen as a process of internationalization (or indeed supranationalization), but as one of altering relationships of power that span what for IR have for a long time been discrete spheres, levels of analysis, and distinct 'actors' (see generally Walker 1993).

Third, this book underlined the relevance of a transnational and relational perspective for understanding the *consequences* of international politics. It also showed how international politics can be shaped by and in turn constitute locales that are – like Madagascar – intuitively (and wrongly so) not considered very relevant in the discipline of IR. African studies indeed offers a long tradition of such a transnational perspective, in thinking of both the state and societies as constituted by transboundary interactions across alleged international and domestic spheres (i.e. understanding the local presence of the international) (Death 2015). In this sense, bridging African studies and IR offers an important way to think social processes *across* boundaries, and it calls for observing their consequences from the bottom up. As demanded by Acharya (2014: 650), bringing experiences from regional worlds into IR should not merely add new empirical insights, but should also challenge theoretical vantage points more generally. Exposing the 'rich kernels of specific junctures' that join global, regional, national, and local ideas, forces, institutions, and capabilities (Latham et al. 2001: 6) helped in this book to shed a different light on what post-coup interventions are and what they do. They might also shed a different light on other processes of apparently 'global' politics, on what they are and what they do. Rather than formulating lessons from one 'discipline' for another, which are often based on sketchy images of what constitutes these respective disciplines, enlivening the conversation between African studies and IR may thus at least reveal the need for a more thorough description of the international and its ambiguous consequences, based on how it unfolds and how it is experienced in very concrete contexts in Africa and across the globe.

So, what to do?

This book does not only add to scholarly debates. Knowledge always has practical implications too (Shapiro 1981: 199). After all, the processes and practices that this study presented shaped the lives and livelihoods, the professional and personal futures of a great number of people, from Antananarivo to Gaborone, Addis Ababa, and Paris. It is quite common to conclude such a research with policy recommendations or some answers to the question of 'what to do now?' This is particularly common in research on the AU and the literature on mediation, peacemaking, and interventions. In fact, and somewhat remarkably, oftentimes even self-described critical, as opposed to so-called problem-solving, academics seem to remain inclined to the idea that their insights have to contribute to making *policy* better. I take inspiration from James Ferguson's (1994: 282) discussion on 'what to do' for a note on the practical implications of this research, beyond policies. As stated in Chapter 1, the critical foundation of this book lies in the conviction that research can contribute to offering *alternative* perspectives to the way we see and think about the world (Tully 2002: 546). This is, to paraphrase Foucault (1994), why it is important to think. This importance does not emanate from a better or more thorough description *of*, but from offering interpretative lenses *to*, the world.

In several instances, this book pointed to the importance of knowledge in accessing and seizing the opportunities of the post-coup intervention in Madagascar. International contacts, familiarity with the institutions and norms of African regional and international organizations, and language skills – all this affected to what extent various Malagasy actors were able to shape Madagascar's return to constitutional order. And it will most probably have a similar effect in the future. The allusion in Chapter 6 to a trend of deepening transnational relationships in Madagascar makes such a conclusion at least compelling. Interpreting what happened in post-March 2009 Madagascar not simply as 'international interference' (*Madagascar Tribune* 2012a), but as an expression of Madagascar's increasing integration into a network of often contradictory webs of ideas, rationalities, institutions, and material forces hence also means revealing where and how these webs may be turned into opportunities. This may have tangible consequences for all those seeking to shape politics on the island and those still to come. At the same time, the preceding chapters repeatedly pointed to a dearth of imagination and creativity in post-coup interventions, restrictions on the play of ideas, the role of unquestioned assumptions underpinning existing policy instruments, and the lack of space to debate alternatives. This leaves an important task to all those involved in creating and contesting knowledge: to think about how this reimagination could be encouraged not as a prescription of alternatives, but as a collective effort to see alternatives at all.

Notes

Introduction

1 Personal conversations, 22 March 2014, Antananarivo. Author's translation.

2 For works on the Americas, see, for instance, Cooper and Legler (2006), McCoy and Diez (2011), and Smith-Cannoy (2012).

1 Norms, interventions, and the making of orders

1 This unfortunate division of labour has also been noted and criticized in a debate on Africa's apparent irrelevance for dominant (theoretical) thinking in IR, which has, however, mainly taken place among 'Africanists' only (see, for instance, Dunn & Shaw 2001; Nkiwane 2001; Smith 2009; Cornelissen et al. 2012; Odoom & Andrews 2017).

2 With regard to Sub-Saharan Africa, this call has, for instance, been taken up in an edited volume by Bischoff et al. (2016) as well as in Aning and Edu-Afful (2016).

3 Nowhere has this effect become more evident than during the decolonization of former colonies in the 1960s, which, rather than fundamentally transforming, actually reproduced and reified the international system of states (Clapham 1996; Clark 2005: 161; Cooper 2008; Scott 2012).

4 Even before this, the English School in IR had developed a different understanding of sovereignty, which for English School scholars was one among several shared principles and thus an institution of 'international society' (see generally Wight 1972; Bull 1977). However, unlike their critical constructivist colleagues later, the English School registered, rather than interrogated, the processes that led to the emergence and change of international legitimacy principles (see also Reus-Smit 2001: 537).

5 For an early exception in IR, see Peter Gourevitch's elaboration of the 'second image reversed', though he decidedly rejects discussing ideas as international structures affecting domestic politics (Gourevitch 1978: 883; see also Cortell & Davis 2000).

6 For exceptions, see Beswick and Hammerstad (2013) and Brown and Harman (2013a).

7 Barnett and Finnemore (2004: 164) in fact noted that IOs also define the purpose of states, because '[as] IO governance activities expand, they are not only helping to create a new structure to world politics but are also working to create and constitute new domestic societies. (…) specifically, all are trying to create durable, modern nation-states that are organized around democracy and markets'. The book's main focus, however, lays on proving autonomy rather than co-constitution or the emergence of new relationships of power.

8 In anthropological accounts of the state in Africa, Thomas Bierschenk (2010: 6), for instance, used the term 'sedimentation' to describe the simultaneity of institutions, practices, and rationalities of the state from precolonial, colonial, and postcolonial times and their gradual expansion (see also Bayart 2010). He understands sedimentation as a metaphor for the layering of old and new, whereas here the term is used as a metaphor for 'thickening' and indeed disappearance from the visible.

9 In this sense, the 'role of intervention in the "ordering" and "reordering" of the modern world' changed according to changing normative and material structures that constituted the international realm (MacMillan 2013: 1040). Changing international purposes, from the fear of revolutionary contagion to the rights of creditors, anti-slavery, the rights of minorities, or 'governance', also meant changing purposes, subjects, and practices of intervention (MacMillan 2013: 1044; see also Finnemore 2003; Williams 2013).

10 Examples for such a perspective on interventions as a social space and an arena in which a variety of actors engage in defining the meaning and purpose of peace and order are by now numerous (see, for example, Heathershaw & Lambach 2008; Heathershaw 2009; Hameiri 2010; Veit 2010; Bliesemann de Guevara 2012; Curtis 2012; Birkholz et al. 2018; Hellmüller 2018). This perspective on interactions contrasts with a purely rationalist one, in which interactions are determined by calculated self-interests of local and international actors who engage in bargaining peace as a 'contract' (Barnett et al. 2014). Here, neither a social (discursive, economic, world society) context nor 'unintended' outcomes and the 'non-plannability' of interventions seem to fit into the research framework (see also Bliesemann de Guevara 2011: 116). It also differs from approaches that conceive of this social field merely in terms of one intervening organization, thus focusing on the practical challenges of how to create consent and legitimacy for a particular intervention (see, for instance, Whalan 2013).

11 This has also been evidenced by very insightful ethnographic studies on the interactions between international interveners and the societies in which they are deployed, as well as the lifeworlds of international interveners more generally (most prominently, see Pouligny 2006; Autesserre 2014a).

12 As mentioned in the first section of this chapter, this division also distinguished the foci IR and African studies developed, respectively, for describing the link between norms and order formation: while African studies interrogated the consequences of international norms on order within the state, IR was more interested in the formation of international orders.

2 Crafting an African anti-coup manual

1 In fact, the assassination of Togo's President Sylvanus Olympio just before the inauguration of the OAU in January 1963 is said to have defined the preparatory debates on the norms and principles of the organization to be established, and that strict adherence to the principle of non-interference was its most crucial

outcome (van Walraven 1996: 129; Makinda & Okumu 2008: 12).

2 R. A. Akinele (1988: 73) identifies regime changes through coups and the question of which norms should guide recognition and representation at the OAU as one of four 'grand debates' that shaped the organization.

3 Apart from these two examples, Kufuor (2002) also lists the following situations as having sparked controversies as to which delegation should be recognized at OAU meetings: the 1980 coup by Samuel Doe against William R. Tolbert in Liberia, the 1982 coup in Chad, the 1989 coup in Liberia in which Doe was in turn toppled by Charles Taylor, and the 1997 coup in Sierra Leone against President Kabbah. One could add the 1987 assassination of Thomas Sankara in Burkina Faso by his compatriot Blaise Compaoré (AFP 1988).

4 This list is based on newspaper articles found in the Factiva database, official OAU documents, and secondary literature (Hartmann 2005). The Factiva search was based on the keywords 'OAU' and 'coup'.

5 In the Factiva search and in the OAU documents, I found evidence for such missions to Burundi (1993 and 1996), Lesotho (1994), the Comoros (1995), Niger (1996 and 1999), Guinea-Bissau (1998), the Comoros (1999), and Côte d'Ivoire (1999). As has often been criticized, these reactions were selective: the 1992 coup in Sierra Leone, for instance, as well as Sani Abacha's 1993 coup in Nigeria, did not provoke comparable reactions (see also Hartmann 2005: 215). In this regard, Burundi's then President Pierre Buyoya, for instance, noted 'two ways of implementing' OAU principles. So, he rejected the strong OAU reaction against his own coup not by questioning the OAU's legitimacy as judge on 'good order', but by demanding 'that OAU principles be applied in the same way [to] everybody' (AFP 1997).

6 The subcommittee suggested the following reaction mechanisms: temporary suspension from the OAU, the possibility of withholding recognition for any would-be or *de facto* government, and the imposition of 'carefully targeted sanctions' against the perpetrators of coups (OAU Secretariat 1999: 3).

7 The subcommittee initially proposed a qualitative difference between these scenarios. In cases of military coups, mercenary interventions, and armed dissidents, the Secretary-General was to be obliged to issue an automatic and immediate condemnation, which would then trigger a meeting of the Central Organ. In all other cases, the Central Organ was only to convene upon request by the OAU Chairman, the Secretary-General, or any OAU member state (OAU 2000b: 12).

8 The meetings covered in the available documents are: a meeting of independent experts on the Draft Charter on Democracy, Elections and Governance (21–23 November 2005, Addis Ababa); a meeting of government experts (3–5 April 2006, Addis Ababa); a first ministerial meeting (6–7 April 2006, Addis Ababa); a meeting of legal experts (25–28 April 2006, Addis Ababa); a second ministerial meeting (9–10 June 2006, Brazzaville), and a meeting of the Committee of African Jurists (19–21 December 2006, Addis Ababa).

9 Interview, UNDP/UNECA official, 26 April 2013, Addis Ababa.

10 The Draft Charter nevertheless prohibited the '[a]mendment or revision of constitutions and

legal instruments, contrary to the provisions of the constitution of the State Party concerned, to prolong the tenure of office for the incumbent government' (AU 2006d: Art. 25(5)). An earlier version of the Charter, unfortunately without date, entailed a provision against the 'manipulation of constitutions and legal instruments for prolongation of tenure of office by incumbent regime' (AU 2005b: 11).

11 Interview, UNDP/UNECA official, 26 April 2013, Addis Ababa.

12 The Charter also lists the five definitions of unconstitutional changes of government as inter alia definitions. Additions in the future are thus possible.

13 As of June 2020, 46 member states have signed the Charter and 34 have deposited their instruments of ratification; six member states have neither signed nor ratified the Charter (Botswana, Egypt, Eritrea, Libya, Morocco, and Tanzania) (AU 2019).

14 The wording of the report was actually much more consequential: 'The AU should not only have a "zero tolerance" policy on coups d'Etat; it should also show the same firmness with regard to transgressions in democratic standards which, if persistent and repeated, could lead to unconstitutional changes of Government. In fact, the relevant AU authorities have to fully play their prevention role, relying on the Union instruments according to which the Member States are committed to abide by democratic principles. Any approach centred solely on the repression of coups would not be in accordance with the relevant AU instruments and would only be of limited effectiveness, since the prevention of coups largely resided in the quality of democratic life in any country and the constitutional functioning of its institutions' (AU Commission 2010: 11).

15 In the Malabo Protocol, adopted in 2014, the AU Assembly extended the jurisdiction of the yet-to-be-established African Court of Justice and Human Rights (ACJHR). In its definition of the 'crime of unconstitutional changes of government', the Protocol adds a sixth scenario to what counts as an unconstitutional change of government: modifications to the electoral laws in the last six months before an election without the consent of the majority of political actors (AU 2014b: Art. 28E (1f)). This was directly taken from the Economic Community of West African States (ECOWAS) Protocol on Democracy and Good Governance (ECOWAS 2001). However, as of June 2020, the Protocol has been signed by 15 member states only and is therefore not in force.

16 With the adoption of the Malabo Protocol (see note 15 above), the legalization even moved one step further in that unconstitutional changes of government were also criminalized (AU 2014b: Art. 28E; Kemp & Kinyunyu 2017).

3 What 'crise malgache'?

1 The Army corps for personnel and administrative and technical services (CAPSAT, *Corps d'armée des personnels et des services administratifs et techniques*) comprises about 600 military personnel; only an estimated 100 of them actively supported the

mutiny (ICG 2010b: 5; Ramasy 2012: 83).
2 Interview, member of the mouvance Zafy, 14 March 2014, Antananarivo; interview, member of the mouvance Zafy, 22 March 2014, Antananarivo.
3 In June 2006, the 3FN nevertheless approached UN Secretary-General Kofi Annan, reminding him that the AU Central Organ in 2003 had, inter alia, demanded the convention of a Round Table 'to address outstanding issues related to human rights, the rule of law as well as the issue of political detainees' (3FN 2006). Like most of the group's attempts to mobilize international support, this effort too remained in vain.
4 Interview, advisor to the AU special envoy, 17 February 2014, Antananarivo.
5 A 2005–2008 Afrobarometer survey, for instance, found that in 2008, the perceived efficiency of local councils had sharply decreased in comparison to 2005 (Afrobarometer 2008). The handling of resources in particular became a major bone of contention (Razafindrakoto et al. 2009: 7). More importantly, however, the survey points towards an increasing distrust and lack of access to local governance structures: only 28 per cent of the respondents felt 'adequately informed about the policies of local authorities', while only '20% of Madagascans claim to be satisfied with the measures taken to ensure that the general public is involved in decisions at a local level' (Razafindrakoto et al. 2009: 8). More than '50% of Madagascans feel that they are not in a position to express a view on these issues' (Razafindrakoto et al. 2009: 7).
6 In a Radio France Internationale (RFI) interview in May 2009, Ravalomanana answered the presenter's question on what his principal error might have been: 'It is this which I don't understand. Because I have done my best to serve the country for the past seven years. We have constructed 10,000 km of paved roads. With regard to education, in 2003 only 63% of Malagasy children were at school, in 2008 it was 92%' [author's translation] (RFI 2009b).
7 In an interview with RFI, the US ambassador Niels Marquardt commented on the pillaging as follows: 'The moment is opportune to listen to what the population says … It is necessary to react with better governance … The choice of shops burned was a clear message, private and public affairs should not be mixed up' [author's translation] (RFI 2009a; see also Galibert 2009a: 144).

4 The intervention scenario

1 Interview, former OIF official, 10 March 2014, Antananarivo; interview, member of the mouvance Zafy, 22 March 2014, Antananarivo.
2 See, for instance, cable from the US embassy in Antananarivo, 8 April 2009, 09ANTANANARIVO261; interview, party leader, 12 March 2014, Antananarivo.
3 Interview, member of the mouvance Ravalomanana, 3 April 2014, Antananarivo.
4 Interview, party leader, 12 March 2014, Antananarivo.
5 Interview, party leader, 12 March 2014, Antananarivo; interview, member of the mouvance Zafy, 14 March 2014, Antananarivo; interview, member of the

NOTES

mouvance Ravalomanana, 3 April 2014, Antananarivo.
6 Interview, member of the HAT, 1 April 2014, Antananarivo.
7 Interview, member of the mouvance Zafy, 14 March 2014, Antananarivo; interview, member of the mouvance Zafy, 22 March 2014, Antananarivo.
8 Interview, former OIF official, 10 March 2014, Antananarivo; interview, party leader, 12 March 2014, Antananarivo; interview, member of the mouvance Zafy, 14 March 2014, Antananarivo; interview, member of the mouvance Zafy, 22 March 2014, Antananarivo.
9 Interview, party leader, 12 March 2014, Antananarivo.
10 Interview, advisor to the AU special envoy, 17 February 2014, Antananarivo; interview, member of the mouvance Ratsiraka, 21 February 2014, Antananarivo.
11 Interview, member of the mouvance Zafy, 14 March 2014, Antananarivo.
12 Interview, member of the mouvance Ravalomanana, 3 April 2014, Antananarivo.
13 See also cable from the US embassy in Maputo, 27 August 2009, 09MAPUTO960.
14 Interview, party leader, 12 March 2014, Antananarivo; interview, member of the mouvance Ravalomanana, 14 March 2014, Antananarivo.
15 Interview, member of the mouvance Zafy, 14 March 2014, Antananarivo; interview, member of the mouvance Zafy, 22 March 2014, Antananarivo; interview, member of the HAT, 1 April 2014, Antananarivo.
16 Interview, member of the mouvance Zafy, 14 March 2014, Antananarivo; interview, member of the mouvance Zafy, 22 March 2014, Antananarivo.

17 Interview, member of the mouvance Zafy, 14 March 2014, Antananarivo; interview, party leader, 31 March 2014, Antananarivo; interview, member of the HAT, 1 April 2014, Antananarivo.
18 Interview, member of the mouvance Ravalomanana, 3 April 2014, Antananarivo.
19 Skype interview, former UN official, 27 August 2014.
20 Interview, South African jurist, 15 May 2014, Pretoria.
21 Interview, member of the mouvance Zafy, 22 March 2014, Antananarivo. Ratsiraka and Ravalomanana also knew Chissano from the 2002 negotiations in Dakar, yet none of my interviewees explicitly mentioned this.
22 Interview, member of the mouvance Ratsiraka, 21 February 2014, Antananarivo; interview, member of the mouvance Ratsiraka, 11 March 2014, Antananarivo; interview, member of the mouvance Zafy, 14 March 2014, Antananarivo; interview, member of the mouvance Zafy, 22 March 2014, Antananarivo.
23 Interview, member of the mouvance Ravalomanana, 14 March 2014, Antananarivo; interview, member of the mouvance Ravalomanana, 3 April 2014, Antananarivo; cable from the US embassy in Antananarivo, 16 July 2009, 09ANTANANARIVO526.
24 Interview, former OIF official, 10 March 2014, Antananarivo; interview, member of the mouvance Ratsiraka, 11 March 2014, Antananarivo; cable from the US embassy in Antananarivo, 8 April 2009, 09ANTANANARIVO261.
25 See, for instance, cable from the US embassy in Maputo, 14 August 2009, 09MAPUTO916,

in which former Mozambican Foreign Minister Leonardo Simão explained how Ravalomanana used his contacts to the King of Swaziland. See also cable from the US embassy in Maseru, 19 June 2009, 09MASERU203; cable from the US embassy in Gaborone, 19 June 2009, 09GABORONE488.

26 Interview, party leader, 31 March 2014, Antananarivo.
27 Interview, member of the HAT, 1 April 2014, Antananarivo.
28 Interview, member of the HAT, 1 April 2014, Antananarivo.
29 In April 2009, Rajoelina was invited to Brussels for the UN donor conference on Somalia and to New York for a UN conference on the global financial crisis. As later in the case of the invitation to South Africa for the ANC's 100th anniversary in January 2012, Rajoelina used both invitations by interpreting them as a sign of international recognition (*L'Express de Madagascar* 2009f). Interview, member of the diplomatic corps, 2 April 2014, Antananarivo.
30 Interview, member of the HAT, 1 April 2014, Antananarivo; interview, party leader, 12 March 2014, Antananarivo.
31 Interview, member of the mouvance Zafy, 14 March 2014, Antananarivo.
32 Interview, member of the mouvance Ratsiraka, 21 February 2014, Antananarivo; interview, former OIF official, 10 March 2014, Antananarivo; interview, former member of the diplomatic corps, 8 July 2015, Paris.
33 Interview, former OIF official, 10 March 2014, Antananarivo; interview, former member of the diplomatic corps, 8 July 2015, Paris. This is also reflected in several US cables. Then US ambassador Niels Marquardt, for instance, noted in September 2009 after he had met Rajoelina: 'Sitting alone, TGV [Rajoelina] opened the meeting with a friendly but naive appeal for international support for elections that he said must be organized as soon as possible (...). TGV remains an exceedingly erratic, unsteady decision-maker (and implementer), as witnessed by the continuing zigzagging over filling the prime ministerial slot'. Cable from the US embassy in Antananarivo, 11 September 2009, 09ANTANANARIVO642.
34 Interview, party leader, 12 March 2014, Antananarivo; interview, member of the mouvance Ravalomanana, 3 April 2014, Antananarivo.
35 Interview, member of the mouvance Ravalomanana, 3 April 2014, Antananarivo.
36 Interview, member of the mouvance Zafy, 14 March 2014, Antananarivo; interview, member of the mouvance Zafy, 22 March 2014, Antananarivo.
37 Interview, member of the mouvance Ratsiraka, 21 February 2014, Antananarivo; interview, member of the HAT, 6 March 2014, Antananarivo; interview, member of the mouvance Zafy, 14 March 2014, Antananarivo; interview, member of the HAT, 1 April 2014, Antananarivo.
38 Interview, party leader, 12 March 2014, Antananarivo; interview, member of the mouvance Zafy, 14 March 2014, Antananarivo (on the emergent 'shadow state' during the transition, see ICG 2010a; ICG 2010b).
39 Interview, member of the mouvance Zafy, 14 March 2014, Antananarivo; interview, member of the mouvance Zafy, 22 March 2014, Antananarivo.
40 Interview, member of the mouvance Zafy, 14 March 2014, Antananarivo.
41 Even before this date, the PSC had already held three sessions on

the case of Madagascar and sent the AU Commissioner for Peace and Security, Ramtane Lamamra, as well as two special envoys to Madagascar in order to assess the situation.
42 Like the AU, SADC had sent three fact-finding missions to Antananarivo even before the official transfer of power.
43 Interview, SADC official, 20 May 2014, Gaborone.
44 The Cotonou Agreement prescribes political values to which the signatories are bound. In case a signatory infringes these 'fundamental principles', EU development cooperation is suspended. The so-called 'appropriate measures' taken in response may include individual targeted sanctions. A consultation process is consequently set up in which a timetable and benchmarks for the return to 'normal relations' are jointly agreed upon. Progress in implementing these decisions is regularly monitored. Subject to an assessment and decision of the EU Council, the suspension is either upheld or withdrawn (Mbangu 2005).
45 Interview, former member of the diplomatic corps, 8 July 2015, Paris.
46 Interview, former member of the diplomatic corps, 8 July 2015, Paris.
47 Interview, member of the diplomatic corps, 26 February 2014, Antananarivo.
48 Interview, member of the diplomatic corps, 29 April 2014, Pretoria.
49 Interview, SADC official, 14 May 2014, Johannesburg; interview, SADC official, 20 May 2014, Gaborone.
50 This initial mistrust towards SADC's potential to be a mediator in the Malagasy crisis is also reflected in the cables from the US embassies in the region. See, for instance, cable from the US embassy in Antananarivo, 25 June 2009, 09ANTANANARIVO477, which reports a meeting with South Africa's ambassador to Madagascar. See also cable from the US embassy in Maseru, 19 June 2009, 09MASERU203; cable from the US embassy in Gaborone, 19 June 2009, 09GABORONE488.
51 Interview, SADC liaison officer, 5 March 2014, Antananarivo; interview, SADC liaison officer, 31 March 2014, Antananarivo.
52 Interview, member of the diplomatic corps, 24 February 2014, Antananarivo; interview, member of the diplomatic corps, 26 February 2014, Antananarivo. A more balanced account is surprisingly given by then US ambassador to Madagascar Niels Marquardt; see cable from the US embassy in Antananarivo, 8 April 2009, 09ANTANANARIVO261.
53 Cable from the US embassy in Antananarivo, 8 April 2009, 09ANTANANARIVO261; interview, member of the diplomatic corps, 24 February 2014, Antananarivo; interview, member of the diplomatic corps, 26 February 2014, Antananarivo; interview, former member of the diplomatic corps, 8 July 2015, Paris.
54 Reflecting the waves of attention, this meant eight meetings in 2009, four meetings in 2010, two meetings in 2011, zero meetings in 2012, four meetings in 2013, and one meeting in 2014, when Madagascar was officially readmitted to the AU.
55 Interview, AU official, 7 May 2013, Addis Ababa.
56 Cable from the US embassy in Antananarivo, 25 June 2009, 09ANTANANARIVO477.
57 Interview, SADC official, 19 May 2014, Gaborone.
58 See, for instance, cable from the US embassy in Gaborone, 19 June 2009, 09GABORONE488; cable

from the US embassy in Maseru, 19 June 2009, 09MASERU203; cable from the US embassy in Antananarivo, 25 June 2009, 09ANTANANARIVO477.
59 That attendance at summit meetings did not always translate into active participation is reflected in one of the US cables. South Africa's then ambassador Monaisa mentioned that 'he felt sorry for the way Ravalomanana had been treated at the Summit. He had been invited to a waiting room, where he worked on remarks he planned to deliver if invited into the plenary. In the event, he was never invited in, and so spent hours waiting while never seeing the heads of state'. Cable from the US embassy in Antananarivo, 25 June 2009, 09ANTANANARIVO477.
60 Until the signing of the Maputo II agreement, there was another officer of the Organ Directorate partly covering Madagascar. Due to financial constraints and an overall shortage of professional staff at the Directorate, however, this was soon scaled down. Interview, SADC official, 20 May 2014, Gaborone.
61 Interview, SADC official, 20 May 2014, Gaborone.
62 Skype interview, former UN official, 27 August 2014.
63 Cable from the US embassy in Antananarivo, 7 October 2009, 09ANTANANARIVO707. In the Malagasy press, the arrival of 48 diplomats was also announced as the arrival of an 'armada', reflecting the already heated and confrontational atmosphere right before the meeting (*Midi Madagasikara* 2009c).
64 Apparently, Japan and the US sent, where possible, their respective ambassadors to Madagascar to participate in ICG-M meetings in Addis Ababa. This, however, remained the diplomatic exception. Interview, member of the diplomatic corps, 26 February 2014, Antananarivo. See also cable from the US embassy in Antananarivo, 16 July 2009, 09ANTANANARIVO526.
65 Interview, member of the diplomatic corps, 24 February 2014, Antananarivo; interview, member of the diplomatic corps, 26 February 2014, Antananarivo.
66 Interview, UNDP official, 11 February 2014, Antananarivo; interview, EU officials, 13 February 2014, Antananarivo; interview, EU official, 21 February 2014, Antananarivo; interview, member of the diplomatic corps, 24 February 2014, Antananarivo; interview, member of the diplomatic corps, 26 February 2014, Antananarivo; interview, member of the diplomatic corps, 28 February 2014, Antananarivo.
67 Interview, EU official, 25 May 2011, Addis Ababa; interview, former OIF official, 16 March 2014, Antananarivo.
68 Interview, former OIF official, 16 March 2014, Antananarivo. See also the account of this situation in the cable from the US embassy in Antananarivo, 22 July 2009, 09ANTANANARIVO548.
69 Cable from the US embassy in Addis Ababa, 7 January 2010, 10ADDISABABA12.
70 For instance, several statements by the ICG-M entailed paragraphs about the status of sanctions and the resumption of development aid that effectively contradicted many of its members' own policies (see ICG-M 2009; ICG-M 2011).
71 Before the appointment of Chissano, Themba Dlamini, former Prime Minister of Swaziland, was sent as special envoy to Antananarivo. However, since SADC's pro-Ravalomanana

position did not include the option of mediation, his presence and his contribution to the intervention dynamics of the first weeks were in fact minimal. See also cable from the US embassy in Antananarivo, 18 May 2009, 09ANTANANARIVO353.
72 Cable from the US embassy in Antananarivo, 8 April 2009, 09ANTANANARIVO261.
73 Cable from the US embassy in Antananarivo, 8 April 2009, 09ANTANANARIVO261.
74 Cable from the US embassy in Antananarivo, 8 April 2009, 09ANTANANARIVO261.
75 See, for instance, cable from the US embassy in Antananarivo, 16 June 2009, 09ANTANANARIVO439.
76 See, for instance, cable from the US embassy in Antananarivo, 3 April 2009, 09ANTANANARIVO247; cable from the US embassy in Antananarivo, 8 April 2009, 09ANTANANARIVO261.
77 Interview, AU official, 11 April 2012, Addis Ababa; interview, advisor to the AU special envoy, 17 February 2014, Antananarivo.
78 Interview, former OIF official, 10 March 2014, Antananarivo; interview, OIF official, 25 February 2014, Antananarivo; Skype interview, former UN official, 27 August 2014.
79 Skype interview, former UN official, 27 August 2014; Skype interview, former expert ICG, 14 October 2014.
80 Interview, advisor to the AU special envoy, 17 February 2014, Antananarivo.
81 Interview, advisor to the AU special envoy, 17 February 2014, Antananarivo.
82 I did not find evidence that any of the four mediators had suggested a fundamental departure from the dominant focus on an intra-elite power-sharing deal and transitional elections. Even though the question of whom to include in the negotiations was contested, none of the mediators propagated, for instance, the equal inclusion of civil society actors, representatives from the regions, or a quota for women. Moreover, I did not find evidence for attempts to integrate the focused mediation into a more comprehensive framework of conflict resolution, as the Carter Center-led mediation did in Venezuela in the early 2000s (McCoy & Diez 2011: 34).
83 Interview, advisor to the AU special envoy, 17 February 2014, Antananarivo.
84 Interview, advisor to the AU special envoy, 17 February 2014, Antananarivo.
85 Interview, former OIF official, 16 March 2014, Antananarivo. During the post-electoral crisis of 2001/2002, both OAU Secretary-General Amara Essy and the then Senegalese President Abdoulaye Wade, who led the negotiations on behalf of the OAU, were explicitly recognized as *ray amandreny* (Rajaonah 2002; Nativel & Rajaonah 2007).
86 This was apparently also the rationale behind SADC's selection of Chissano. Interview, former OIF official, 10 March 2014, Antananarivo. See also cable from the US embassy in Antananarivo, 25 June 2009, 09ANTANANARIVO477; cable from the US embassy in Maputo, 14 August 2009, 09MAPUTO916.
87 Interview, member of the mouvance Zafy, 14 March 2014, Antananarivo; interview, former OIF official, 16 March 2014, Antananarivo; interview, member of the mouvance Ravalomanana, 3 April 2014, Antananarivo.

88 Interview, member of ESCOPOL, 12 March 2014, Antananarivo; interview, member of the mouvance Zafy, 14 March 2014, Antananarivo; interview, member of ESCOPOL, 21 March 2014, Antananarivo; interview, member of the mouvance Ravalomanana, 3 April 2014, Antananarivo; interview, advisor to mediator Chissano, 29 May 2014, Pretoria.

89 The accounts of several interviewees reflected this: they merged high respect and yet a certain degree of mockery about the 'therapist' Chissano, as depicted by one interviewee. Interview, member of ESCOPOL, 12 March 2014, Antananarivo; interview, member of the mouvance Zafy, 14 March 2014, Antananarivo; interview, member of ESCOPOL, 21 March 2014, Antananarivo; interview, member of the mouvance Ravalomanana, 3 April 2014, Antananarivo.

90 Interview, advisor to mediator Chissano, 29 May 2014, Pretoria; interview, member of the diplomatic corps, 29 April 2014, Pretoria.

91 Interview, former OIF official, 10 March 2014, Antananarivo.

92 Interview, advisor to mediator Chissano, 29 May 2014, Pretoria.

93 As explained by one interviewee, this decision was based on the observation that all Malagasies were biased in one way or another. Even interpreters were biased. SADC, however, wanted to stay neutral. The decision not to work with local interlocutors thus once again underscores the mutual suspicion that initially defined SADC's relations to the Malagasy parties, as explicated in the preceding section. Interview, SADC official, 20 May 2014, Gaborone.

94 Interview, advisor to mediator Chissano, 29 May 2014, Pretoria.

95 Interview, former OIF official, 16 March 2014, Antananarivo; cable from the US embassy in Antananarivo, 22 July 2009, 09ANTANANARIVO548.

96 See also cable from the US embassy in Antananarivo, 25 June 2009, 09ANTANANARIVO477, in which the then South African ambassador Monaisa noted a 'tension between SADC and the AU over SADC's takeover of the mediation. (…) The AU would remain engaged but had no choice but to accept this change'.

97 Interview, AU official, 10 April 2012, Addis Ababa; Skype interview, former UN official, 24 August 2014. See also cable from the US embassy in Addis Ababa, 17 December 2009, 09ADDISABABA2952.

98 Interview, former OIF official, 10 March 2014, Antananarivo; interview, member of the mouvance Ravalomanana, 3 April 2014, Antananarivo.

99 Interview, member of the HAT, 1 April 2014, Antananarivo; interview, member of the mouvance Ravalomanana, 3 April 2014, Antananarivo.

100 Interview, former OIF official, 10 March 2014, Antananarivo.

101 Interview, member of the diplomatic corps, 29 April 2014, Pretoria; interview, SADC official, 14 May 2014, Johannesburg; interview, advisor to mediator Chissano, 29 May 2014, Pretoria.

102 Interview, member of the diplomatic corps, 29 April 2014, Pretoria; interview, SADC official, 19 May 2014, Gaborone; interview, SADC official, 20 May 2014, Gaborone.

103 Interview, SADC official, 19 May 2014, Gaborone; interview,

SADC official, 20 May 2014, Gaborone.
104 See, for instance, cable from the US embassy in Addis Ababa, 7 January 2010, 10ADDISABABA12. See also cable from the US embassy in Paris, 25 February 2010, 10PARIS232, in which the Africa Advisor at the French Presidency is cited saying that Chissano is 'not displaying the requisite energy' and that his 'failure to capture in Maputo III elements such as this that the parties had earlier accepted was a major error (...) and provided Rajoelina ample grounds for considering Maputo III a repudiation of the earlier agreements'.
105 Cable from the US embassy in Maputo, 22 January 2010, 10MAPUTO75. That the French policy subverted his mediation strategy, however, continued to be an issue. In his report to the SADC summit in August 2010, he complained that France, Senegal, and the OIF were the ones immediately appreciating Rajoelina's decision of May 2010 to dissolve his mouvance and to launch a unilateral transitional process (Chissano 2010: 9).
106 Interview, member of the mouvance Zafy, 14 March 2014, Antananarivo; interview, member of the mouvance Ravalomanana, 14 March 2014, Antananarivo; interview, former OIF official, 16 March 2014, Antananarivo.

5 The logic of intervention

1 As criticized by the mouvance Ravalomanana, this article was indeed copied from *ordonnance 2010-010* of October 2010 with which the HAT had set up the transitional parliament (République de Madagascar 2010a). The mouvance thus commented, 'This removes any meaning and foundation from Article 7 [actually Art. 9] of the roadmap, which states "The Transitional Parliament shall oversee the work of the Transitional Government"' [author's translation] (Mouvance Ravalomanana 2011a: 12).
2 In most of these suggestions, reconciliation and transition therefore became almost synonymous processes. Transition was not merely the path to elections or the formation of a new government, but rather the *search* for 'state and institutional structures guaranteeing the equitable sharing of power and wealth with mutual respect for diversity in unity' [author's translation] (Mouvance Zafy 2009c). As stipulated in a preparatory note for mediator Chissano, 'national reconciliation begins in the architecture of the transition' [author's translation] (Mouvance Zafy 2009e).
3 This has already been evidenced by the way in which the SADC mediation team presented the first version of the roadmap to the potential signatories as well as the wider Malagasy public: as a largely uncontroversial document. The press statement thus noted with satisfaction that the majority of the party leaders had reacted in a similarly uncontroversial way (*Madagascar Tribune* 2011g).
4 Even party members willing to sign the roadmap did not recall having contributed to its content or having been approached by the

mediators to make substantive contributions. Interview, member of the HAT, 18 February 2014, Antananarivo; interview, member of the mouvance Zafy, 14 March 2014, Antananarivo; interview, member of ESCOPOL, 21 March 2014, Antananarivo; interview, party leader, 31 March 2014, Antananarivo; interview, member of the mouvance Ravalomanana, 3 April 2014, Antananarivo.
5 Interview, SADC liaison officer, 31 March 2014, Antananarivo.
6 The complaint also noted that 'several of the most controversial and repressive members of the former government were simply reappointed to their positions' and demanded an 'arbitration' by the SADC liaison office (Mouvance Ravalomanana 2011b: 6).
7 Interview, party leader, 12 March 2014, Antananarivo.
8 Interview, member of CNOSC, 13 March 2014, Antananarivo; interview, member of CNOSC, 17 March 2014, Antananarivo.
9 Interview, member of the diplomatic corps, 26 February 2014, Antananarivo; Skype interview, former UN official, 27 August 2014; Skype interview, former member of the diplomatic corps, 6 November 2014.
10 Interview, member of the mouvance Ratsiraka, 21 February 2014, Antananarivo; interview, member of the mouvance Zafy, 22 March 2014, Antananarivo; interview, member of the mouvance Ravalomanana, 3 April 2014, Antananarivo.
11 Interview, AU liaison officer, 21 February 2014, Antananarivo; interview, SADC liaison officer, 5 March 2014, Antananarivo; interview, member of the diplomatic corps, 2 April 2014, Antananarivo; interview, SADC official, 14 May 2014, Johannesburg.
12 The signatory parties were ESCOPOL, Rajoelina's TGV, the Union of Democrats and Republicans for Change (*Union des démocrates et républicains pour le changement*, UDR-C), the Movement for Democracy in Madagascar (*Mouvement pour la démocratie à Madagascar*, MDM), the HPM, the so-called Other Sensibilities (*Autres sensibilités*, AS), MONIMA-Uamad – a faction of the historical Nationalist and Independent Movement of Madagascar (*Madagasikara otronin'ny Malagasy*, MONIMA) led by Monja Roindefo – and AREMA.
13 Interview, member of ESCOPOL, 21 March 2014, Antananarivo.
14 Interview, member of ESCOPOL, 21 March 2014, Antananarivo.
15 Interview, advisor to mediator Chissano, 29 May 2014, Pretoria.
16 Interview, party leader, 12 March 2014, Antananarivo.
17 Interview, EKAR official, 17 March 2014, Antananarivo; interview, member of CNOSC, 17 March 2014, Antananarivo; interview, expert KMF/CNOE, 4 April 2014, Antananarivo. A Roadmap Implementation Monitoring and Control Committee (*Comité de suivi et de contrôle de la mise en œuvre de la Feuille de route*, CSC) was set up only in July 2012 (*Midi Madagasikara* 2012a). It never played a significant role since and was split over questions of leadership (*Midi Madagasikara* 2012b).
18 Interview, member of the mouvance Zafy, 22 March 2014, Antananarivo.
19 Interview, member of the mouvance Ratsiraka, 21 February 2014, Antananarivo; interview, member of the mouvance Zafy, 22 March 2014, Antananarivo; interview, member of the

mouvance Ravalomanana, 3 April 2014, Antananarivo.
20 Interview, gendarmerie, 18 March 2014, Antananarivo; interview, member of ESCOPOL, 21 March 2014, Antananarivo; interview, member of the mouvance Zafy, 15 April 2014, Antananarivo.
21 Interview, member of the mouvance Zafy, 15 April 2014, Antananarivo.
22 Interview, member of the HAT, 18 February 2014, Antananarivo; interview, member of the mouvance Ratsiraka, 21 February 2014, Antananarivo; interview, party leader, 12 March 2014, Antananarivo.
23 Interview, party leader, 12 March 2014, Antananarivo.
24 Interview, party leader, 12 March 2014, Antananarivo; interview, member of ESCOPOL, 21 March 2014, Antananarivo.
25 Interview, party leader, 31 March 2014, Antananarivo.
26 Interview, EU officials, 13 February 2014, Antananarivo; interview, member of the diplomatic corps, 26 February 2014, Antananarivo; interview, SADC liaison officer, 31 March 2014, Antananarivo; interview, advisor to mediator Chissano, 29 May 2014, Pretoria; interview, former member of the diplomatic corps, 8 July 2015, Paris.
27 Interview, member of the diplomatic corps, 24 February 2014, Antananarivo; interview, AU official, 13 May 2013, Addis Ababa.
28 Interview, member of the diplomatic corps, 24 February 2014, Antananarivo; interview, member of the diplomatic corps, 2 April 2014, Antananarivo.
29 Interview, member of the diplomatic corps, 26 February 2014, Antananarivo; interview, member of the diplomatic corps, 21 March 2014, Antananarivo; interview, member of the diplomatic corps, 2 April 2014, Antananarivo.
30 Interview, UNDP official, 11 February 2014, Antananarivo; interview, OIF official, 25 February 2014, Antananarivo; Skype interview, former UN official, 27 August 2014.
31 Interview, party leader, 31 March 2014, Antananarivo.
32 Interview, SADC liaison officer, 5 March 2014, Antananarivo; interview, SADC liaison officer, 31 March 2014, Antananarivo.
33 Interview, member of the mouvance Zafy, 14 March 2014, Antananarivo; interview, member of the mouvance Zafy, 22 March 2014, Antananarivo.
34 Interview, member of PFNOSC, 20 February 2014, Antananarivo; interview, member of CNOSC, 17 March 2014, Antananarivo; interview, member of the gendarmerie, 18 March 2014, Antananarivo.
35 Interview, SADC official, 19 May 2014, Gaborone; interview, SADC official, 20 May 2014, Gaborone.
36 In fact, reflecting the above-mentioned division between the Malagasy parties' demand for an accessible international mediator and SADC's actual commitment, it is also telling that apart from Chissano, both the HAT and several other parties to the negotiations had demanded the establishment of such an office for a long time as well (Chissano 2011a: 1; Mouvance Zafy 2010b).
37 Interview, SADC liaison officer, 5 March 2014, Antananarivo; interview, SADC liaison officer, 31 March 2014, Antananarivo; interview, SADC official, 14 May 2014, Johannesburg.
38 Interview, AU liaison officer, 21 February 2014, Antananarivo;

interview, SADC liaison officer, 5 March 2014, Antananarivo; interview, SADC liaison officer, 31 March 2014, Antananarivo.
39 Interview, SADC official, 14 May 2014, Johannesburg.
40 Interview, SADC official, 14 May 2014, Johannesburg.
41 Several members of the diplomatic community described SADC as a child that needs to be enabled to carry out its task. Interview, EU official, 21 February 2014, Antananarivo; interview, member of the diplomatic corps, 24 February 2014, Antananarivo; interview, member of the diplomatic corps, 26 February 2014, Antananarivo.
42 Interview, EU officials, 13 February 2014, Antananarivo; interview, member of the diplomatic corps, 24 February 2014, Antananarivo; interview, member of the diplomatic corps, 29 April 2014, Pretoria.
43 Interview, party leader, 12 March 2014, Antananarivo; interview, member of ESCOPOL, 21 March 2014, Antananarivo; interview, member of the HAT, 1 April 2014, Antananarivo.
44 Interview, UNDP official, 11 February 2014, Antananarivo; interview, OIF official, 25 February 2014, Antananarivo; interview, member of the diplomatic corps, 26 February 2014, Antananarivo; interview, member of the diplomatic corps, 3 March 2014, Antananarivo.
45 Interview, member of the diplomatic corps, 26 February 2014, Antananarivo.
46 Interview, expert ECES, 3 March 2014, Antananarivo; interview, CENI-T official, 6 March 2014, Antananarivo.
47 See www.mg.undp.org/content/madagascar/fr/home/operations/projects/democratic_governance/projet-d_appui--au-cycle-electoral-2012--2014--a--madagascar--.html (last access 20 December 2017).
48 Interview, expert SADC CNGO, 19 May 2014, Gaborone; interview, expert KMF/CNOE, 4 April 2014, Antananarivo.
49 Interview, CENI-T official, 6 March 2014, Antananarivo.
50 Camille Vital later noted that in contrast to the supporters of other candidates, his 'friend' is neither the Central Bank, Jirama (the national electricity company), Aid Mad, or BNI-Madagascar, nor are his funds coming from illegal rosewood traffic or the public treasury (*Madagascar Tribune* 2013d). This underlines how openly issues of illegal economic activities were discussed in public.
51 Interview, party leader, 21 February 2014, Antananarivo; interview, member of ESCOPOL, 2 April 2014, Antananarivo.
52 In early 2011, the conditions for free and fair elections had led to two strongly diverging assessments from the OIF and the UN, respectively: while the first proposed that elections could be held in four months, the latter insisted that at least 11 months would be required (Marcus 2011).
53 The pro-Ravalomanana camp undertook several attempts to lobby international support against the election results, though in vain (*Madagascar Tribune* 2014b; *Madagascar Tribune* 2014c; *Madagascar Tribune* 2014d). Interview, SADC liaison officer, 31 March 2014, Antananarivo.
54 Interview, member of the diplomatic corps, 24 February 2014, Antananarivo; interview, member of the diplomatic corps, 26 February 2014, Antananarivo; interview, expert ECES, 3 March 2014, Antananarivo.
55 Interview, FFM official, 26 March 2014, Antananarivo.

6 Reproducing old, legitimating new orders

1 Interview, member of CCOC, 25 March 2014, Antananarivo.
2 It is an irony of history that this wording is in fact reminiscent of what the AU Assembly had concluded in early 2003, when it finally recognised Ravalomanana as president (AU Assembly 2003).
3 Despite great efforts, I could not obtain a copy of the official register of parties.
4 Interview, EU officials, 13 February 2014, Antananarivo; interview, member of the diplomatic corps, 26 February 2014, Antananarivo; interview, member of the diplomatic corps, 28 February 2014, Antananarivo; interview, member of the diplomatic corps, 21 March 2014, Antananarivo; interview, member of the diplomatic corps, 2 April 2014, Antananarivo.
5 Interview, member of the diplomatic corps, 2 April 2014, Antananarivo.
6 Interview, SADC liaison officer, 5 March 2014, Antananarivo; interview, SADC official, 20 May 2014, Gaborone.
7 Interview, SADC liaison officer, 5 March 2014, Antananarivo; interview, member of the gendarmerie, 18 March 2014, Antananarivo; interview, SADC liaison officer, 31 March 2014, Antananarivo.
8 Interview, member of the diplomatic corps, 28 May 2014, Pretoria.
9 Interview, member of the diplomatic corps, 3 March 2014, Antananarivo; interview, member of the diplomatic corps, 28 May 2014, Pretoria.
10 Interview, member of the diplomatic corps, 28 May 2014, Pretoria.
11 Interview, member of the diplomatic corps, 3 March 2014, Antananarivo; interview, member of the diplomatic corps, 28 May 2014, Pretoria.
12 Interview, OIF official, 25 February 2014, Antananarivo.
13 Interview, member of the diplomatic corps, 2 April 2014, Antananarivo; interview, SADC official, 14 May 2014, Johannesburg; interview, SADC official, 19 May 2014, Gaborone.
14 The 2014 SADC summit nevertheless reiterated SADC's 'commitment to support Madagascar in the context of dialogue, national reconciliation and national building processes (…)' (SADC 2014: 2), and in 2015 'called upon the Government of Madagascar and all political key stakeholders to safeguard achievements made in nation building and reconciliation by fully implementing the SADC roadmap' (SADC 2015: 3).
15 Interview, AU liaison officer, 21 February 2014, Antananarivo.

7 Politics and power of post-coup interventions

1 The most recent case of the Sudan somewhat diverges from this pattern in that – unlike in all other cases before – the AU sanctioned the organization of a long, three-year transition period. Upon the appointment of the new transitional government, like in Burkina Faso four years earlier, the AU lifted the

country's suspension. Whether this introduced a new pattern of AU intervention practice, whether the latter is a recognition of the popular movement behind the Sudanese transitional authorities and the undemocratic character of the ousted regime, as well as to what extent the Sudanese transition will accomplish the set objectives, is, at the time of writing, still too early to tell.

2 See also the entire special issue of the *South African Journal of International Affairs* on 'African peace interventions seen from below' (Vol. 25:1).

3 See the otherwise very innovative and valuable special issue on 'Decentering intervention' (*Cooperation & Conflict*, Vol. 53:2) and the forum on '"The West" and "The Rest" in International Interventions' (*Conflict, Security & Development*, Vol. 19:3).

References

3FN. 2005. *Conférence nationale unique 2005: résolutions*. Antananarivo: mimeo.
3FN. 2006. *Lettre envoyée par le groupe 3FN au Secrétaire Général des Nations Unies*. Antananarivo: mimeo.
Aalberts, Tanja E. 2012. Patterns of global governmentality and sovereignty. In: Guzzini, Stefano & Iver B. Neumann (eds.): *The Diffusion of Power in Global Governance: International Political Economy Meets Foucault*. Basingstoke: Palgrave, 229–255.
Abrahamsen, Rita. 2000. *Disciplining Democracy: Development Discourse and Good Governance in Africa*. London: Zed Books.
Abrahamsen, Rita. 2003. African studies and the postcolonial challenge, *African Affairs* 102:407, 189–210.
Abrahamsen, Rita. 2016. Africa and international relations: Assembling Africa, studying the world, *African Affairs* 116:462, 125–139.
Abu-Lughod, Lila. 1990. The romance of resistance: Tracing transformations of power through Bedouin women, *American Ethnologist* 17:1, 41–55.
Acharya, Amitav. 2014. Global International Relations (IR) and regional worlds: A new agenda for international studies, *International Studies Quarterly* 58:4, 647–659.
ACHPR. 2010. *Resolution on the Political Situation in Niger*. Resolution 162. Banjul: African Commission on Human and Peoples' Rights.
ACHPR. 2012. *Resolution on the Unconstitutional Change of Governments*. Resolution 213. Banjul: African Commission on Human and Peoples' Rights.
AfDB, OECD, UNDP, & UNECA. 2013. *African Economic Outlook 2013: Structural Transformation and Natural Resources*. Tunis: African Development Bank.
AFP. 1988. Sankara's ghost haunts his successor, https://global.factiva.com/ha/default.aspx#./!?&_suid=144847422799709106406606733799 (last access 24 November 2015).
AFP. 1996. Burundi coup is 'illegal, unacceptable': OAU chief, https://global.factiva.com/ha/default.aspx#./!?&_suid=14486221851160980090620694682 (last access 17 November 2015).
AFP. 1997. OAU accused of applying double standards, https://global.factiva.com/ha/default.aspx#./!?&_suid=144862335075608651741833389172 (last access 17 November 2015).
Africa Confidential. 1999. Tougher talk, *Africa Confidential* 40:5, 1–2.
Afrik-News. 2009. 19 COMESA states to intervene militarily in Madagascar?, www.afrik-news.com/article15787.html (last access 9 July 2019).
Afrobarometer. 2008. *Popular Attitudes Toward Democracy in Madagascar: A Summary of Afrobarometer Indicators, 2005–2008*. Accra: Afrobarometer.
Afrobarometer. 2018. Resumé des resultats: 7ème série de l'enquête Afrobaromètre à Madagascar, http://afrobarometer.org/sites/default/files/publications/Summary%20of%20results/mad_r7_sor_fre.pdf (last access 31 July 2019).
Agnew, John. 2009. *Globalization and Sovereignty*. Lanham: Rowman & Littlefield.

Aidoo, Akwasi. 1993. Africa: Democracy without human rights, *Human Rights Quarterly* 15:4, 703-715.
AIM. 2010. Madagascar: Impasse in negotiations, http://allafrica.com/stories/201006141546.html (last access 9 July 2019).
Akinele, R.A. 1988. The Organization of African Unity: Four grand debates among African leaders revisited, *Nigerian Journal of International Affairs* 14:1, 73-94.
Allen, Philip M. 1995. *Madagascar: Conflicts of Authority in the Great Island*. Boulder: Westview Press.
Allen, Philip M. 2003. Madagascar: Impeachment as parliamentary coup d'état. In: Baumgartner, Jody C. & Naoko Kada (eds.): *Checking Executive Power: Presidential Impeachment in Comparative Perspective*. Westport: Praeger, 81-94.
Ambassade de France. 2010. *Suggestions pour un accompagnement conditionné d'une transition malgache par la communauté internationale*. Antananarivo: mimeo.
Ambrosetti, David & Yves Buchet de Neuilly. 2009. Les organisations internationales au cœur des crises, *Cultures & Conflits* 75, 7-14.
Amnesty International. 2010. *Madagascar: Urgent Need for Justice. Human Rights Violations During the Political Crisis*. London: Amnesty International.
Amnesty International. 2011. *Madagascar: Human Rights Must Be at the Heart of the Roadmap to End the Crisis*. London: Amnesty International.
Amnesty International. 2012. *Madagascar Must End Killings and Investigate Security Forces*. London: Amnesty International.
Andersen, Louise Riis. 2012. Statebuilding as tacit trusteeship: The case of Liberia. In: Bliesemann de Guevara, Berit (ed.): *Statebuilding and State-Formation: The Political Sociology of Intervention*. Abingdon: Routledge, 132-148.
Andrianarimanana, Mboara. 2012. Les jeunes de Tananarive comme exutoire. In: Randrianja, Solofo (ed.): *Madagascar: le coup d'État de mars 2009*. Paris: Karthala, 179-186.
Aning, Kwesi & Fiifi Edu-Afful. 2016. African agency in R2P: Interventions by African Union and ECOWAS in Mali, Côte d'Ivoire, and Libya, *International Studies Review* 18:1, 120-133.
Ansoms, An. 2013. Dislodging power structures in rural Rwanda: From 'disaster tourist' to 'transfer gate'. In: Thomson, Susan, An Ansoms, & Jude Murison (eds.): *Emotional and Ethical Challenges for Field Research in Africa*. Basingstoke: Palgrave Macmillan, 42-55.
APN. 1999. African leaders reject governments that take power by force, https://global.factiva.com/ha/default.aspx#./!?&_suid=1448623 7379690895489674527198 1 (last access 17 November 2015).
ARB. 2012. Madagascar: First direct talks, *Africa Research Bulletin: Political, Social and Cultural Series* 49:7, 19345.
ARB. 2013. Madagascar: Rajoelina withdrawn, *Africa Research Bulletin: Political, Social and Cultural Series* 50:8, 19809-19810.
Asante-Darko, Kwaku. 2012. The African Union and the challenge of international mediation in Niger. In: Engel, Ulf (ed.): *New Mediation Practices in African Conflicts*. Leipzig: Leipziger Universitätsverlag, 83-98.
AU. 2002. *Protocol Relating to the Establishment of the Peace and Security Council of the African Union*. Durban: African Union.
AU. 2003. *Communiqué of the 93rd Ordinary Session at Ambassadorial Level of the Central Organ of the Mechanism for Conflict Prevention, Management and Resolution*. Central Organ/MEC/AMB/COMM. (XCIII). Addis Ababa: African Union.

REFERENCES

AU. 2005a. *Report on the Meeting of Independent Experts on the Draft Charter on Democracy, Elections and Governance*. Addis Ababa: African Union.

AU. 2005b. *Draft African Charter on Democracy, Elections and Governance*. Addis Ababa: African Union.

AU. 2005c. *Report on the Review of the Lomé Declaration of July 2000 on Unconstitutional Changes of Government in Africa*. Addis Ababa: African Union.

AU. 2006a. *Report of the Ministerial Meeting on the Draft African Charter on Democracy, Elections and Governance and on the Revision of the Lomé Declaration on Unconstitutional Changes of Government in Africa*. Ex.CL/258(IX). Banjul: African Union.

AU. 2006b. *Report of the Meeting of Government Experts on the Draft African Charter on Democracy, Elections and Governance and on the Lomé Declaration on Unconstitutional Changes of Government*. Addis Ababa: African Union.

AU. 2006c. *Report of the Ministerial Meeting on the Draft Charter on Democracy, Elections and Governance*. Draft/Min/RPT/II. Brazzaville: African Union.

AU. 2006d. *Draft African Charter on Democracy, Elections and Governance*. Draft/Charter/II/Rev.2. Addis Ababa: African Union.

AU. 2006e. *Report of the Ministerial Meeting on the Draft African Charter on Democracy, Elections and Governance*. Addis Ababa: African Union.

AU. 2006f. *Report of the Ministerial Meeting on the African Draft Charter on Democracy, Elections and Governance and the Lomé Declaration*. Addis Ababa: African Union.

AU. 2007. *African Charter on Democracy, Elections and Governance*. Addis Ababa: African Union.

AU. 2009. *Madagascar: Statement on the Transition in Madagascar, 23 May 2009*. Antananarivo: African Union.

AU. 2014a. AU and partners end joint security sector assessment mission to Madagascar, www.peaceau.org/uploads/joint-pressrelease-madagascar-eng.pdf (last access 31 July 2019).

AU. 2014b. *Protocol on Amendments to the Protocol on the Statute of the African Court of Justice and Human Rights*. Malabo: African Union.

AU. 2015. The African Union supports civil society and women of Madagascar within the framework of reconciliation and peacebuilding, www.peaceau.org/uploads/mad-communique-de-presse-de-l-ua-et-gender-links-version-finale1-25-03-2015-rev2.pdf (last access 31 July 2019).

AU. 2018. AU Commission convenes a high-level sensitization and training workshop on the national security sector reform process in Madagascar, www.peaceau.org/uploads/pr-auc-madagascar-ssr-10-august-2018-.pdf (last access 31 July 2019).

AU. 2019. List of countries which have signed and ratified/acceded to the African Charter on Democracy, Elections and Governance, https://au.int/sites/default/files/treaties/36384-sl-African%20Charter%20on%20Democracy%2C%20Elections%20and%20Governance.pdf (last access 29 June 2019).

AU Assembly. 2002. *OAU/AU Declaration on the Principles Governing Democratic Elections in Africa*. AHG/Decl. 1 (XXXVIII). Durban: African Union.

AU Assembly. 2003. *Decision on Madagascar*. Assembly/AU/Dec.6 (II). Addis Ababa: African Union.

AU Assembly. 2009a. *Decision on the Report of the Peace and Security Council on its Activities and the State of Peace and Security in Africa*. Assembly/AU/Dec.252(XIII). Sirte: African Union.

AU Assembly. 2009b. *Decision on the Resurgence of the Scourge of*

Coups d'État in Africa. Assembly/AU/Dec.220(XII). Addis Ababa: African Union.

AU Assembly. 2010a. *Decision on the Prevention of Unconstitutional Changes of Government and Strengthening the Capacity of the African Union to Manage Such Situations*. Assembly/AU/Dec.269(XIV) Rev.1. Addis Ababa: African Union.

AU Assembly. 2010b. *Decision on the Report of the Peace and Security Council on Its Activities and the State of Peace and Security in Africa*. Assembly/AU/Dec.294(XV).2. Kampala: African Union.

AU Assembly. 2010c. *Decision on Madagascar*. Assembly/AU/Dec.279(XIV). Addis Ababa: African Union.

AU Assembly. 2011. *Declaration on the Theme of the Summit: 'Towards Greater Unity and Integration Through Shared Values'*. Assembly/AU/ Decl.1(XVI). Addis Ababa: African Union.

AU Assembly. 2013a. *Declaration on the Report of the Peace and Security Council on Its Activities and the State of Peace and Security in Africa*. Assembly/AU/Decl.1(XXI). Addis Ababa: African Union.

AU Assembly. 2013b. *50th Anniversary Solemn Declaration*. Addis Ababa: African Union.

AU Commission. 2003. *Report of the Interim Chairperson on the Proceedings of the African Conference on Elections, Democracy and Good Governance*. EX/CL/35 IIII. Maputo: African Union.

AU Commission. 2005. *Report of the Chairperson of the Commission on the Situation in the Islamic Republic of Mauritania*. PSC/PR/2(XXXVII). Addis Ababa: African Union.

AU Commission. 2009. *Interim Report of the Chairperson of the Commission on the Prevention of Unconstitutional Changes of Government Through Appropriate Measures and Strengthening the Capacity of the African Union to Manage Such Situations*. Assembly/AU/7(XIII). Sirte: African Union.

AU Commission. 2010. *Report of the Chairperson of the Commission on the Prevention of Unconstitutional Changes of Government and Strengthening the Capacities of the African Union to Manage Such Situations*. EX.CL/566 (XVI). Addis Ababa: African Union.

AU Commission. 2013a. *Report of the Chairperson of the Commission on the Situation in Madagascar*. Addis Ababa: African Union.

AU Commission. 2013b. *Aide-Mémoire: plan en sept points pour sortir le processus électoral à Madagascar de l'impasse*. Addis Ababa: African Union.

AU Commission. 2014a. *Unconstitutional Changes of Governments: Revisiting the AU Normative Framework*. Addis Ababa: African Union.

AU Commission. 2014b. *Rapport final de la mission d'observation de l'Union Africaine pour le deuxième tour de l'élection présidentielle couplée aux élections législatives du 20 Décembre 2013 en République de Madagascar*. Addis Ababa: African Union.

AU Executive Council. 2003. *Decision on the Report of the Interim Chairperson on the Conference on Elections, Democracy and Good Governance*. EX/CL/Dec.31 (III). Maputo: African Union.

AU Executive Council. 2006. *Decision on the Report of the Ministerial Conference on the African Charter on Democracy, Elections and Governance Doc.Ex.CL/258 (IX)*. EX.CL/Dec.288 (IX). Banjul: African Union.

AU Panel of the Wise. 2012. *Discussion Paper: Workshop of the Panel of the Wise on Strengthening Political Governance for Peace, Security and Stability in Africa*. Addis Ababa: African Union.

REFERENCES

AU PSC. 2009a. *Communiqué of the 180th Meeting of the Peace and Security Council.* PSC/PR/COMM. (CLXXX). Addis Ababa: African Union.

AU PSC. 2009b. *Communiqué of the 181st Meeting of the Peace and Security Council.* PSC/PR/COMM. (CLXXXI). Addis Ababa: African Union.

AU PSC. 2009c. *Ezulwini Framework for the Enhancement of the Implementation of African Union Sanctions in Situations of Unconstitutional Changes of Government in Africa.* PSC/PR/(CCXIII). Ezulwini: African Union.

AU PSC. 2009d. *Communiqué of the 208th Meeting of the Peace and Security Council.* PSC/PR/Comm. (CCVIII). Addis Ababa: African Union.

AU PSC. 2009e. *Press Statement of the 200th Meeting of the Peace and Security Council.* PSC/PR/BR(CC). Addis Ababa: African Union.

AU PSC. 2010a. *Communiqué of the 221st Meeting of the Peace and Security Council.* PSC/PR/COMM. (CCXXI). Addis Ababa: African Union.

AU PSC. 2010b. *Press Statement of the 237th Meeting of the Peace and Security Council.* PSC/PR/COMM-2(CCXXXVII). Kampala: African Union.

AU PSC. 2011a. *Declaration of the Ministerial Meeting of the Peace and Security Council on the State of Peace and Security in Africa.* PSC/MIN/BR.1(CCLXXV). Addis Ababa: African Union.

AU PSC. 2011b. *Communiqué of the 275th Meeting of the Peace and Security Council.* PSC/MIN/COMM.2(CCLXXV). Addis Ababa: African Union.

AU PSC. 2011c. *Communiqué of the 260th Meeting of the Peace and Security Council.* PSC/PR/COMM. (CCLX). Addis Ababa: African Union.

AU PSC. 2011d. *Communiqué of the 261st Meeting of the Peace and Security Council.* PSC/PR/COMM(CCLXI). Addis Ababa: African Union.

AU PSC. 2011e. *Communiqué of the 303rd Meeting of the Peace and Security Council.* PSC/PR/COMM.1 (CCCIII). Addis Ababa: African Union.

AU PSC. 2013a. *Communiqué of the 355th Meeting of the Peace and Security Council.* PSC/PR/COMM.1 (CCCLV). Addis Ababa: African Union.

AU PSC. 2013b. *Communiqué of the 368th Meeting at Ministerial Level of the Peace and Security Council.* PSC/MIN/COMM. (CCCLXVIII). Dar es Salaam: African Union.

AU PSC. 2013c. *Communiqué of the 376th Meeting of the Peace and Security Council.* PSC/PR/COMM. (CCCLXXVI). Addis Ababa: African Union.

AU PSC. 2013d. *Communiqué of the 394th Meeting of the Peace and Security Council.* PSC/PR/COMM. (CCCXCIV). Addis Ababa: African Union.

AU PSC. 2013e. *Report of the Peace and Security Council on its Activities and the State of Peace and Security in Africa.* Assembly/AU/5(XXI). Addis Ababa: African Union.

AU PSC. 2014a. *Communiqué of the 415th Meeting of the Peace and Security Council.* PSC/PR/COMM. (CDXV). Addis Ababa: African Union.

AU PSC. 2014b. *Final Report of the African Union High-Level Panel for Egypt.* PSC/AHG/4.(CDXVI). Addis Ababa: African Union.

AU PSC. 2014c. *Press Statement of the 432nd Meeting of the Peace and Security Council.* PSC/PR/BR.(CDXXXII). Addis Ababa: African Union.

AU PSC. 2014d. *Communiqué of the 465th Meeting of the Peace and

Security Council. PSC/PR/COMM. (CDLXV). Addis Ababa: African Union.

AU PSC. 2015. Communiqué de la 545ème réunion du Conseil de paix et de sécurité. PSC/PR/COMM.1(DXLV). Addis Ababa: African Union.

Autesserre, Séverine. 2014a. *Peaceland: Conflict Resolution and the Everyday Politics of International Intervention.* New York: Cambridge University Press.

Autesserre, Séverine. 2014b. Going micro: Emerging and future peacekeeping research, *International Peacekeeping* 21:4, 492–500.

Avant, Deborah D., Martha Finnemore, & Susan K. Sell (eds.). 2010. *Who Governs the Globe?* Cambridge: Cambridge University Press.

Bacchi, Carol. 2009. *Analysing Policy: What's the Problem Represented to Be?* Frenchs Forest: Pearson.

Bachelard, Jérôme. 2014. *Governance Reform in Africa: International and Domestic Pressures and Counter-Pressures.* London: Routledge.

Barkin, Samuel J. 1998. The evolution of the constitution of sovereignty and the emergence of human rights norms, *Millennium: Journal of International Studies* 27:2, 229–252.

Barkin, Samuel J. & Bruce Cronin. 1994. The state and the nation: Changing norms and the rules of sovereignty in international relations, *International Organization* 48:1, 107–130.

Barnett, Michael & Martha Finnemore. 2004. *Rules for the World: International Organizations in Global Politics.* Ithaca: Cornell University Press.

Barnett, Michael, Songying Fang, & Christoph Zürcher. 2014. Compromised peacebuilding, *International Studies Quarterly* 58:3, 608–620.

Barry, Boubacar. 2009. 'We must move towards a conference of national reconciliation …' – Professor Boubacar Barry on the Guinea crisis, *Africa Spectrum* 44:2, 149–159.

Bartelson, Jens. 2014. *Sovereignty as Symbolic Form.* London: Routledge.

Bayart, Jean-François. 2000. Africa in the world: A history of extraversion, *African Affairs* 99:395, 217–267.

Bayart, Jean-François. 2010. *The State in Africa: The Politics of the Belly.* 2nd edition. Malden: Polity Press.

BBC. 1993. OAU Secretary-General in Rwanda, says that something has to be done for Burundi, https://global.factiva.com/ha/default.aspx#./!?&_suid=14486219440580 3351135831326246 (last access 17 November 2015).

Behrends, Andrea, Sung-Joon Park, & Richard Rottenburg. 2014. Travelling models: Introducing an analytical concept to globalisation studies. In: Behrends, Andrea, Sung-Joon Park, & Richard Rottenburg (eds.): *Travelling Models in African Conflict Management: Translating Technologies of Social Ordering.* Leiden: Brill, 1–40.

Bellamy, Alex J. 2014. *The Responsibility to Protect: A Defense.* Oxford: Oxford University Press.

Bercovitch, Jacob & Richard Jackson. 2001. Negotiation or mediation? An exploration of factors affecting the choice of conflict management in international conflict, *Negotiation Journal* 17:1, 59–77.

Berridge, Willow J. 2020. Briefing: Uprising in Sudan, *African Affairs*, 119:474, 164–176.

Beswick, Danielle & Anne Hammerstad. 2013. African agency in a changing security environment: Sources, opportunities and challenges, *Conflict, Security & Development* 13:5, 471–486.

Bierschenk, Thomas. 2010. *States at Work in West Africa: Sedimentation, Fragmentation and Normative Double-Binds*. Arbeitspapier Institut für Ethnologie und Afrikastudien Nr. 113. Mainz: Johannes Gutenberg Universität.

Biersteker, Thomas J. & Cynthia Weber. 1996. The social construction of state sovereignty. In: Biersteker, Thomas J. & Cynthia Weber (eds.): *State Sovereignty as Social Construct*. Cambridge: Cambridge University Press, 1–21.

Birkholz, Sina, Tilmann Scherf, & Ursula Schroeder. 2018. International interventions seen from the 'middle': Perceptions of intermediary actors in Côte d'Ivoire and Lebanon, *Cooperation & Conflict* 53:2, 173–192.

Bischoff, Paul-Henri, Kwesi Aning, & Amitav Acharya (eds.). 2016. *Africa in Global International Relations: Emerging Approaches to Theory and Practice*. London: Routledge.

Björkdahl, Annika & Kristine Höglund. 2013. Precarious peacebuilding: Friction in global–local encounters, *Peacebuilding* 3:1, 289–299.

Björkdahl, Annika, Kristine Höglund, Gearoid Millar, Jaïr van der Lijn, & Willemijn Verkoren. 2016. Introduction: Peacebuilding through the lens of friction. In: Björkdahl, Annika, Kristine Höglund, Gearoid Millar, Jaïr van der Lijn, & Willemijn Verkoren (eds.): *Peacebuilding and Friction: Global and Local Encounters in Post-Conflict Societies*. Abingdon: Routledge, 1–16.

Bliesemann de Guevara, Berit. 2011. Peace, intervention and legitimate order: Book review, *International Peacekeeping* 18:1, 114–119.

Bliesemann de Guevara, Berit (ed.). 2012. *Statebuilding and State-Formation: The Political Sociology of Intervention*. London: Routledge.

Bliesemann de Guevara, Berit. 2014. Studying the international crisis group, *Third World Quarterly* 35:4, 545–562.

Bonnecase, Vincent. 2015. Sur la chute de Blaise Compaoré: autorité et colère dans les derniers jours d'un régime, *Politique africaine* 137, 151–168.

Börzel, Tanja A. & Vera van Hüllen (eds.). 2015. *Governance Transfer by Regional Organizations: Patching Together a Global Script*. Basingstoke: Palgrave Macmillan.

Bowden, Brett. 2004. In the name of progress and peace: The 'standard of civilization' and the universalizing project, *Alternatives: Global, Local, Political* 29:1, 43–68.

Brosig, Malte. 2015. *Cooperative Peacekeeping in Africa: Exploring Regime Complexity*. Abingdon: Routledge.

Brown, William & Sophie Harman (eds.). 2013a. *African Agency in International Politics*. London: Routledge.

Brown, William & Sophie Harman. 2013b. African agency in international politics. In: Brown, William & Sophie Harman (eds.): *African Agency in International Politics*. London: Routledge, 1–15.

Bryceson, Deborah F. 2012. Discovery and denial: Social science theory and interdisciplinarity in African studies, *African Affairs* 111:443, 281–302.

Bukovansky, Mlada. 2002. *Legitimacy and Power Politics: The American and French Revolutions in International Political Culture*. Princeton: Princeton University Press.

Bull, Hedley. 1977. *The Anarchical Society: A Study of Order in World Politics*. New York: Columbia University Press.

Bull, Hedley. 1984. Introduction. In: Bull, Hedley (ed.): *Intervention in World Politics*. Oxford: Clarendon Press, 1–6.

Burnod, Perrine, Mathilde Gingembre, & Rivo Andrianirina Ratsialonana. 2013. Competition over authority and access: International land deals in Madagascar, *Development & Change* 44:2, 357–379.

Butedi, François. 2018. The work of the African Union liaison office in building peace on the ground: A case study of Madagascar, *South African Journal of International Affairs* 25:1, 99–116.

Call, Charles T. 2012. *UN Mediation and the Politics of Transition After Constitutional Crises*. New York: International Peace Institute.

Campbell, Susanna, David Chandler, & Meera Sabaratnam (eds.). 2011. *A Liberal Peace? The Problems and Practices of Peacebuilding*. London: Zed Books.

Carter Center. 2013. *Carter Center Election Observation Mission: Preliminary Statement – Legislative and Second Round Presidential Elections*. Antananarivo: Carter Center.

Cawthra, Gavin. 2010. *The Role of SADC in Managing Political Crisis and Conflict: The Cases of Madagascar and Zimbabwe*. Maputo: Friedrich-Ebert-Stiftung.

Chandler, David. 2013. Peacebuilding and the politics of non-linearity: Rethinking 'hidden' agency and 'resistance', *Peacebuilding* 1:1, 17–32.

Châtaigner, Jean-Marc. 2014. Madagascar: le développement contrarié, *Afrique contemporaine* 251, 107–124.

Chesterman, Simon. 2004. *You, the People: The United Nations, Transitional Administration, and State-Building*. Oxford: Oxford University Press.

Chissano, Joaquim. 2010. *Report of the SADC Mediator on the Crisis in Madagascar*. Windhoek: Southern African Development Community.

Chissano, Joaquim. 2011a. *Report du médiateur HE Joaquim Chissano preparé pour la réunion du sommet de la Troïka de l'Organe de Coopération en Matière de Politique, Défense et Sécurité de la SADC*. Livingstone: Southern African Development Community.

Chissano, Joaquim. 2011b. *Statement of the SADC Mediator on the Mediation Process in Madagascar*. Addis Ababa: African Union.

Chouli, Lila. 2015. The popular uprising in Burkina Faso and the transition, *Review of African Political Economy* 42:144, 325–333.

Clapham, Christopher. 1996. *Africa and the International System: The Politics of Survival*. Cambridge: Cambridge University Press.

Clark, Ian. 2005. *Legitimacy in International Society*. Oxford: Oxford University Press.

Claude, Inis L. 1966. Collective legitimization as a political function of the United Nations, *International Organization* 20:3, 367–379.

CNOSC. 2010a. *Rapport d'activités 1*. Antananarivo: Coordination nationale des organisations de la société civile.

CNOSC. 2010b. *Rapport d'activités 2*. Antananarivo: Coordination nationale des organisations de la société civile.

CNOSC. 2011. *Rapport d'activités 4*. Antananarivo: Coordination nationale des organisations de la société civile.

COI. 2010a. *Résolution de la Commission de l'Océan Indien sur la situation à Madagascar*. Saint Denis: Commission de l'Océan Indien.

COI. 2010b. *Madagascar: Contribution régionale de la COI dans le cadre d'un accompagnement international du processus de sortie de crise*. Ebène: Commission de l'Océan Indien.

COI. 2010c. *Rapport annuel 2009*. Ebène: Commission de l'Océan Indien.

COI. 2011. *Relève des décisions: 27ᵉᵐᵉ session du Conseil des Ministres de la COI*. Quatre Bornes: Commission de l'Océan Indien.

COI. 2012. *Rapport annuel 2012*. Ebène: Commission de l'Océan Indien.

COI. 2013a. *Rapport annuel 2013*. Ebène: Commission de l'Océan Indien.

COI. 2013b. *Note de synthèse du Plan de Développement Stratégique 2013-2016 et du Plan d'Actions Prioritaires 2013-2015*. Ebène: Commission de l'Océan Indien.

COI. 2014. *Rapport annuel 2014*. Ebène: Commission de l'Océan Indien.

COI. 2018. *Rapport annuel 2017*. Ebène: Commission de l'Océan Indien.

Comaroff, Jean & John L. Comaroff. 2011. *Theory from the South. Or, How Euro-America is Evolving Towards Africa*. Boulder: Paradigm.

CONECS. 2008. Message du Président CONECS Madagascar, http://conecs.canalblog.com (last access 9 July 2019).

Cooper, Andrew F. & Thomas Legler. 2005. A tale of two mesas: The OAS defense of democracy in Peru and Venezuela, *Global Governance* 11:4, 425-444.

Cooper, Andrew F. & Thomas Legler. 2006. *Intervention without Intervening: The OAS and Defense and Promotion of Democracy in the Americas*. New York: Palgrave Macmillan.

Cooper, Frederick. 2008. Possibility and constraint: African independence in historical perspective, *Journal of African History* 49:2, 167-196.

Cornelissen, Scarlett, Fantu Cheru, & Timothy M. Shaw (eds.). 2012. *Africa and International Relations in the 21st Century*. Basingstoke: Palgrave Macmillan.

Cornwell, Richard. 2003. Madagascar: First test for the African Union, *African Security Review* 12:1, 40-53.

COSC. 2010. *Résultats du Dinika Santatra*. Antananarivo: Coalition des organisations de la société civile.

Cowell, Frederick. 2011. Preventing coups in Africa: Attempts at the protection of human rights and constitutions, *International Journal of Human Rights* 15:15, 749-764.

CRN. 2003. *Feuille de route pour une sortie non violente des effects de la crise de 2002 à Madagascar*. Antananarivo: mimeo.

Cortell, Andrew P. & James W. Davis. 2000. Understanding the domestic impact of international norms: A research agenda, *International Studies Review* 2:1, 65-87.

Curtis, Devon. 2012. Introduction: The contested politics of peacebuilding in Africa. In: Curtis, Devon & Gwinyayi A. Dzinesa (eds.): *Peacebuilding, Power, and Politics in Africa*. Athens: Ohio University Press, 1-28.

d'Ersu, Laurent. 2009. Changement d'homme providentiel à Madagascar, *Études* 411:11, 451-461.

Daase, Christopher & Nicole Deitelhoff. 2019. Opposition and dissidence: Two modes of resistance against international rule, *Journal of International Political Theory* 15:1, 11-30.

Dalichau, Oliver & Jean-Aimé Raveloson. 2009. *Machtkampf in Madagaskar: Erste Ergebnisse der nationalen Tagung*. Antananarivo: Friedrich-Ebert-Stiftung.

de Coning, Cedric, Linnéa Gelot, & John Karlsrud (eds.). 2016. *The Future of African Peace Operations*. London: Zed Books.

de Waal, Alex & Rahel Ibreck. 2013. Alem Bekagn: The African Union's accidental human rights memorial, *African Affairs* 112:447, 191-215.

Dean, Mitchell. 2010. *Governmentality: Power and Rule in Modern Society*. 2nd edition. Los Angeles: SAGE.

Death, Carl. 2013. Governmentality and the limits of the international: African politics and Foucauldian theory, *Review of International Studies* 39:3, 763–787.

Death, Carl. 2015. Introduction: Africa's international relations, *African Affairs*, http://afraf.oxfordjournals.org/content/early/2015/08/11/afraf.advo41. extract (last access 9 July 2019).

Decalo, Samuel. 1990. *Coups and Army Rule in Africa*. 2nd edition. New Haven: Yale University Press.

Deitelhoff, Nicole & Michael Zürn. 2015. Internationalization of the state: Sovereignty as the external side of modern statehood. In: Leibfried, Stephan, Evelyne Huber, Matthew Lange, Jonah D. Levy, & John D. Stephens (eds.): *The Oxford Handbook of Transformations of the State*. Oxford: Oxford University Press, 193–217.

Dersso, Solomon A. 2017. Defending constitutional rule and a peacemaking enterprise: The case of the AU's ban of unconstitutional changes of government, *International Peacekeeping* 24:4, 639–660.

Dersso, Solomon A. 2019. The status and legitimacy of popular uprisings in the AU norms on democracy and constitutional governance, *Journal of African Law* 63:S1, 107–130.

Dewar, Bob, Simon Massey, & Bruce Baker. 2012. *Madagascar: Time to Make a Fresh Start*. London: Chatham House.

Duffield, Mark. 2001. *Global Governance and the New Wars: The Merging of Development and Security*. London: Zed Books.

Dunn, Kevin C. & Timothy M. Shaw (eds.). 2001. *Africa's Challenge to International Relations Theory*. Basingstoke: Palgrave Macmillan.

ECOWAS. 2001. *Protocol A/SP1/12/01 on Democracy and Good Governance Supplementary to the Protocol Relating to the Mechanism for Conflict Prevention, Management, Resolution, Peacekeeping and Security*. Dakar: Economic Community of West African States.

Edozie, Rita Kiki & Keith Gottschalk. 2014. *The African Union's Africa: New Pan-African Initiatives in Global Governance*. East Lansing: Michigan State University Press.

EIA. 2014. *The Ongoing Illegal Logging Crisis in Madagascar: An EIA Briefing for CITES SC65*. London: Environmental Investigation Agency.

Engel, Ulf & João Gomes Porto (eds.). 2010. *Africa's New Peace and Security Architecture: Promoting Norms, Institutionalizing Solutions*. Farnham: Ashgate.

Engel, Ulf & João Gomes Porto (eds.). 2013. *Towards an African Peace and Security Regime: Continental Embeddedness, Transnational Linkages, Strategic Relevance*. Farnham: Ashgate.

Engel, Ulf & João Gomes Porto. 2014. Imagining, implementing, and integrating the African Peace and Security Architecture: The African Union's challenges, *African Security* 7:3, 135–146.

Engel, Ulf. 2012a. The African Union and mediation in cases of unconstitutional changes of government, 2008–2011. In: Engel, Ulf (ed.): *New Mediation Practices in African Conflicts*. Leipzig: Leipziger Universitätsverlag, 55–82.

Engel, Ulf. 2012b. Ambitions, constraints and opportunities: Some tentative conclusions on new mediation practices in African conflicts. In: Engel, Ulf (ed.): *New Mediation Practices in African Conflicts*. Leipzig: Leipziger Universitätsverlag, 255–261.

Engel, Ulf. 2013. The changing role of the AU Commission in inter-African relations: The case of

APSA and AGA. In: Harbeson, John H. & Donald Rothchild (eds.): *Africa in World Politics: Engaging a Changing Global Order*. Boulder: Westview Press, 186–206.

Engel, Ulf. 2019. The 2007 African Charter on Democracy, Elections and Governance: Trying to make sense of the late ratification of the African Charter and non-implementation of its compliance mechanism, *Africa Spectrum* 54:2, 127–146.

Englebert, Pierre. 2009. *Africa: Unity, Sovereignty, and Sorrow*. Boulder: Lynne Rienner.

Eriksson, Mikael. 2010. *Supporting Democracy in Africa: African Union's Use of Targeted Sanctions to Deal with Unconstitutional Changes of Government*. Stockholm: Swedish Defence Research Agency.

ESCOPOL. 2011. *Espace de concertation des organisations et partis politiques: Documentation du travail*. Antananarivo: mimeo.

EU. 2014. Déclaration du porte-parole de Catherine Ashton, Haute Représentant de l'UE, sur les élections présidentielles et législatives à Madagascar, https://reliefweb.int/report/madagascar/d-claration-du-porte-parole-de-catherine-ashton-haute-repr-sentante-de-lue-sur-les (last access 9 July 2019).

EU Commission. 2013. *African Peace Facility Evaluation. Part 2: Reviewing the Overall Implementation of the APF as an Instrument for African Efforts to Manage Conflicts on the Continent*. Brussels: European Union.

EU EOM. 2014. *Union Européenne Mission d'observation électorale Madagascar 2013: Rapport final*. Antananarivo: European Union.

Fabricius, Peter. 2015. Ravalomanana's gamble pays off, but Hery's bigger challenge now is Rajoelina, www.issafrica.org/iss-today/ravalomananas-gamble-pays-off-but-herys-bigger-challenge-now-is-rajoelina (last access 9 July 2019).

Ferguson, James. 1994. *The Anti-Politics Machine: 'Development', Depoliticization, and Bureaucratic Power in Lesotho*. Minneapolis: University of Minnesota Press.

FES. 2009. *Journal des événements socio-politiques à Madagascar: Une sélection d'articles de mars 2009 à décembre 2009*. Antananarivo: Friedrich-Ebert-Stiftung.

Finnemore, Martha. 2003. *The Purpose of Intervention: Changing Beliefs About the Use of Force*. Ithaca: Cornell University Press.

Fisher, Jonathan. 2014. When it pays to be a 'fragile state': Uganda's use and abuse of a dubious concept, *Third World Quarterly* 35:2, 316–332.

Foucault, Michel. 1982. The subject and power, *Critical Inquiry* 8:4, 777–795.

Foucault, Michel. 1994 [1981]. So is it important to think? In: Faubion, James D. (ed.): *Essential Works of Michel Foucault 1954–1984. Volume 3: Power*. London: Penguin, 454–458.

Foucault, Michel. 2004 [1978]. *Sicherheit, Territorium, Bevölkerung. Geschichte der Gouvernementalität I*. Frankfurt am Main: Suhrkamp.

France Diplomatie. 2009a. Audition du Ministre des affaires étrangères et européennes, Bernard Kouchner, devant la Commission des affaires étrangères de l'Assemblée nationale, 18 March 2009, www.diplomatie.gouv.fr/fr/salle-de-presse/ (last access 9 July 2019).

France Diplomatie. 2009b. Madagascar: point de presse, 20 March 2009, www.diplomatie.gouv.fr/fr/salle-de-presse/ (last access 9 July 2019).

France Diplomatie. 2009c. Madagascar: point de presse, 11 March 2009, www.diplomatie.gouv.fr/fr/salle-de-presse/ (last access 9 July 2019).

France Diplomatie. 2009d. Madagascar: point de presse, 23 December 2009, www.diplomatie.

gouv.fr/fr/salle-de-presse/ (last access 9 July 2019).
France Diplomatie. 2009e. Madagascar: point de presse, 13 May 2009, www.diplomatie.gouv.fr/fr/salle-de-presse/ (last access 9 July 2019).
France Diplomatie. 2009f. Audition du Secrétaire d'Etat chargé de la coopération et de la Francophonie, Alain Joyandet, devant la Commission des affaires étrangères de l'Assemblée nationale, 27 May 2009, www.diplomatie.gouv.fr/fr/salle-de-presse/ (last access 9 July 2019).
France Diplomatie. 2009g. Audition du Ministre des affaires étrangères et européennes, Bernard Kouchner, devant la Commission des affaires étrangères, de la défense et des forces armées du Senat, 18 March 2009, www.diplomatie.gouv.fr/fr/salle-de-presse/ (last access 9 July 2019).
France Diplomatie. 2009h. Conseil Européen: conference de presse du Président de la République, Nicolas Sarkozy, 20 March 2009, www.diplomatie.gouv.fr/fr/salle-de-presse/ (last access 9 July 2019).
France Diplomatie. 2009i. Conséquences de la crise économique et financière en matière de sécurité et de défense, audition du Ministre des affaires étrangères et européennes, Bernard Kouchner, devant la Commission des affaires étrangères, de la défense et des forces armées du Senat, 2 April 2009, www.diplomatie.gouv.fr/fr/salle-de-presse (last access 9 July 2019).
France Diplomatie. 2009j. Communiqué d'Alain Joyandet, Secrétaire d'Etat chargé de la coopération et de la Francophonie sur l'aide française à Madagascar, 3 April 2009, www.diplomatie.gouv.fr/fr/salle-de-presse/ (last access 9 July 2019).
France Diplomatie. 2009k. Madagascar: point de presse, 30 March 2009, www.diplomatie.gouv.fr/fr/salle-de-presse (last access 9 July 2019).
France Diplomatie. 2009l. Madagascar: point de presse, 18 March 2009, www.diplomatie.gouv.fr/fr/salle-de-presse (last access 9 July 2019).
France Diplomatie. 2010. Entretien du Président de la République, Nicolas Sarkozy, avec l'hebdomadaire 'Les Afriques', 27 May 2010, www.diplomatie.gouv.fr/fr/salle-de-presse/ (last access 9 July 2019).
Franck, Thomas M. 1992. The emerging right to democratic governance, *American Journal of International Law* 86:1, 46–91.
Fremigacci, Jean. 2014. Madagascar ou l'éternel retour de la crise, *Afrique contemporaine* 251, 125–142.
Frère, Marie-Soleil & Pierre Englebert. 2015. Briefing: Burkina Faso – The fall of Blaise Compaoré, *African Affairs* 114:455, 295–307.
Friends of the Earth. 2007. *Mining Madagascar: Forests, Communities, and Rio Tinto's White Wash. Media Briefing*. London: Friends of the Earth.
Fujii, Lee Ann. 2018. *Interviewing in Social Science Research: A Relational Approach*. New York: Routledge.
Gabay, Clive & Carl Death. 2014. Introduction: Critical perspectives on liberal interventions and governmentality in Africa. In: Gabay, Clive & Carl Death (eds.): *Critical Perspectives on African Politics: Liberal Interventions, State-Building and Civil Society*. Oxon: Routledge, 1–17.
Galibert, Didier. 2009a. Mobilisation populaire et répression à Madagascar: La transgression de la cité culturelle, *Politique africaine* 113, 139–151.
Galibert, Didier. 2009b. *Les gens du pouvoir à Madagascar: État postcolonial, légitimités et territoire (1956–2002)*. Paris: Karthala.
Galibert, Didier. 2011. Rigidités et 'glocalisation': un regard

anthropologique sur la crise malgache (2009–2011), *Les Cahiers d'Outre-Mer* 255, 413–426.

Gavigan, Patrick. 2010. *The 2009 Madagascar Crisis and International Mediation*. Paper Prepared for the Conflict Prevention and Peace Forum. New York: mimeo.

Gelot, Linnéa. 2012. *Legitimacy, Peace Operations and Global-Regional Security: The African Union–United Nations Partnership in Darfur*. Oxon: Routledge.

Gingembre, Mathilde. 2010. Madagascar: les aspirations confisquées du mouvement de 2009, *Alternatives Sud* 17:4, 187–193.

Gingembre, Mathilde. 2011. Match religieux en terrain politique: Compétition entre Églises chrétiennes et chute du régime Ravalomanana à Madagascar, *Politique africaine* 123, 51–72.

Glen, Patrick J. 2012. Institutionalizing democracy in Africa: A comment on the African Charter for Democracy, Elections and Governance, *African Journal of Legal Studies* 5, 119–146.

Gourevitch, Peter. 1978. The second image reversed: The international structure of domestic politics, *International Organization* 32:4, 881–912.

Grovogui, Siba N. 2002. Regimes of sovereignty: International morality and the African condition, *European Journal of International Relations* 8:3, 315–338.

Grund, Constantin. 2010. *Auf der Suche nach Kontrolle: Die politische Krise in Madagaskar 2009/2010*. Antananarivo: Friedrich-Ebert-Stiftung.

Guzzini, Stefano. 2005. The concept of power: A constructivist analysis, *Millennium: Journal of International Studies* 33:3, 495–521.

Hagberg, Sten & Gabriella Körling. 2012. Socio-political turmoil in Mali: The public debate following the coup d'état on 22 March 2012, *Africa Spectrum* 47:2–3, 111–125.

Hagmann, Tobias & Didier Péclard. 2010. Negotiating statehood: Dynamics of power and domination in Africa, *Development & Change* 41:4, 539–562.

Hameiri, Shahar. 2010. *Regulating Statehood: State Building and the Transformation of the Global Order*. Basingstoke: Palgrave Macmillan.

Hammerstad, Anne. 2005. Rejoining the continent: Madagascar and SADC, *SADC Barometer* 8, 2–3.

Harbison, Rod. 2007. *A Mine of Information? Improving Communication Around the Rio Tinto Ilmenite Mine in Madagascar*. London: Panos.

Harman, Sophie & David Williams (eds.). 2013. *Governing the World? Cases in Global Governance*. Abingdon: Routledge.

Hartmann, Christof. 2005. Demokratie als Leitbild der afrikanischen Staatengemeinschaft? *Verfassung und Recht in Übersee* 38:2, 201–220.

Hartmann, Christof. 2017. ECOWAS and the restoration of democracy in The Gambia, *Africa Spectrum* 52:1, 85–99.

HAT. 2009a. *Note sur le dénouement de la crise malgache et sur les perspectives d'avenir de la transition*. Antananarivo: mimeo.

HAT. 2009b. *Communiqué Maputo No. 3*. Maputo: mimeo.

HAT. 2009c. *Communiqué Maputo No. 4*. Maputo: mimeo.

HAT. 2009d. *Communiqué Maputo No. 5*. Maputo: mimeo.

HAT. 2009e. *Communiqué Maputo No. 6*. Maputo: mimeo.

HAT. 2010. *Communiqué de la Présidence de la Haute Autorité de la Transition sur la rencontre de Pretoria du 28 au 29 Avril 2010*. Antananarivo: mimeo.

HAT. 2011. *Mémorandum sur l'évolution de la situation de crise à Madagascar*. Antananarivo: mimeo.

Heathershaw, John. 2009. *Post-Conflict Tajikistan: The Politics of Peacebuilding and the Emergence of Legitimate Order*. London: Routledge.

Heathershaw, John & Daniel Lambach. 2008. Introduction: Post-conflict spaces and approaches to statebuilding, *Journal of Intervention and Statebuilding* 2:3, 269–289.

Hellmüller, Sara. 2018. *The Interaction Between Local and International Peacebuilding Actors: Partners for Peace*. Cham: Palgrave.

Herbst, Jeffrey. 2000. *States and Power in Africa: Comparative Lessons in Authority and Control*. Princeton: Princeton University Press.

Hindess, Barry. 2005. Politics as government: Michael Foucault's analysis of political reason, *Alternatives: Global, Local, Political* 30:4, 389–413.

Hinthorne, Lauren L. 2011. Democratic crisis or crisis of confidence? What local perceptual lenses tell us about Madagascar's 2009 political crisis, *Democratization* 18:2, 535–561.

Hofmann, Gregor P. & Lisbeth Zimmermann. 2019. Norm contestation and its effects: Challenges to the responsibility to protect and the responsibility to prosecute, *Global Responsibility to Protect* 11:2, 137–148.

Hooghe, Lisbet, Gary Marks, Tobias Lenz, Jeanine Bezuijen, Besir Ceka, & Svet Derderyan. 2017. *Measuring International Authority: A Postfunctionalist Theory of Governance, Volume III*. Oxford: Oxford University Press.

Howarth, David. 2009. Power, discourse, and policy: Articulating a hegemony approach to critical policy studies, *Critical Policy Studies* 3:3–4, 309–335.

Hurd, Ian. 2014. *International Organizations: Politics, Law, Practice*. 2nd edition. Cambridge: Cambridge University Press.

ICG. 2010a. *Madagascar: Crisis Heating Up?* Africa Report No. 166. Brussels: International Crisis Group.

ICG. 2010b. *Madagascar: sortir du cycle de crises*. Africa Report No. 156. Brussels: International Crisis Group.

ICG. 2014. *A Cosmetic End to Madagascar's Crisis?* Africa Report No. 218. Brussels: International Crisis Group.

ICG-M. 2009. *Communiqué of the Consultative Meeting on the Situation in Madagascar 30 April 2009*. Addis Ababa: International Contact Group on Madagascar.

ICG-M. 2010. *4th Meeting of the International Contact Group on Madagascar (ICG-M)*. Addis Ababa: International Contact Group on Madagascar.

ICG-M. 2011. *6th Consultative Meeting of the International Contact Group on Madagascar (ICG-M)*. Addis Ababa: International Contact Group on Madagascar.

ICG-M. 2013a. *7th Meeting of the International Contact Group on Madagascar (ICG-M)*. Addis Ababa: International Contact Group on Madagascar.

ICG-M. 2013b. *8th Consultative Meeting of the International Contact Group on Madagascar (ICG-M)*. Addis Ababa: International Contact Group on Madagascar.

ICG-M. 2014. *9ème réunion consultative du Groupe International de Contact sur Madagascar (GIC-M)*. Antananarivo: International Contact Group on Madagascar.

Ikome, Francis. 2007. *Good Coups and Bad Coups: The Limits of the AU's Injunction on Unconstitutional Changes of Government*. Occasional Paper No. 55. Johannesburg: Institute for Global Dialogue.

Imbiki, Anaclet. 2014. *La réconciliation nationale à Madagascar: Une perspective complexe et difficile*. Paris: L'Harmattan.

Indian Ocean Newsletter. 2012a. EU negotiating a new fishing agreement with Madagascar, www.africaintelligence.com/ION/politics-power/on-the-line/2012/05/12/eu-negotiating-a-new-fishing-agreement-with-madagascar,101805463-BRE (last access 9 July 2019).

Indian Ocean Newsletter. 2012b. Deep financial trouble before elections, www.africaintelligence.com/ION/politics-power/2012/06/23/deep-financial-trouble-before-elections,103485981-EVE (last access 9 July 2019).

Indian Ocean Newsletter. 2013a. Presidential election is reviving business, www.africaintelligence.com/ION/politics-power/2013/10/25/presidential-election-is-reviving-business,107991613-EVE (last access 9 July 2019).

Indian Ocean Newsletter. 2013b. TGV lurches his way out of the road map, www.africaintelligence.com/ION/politics-power/2013/07/26/tgv-lurches-his-way-out-of-the-road-map,107971112-EVE (last access 9 July 2019).

IOL News. 2011. Ravalomanana shocked by barring, www.iol.co.za/news/africa/ravalomanana-shocked-by-barring-1.1029058?showComments=true#.VIqlfktyeDo (last access 9 July 2019).

Isbell, Thomas. 2018. Note to Madagascar's election winner: Crime, infrastructure, and food insecurity most important issues for government to fix, http://afrobarometer.org/sites/default/files/publications/Dispatches/ab_r7_dipatchno255_citizen_priorities_for_madagascar_government.pdf (last access 31 July 2019).

Jabri, Vivienne. 2013. Peacebuilding, the local and the international: A colonial or a postcolonial rationality?, *Peacebuilding* 1:1, 3–16.

Jackson, Jennifer. 2013. *Political Oratory and Cartooning: An Ethnography of Democratic Processes in Madagascar*. Oxford: Wiley.

Jackson, Robert H. & Carl G. Rosberg. 1982. Why Africa's weak states persist: The empirical and the juridical in statehood, *World Politics* 35:1, 1–24.

Jahn, Beate. 2007a. The tragedy of liberal diplomacy: Democratization, intervention, statebuilding (part I), *Journal of Intervention and Statebuilding* 1:1, 87–106.

Jahn, Beate. 2007b. The tragedy of liberal diplomacy: Democratization, intervention, statebuilding (part II), *Journal of Intervention and Statebuilding* 1:2, 211–229.

Jeune Afrique. 2003. «J'entends gérer mon pays comme une entreprise», interview avec Marc Ravalomanana, www.jeuneafrique.com/Article/LIN23113jenteesirpeo/actualite-afrique---j-entends-g-rer-mon-pays-comme-une-entreprise.html (last access 9 July 2019).

Johnson, Jaclyn & Clayton L. Thyne. 2018. Squeaky wheels and troop loyalty: How domestic protests influence coups d'état, 1951–2005, *Journal of Conflict Resolution* 62:3, 597–625.

Jütersonke, Oliver. 2011. Ethos of exploitation: Insecurity and predation in Madagascar. In: Berman, Eric G., Keith Krause, Emile LeBrun, & Glenn McDonald (eds.): *Small Arms Survey 2011: States of Security*. Cambridge: Cambridge University Press, 167–191.

Jütersonke, Oliver & Moncef Kartas. 2010. *Peace and Conflict Impact Assessment (PCIA) Madagascar*. Geneva: Geneva Centre on Conflict, Development and Peacebuilding.

Kane, Ibrahima. 2008. The implementation of the African Charter on Democracy, Elections and Governance, *African Security Review* 17:4, 43–62.

Kassimir, Ronald & Robert Latham. 2001. Toward a new research agenda. In: Callaghy, Thomas M., Ronald Kassimir, & Robert Latham (eds.): *Intervention and Transnationalism in Africa: Global–Local Networks of Power*. Cambridge: Cambridge University Press, 267–278.

Kemp, Gerhard & Selemani Kinyunyu. 2017. The crime of unconstitutional changes of government. In: Werle, Gerhard & Moritz Vormbaum (eds.): *The African Criminal Court*. The Hague: Asser Press, 57–70.

Khadiagala, Gilbert M. 2011. Mediators in current African conflicts. In: Oslo Forum Network of Mediators (ed.): *Africa Mediators' Retreat 2011*. Oslo: Oslo Forum Network of Mediators, 22–32.

KMF/CNOE. 2014. *Atelier de réflexion sur le processus électoral 2013*. Antananarivo: KMF/CNOE.

Kotzé, Dirk. 2013a. The government of national unity as a transitional power-sharing institution in Madagascar, *Southern African Peace and Security Studies* 2:1, 9–22.

Kotzé, Dirk. 2013b. Africa's concept of 'unconstitutional change of government': How appropriate? *Conflict Trends* 4, 3–10.

Krasner, Stephen D. 2001. Problematic sovereignty. In: Krasner, Stephen D. (ed.): *Problematic Sovereignty: Contested Rules and Political Possibilities*. New York: Columbia University Press, 1–23.

Kufuor, Kofi Oteng. 2002. The OAU and the recognition of governments in Africa: Analyzing its practice and proposals for the future, *American University International Law Review* 17:2, 369–401.

Kühn, Florian P. 2012. The peace prefix: Ambiguities of the word 'peace', *International Peacekeeping* 19:4, 396–409.

Kvale, Steinar. 2011. *Doing Interviews: The SAGE Qualitative Research Kit*. London: SAGE.

L'Express. 2011. Madagascar: Andry Rajoelina pourrait assouplir sa position après son voyage en Europe, http://fr.allafrica.com/stories/201002010801.html (last access 9 July 2019).

L'Express de Madagascar. 2007. Madagascar: Andry Rajoelina déterminé, http://fr.allafrica.com/stories/200712101548.html (last access 9 July 2019).

L'Express de Madagascar. 2009a. Madagascar: Rajoelina rassure l'Afrique, http://fr.allafrica.com/stories/200903260266.html (last access 9 July 2019).

L'Express de Madagascar. 2009b. Madagascar: Le GIC désavoue Ravalomanana, http://fr.allafrica.com/stories/200910280251.html (last access 9 July 2019).

L'Express de Madagascar. 2009c. Madagascar: Incertitudes à Addis-Abeba, http://fr.allafrica.com/stories/200911030280.html (last access 9 July 2019).

L'Express de Madagascar. 2009d. Madagascar: Le pouvoir confié à Andry Rajoelina, http://fr.allafrica.com/stories/200903180421.html (last access 9 July 2019).

L'Express de Madagascar. 2009e. Madagascar: Andry Rajoelina maintient la pression, http://fr.allafrica.com/stories/200901300206.html (last access 9 July 2019).

L'Express de Madagascar. 2009f. Madagascar: Andry Rajoelina invité aux Nations unies, http://fr.allafrica.com/stories/200904280125.html (last access 9 July 2019).

L'Express de Madagascar. 2013. Madagascar: Sortie de crise – Les sept commandements du GIC, http://fr.allafrica.com/stories/201307181299.html (last access 9 July 2019).

REFERENCES

L'*Express de Madagascar*. 2014. Madagascar: Mapar-Indépendants dans un mouchoir, http://fr.allafrica.com/stories/201402071204.html (last access 9 July 2019).

L'*Express de Madagascar*. 2015. Afrique de l'Est: Coopération régionale – Le sommet Comesa à Madagascar, http://fr.allafrica.com/stories/201503311463.html?aa_source=nwsltr-madagascar-fr (last access 9 July 2019).

Lanz, David & Rachel Gasser. 2013. *A Crowded Field: Competition and Coordination in International Peace Mediation*. Mediation Arguments No. 2. Pretoria: Centre for Mediation in Africa.

Latham, Robert. 1999. Politics in a floating world: Toward a critique of global governance. In: Hewson, Martin & Timothy J. Sinclair (eds.): *Approaches to Global Governance Theory*. New York: State University of New York Press, 23–53.

Latham, Robert. 2001. Identifying the contours of transboundary political life. In: Callaghy, Thomas M., Ronald Kassimir, & Robert Latham (eds.): *Intervention and Transnationalism in Africa: Global-Local Networks of Power*. Cambridge: Cambridge University Press, 69–92.

Latham, Robert, Ronald Kassimir, & Thomas M. Callaghy. 2001. Introduction: Transboundary formations, intervention, order, and authority. In: Callaghy, Thomas M., Ronald Kassimir, & Robert Latham (eds.): *Intervention and Transnationalism in Africa: Global-Local Networks of Power*. Cambridge: Cambridge University Press, 1–20.

Lavrard-Meyer, Cécile. 2015. *Didier Ratsiraka: Transition démocratique et pauvreté à Madagascar: Entretiens avec un Président de la République de Madagascar*. Paris: Karthala.

Lawson, George & Luca Tardelli. 2013. The past, present, and future of intervention, *Review of International Studies* 39:5, 1233–1253.

Le Monde. 2008. L'ambassadeur de France renvoyé de Madagascar pour conjurer son mauvais œil, www.lemonde.fr/afrique/article/2008/07/15/l-ambassadeur-de-france-renvoye-de-madagascar-pour-conjurer-son-mauvais-oeil_1073491_3212.html (last access 9 July 2019).

Lederach, John Paul. 2005. *The Moral Imagination: The Art and Soul of Building Peace*. Oxford: Oxford University Press.

Legler, Thomas. 2012. The democratic charter in action: Reflections on the Honduran crisis, *Latin American Policy* 3:1, 74–87.

Legler, Thomas & Thomas K. Tieku. 2010. What difference can a path make? Regional democracy promotion regimes in the Americas and Africa, *Democratization* 17:3, 465–491.

Leininger, Julia. 2014. *A Strong Norm for Democratic Governance in Africa*. Stockholm: International IDEA.

Lemay-Hébert, Nicolas. 2011. The 'empty shell' approach: The setup process of international administrations in Timor-Leste and Kosovo, its consequences and lessons, *International Studies Perspectives* 12:2, 190–211.

Levitt, Jeremy L. 2008. Pro-democratic intervention in Africa. In: Levitt, Jeremy L. (ed.): *Africa: Mapping New Boundaries in International Law*. Oxford: Hart Publishing, 103–148.

Liberty 32. 2013. *Sondage sur la participation politique du citoyen*. Antananarivo: Liberty 32.

Lobo-Guerrero, Luis. 2013. Wondering as research attitude. In: Salter, Mark B. & Can E. Mutlu (eds.): *Research Methods in*

Critical Security Studies. London: Routledge, 25–28.
Mac Ginty, Roger. 2011. *International Peacebuilding and Local Resistance*. Basingstoke: Palgrave Macmillan.
MacMillan, John. 2013. Intervention and the ordering of the modern world, *Review of International Studies* 39:5, 1039–1056.
Madagascar Tribune. 2007. Plateforme de l'opposition «Plutôt un monologue présidentiel», www.madagascar-tribune.com/Plutot-un-monologue-presidentiel,3097.html (last access 9 July 2019).
Madagascar Tribune. 2008. Andry Rajoelina: Leader naturel de l'opposition, www.madagascar-tribune.com/Leader-naturel-de-l-opposition,10402.html (last access 9 July 2019).
Madagascar Tribune. 2009a. Signature d'adhésion aux accords de Maputo, www.madagascar-tribune.com/Signature-d-adhesion-aux-accords,12575.html (last access 26 July 2019).
Madagascar Tribune. 2009b. Armée «réconciliée»: Solidaire contre d'éventuelles interventions armées de la SADC, www.madagascar-tribune.com/Solidaire-contre-d-eventuelles,11539.html (last access 9 July 2019).
Madagascar Tribune. 2010a. Rapport d'observation du KMF/CNOE «C'est la pire des élections observées», www.madagascar-tribune.com/C-est-la-pire-des-elections,15118.html (last access 9 July 2019).
Madagascar Tribune. 2010b. Raymond Ranjeva: «Ce n'est plus une crise, c'est une maladie», www.madagascar-tribune.com/Ce-n-est-plus-une-crise-c-est-une,14854.html (last access 9 July 2019).
Madagascar Tribune. 2010c. Voninahitsy qualifie Raharinaivo de traître, www.madagascar-tribune.com/Voninahitsy-qualifie-Raharinaivo,15255.html (last access 9 July 2019).
Madagascar Tribune. 2010d. Le TIM se déchire, www.madagascar-tribune.com/Le-TIM-se-dechire,14637.html (last access 9 July 2019).
Madagascar Tribune. 2011a. Mission technique de la Troïka: «Il y a erreur de Tomaz Salomao», www.madagascar-tribune.com/Il-y-a-erreur-de-Tomaz-Salomao,16400.html (last access 9 July 2019).
Madagascar Tribune. 2011b. Afrique australe et Océan Indien: La COI veut intégrer l'Union africaine, www.madagascar-tribune.com/La-COI-veut-integrer-l-Union,16513.html (last access 9 July 2019).
Madagascar Tribune. 2011c. Lettre envoyée par Tomaz Salomão aux parties prenantes malgaches, www.madagascar-tribune.com/Lettre-envoye-par-Tomaz-Salomao,16065.html (last access 9 July 2019).
Madagascar Tribune. 2011d. SADC: divisée? www.madagascar-tribune.com/SADC-divisee,16074.html (last access 9 July 2019).
Madagascar Tribune. 2011e. Vaovao Benjamin et consorts: «Pierrot Rajaonarivelo est le patron du parti AREMA», www.madagascar-tribune.com/Pierrot-Rajaonarivelo-est-le,15308.html (last access 9 July 2019).
Madagascar Tribune. 2011f. Les querelles sur l'héritage AREMA se perpétuent, www.madagascar-tribune.com/Les-querelles-sur-l-heritage-AREMA,15400.html (last access 9 July 2019).
Madagascar Tribune. 2011g. Communiqué de presse: Médiation de la SADC, www.madagascar-tribune.com/Mediation-de-la-SADC,15435.html (last access 9 July 2019).
Madagascar Tribune. 2011h. Les signataires de la Feuille de route, www.madagascar-tribune.com/Les-signataires-de-la-Feuille-de,16416.html (last access 9 July 2019).

Madagascar Tribune. 2011i. Mission de la SADC: Consultations avant toute signature, www.madagascar-tribune.com/Consultations-avant-toute,16389.html (last access 9 July 2019).

Madagascar Tribune. 2012a. «Ni, ni»: Inadmissible, c'est de l'ingérence, www.madagascar-tribune.com/Inadmissible-c-est-de-l-ingerence,18272.html (last access 9 July 2019).

Madagascar Tribune. 2012b. Mise en œuvre de la feuille de route: L'OIF est dans nos murs, www.madagascar-tribune.com/L-OIF-est-dans-nos-murs,17188.html (last access 9 July 2019).

Madagascar Tribune. 2013a. Résolutions de la réunion d'Ivato conduite par le FFKM: Pour un gouvernement neutre et une autre transition, www.madagascar-tribune.com/IMG/article_PDF/Pour-un-gouvernement-neutre-et-une_a18687.pdf (last access 9 July 2019).

Madagascar Tribune. 2013b. Détournements de vote et fraudes électorales: Béatrice Atallah promet des enquêtes, www.madagascar-tribune.com/Beatrice-Atallah-promet-des,19475.html (last access 9 July 2019).

Madagascar Tribune. 2013c. Observation des élections: Le Groupe des experts nationaux suggère, www.madagascar-tribune.com/Le-Groupe-des-experts-nationaux,19287.html (last access 9 July 2019).

Madagascar Tribune. 2013d. 350 véhicules 4×4 destinés à la propagande, bloqués au port de Toamasina: Camille Vital est monté au créneau, www.madagascar-tribune.com/Camille-Vital-est-monte-au-creneau,19179.html (last access 9 July 2019).

Madagascar Tribune. 2014a. Assemblée nationale: La majorité des sièges au Mapar, suivi de près par les indépendants, www.madagascar-tribune.com/La-majorite-des-sieges-au-Mapar,19621.html (last access 9 July 2019).

Madagascar Tribune. 2014b. Résultats de la présidentielle: L'ombre de la Côte d'Ivoire plane, www.madagascar-tribune.com/L-ombre-de-la-Cote-d-Ivoire-plane,19506.html (last access 9 July 2019).

Madagascar Tribune. 2014c. La Cour électorale spéciale: Pour la transparence, www.madagascar-tribune.com/Pour-la-transparence,19529.html (last access 9 July 2019).

Madagascar Tribune. 2014d. Jean Louis Robinson et la mouvance Ravalomanana: Des centaines de requêtes pour un autre résultat, www.madagascar-tribune.com/Des-centaines-de-requetes-pour-un,19501.html (last access 9 July 2019).

Madagascar Tribune. 2015a. Réconciliation: Qui fait quoi?, http://madagascar-tribune.com/Qui-fait-quoi,20864.html (last access 9 July 2019).

Madagascar Tribune. 2015b. La reconnaissance internationale toujours en marche, www.madagascar-tribune.com/La-reconnaissance-internationale,20959.html (last access 9 July 2019).

Madagascar Tribune. 2019. Andry Rajoelina promet un changement, www.madagascar-tribune.com/Andry-Rajoelina-promet-un-changement.html (last access 31 July 2019).

Mahitsy Fijery. 2013. *Déclaration préliminaire de la Plateforme Mahitsy Fijery*. Antananarivo: Mahitsy Fijery.

Makinda, Samuel M. & Wafula F. Okumu. 2008. *The African Union: Challenges of Globalization, Security and Governance*. London: Routledge.

Malmvig, Helle. 2014. Free us from power: Governmentality, counter-conduct, and simulation in European democracy and reform promotion in the Arab world, *International Political Sociology* 8:3, 293–310.

Marcus, George E. 1995. Ethnography in/of the world system: The emergence of multi-sited ethnography, *Annual Review of Anthropology* 24, 95–117.

Marcus, Richard R. 2007. Madagascar. In: Mehler, Andreas, Henning Melber, & Klaas van Walraven (eds.): *Africa Yearbook Online Vol. 4*, http://referenceworks.brillonline.com/entries/africa-yearbook-online/madagascar-vol-4-2007-ayb2007_COM_0046 (last access 9 July 2019).

Marcus, Richard R. 2008. Madagascar. In: Mehler, Andreas, Henning Melber, & Klaas van Walraven (eds.): *Africa Yearbook Online Vol. 5*, http://referenceworks.brillonline.com/entries/africa-yearbook-online/madagascar-vol-5-2008-ayb2008_COM_0047?s.num=0 (last access 9 July 2019).

Marcus, Richard R. 2010a. Marc the medici? The failure of a new form of neopatrimonial rule in Madagascar, *Political Science Quarterly* 125:1, 111–131.

Marcus, Richard R. 2010b. Madagascar. In: Mehler, Andreas, Henning Melber, & Klaas van Walraven (eds.): *Africa Yearbook Online Vol. 7*, http://referenceworks.brillonline.com/entries/africa-yearbook-online/madagascar-vol-7-2010-ayb2010_COM_0047?s.num=6 (last access 9 July 2019).

Marcus, Richard R. 2011. Madagascar. In: Mehler, Andreas, Henning Melber, & Klaas van Walraven (eds.): *Africa Yearbook Online Vol. 8*, http://referenceworks.brillonline.com/entries/africa-yearbook-online/madagascar-vol-8-2011-ayb2011_COM_0046 (last access 9 July 2019).

Marcus, Richard R. 2015. Madagascar. In: Mehler, Andreas, Henning Melber, & Klaas van Walraven (eds.): *Africa Yearbook Online Vol. 12*, http://dx.doi.org/10.1163/1872-9037_ayb_ayb2015_COM_0047 (last access 31 July 2019).

Marcus, Richard R. 2016. *The Politics of Institutional Failure in Madagascar's Third Republic*. Lanham: Lexington Books.

Marcus, Richard R. & Adrien M. Ratsimbaharison. 2005. Political parties in Madagascar: Neopatrimonial tools or democratic instruments?, *Party Politics* 11:4, 495–512.

Matlosa, Khabele. 2008. *The African Charter on Democracy, Elections and Governance: Declaration vs. Policy Practice*. Policy Brief 53. Johannesburg: Centre for Policy Studies.

Maundi, Mohammed O., William I. Zartman, Gilbert M. Khadiagala, & Kwaku Nuamah. 2006. *Getting In: Mediator's Entry into the Settlement of African Conflicts*. Washington, DC: United States Institute for Peace.

Mbangu, Lydie. 2005. *Recent Cases of Article 96 Consultations*. Discussion Paper No. 64C. Maastricht: ECDPM.

McCoy, Jennifer & Francisco Diez. 2011. *International Mediation in Venezuela*. Washington, DC: United States Institute of Peace.

McGowan, Patrick J. 2003. African military coups d'état 1956–2001: Frequency, trends and distribution, *Journal of Modern African Studies* 41:3, 339–370.

McMahon, Edward R. 2007. *The African Charter on Democracy, Elections and Governance: A Positive Step on a Long Path*. Nairobi: Open Society Institute.

McMahon, Edward R. & Scott H. Baker. 2006. *Piecing a Democratic Quilt? Regional Organizations and*

REFERENCES

Universal Norms. Bloomfield: Kumarian Press.

Mearsheimer, John J. 1995. The false promise of international institutions, *International Security* 19:3, 5–49.

Merlingen, Michael. 2003. Governmentality: Towards a Foucauldian framework for the study of IGOs, *Cooperation & Conflict* 38:4, 361–384.

Merlingen, Michael. 2011. From governance to governmentality in CSDP: Towards a Foucauldian research agenda, *Journal of Common Market Studies* 49:1, 149–169.

Merlingen, Michael & Rosa Ostrauskaite. 2005. Power/knowledge in international peacebuilding: The case of the EU Police Mission in Bosnia, *Alternatives: Global, Local, Political* 30:3, 297–323.

Midi Madagasikara. 2009a. Madagascar: Sortie de crise – Andry Rajoelina consulte l'Elysée, http://fr.allafrica.com/stories/200910010447.html (last access 9 July 2019).

Midi Madagasikara. 2009b. Madagascar: CAPSAT – Les militaires campent sur leur position, http://fr.allafrica.com/stories/200903100635.html (last access 9 July 2019).

Midi Madagasikara. 2009c. Madagascar: GIC – Armada de 48 diplomates, http://fr.allafrica.com/stories/200910060541.html (last access 9 July 2019).

Midi Madagasikara. 2010. Madagascar: Ambassadeurs limogés – Salaires suspendus par la HAT!, http://fr.allafrica.com/stories/201007310112.html (last access 9 July 2019).

Midi Madagasikara. 2012a. Madagascar: Feuille de route – la CNOSC réintègre le processus, http://fr.allafrica.com/stories/201207310488.html (last access 9 July 2019).

Midi Madagasikara. 2012b. Madagascar: Violation de la FDR – Une plainte reçue par le CSC, http://fr.allafrica.com/stories/201208150929.html (last access 9 July 2019).

Midi Madagasikara. 2014a. Madagascar: Peste, dahalo, montée des eaux, délestage – Tanà menacée par mille dangers, http://fr.allafrica.com/stories/201412021405.html?aa_source=nwsltr-madagascar-fr (last access 9 July 2019).

Midi Madagasikara. 2014b. Madagascar: Grève à Ankatso – «Les forces de l'ordre pénètrent même dans les salles d'examens», http://fr.allafrica.com/stories/201407250783.html (last access 9 July 2019).

Midi Madagasikara. 2014c. Madagascar: Une année riche en grèves et manifestations, http://fr.allafrica.com/stories/201412222842.html (last access 9 July 2019).

Migdal, Joel & Klaus Schlichte. 2005. Rethinking the state. In: Schlichte, Klaus (ed.): *The Dynamics of States: The Formation and Crises of State Domination*. Aldershot: Ashgate, 1–40.

Millar, Gearoid, Jaïr van der Lijn, & Willemijn Verkoren. 2013. Peacebuilding plans and local reconfigurations: Frictions between imported processes and indigenous practices, *International Peacekeeping* 20:2, 137–143.

Moore, Christopher W. 2003. *The Mediation Process. Practical Strategies for Resolving Conflict*. 3rd edition. San Francisco: Jossey-Bass.

Morel, Claude. 2014. *Cérémonie de remise des insignes de chevalier de l'ordre national à l'Ambassadeur Claude Morel, Chef du bureau de liaison de la Commission de l'Océan indien, le 15 janvier 2014*. Antananarivo: mimeo.

Mouvance Ravalomanana. 2011a. *Feuille de Route sortie de crise*

à Madagascar. *Observations et propositions*. Antananarivo: mimeo.
Mouvance Ravalomanana. 2011b. *Complaint in Terms of Clause 32 and Clause 43 of the SADC Roadmap to End the Crisis in Madagascar*. Antananarivo: mimeo.
Mouvance Ravalomanana. 2011c. *Report to the Southern African Development Community Extraordinary Summit on Madagascar*. Antananarivo: mimeo.
Mouvance Ravalomanana. 2012. *Report to the Southern African Development Community (SADC) on the Occasion of the SADC Summit in Maputo on Madagascar*. Antananarivo: mimeo.
Mouvance Ravalomanana. 2013. *Report to GIC Madagascar on the Occasion of the GIC Meeting in Addis Ababa on Madagascar*. Antananarivo: Mimeo.
Mouvance Zafy. 2009a. *Procès verbal des résultats des pourparlers du Carlton, Antananarivo, 20–22 mai 2009*. Antananarivo: mimeo.
Mouvance Zafy. 2009b. *Compte rendu des rencontres du Carlton, vendredi 12 et samedi 13 juin 2009*. Antananarivo: mimeo.
Mouvance Zafy. 2009c. *Convention en vue d'une sortie de crise et d'une réconciliation nationale*. Antananarivo: mimeo.
Mouvance Zafy. 2009d. *Propositions d'amendements d'une 'Charte' proposée par la Médiation Dramé-Ouédraogo*. Antananarivo: mimeo.
Mouvance Zafy. 2009e. *Mémorandum de la Mouvance Albert Zafy à SEM J. Chissano, nouveau Médiateur, sur la situation de la crise et des négociations en juillet 2009*. Antananarivo: mimeo.
Mouvance Zafy. 2009f. *Aide-mémoire par la Mouvance Albert Zafy sur la situation des négociations en vue de la reprise des pourparlers à Maputo, juillet 2009*. Antananarivo: mimeo.
Mouvance Zafy. 2010a. *Mémorandum par la Mouvance Albert Zafy pour une délégation de parlementaires UE-ACP sur la situation de la crise, juillet 2010*. Antananarivo: mimeo.
Mouvance Zafy. 2010b. *Réponse de la Mouvance Albert Zafy au Projet d'Accord soumis par SEM J. Chissano après le Sommet de Pretoria, mai 2010*. Antananarivo: mimeo.
Mouvance Zafy. 2011a. *Procès verbal de la rencontre des trois mouvances avec la médiation le 18 janvier 2011*. Antananarivo: mimeo.
Mouvance Zafy. 2011b. *Nouvelles propositions en vue d'une solution de sortie à la crise malgache*. Antananarivo: mimeo.
Mouvance Zafy. 2011c. *Réaction de la mouvance Albert Zafy à la 'Feuille de Route' du 31 janvier 2011*. Antananarivo: mimeo.
Mouvance Zafy. 2011d. *Letter to His Excellency Mr Joaquim Alberto Chissano*. Antananarivo: mimeo
Murphy, Alexander B. 1996. The sovereign state system as political-territorial ideal: Historical and contemporary considerations. In: Biersteker, Thomas J. & Cynthia Weber (eds.): *State Sovereignty as Social Construct*. Cambridge: Cambridge University Press, 81–120.
Murray, Rachel. 2004. *Human Rights in Africa: From the OAU to the African Union*. Cambridge: Cambridge University Press.
Mwanasali, Musifiky. 2006. Africa's responsibility to protect. In: Adebajo, Adekeye & Helen Scanlon (eds.): *A Dialogue of the Deaf: Essays on Africa and the United Nations*. Sunnyside: Jacana Media, 89–110.
N'Diaye, Boubacar. 2006. Mauritania, August 2005: Justice and democracy, or just another coup?, *African Affairs* 105:420, 421–441.
Nathan, Laurie. 2012. *Community of Insecurity: SADC's Struggle for Peace and Security in Southern Africa*. Farnham: Ashgate.

REFERENCES

Nathan, Laurie. 2013. *A Clash of Norms and Strategies in Madagascar: Mediation and the AU Policy on Unconstitutional Change of Government*. Mediation Arguments No. 4. Pretoria: Centre for Mediation in Africa.

Nathan, Laurie. 2017. *A Survey of Mediation in African Coups*. APN Working Papers No. 15. New York: African Peacebuilding Network.

Nativel, Didier & Faranirina V. Rajaonah. 2007. L'île et son continent. In: Nativel, Didier & Faranirina V. Rajaonah (eds.): *Madagascar et l'Afrique: Entre identité insulaire et appartenances historiques*. Paris: Karthala, 9–25.

Ndulo, Muna. 2012. The prohibition of unconstitutional change of government. In: Yusuf, Abdulqawi A. & Fatsah Ouguergouz (eds.): *The African Union: Legal and Institutional Framework. A Manual on the Pan-African Organization*. Leiden: Martinus Nijhoff, 251–274.

Neal, Andrew W. 2013. Empiricism without positivism: King Lear and critical security studies. In: Salter, Mark B. & Can E. Mutlu (eds.): *Research Methods in Critical Security Studies*. London: Routledge, 42–45.

Neumann, Iver B. & Ole Jacob Sending. 2007. 'The international' as governmentality, *Millennium: Journal of International Studies* 35:3, 677–701.

Neumann, Iver B. & Ole Jacob Sending. 2010. *Governing the Global Polity: Practice, Mentality, Rationality*. Ann Arbor: University of Michigan Press.

Nkiwane, Tandeka C. 2001. Africa and international relations: Regional lessons for a global dialogue, *International Political Science Review* 22:3, 279–290.

Novicki, Margaret A. 1992. Interview Salim Ahmed Salim: A new agenda for the OAU, *Africa Report* 37:3, 36–39.

OAU. 1963. *OAU Charter*. Addis Ababa: Organisation of African Unity.

OAU. 1977. *OAU Convention for the Elimination of Mercenarism in Africa*. CM/817 (XXIX) Annex II Rev.1. Addis Ababa: Organisation of African Unity.

OAU. 2000a. *Declaration on the Framework for an OAU Response to Unconstitutional Changes of Government*. AHG/Decl.5 (XXXVI). Lomé: Organisation of African Unity.

OAU. 2000b. *Report of the Sub-Committee of the Central Organ on Unconstitutional Changes of Government*. Addis Ababa: Organisation of African Unity.

OAU. 2000c. *Framework for an OAU Response to Unconstitutional Changes of Government*. CM/2166(LXXII) Rev. 2 Annex D. Addis Ababa: Organisation of African Unity.

OAU. 2000d. *Report of the Sub-Committee of the Central Organ on Unconstitutional Changes in Africa*. Lomé: Organisation of African Unity.

OAU. 2000e. *Constitutive Act of the African Union*. Lomé: Organisation of African Unity.

OAU Assembly. 1999. *Decision by the OAU Assembly of Heads of State and Government*. AHG/Dec.142 (XXXV). Algiers: Organisation of African Unity.

OAU Council of Ministers. 1997. *Decision on Sierra Leone*. CM/Dec.356 (LXVI). Harare: Organisation of African Unity.

OAU Council of Ministers. 1999. *Decision by the Council of Ministers on Un-Constitutional Changes in Member States*. CM/Dec.483 (LXX). Algiers: Organisation of African Unity.

OAU Secretariat. 1999. *Report of the Secretary-General on the Follow-Up on Decisions of the Council and Summit on Unconstitutional Changes of Government*. Central Organ/

MEC/AMB/2 (LIX). Addis Ababa: Organisation of African Unity.
OAU Secretariat. 2000. *Report of the Secretary-General on the Implementation of the Algiers Decisions of the Assembly of Heads of State and Government and the Council of Ministers on Unconstitutional Changes of Government.* CM/2166(LXXII) Rev. 2. Lomé: Organisation of African Unity.
OAU Secretariat. 2002. *Report of the Secretary-General on the Situation in Madagascar: Sixth Session of the Central Organ of the OAU Mechanism for Conflict Prevention, Management and Resolution at Summit Level.* Central/MEC/AHG/2 (VI). Addis Ababa: Organisation of African Unity.
Odoom Isaac & Nathan Andrews. 2017. What/who is still missing in international relations scholarship? Situating Africa as an agent in IR theorising, *Third World Quarterly* 38:1, 42–60.
OECD. 2015. *Development Aid at a Glance: Statistics by Region.* Paris: Organisation for Economic Co-operation and Development.
OIF. 2000. *Déclaration de Bamako.* Bamako: Organisation Internationale de la Francophonie.
OIF. 2009. Le Conseil permanent de la Francophonie suspend Madagascar, www.francophonie. org/Le-Conseil-permanent-de-la-28269.html (last access 9 July 2019).
OIF. 2011. *Rapport d'évaluation du processus électoral à Madagascar. Rapport d'étape.* Paris: Organisation Internationale de la Francophonie.
OIF. 2012. *Mission d'assistance et d'évaluation des besoins du processus électoral à Madagascar effectuée à Madagascar du 22 avril au 9 mai 2012. Rapport au Secrétaire générale de la Francophonie.* Paris: Organisation Internationale de la Francophonie.
Omorogbe, Yemisi. 2011. A club of incumbents? The African Union and coups d'état, *Vanderbilt Journal of Transnational Law* 44:123, 123–154.
Onuf, Nicolas & Frank F. Klink. 1989. Anarchy, authority, rule, *International Studies Quarterly* 33:2, 149–173.
Oosthuizen, Gabriël H. 2006. *The Southern African Development Community: The Organisation, Its Policies and Prospects.* Midrand: Institute for Global Dialogue.
Orford, Anne. 2011. *International Authority and the Responsibility to Protect.* Cambridge: Cambridge University Press.
PACTE. 2013. *Madagascar processus électoral 2013: Manuel pour la mission d'observation électoral du SADC-ECF.* Antananarivo: Projet d'Appui à la Crédibilité et à la Transparence des Elections.
Paffenholz, Thania. 2014. Civil society in peace negotiations: Beyond the inclusion–exclusion dichotomy, *Negotiation Journal* 30:1, 69–91.
PANA. 2000. African Union to refuse putsches, political assassinations, https://global.factiva.com/ha/default.aspx#./!?&_suid=1448623 45372900695468035992235 (last access 17 November 2015).
Panos. 2009. *Voices of Change: Oral Testimony of the Antanosy People.* London: Panos.
PAP. 2013. *Report of the Pan-African Parliament for the Period July 2012 to May 2013.* Midrand: Pan-African Parliament.
Paris, Roland. 2002. International peacebuilding and the 'mission civilisatrice', *Review of International Studies* 28:4, 637–656.
Pearlman, Wendy. 2008. Spoiling inside and out: International political contestation and the Middle East peace process, *International Security* 33:3, 79–109.
Pellerin, Matthieu. 2009a. Madagascar: un conflit d'entrepreneurs? Figures de la

réussite économique et rivalités politiques, *Politique africaine* 113, 152–165.
Pellerin, Matthieu. 2009b. Crise malgache: interview avec Sylvain Touati, www.ifri.org/fr/publications/editoriaux/lafrique-questions/lafrique-questions-ndeg5-crise-malgache (last access 9 July 2019).
Pellerin, Matthieu. 2011. *Le nouvel essor des relations entre la Chine et Madagascar*. Paris: Institut français des relations internationales.
Pellerin, Matthieu. 2014a. La rupture en demi-teinte du nouveau président malgache, https://afriquedecryptages.wordpress.com/2014/08/28/la-rupture-en-demi-teinte-du-nouveau-president-malgache/ (last access 9 July 2019).
Pellerin, Matthieu. 2014b. *Madagascar: gérer l'héritage de la transition*. Note de l'Ifri. Paris: Institut français des relations internationales.
Peterson, Spike V. 1990. Whose rights? A critique of the 'givens' in human rights discourse, *Alternatives: Global, Local, Political* 15:3, 303–344.
Pevehouse, Jon C. 2005. *Democracy from Above: Regional Organizations and Democratization*. Cambridge: Cambridge University Press.
Picard, Louis A. & Ezzedine Moudoud. 2010. The 2008 Guinea coup: Neither inevitable nor inexorable, *Journal of Contemporary African Studies* 28:1, 51–69.
Piccolino, Giulia. 2012. David against Goliath in Côte d'Ivoire? Laurent Gbagbo's war against global governance, *African Affairs* 111:442, 1–23.
Posner, Daniel N. & Daniel J. Young. 2007. The institutionalization of political power in Africa, *Journal of Democracy* 18:3, 126–140.
Pouligny, Béatrice. 2006. *Peace Operations Seen from Below: UN Missions and Local People*. Bloomfield: Kumarian Press.

Powell, Jonathan M. 2014. An assessment of the 'democratic' coup theory: Democratic trajectories in Africa, 1952–2012, *African Security Review* 23:3, 213–224.
Powell, Jonathan, Trace Lasley, & Rebecca Schiel. 2016. Comparing coups d'état in Africa, 1950–2014, *Studies in Comparative International Development* 51:4, 482–502.
Rabanirinirarison, Rindra Hasimbelo & Jean-Aimé Raveloson. 2011. *Les partis politiques malgaches à travers les régimes et gouvernements successifs*. Antananarivo: Friedrich-Ebert-Stiftung.
Rabemananoro, Erick A. 2014. Le drame des «investissements irréversibles» à Madagascar: Quand la comédie se mue en tragédie, *Afrique contemporaine* 251, 51–68.
Raison, Françoise. 2007. L'Afrique de Didier Ratsiraka, lieu de passage vers la cour des grands. In: Nativel, Didier & Faranirina V. Rajaonah (eds.): *Madagascar et l'Afrique. Entre identité insulaire et appartenances historiques*. Paris: Karthala, 345–362.
Rajaonah, Faranirina V. 2002. Les imaginaires de l'étranger dans la crise Malgache, *Politique africaine* 86, 152–170.
Rajerison, Olivia. 2013. *La légitimation démocratique du pouvoir à Madagascar*. Antananarivo: Friedrich-Ebert-Stiftung.
Rakoto, Ignace & Sylvain Urfer (eds.). 2014. *Esclavage et libération à Madagascar*. Paris: Karthala.
Rakotomalala, Patrick. 2012. Implicites de la crise malgache et diplomatie française. In: Randrianja, Solofo (ed.): *Madagascar: le coup d'État de mars 2009*. Paris: Karthala, 211–238.
Rakotomalala, Patrick. 2014. Madagascar: la crise de 2009 ou les aléas de la diplomatie française, *Afrique contemporaine* 251, 93–105.
Rakotomamonjy, Joël, Laetitia Razafimamonjy, Mireille

Razafindrakoto, Désiré Razafindrazaka, François Roubaud, & Jean-Michel Wachsberger. 2014a. *Gouvernance, corruption et confiance à l'égard des institutions à Madagascar: expérience, perception et attentes de la population.* Afrobarometer Briefing Papers No. 140. Accra: Afrobarometer.

Rakotomamonjy, Joël, Laetitia Razafimamonjy, Mireille Razafindrakoto, Désiré Razafindrazaka, François Roubaud, & Jean-Michel Wachsberger. 2014b. *Redevabilité sociale et attentes des Malgaches envers leurs dirigeants.* Afrobarometer Briefing Papers No. 141. Accra: Afrobarometer.

Ralambomahay, Toavina. 2011. *Madagascar dans une crise interminable.* Paris: L'Harmattan.

Ralambomahay, Toavina. 2012. *Des entorses aux droits de l'Homme et aux principes démocratiques dans la feuille de route*, www.pambazuka.org/fr/governance/madagascar-des-entorses-aux-droits-de-l%E2%80%99homme-et-aux-principes-d%C3%A9mocratiques-dans-la (last access 9 July 2019).

Ralambomahay, Toavina. 2014. *Pratiques politiques: expériences des candidats à l'élection législative de 2013.* Antananarivo: Friedrich-Ebert-Stiftung.

Ramasy, Juvence. F. 2012. Militaires et système politique. In: Randrianja, Solofo (ed.): *Madagascar: le coup d'État de mars 2009.* Paris: Karthala, 67–96.

Ramasy, Juvence F. & Olivier Vallée. 2014. *Transition électorale à Madagascar et enjeux sécuritaires.* Paris: Fondation pour la Recherche Stratégique.

Randrianasolo, José & Toky Ravoavy. 2007. *Madagascar: absence de dialogue sur le projet minier de Rio Tinto à Taolagnaro (Ex-Fort-Dauphin)*, www.afaspa.com/article.php3?id_article=140 (last access 9 July 2019).

Randrianja, Solofo. 2003. 'Be not afraid: Only believe': Madagascar 2002, *African Affairs* 102:407, 309–329.

Randrianja, Solofo. 2012a. Le coup d'Etat de mars 2009, chronologie et causes. In: Randrianja, Solofo (ed.): *Madagascar: le coup d'État de mars 2009.* Paris: Karthala, 13–41.

Randrianja, Solofo. 2012b. Les années Ravalomanana (2002–2009): Politique et libéralisme économique. In: Randrianja, Solofo (ed.): *Madagascar: le coup d'État de mars 2009.* Paris: Karthala, 239–277.

Randrianja, Solofo & Stephen Ellis. 2009. *Madagascar: A Short History.* Chicago: University of Chicago Press.

Ranjeva, Raymond. 2012. Constitutionalismes et sorties de crise à Madagascar. In: Randrianja, Solofo (ed.): *Madagascar: le coup d'État de mars 2009.* Paris: Karthala, 279–284.

Ratsimbaharison, Adrien M. 2017. *The Political Crisis of March 2009 in Madagascar: A Case Study of Conflict and Conflict Mediation.* Lanham: Rowman & Littlefield.

Razafindrakoto, Mireille, Désiré Razafindrazaka, & François Roubaud. 2009. *Governance in Madagascar: Scope and Limits of the Fight Against Corruption and of Decentralization.* Afrobarometer Briefing Paper No. 63. Accra: Afrobarometer.

Razafindrakoto, Mireille, François Roubaud, & Jean-Michel Wachsberger. 2014a. Introduction thématique, *Afrique contemporaine* 251, 13–22.

Razafindrakoto, Mireille, François Roubaud, & Jean-Michel Wachsberger. 2014b. Élites, pouvoir et régulation à Madagascar: Une lecture de l'histoire à l'aune de l'économie politique, *Afrique contemporaine* 251, 25–50.

Razafindrakoto, Mireille, François Roubaud, & Jean-Michel Wachsberger (eds.). 2018. *Madagascar, d'une crise l'autre: ruptures et continuité*. Paris: Karthala/IRD.

Razafindrakoto, Mireille, François Roubaud, & Jean-Michel Wachsberger. 2020. *Puzzle and Paradox: A Political Economy of Madagascar*. Cambridge: Cambridge University Press.

République de Madagascar. 2009a. *Ordonnance No 2009-001 du 17 mars 2009 conférant les pleins pouvoirs à un Directoire Militaire*. Antananarivo: mimeo.

République de Madagascar. 2009b. *Ordonnance No 2009-002 du mars 2009 portant le transfère des pleins pouvoirs à Andry Rajoelina*. Antananarivo: mimeo.

République de Madagascar. 2009c. *Charte de la transition*. Maputo: mimeo.

République de Madagascar. 2009d. *Accord politique de Maputo*. Maputo: mimeo.

République de Madagascar. 2010a. *Ordonnance No. 2010-010 relative à la mise en place du Parlement de la Transition*. Antananarivo: mimeo.

République de Madagascar. 2010b. *Accord politique d'Ivato du 13 août 2010*. Antananarivo: mimeo

Reus-Smit, Christian. 1999. *The Moral Purpose of the State: Culture, Social Identity, and Institutional Rationality in International Relations*. Princeton: Princeton University Press.

Reus-Smit, Christian. 2001. Human rights and the social construction of sovereignty, *Review of International Studies* 27:4, 519–538.

Reus-Smit, Christian. 2004. The politics of international law. In: Reus-Smit, Christian (ed.): *The Politics of International Law*. Cambridge: Cambridge University Press, 14–44.

Reus-Smit, Christian. 2013. The concept of intervention, *Review of International Studies* 39:5, 1057–1076.

Reuters. 1993. OAU condemns coup in Burundi, https://global.factiva.com/ha/default.aspx#./!?&_suid=14 4862119146401004177967552095 7 (last access 17 November 2015).

Reuters. 1995. OAU condemns coup in Sao Tomé et Principe, https://global.factiva.com/ha/default.aspx#./!?&_suid=14486215212770 2612080422695726 (last access 25 November 2015).

Reuters. 1996a. African body stands firm on Burundi, https://global.factiva.com/ha/default.aspx#./!?&_suid=14486217149970025250 931037589908 (last access 17 November 2015).

Reuters. 1996b. OAU says coup in Burundi will be met with force, https://global.factiva.com/ha/default.aspx#./!?&_suid=1448622 5507880369647266110405 3 (last access 27 November 2015).

Reuters. 1997. OAU condemns coups, seeks democracy for all, https://global.factiva.com/ha/default.aspx#./!?&_suid=1448621 3581580576013048877939 6 (last access 17 November 2015).

RFI. 2009a. Madagascar: Les avertissements du FMI et de la communauté internationale, www1.rfi.fr/actufr/articles/110/article_78082.asp (last access 9 July 2019).

RFI. 2009b. Ravalomanana affirme qu'il rentrera «le plus tôt possible» dans son pays, www1.rfi.fr/actufr/articles/113/article_81022.asp (last access 9 July 2019).

RFI. 2013. Ablassé Ouedraogo sur RFI: «surtout ne pas faire le choix à la place du peuple malgache», www.rfi.fr/afrique/20130623-ablasse-ouedraogo-madagascar-rajoelina-ratsiraka-sadc-ratsiraka/ (last access 9 July 2019).

RFI. 2014. Madagascar: pourquoi les dahalos volent-ils des zébus?, www.rfi.fr/afrique/20140430-

madagascar-questionnements-autour-trafic-zebus-dahalos/ (last access 9 July 2019).
RFI. 2015. Afrique: Madagascar célèbre la Francophonie et son retour dans l'OIF, www.rfi.fr/afrique/20150316-madagascar-celebre-francophonie-son-retour-oif (last access 9 July 2019).
Richmond, Oliver P. & Audra Mitchell. 2011. Peacebuilding and critical forms of agency: From resistance to subsistence, *Alternatives: Global, Local, Political* 36:4, 326–344.
Richmond, Oliver P. & Roger Mac Ginty. 2015. Where now for the critique of the liberal peace?, *Cooperation & Conflict* 50:2, 171–189.
Roth, Brad R. 1999. *Governmental Illegitimacy in International Law*. Oxford: Clarendon Press.
Sabaratnam, Meera. 2013. Avatars of Eurocentrism in the critique of the liberal peace, *Security Dialogue* 44:3, 259–278.
SADC. 2001. *Protocol on Politics, Defence and Security in the Southern African Development Community (SADC) Region*. Blantyre: Southern African Development Community.
SADC. 2009a. *Communiqué of an Extraordinary Summit of SADC Heads of State and Government of 20 June 2009*. Sandton: Southern African Development Community.
SADC. 2009b. *Communiqué of the Extraordinary Summit of SADC Heads of State and Government 30 March 2009*. Mbabane: Southern African Development Community.
SADC. 2009c. *Extraordinary SADC Summit of Troika of the Organ on Politics, Defence and Security Cooperation of 19 March*. Ezulwini: Southern African Development Community.
SADC. 2009d. *SADC Mediation Efforts in Madagascar. Draft Report, 7 July–10 August 2009*. SC-A87.3.

Gaborone: Southern African Development Community.
SADC. 2010a. *Double Troika Summit Communiqué*. Maputo: Southern African Development Community.
SADC. 2010b. *30th Jubilée Summit: Communiqué*. Windhoek: Southern African Development Community.
SADC. 2010c. *Communiqué of the Extraordinary Summit of SADC Heads of State and Government*. Gaborone: Southern African Development Community.
SADC. 2011a. *SADC Roadmap for Ending the Crisis in Madagascar*. Antananarivo: Southern African Development Community.
SADC. 2011b. *Réunion du sommet de la Troïka de l'Organe de coopération en matière de politique, défense et sécurité de la SADC*. Livingstone: Southern African Development Community.
SADC. 2011c. *Extraordinary Summit of Heads of State and Government of the Southern African Development Community*. Sandton: Southern African Development Community.
SADC. 2011d. *Communiqué Extraordinary Summit Heads of State and Government of the Southern Africa Development Community*. Windhoek: Southern African Development Community.
SADC. 2011e. *Madagascar Roadmap Implementation Framework*. Gaborone: Southern African Development Community.
SADC. 2013a. *Extra-Ordinary Summit of the SADC Heads of State and Government*. Addis Ababa: Southern African Development Community.
SADC. 2013b. *Extra-Ordinary Summit of the SADC Heads of State and Government*. Maputo: Southern African Development Community.
SADC. 2013c. *Summit of the SADC Troika of the Organ on Politics, Defence and Security Cooperation*. Cape Town: Southern African Development Community.

SADC. 2014. *Communiqué of the 34th Summit of SADC Heads of State and Government*. Victoria Falls: Southern African Development Community.

SADC. 2015. *Communiqué of the 35th Summit of Heads of State and Government*. Gaborone: Southern African Development Community.

Sampson, Peter R. 2012. Conceptual shifts in multi-track mediation in Sub-Saharan Africa. In: Engel, Ulf (ed.): *New Mediation Practices in African Conflicts*. Leipzig: Leipziger Universitätsverlag, 237–254.

Sandholtz, Wayne & Kendall Stiles. 2008. *International Norms and Cycles of Change*. Oxford: Oxford University Press.

Saungweme, Sekai. 2007. *A Critical Look at the Charter on Democracy, Elections and Governance in Africa*. Nairobi: Open Society Institute.

Schattschneider, Elmer E. 1960. *The Semisovereign People: A Realist's View of Democracy in America*. New York: Holt, Rinehart & Winston.

Schlichte, Klaus. 2012. Der Streit der Legitimitäten: Der Konflikt als Grund einer historischen Soziologie des Politischen, *Zeitschrift für Friedens- und Konfliktforschung* 1:1, 9–43.

Schroeder, Ursula. 2018. Introduction: Decentring the study of international interventions, *Cooperation & Conflict* 53:2, 139–153.

Schwartz-Shea, Peregrine & Dvora Yanow. 2012. *Interpretative Research Design: Concepts and Processes*. New York: Routledge.

Scott, David. 2012. Norms of self-determination: Thinking sovereignty through, *Middle East and Governance* 4:2–3, 195–224.

SeFaFi. 2014a. De la véritable décentralisation, 1 octobre 2004. In: SeFaFi (ed.): *L'Observatoire de la vie publique à Madagascar. D'une crise à l'autre (2001–2013)*. Paris: Karthala, 94–101.

SeFaFi. 2014b. Décentralisation ou centralisation? 4 mars 2005. In: SeFaFi (ed.): *L'Observatoire de la vie publique à Madagascar. D'une crise à l'autre (2001–2013)*. Paris: Karthala, 110–113.

SeFaFi. 2014c. Sefo Fokotany: Où allons-nous? 18 octobre 2007. In: SeFaFi (ed.): *L'Observatoire de la vie publique à Madagascar. D'une crise à l'autre (2001–2013)*. Paris: Karthala, 199–204.

SeFaFi. 2014d. Quelle décentralisation pour Madagascar? 28 mars 2008. In: SeFaFi (ed.): *L'Observatoire de la vie publique à Madagascar. D'une crise à l'autre (2001–2013)*. Paris: Karthala, 218–226.

SeFaFi. 2014e. Les ressources minières au profit de quels intérêts? In: SeFaFi (ed.): *L'Observatoire de la vie publique à Madagascar. D'une crise à l'autre (2001–2013)*. Paris: Karthala, 226–232.

SeFaFi. 2014f. Pour une nouvelle politique minière à Madagascar. In: SeFaFi (ed.): *L'Observatoire de la vie publique à Madagascar. D'une crise à l'autre (2001–2013)*. Paris: Karthala, 240–242.

SeFaFi. 2014g. La hausse du cout de la vie, 12 septembre 2008. In: SeFaFi (ed.): *L'Observatoire de la vie publique à Madagascar. D'une crise à l'autre (2001–2013)*. Paris: Karthala, 232–237.

SeFaFi. 2014h. Pour la défense des valeurs Républicaines et la consolidation de la démocratie à Madagascar, 21 janvier 2009. In: SeFaFi (ed.): *L'Observatoire de la vie publique à Madagascar. D'une crise à l'autre (2001–2013)*. Paris: Karthala, 253–255.

SeFaFi. 2014i. Comment gérer nos terres? 8 décembre 2008. In: SeFaFi (ed.): *L'Observatoire de la vie publique à Madagascar. D'une crise à l'autre (2001–2013)*. Paris: Karthala, 243–246.

SeFaFi. 2014j. Communauté internationale et solution

malgacho-malgache, 28 novembre 2012. In: SeFaFi (ed.): *L'Observatoire de la vie publique à Madagascar. D'une crise à l'autre (2001–2013)*. Paris: Karthala, 384–392.

SeFaFi. 2014k. Transition: Rappel des vrais objectifs, 23 novembre 2009. In: SeFaFi (ed.): *L'Observatoire de la vie publique à Madagascar. D'une crise à l'autre (2001–2013)*. Paris: Karthala, 284–287.

SeFaFi. 2014l. Élections de sortie de transition: les obstacles à surmonter, 23 mars 2013. In: SeFaFi (ed.): *L'Observatoire de la vie publique à Madagascar. D'une crise à l'autre (2001–2013)*. Paris: Karthala, 400–404.

SeFaFi. 2014m. Arrêter la pagaille, sortir du transitoire, 1 juin 2011. In: SeFaFi (ed.): *L'Observatoire de la vie publique à Madagascar. D'une crise à l'autre (2001–2013)*. Paris: Karthala, 341–345.

SeFaFi. 2014n. La «feuille de route», et après? 21 octobre 2011. In: SeFaFi (ed.): *L'Observatoire de la vie publique à Madagascar. D'une crise à l'autre (2001–2013)*. Paris: Karthala, 352–354.

SeFaFi. 2014o. Impunité, amnistie et réconciliation. Bilan des ateliers du SeFaFi, 7 novembre 2012. In: SeFaFi (ed.): *L'Observatoire de la vie publique à Madagascar. D'une crise à l'autre (2001–2013)*. Paris: Karthala, 378–383.

SeFaFi. 2015a. Les dysfonctionnements de l'Etat, 7 février 2015, http://sefafi.mg/fr/posts/les-dysfonctionnements-de-letat (last access 9 July 2019).

SeFaFi. 2015b. Pour que le pire ne soit pas à venir ..., 12 septembre 2015, http://sefafi.mg/fr/posts/pour-que-le-pire-ne-soit-pas-a-venir (last access 9 July 2019).

Sellström, Tor. 2015. *Africa in the Indian Ocean: Islands in Ebb and Flow*. Leiden: Brill.

Sending, Ole Jacob. 2015. *The Politics of Expertise: Competing for Authority in Global Governance*. Ann Arbor: University of Michigan Press.

Seybolt, Taylor B. 2016. The use of force. In: Bellamy, Alex J. & Tim Dunne (eds.): *The Oxford Handbook of the Responsibility to Protect*, Oxford: Oxford University Press, 561–580.

Shannon, Megan, Thyne Clayton, Sarah Hayden, & Amanda Dugan. 2015. The international community's reaction to coups, *Foreign Policy Analysis* 11:4, 363–376.

Shapiro, Michael J. 1981. *Language and Political Understanding: The Politics of Discursive Practices*. New Haven: Yale University Press.

Shore, Chris & Susan Wright. 1997. *Anthropology of Policy: Critical Perspectives on Governance and Power*. London: Routledge.

Simão, Leonardo. 2011. *Letter to the Three Mouvances*. Maputo: mimeo.

Smith, Karen. 2009. Has Africa got anything to say? African contributions to the theoretical development of international relations, *The Round Table* 98:402, 269–284.

Smith-Cannoy, Heather. 2012. Defending democracy? Assessing the OAS's 2002 diplomatic intervention in Haiti, *Civil Wars* 14:3, 431–450.

Söderbaum, Fredrik & Rodrigo Tavares (eds.). 2011. *Regional Organizations in African Security*. Abingdon: Routledge.

Souaré, Issaka K. 2009. *The AU and the Challenge of Unconstitutional Changes of Government in Africa*. ISS Paper 197. Pretoria: Institute for Security Studies.

Souaré, Issaka K. 2014. The African Union as a norm entrepreneur on military coups d'état in Africa (1952–2012): An empirical assessment, *Journal of Modern African Studies* 52:1, 69–94.

Stepputat, Finn & Jessica Larsen. 2015. *Global Political Ethnography: A Methodological Approach to Studying Global Policy Regimes*. DIIS Working Paper. Copenhagen: Danish Institute for International Studies.

Sturman, Kathryn. 2008. The use of sanctions by the African Union: Peaceful means to peaceful ends? In: Wheeler, Tom (ed.): *South African Yearbook of International Affairs*. Johannesburg: South African Institute of International Affairs, 97–108.

Svensson, Isak & Peter Wallensteen. 2010. *The Go-Between: Jan Eliasson and the Styles of Mediation*. Washington, DC: United States Institute of Peace.

Tansey, Oisín. 2017. The fading of the anti-coup norm, *Journal of Democracy* 28:1, 144–156.

TANY. 2013. *Land Grabbing in Madagascar: Echoes and Testimonies from the Field*. Antananarivo: Collectif pour la Défense des Terres Malgaches.

Tarabey, Bilal. 2014. *Madagascar dahalo*. Antananarivo: no comment editions.

Tavares, Rodrigo & Luís B. Bernadino. 2011. Speaking the language of security: The commonwealth, the Francophonie and the CPLP in conflict management in Africa, *Conflict, Security & Development* 11:5, 607–636.

Tieku, Thomas K. 2009. Multilateralization of democracy promotion and defense in Africa, *Africa Today* 56:2, 75–91.

Tieku, Thomas K. 2016. *Governing Africa: 3D Analysis of the African Union's Performance*. Lanham: Rowman & Littlefield.

Trois Mouvances. 2010. *Résolutions des trois mouvances, 13–14 août 2010 Carlton Madagascar*. Antananarivo: mimeo.

Tully, James. 2002. Political philosophy as a critical activity, *Political Theory* 30:4, 533–555.

Turner, Mandy & Florian Kühn. 2019. 'The West' and 'The Rest' in international interventions: Eurocentrism and the competition for order, *Conflict, Security & Development* 19:3, 237–243.

UN. 2012. *Report of the Electoral Needs Assessment Mission to Madagascar*. New York: United Nations.

UN DPA. 2011. *Mediation Support Unit Annual Report 2010*. New York: United Nations Department for Political Affairs.

UN General Assembly. 2011. *Rapport du Rapporteur spécial sur le droit à l'alimentation, Olivier De Schutter: Mission à Madagascar (18 au 22 juillet 2011)*. A/HRC/19/59/Add.4. New York: United Nations.

UN News. 2009. Madagascar: General Assembly denies delegation permission to address forum, www.un.org/apps/news/story.asp?NewsID=32270#.VGN7ootyeDo (last access 9 July 2019).

UNDP. 2013. *Rapport d'activités*. Antananarivo: United Nations Development Programme.

Urfer, Sylvain. 2009. Églises et politique à Madagascar, un éclairage historique, *Doctrine sociale de l'Église catholique*, www.doctrine-sociale-catholique.fr/la-doctrine-sociale-en-debat/154-eglises-et-politique-a-madagascar#%C3%89glises%20et%20politique%20%C3%A0%20Madagascar (last access 9 July 2019).

US Government. 2010. *Non-Paper: Restauration de la Démocratie à Madagascar*. Antananarivo: mimeo.

van Walraven, Klaas. 1996. *Dreams of Power: The Role of the Organization of African Unity in the Politics of Africa, 1963-1993*. Ridderkerk: mimeo.

Vandeginste, Stef. 2013. The African Union, constitutionalism and power-sharing, *Journal of African Law* 57:1, 1–28.

Various. 2009. *Assises nationales 2–3 avril 2009: résolutions*. Antananarivo: mimeo.

Veit, Alex. 2010. *Intervention as Indirect Rule: Civil War and Statebuilding in the Democratic Republic of Congo*. Frankfurt am Main: Campus Verlag.
Veit, Alex & Klaus Schlichte. 2012. Three arenas: The conflictive logic of external statebuilding. In: Bliesemann de Guevara, Berit (ed.): *Statebuilding and State-Formation: The Political Sociology of Intervention*. London: Routledge, 167–181.
Véron, Jean-Bernard. 2010. L'Afrique post-indépendances: 50 ans de crises? L'exemple de Madagascar, *Afrique contemporaine* 235, 115–126.
Vigh, Henrik. 2008. Crisis and chronicity: Anthropological perspectives on continuous conflict and decline, *Ethnos: Journal of Anthropology* 73:1, 5–24.
Vivier, Jean-Loup. 2010. *Madagascar, une île à la dérive. Les années 2007–2010 de Ravalomanana à Rajoelina*. Paris: L'Harmattan.
Wachira, George Mukundi. 2014. The role of the African Union in strengthening the rule of law and constitutional order. In: Cordenillo, Raul & Kristen Samle (eds.): *Rule of Law and Constitution Building: The Role of Regional Organizations*. Stockholm: International IDEA, 9–30.
Walker, R.B.J. 1993. *Inside/Outside: International Relations as Political Theory*. Cambridge: Cambridge University Press.
Wall, James A. 1981. Mediation: An analysis, review, and proposed research, *Journal of Conflict Resolution* 25:1, 157–180.
Wallner, Ingo. 2012. *Kultur- und Nationalbewusstsein: Zur Gestaltung einer nationalen Identität Madagaskars*. Dissertationsschrift. Münster: Universität Münster.
Walters, William. 2012. *Governmentality: Critical Encounters*. Oxon: Routledge.

Wanis-St. John, Anthony. 2006. Back-channel negotiation: International bargaining in the shadows, *International Negotiation* 22:2, 119–144.
Weber, Max. 2006 [1922]. *Wirtschaft und Gesellschaft*. Paderborn: voltmedia.
Welch, Claude E. Jr. 1975. The OAU and international recognition: Lessons from Uganda. In: El-Ayouty, Yassin (ed.): *The Organization of African Unity After Ten Years: Comparative Perspectives*. New York: Praeger, 103–117.
Whalan, Jeni. 2013. *How Peace Operations Work: Power, Legitimacy and Effectiveness*. Oxford: Oxford University Press.
Whitehouse, Bruce. 2013. 'A festival of brigands': In search of democracy and political legitimacy in Mali, *Strategic Review for Southern Africa* 35:2, 35–52.
Wiebusch, Micha, Chika Charles Aniekwe, Lutz Oette, & Stef Vandeginste. 2019. The African Charter on Democracy, Elections and Governance: Past, present and future, *Journal of African Law* 63:S1, 9–38.
Wight, Martin. 1972. International legitimacy, *International Relations* 4:1, 1–28.
Wilén, Nina & Paul D. Williams. 2018. The African Union and coercive diplomacy: The case of Burundi, *Journal of Modern African Studies* 56:4, 673–696.
Williams, David. 2013. Development, intervention, and international order, *Review of International Studies* 39:5, 1213–1231.
Williams, Paul D. 2007. From non-intervention to non-indifference: The origins and development of the African Union's security culture, *African Affairs* 106:423, 253–279.
Williams, Paul D. 2014. Reflections on the evolving African Peace and Security Architecture, *African Security* 7:3, 147–162.

Williams, Paul D. 2018. *Fighting for Peace in Somalia: A History and Analysis of the African Union Mission (AMISOM), 2007–2017*. Oxford: Oxford University Press.

Witt, Antonia. 2012a. *Negotiating Political Order(s): The Politics of Unconstitutional Changes of Government*. CAS Working Paper Series No. 2. Leipzig: Leipziger Universitätsverlag.

Witt, Antonia. 2012b. A constructive engagement? The European Union's contributions to mediating coups d'état in Africa. In: Engel, Ulf (ed.): *New Mediation Practices in African Conflicts*. Leipzig: Leipziger Universitätsverlag, 211–236.

Witt, Antonia. 2013a. The African Union and contested political order(s). In: Engel, Ulf & João Gomes Porto (eds.): *Towards an African Peace and Security Regime: Continental Embeddedness, Transnational Linkages, Strategic Relevance*. Farnham: Ashgate, 11–30.

Witt, Antonia. 2013b. Convergence on whose terms? Reacting to coups d'état in Guinea and Madagascar, *African Security* 6:3–4, 257–275.

Witt, Antonia. 2019. Between the shadow of history and the 'Union of People': Legitimating the Organisation of African Unity and the African Union. In: Dingwerth, Klaus, Antonia Witt, Ina Lehmann, Ellen Reichel, & Tobias Weise: *International Organizations Under Pressure: Legitimating Global Governance in Challenging Times*. Oxford: Oxford University Press, 98–129.

Witt, Antonia & Gilbert Khadiagala. 2018. Towards studying African interventions 'from below': A short conclusion, *South African Journal of International Affairs* 25:1, 133–139.

Wodrig, Stefanie. 2017. *Regional Intervention Politics in Africa: Crisis, Hegemony, and the Transformation of Subjectivity*. Abingdon: Routledge.

Woodward, Susan L. 2007. Do the root causes of civil war matter? On using knowledge to improve peacebuilding interventions, *Journal of Intervention and Statebuilding* 1:2, 143–170.

World Bank. 2013. *Madagascar 2013: La Banque mondiale en action*. Antananarivo: World Bank.

World Bank. 2015. *Madagascar: Systematic Country Diagnostic*. Antananarivo: World Bank.

Yabi, Gilles O. 2010. *The Role of ECOWAS in Managing Political Crisis and Conflict: The Cases of Guinea and Guinea-Bissau*. Abuja: Friedrich-Ebert-Stiftung.

Zafimahova, Serge. 2009. *Note de présentation: projet vérité et réconciliation*. Antananarivo: mimeo.

Zanker, Franzisca. 2018. *Legitimacy in Peacebuilding: Rethinking Civil Society Involvement in Peace Negotiations*. Abingdon: Routledge.

Zanotti, Laura. 2011. *Governing Disorder: UN Peace Operations, International Security, and Democratization in the Post-Cold War Era*. University Park: Pennsylvania State University Press.

Zürn, Michael. 2018. *A Theory of Global Governance: Authority, Legitimacy, and Contestation*. Oxford: Oxford University Press.

Interviews

Interview partner	Place	Date
EU official	Addis Ababa	25 May 2011
EU official	Addis Ababa	7 June 2011
EU official	Addis Ababa	14 June 2011
AU official	Addis Ababa	10 April 2012
AU official	Addis Ababa	11 April 2012
UNDP/UNECA official	Addis Ababa	26 April 2013
EU official	Addis Ababa	30 April 2013
AU official	Addis Ababa	7 May 2013
AU official	Addis Ababa	13 May 2013
AU official	Addis Ababa	14 May 2013
EU official	Addis Ababa	15 May 2013
AU official	Addis Ababa	17 May 2013
Official International IDEA	Addis Ababa	20 May 2013
AU official	Addis Ababa	20 May 2013
AU official	Addis Ababa	24 May 2013
FES officer	Antananarivo	11 February 2014
UNDP official	Antananarivo	11 February 2014
EU officials	Antananarivo	13 February 2014
Malagasy academic	Antananarivo	13 February 2014
Missionary FJKM	Antananarivo	14 February 2014
Advisor to the AU special envoy	Antananarivo	17 February 2014
Member of the *Haute autorité de la transition* (HAT)	Antananarivo	18 February 2014
Member of the *Plateforme nationale des organisations de la société civile* (PFNOSC)	Antananarivo	20 February 2014

INTERVIEWS

Interview partner	Place	Date
EU official	Antananarivo	21 February 2014
Member of the mouvance Ratsiraka	Antananarivo	21 February 2014
AU liaison officer	Antananarivo	21 February 2014
Party leader	Antananarivo	21 February 2014
Member of the diplomatic corps	Antananarivo	24 February 2014
World Bank official	Antananarivo	24 February 2014
Cartoonist	Antananarivo	24 February 2014
OIF official (re-sit same day)	Antananarivo	25 February 2014
Member of the diplomatic corps	Antananarivo	26 February 2014
Member of the diplomatic corps	Antananarivo	28 February 2014
American academic	Antananarivo	28 February 2014
Member of the diplomatic corps	Antananarivo	3 March 2014
Expert, *European Centre for Electoral Support* (ECES)	Antananarivo	3 March 2014
Cartoonist	Antananarivo	4 March 2014
SADC liaison officer	Antananarivo	5 March 2014
Member of the *Haute autorité de la transition* (HAT) (re-sit)	Antananarivo	6 March 2014
Official, *Commission électorale nationale indépendante pour la transition* (CENI-T)	Antananarivo	6 March 2014
Official, *Conseil de la réconciliation Malagasy* (FFM)	Antananarivo	10 March 2014
Former OIF official	Antananarivo	10 March 2014
Member of the *Collectif des citoyens et des organisations citoyennes* (CCOC)	Antananarivo	11 March 2014
Member of the mouvance Ratsiraka (re-sit)	Antananarivo	11 March 2014
Member of *Tangalamena* (Notables de Madagascar)	Antananarivo	12 March 2014
Party leader	Antananarivo	12 March 2014
Member of ESCOPOL	Antananarivo	12 March 2014

(continued)

(continued)

Interview partner	Place	Date
Member of the *Coordination nationale des organisations de la société civile* (CNOSC)	Antananarivo	13 March 2014
Member of the *mouvance* Zafy	Antananarivo	14 March 2014
Member of the *mouvance* Ravalomanana	Antananarivo	14 March 2014
Member of the *mouvance* Zafy	Antananarivo	15 March 2014
Former OIF official (re-sit)	Antananarivo	16 March 2014
Member of the *Coordination nationale des organisations de la société civile* (CNOSC)	Antananarivo	17 March 2014
Official, Catholic Church (EKAR)	Antananarivo	17 March 2014
Member of the gendarmerie	Antananarivo	18 March 2014
Member of the *Collectif des citoyens et des organisations citoyennes* (CCOC)	Antananarivo	18 March 2014
Malagasy academic	Antananarivo	19 March 2014
Member of the diplomatic corps	Antananarivo	21 March 2014
Member of ESCOPOL	Antananarivo	21 March 2014
Member of the *mouvance* Zafy	Antananarivo	22 March 2014
Member of the *Coordination nationale des organisations de la société civile* (CNOSC) (re-sit)	Antananarivo	25 March 2014
Member of SeFaFi	Antananarivo	25 March 2014
Member of the *Collectif des citoyens et des organisations citoyennes* (CCOC)	Antananarivo	25 March 2014
Official, *Conseil de la réconciliation Malagasy* (FFM) (re-sit)	Antananarivo	26 March 2014
Member of Liberty 32; Wake up Madagascar	Antananarivo	26 March 2014
Family member of Marc Ravalomanana	Antananarivo	27 March 2014
Member of the *Coalition des organisations de la société civile* (COSC)	Antananarivo	27 March 2014
Party leader	Antananarivo	31 March 2014

INTERVIEWS

Interview partner	Place	Date
SADC liaison officer	Antananarivo	31 March 2014
Member of the *Haute autorité de la transition* (HAT)	Antananarivo	1 April 2014
Official, Malagasy Church of Jesus Christ (FJKM)	Antananarivo	1 April 2014
Cartoonist	Antananarivo	2 April 2014
Member of the diplomatic corps	Antananarivo	2 April 2014
Party leader	Antananarivo	2 April 2014
Member of ESCOPOL	Antananarivo	2 April 2014
Member of the mouvance Ravalomanana	Antananarivo	3 April 2014
Expert KMF/CNOE	Antananarivo	4 April 2014
Member of the diplomatic corps	Pretoria	29 April 2014
Expert, *Electoral Institute for Sustainable Democracy in Africa* (EISA)	Johannesburg	12 May 2014
Legal advisor to Marc Ravalomanana	Pretoria	13 May 2014
Expert, *International Crisis Group* (ICG)	Johannesburg	14 May 2014
SADC official	Johannesburg	14 May 2014
South African jurist	Pretoria	15 May 2014
Expert, *SADC Council of NGOs* (SADC CNGO)	Gaborone	19 May 2014
SADC official	Gaborone	19 May 2014
SADC official	Gaborone	19 May 2014
SADC official	Gaborone	20 May 2014
Member of the diplomatic corps	Gaborone	21 May 2014
Expert, GIZ programme with SADC	Gaborone	21 May 2014
Expert, GIZ programme with SADC	Gaborone	21 May 2014
Member of the diplomatic corps (formerly Antananarivo)	Pretoria	28 May 2014
Expert, *Institute for Security Studies* (ISS)	Pretoria	28 May 2014

(continued)

(continued)

Interview partner	Place	Date
Advisor to mediator Chissano	Pretoria	29 May 2014
Former UN official	Skype	27 August 2014
Former expert, *International Crisis Group* (ICG)	Skype	14 October 2014
Former member of the diplomatic corps	Skype	6 November 2014
Former member of the diplomatic corps	Paris	8 July 2015

Index

Note: Page numbers in italic indicate figures or tables and page numbers followed by *n* indicate an endnote with relevant number.

Abrahamsen, Rita, 22
Acharya, Amitav, 21–2, 213, 216
African agency, 203, 214
African Association of Electoral Authorities, 56
African Charter on Democracy, Elections and Governance: anti-coup norm, 5; Malagasy activism, 1–2; negotiation participants, 61–2; negotiations, 56–61; ratifications, 62, 221*n*13; shortcomings, 10
African Commission on Human and Peoples' Rights (ACHPR), 68
African Governance Architecture (AGA), 64
African Peace and Security Architecture (APSA), 5, 209–10, 212
African studies: and IR (International Relations), 216; and principles of legitimate authority, 25–9; and sovereignty, 26–8; theoretical approach, 22
Afrobarometer, 96, 182, 189
agreements, Addis Ababa and Maputo, 11, 105, 136, 137, 153
agriculture, 94
Air Force One II scandal, 73
Amin, Idi, 47
amnesty, 103, 104, 146, 148, 149
Andriamanjato, Ny Hasina, 88
anti-corruption campaigns, 33, 86
anti-coup norm: aims and effects, 8–10; ambiguous rationale, 6; AU's zero tolerance policy, 2, 9–10, 62–3, 198, 221*n*14; early experiments, 46–50; enabling factor for international action, 202–3; evolution, 18–19, 45–6; expansion, 66, 69–71; inconsistent implementation and response, 7–10; legally binding status, 5; local dynamics, 8; shortcomings and indecisiveness, 9–10
anti-imperialism, 47, 68
APSA (African Peace and Security Architecture), 5, 209–10, 212
Arab Spring, 64, 67, 69–70
AREMA (Association for the Rebirth of Madagascar), 101, 104, 159–60
AS (Other Sensibilities), 159, 230*n*12
Ashton, Catherine, 189, 204
Assises nationales (April 2009), 131, 147, 160–1
Association for the Rebirth of Madagascar (AREMA), 101, 104, 159–60, 230*n*12
AU: Constitutive Act, 55; coup prevention measures, 63–4, 210; expanding mission, 69–71; Madagascar intervention, 113–14; Madagascar liaison office, 196–7; Madagascar suspension, 10–11; Madagascar suspension lifted, 182; Malagasy crisis (2001/02), 117–18; mandate, 5–6, 132; police or social worker role, 69; post-coup interventions, 205, 206–8, 207; recognition of delegations, 220*n*3; reconciliation activities, 197; responsibility to protect (R2P), 30; SADC-AU liaison office, 122–3, 124, 171, 191–2; as a suprastate, 211; on unconstitutional changes of government, 2; *see also* African Charter on Democracy, Elections and Governance
AU Assembly, 62, 64, 121
AU Commission: Draft Declaration on Democracy, Elections and Governance in Africa, 56;

INDEX

Madagascar mediation, 121–2; Peace and Security Department, 122; role, 61, 69
AU Economic, Social and Cultural Council, 65

Barkin, Samuel, 26
Barnett, Michael, 33–5
Bayart, Jean-François, 27–8
Biersteker, Thomas, 25
Bukovansky, Mlada, 24
Burkina Faso, 2, 64, 70, 205–6, 207, 208, 220n3
Burundi, 48

capacity-building, 33, 195
CAPSAT mutiny, 72, 89, 221n1
Catholic Church, 89–90
cattle raids (*dahalo*), 188
CENI-T (Independent National Electoral Commission for the Transition), 173, 174, 175, 177
Central African Republic (CAR), 2, 55, 207
Châtaigner, Jean-Marc, 120
Chiluba, Frederick, 51
China, development cooperation, 116
Chissano, Joaquim: ambiguous role, 136–7; contradictory expectations, 119; financial issues, 137; FRELIMO member, 107, 129; on HAT presidency, 104; and the ICG-M, 126, 136–7; links with Ratsiraka and Zafy, 106–7; mediation and peace negotiation background, 129, 135; mediation process, 155–6; power-sharing agreement, 11; SADC roadmap, 157–9; status as former head of state, 129, 134–5; support from Malagasy parties, 134–5; support structure, 135; withdrawal from mediation, 137–8
church: Catholic Church, 89–90; Malagasy Council of Christian Churches (FFKM), 153, 160, 177–8
civil society: CNOSC (National Coordination of Civil Society Organizations), 155; Coalition of Civil Society Organizations, 147–8; mediator consultations, 153; opposition to Ravalomanana, 82; and reconciliation, 147–8; roadmap implementation, 160; SeFaFi, 82, 87, 88, 90, 93–4, 153, 174
Clapham, Christopher, *Africa and the International System*, 27
Claude, Inis, 33
Club for Development and Ethics (CDE), 82
CNOSC (National Coordination of Civil Society Organizations), 155, 160
COI (Indian Ocean Commission), 113, 125, 156, 168, 172, 173, 192–5
COMESA (Common Market for Eastern and Southern Africa), 113, 115, 192, 196
Comité national pour l'observation des élections (KMF/CNOE), 82, 153, 174
Committee for National Reconciliation (CRN), 81, 101, 146, 147
Common Market for Eastern and Southern Africa (COMESA), 113, 115, 192, 196
common values and principles, 52, 53, 70
Comoros, 48, 50, 51–2, 195
Compaoré, Blaise, 64, 205, 220n3
conceptual resources, 18, 22–3
CONECS (National Economic and Social Council), 82, 88
Congrès see transitional parliament
constitution, Madagascar, 143
constitutional manipulation, 53, 59–60, 84–5, 91; *see also* unconstitutional changes of government
Cooper, Frederick, 27
corruption, 84, 96, 176, 182
Côte d'Ivoire, 55
coup perpetrators: AU punitive measures, 63; inconsistent treatment, 7; participation in transitional elections barred, 58, 165–6, 207; withdrawal of recognition, 47

coups: in Africa, 47–8, 55, 62, 198; AU's zero tolerance policy, 2, 9–10, 62–3, 198, 221*n*14; culmination of crises, 205–6; preventive measures, 63–4, 69; in the public interest, 57, 60–1; solutions, 68; *see also* anti-coup norm
critical constructivism, 25–6, 29, 37
CRN (Committee for National Reconciliation), 81, 101, 146, 147
Cronin, Bruce, 26
Currin, Brian, 110

Daewoo Logistics, 73, 92–3
dahalo (cattle raids), 188
democracy: common values and principles, 52, 53, 70; OAU action, 54; people's right to choose government, 48–9, 49–50, 60, 66; public disillusion, 95–6
democratization, 46, 49, 64
depoliticization, 94–5, 150–2, 184
development aid, 73, 116; for transitional elections, 173
Doe, Samuel, 220*n*3
Dramé, Tiébilé: competition with Ouédraogo, 130; and fifth mouvance, 153; mandate ends, 136–7; political background, 129; UN appointment, 113, 115, 124, 131

ecological destruction, 176, 182
economic sanctions *see* sanctions
economy: excluded cadres, 81–3, 88, 91; Rajoelina's business interests, 80–1; restrictions under Ravalomanana, 83–4
Edozie, Rita Kiki, 210–11
Egypt, 2, 64, 207, 208
election observation, 33, 56, 195; Madagascar, 173, 174, 175–6
elections: Declaration on the Principles Governing Democratic Elections in Africa (2002), 56; malpractice, 53–4; refusal of government to organise, 50, 53; refusal to relinquish power, 50, 52, 59
elections (Madagascar): (1993), 75; (1996), 75; (2001), 75–6; (2018), 189; electoral fatigue, 95; French

position, 117; postponement of local elections, 188; Ravalomanana's reforms, 86–7; *see also* transitional elections (2013)
Electoral Institute for Sustainable Democracy in Africa (EISA), 57, 62
elite: access to state institutions, 13, 76; benefit from constitutional settlement, 184; competition between, 77; opposition to Ravalomanana, 81–3; personal ambitions, 77–8; power-sharing negotiations, 142–3
Ellis, Stephen, 75
Englebert, Pierre, 27
ESCOPOL (Space for Consultation of Political Organizations and Parties), 154–5, 157, 159, 170, 230*n*12
European Union (EU): Cotonou Agreement, 115, 225*n*44; fisheries agreement, 187; regional capacity building, 195; and transitional election, 173, 175–6
extractive industries, 93–4, 187

Federation of Professional Mining Associations (FEDMINES), 82
Ferguson, James, 217
FFKM (Malagasy Council of Christian Churches), 153, 160, 167, 177–8
FFM (Malagasy Reconciliation Council), 148–9, 161, 167, 177–8
Finnemore, Martha, 33–5
FISEMA, 93
fisheries, 187
flour, 84
FNS (National Solidarity Fund), 148, 161, 177
foreign investments, 73, 92–3, 94, 187–8
Foucault, Michel, 18, 36, 211, 215, 217
France: alleged support for Rajoelina, 119–20, 137–8, 140; ambiguous negotiation messages, 116–17, 120–1; important bilateral partner, 113, 119; negotiations, 163; Rajoelina's participation in elections, 202; Rajoelina's visit,

108; security cooperation, 116; support for Ratsiraka, 110
Fransman, Marius, 169, 172
Friends of the Earth, 93

Galibert, Didier, 86, 97, 159
Gambia, 2, 207
Gayama, Pascal, 48
Germany, 113, 116, 125
Ghana, coup, 47
good governance, 54, 57, 59
Gottschalk, Keith, 210–11
government by decrees, 50, 54
Guinea, 2, 62, 192, 207, 208
Guinea-Bissau, 2, 51–2, 55, 207

HAT (High Authority of the Transition): *Assises nationales* (April 2009), 131, 147, 160–1; diplomatic inexperience, 109, 118; handed power, 72; international links, 109; lack of international recognition, 153; mediation efforts, 11, 132; membership, 102; military members, 89; and Ouédraogo, 131; popular consultations, 160–1; Rajoelina as President, 10, 72, 136, 143–4; sanctions against members, 11, 166; transitional programme, 154
Heathershaw, John, 39, 40
Hinthorne, Lauren, 95–6
HPM (Rally of Political Forces), 101, 159, 230*n*12
human rights, 30, 33, 61, 149

I Love Madagascar (TIM) party, 84, 85, 101, 159–60
ICG-M (International Contact Group on Madagascar), 125–7; becomes International Support Group for Madagascar, 191; and Chissano, 126, 136, 137; and development aid, 190; disconnect from developments in Madagascar, 125–6; internal conflicts, 126–7; local chapter, 126; mandate, 125; membership, 125; seven-point plan for SADC roadmap, 166–7; and transitional elections, 166–7, 173, 179
Ikome, Francis, 57

Independent Electoral Commission of South Africa, 56
Independent National Electoral Commission for the Transition (CENI-T), 173, 174, 175, 177
Indian Ocean Commission (COI), 113, 125, 156, 168, 172, 173, 192–5
INJET, 80–1
international actors: ambiguity of African agency, 202–3; coercion in negotiations, 163–8; contradictory mandates, 199–200; overlapping mandates and responsibilities, 212; post-coup opportunities, 180–1, 190–7; and SADC implementation, 161, 162
International Contact Group on Madagascar *see* ICG-M
International IDEA, 62
international norms, 31–3, 201; *see also* anti-coup norm; legitimate authority; sovereignty
International Organisation of La Francophonie (OIF), 62, 113, 114–15, 192, 195–6
international organizations (IO): as bureaucracies, 33, 34; disseminators of knowledge regimes, 36–7; effects of mediation, 13–14; expanded reach and depth, 201; expansion of legitimacy principles, 29–32; guarantors of legitimacy principles, 18, 32–7; legitimacy achieved by membership, 27; new roles and responsibilities, 214–15; and state authority, 34–5, 215
interventions: concept, 38–9; hybridity, 39–40; justification of choice of actors, 44; multiplicity of actors, 42–3; rationality, 142; as social space and practice, 38–41; unintended consequences, 39–40; *see also* post-coup intervention (general); post-coup intervention (Madagascar)
IR (International Relations): and African agency, 214; and African studies, 216; neglect of African intervention practices, 198; and sovereignty, 25–7; standards

for legitimate authority, 25–9;
theoretical approach, 14, 21–2

Jackson, Jennifer, 87
Jackson, Robert H., 26–7
Japan, 116, 125
Jütersonke, Oliver, 91

Kabbah, Ahmad Tejan, 46
Kartas, Moncef, 91
Kassimir, Ronald, 42
Klink, Frank, 33–4
KMF/CNOE (National Election Observation Committee – Citizen Education), 82, 153, 174
knowledge regimes, 18, 36
Kobama flour mill, 84, 88
Kodjo, Edem, 113, 129, 131
Kouchner, Bernard, 116, 120–1
Kufuor, Kofi Oteng, 47

Lahiniriko, Jean, 88, 159
Lamamra, Ramtane, 70, 122, 169
land rights, 73, 92–3, 187
language: field research, 17; importance in negotiations, 110, 133–4, 136
Latham, Robert, 41–2
Lawson, George, 38
legitimate authority: and democracy, 61; expansion of principles, 29–32; international organizations as guarantors, 32–7; in IR and African studies, 23–9; negated by violence, 76; public alienation, 94–6; and sovereignty, 25–7, 201–2; standards, 23–5; Weber's three types, 24
Lesotho, 48
Liberia, 220n3
Libya, Arab Spring, 64
local actors: agency, 40; financial resource inequality, 110–11; international access, 106–8; mouvance formation, 99–103; mouvance interests and strategies, 103–6; varied human capital, 108–10
local cultural sensitivity, 132, 133, 139, 140, 141, 205
local government reforms, 86, 94–5, 222n5

locality issues, 8, 43, 106
Lomé Declaration (2000): adoption, 4, 52; and Madagascar, 113, 114; provisions, 4–5, 52–4; rationale, 5–6; shortcomings, 9–10, 55–6, 57

Mac Ginty, Roger, 39
Madagascar Action Plan (MAP), 85, 88
Magro, 83
Malagasy army, 72, 89
Malagasy Broadcasting System (MBS), 80
Malagasy Council of Christian Churches (FFKM), 153, 160, 167, 177–8
Malagasy crisis (2001/02), 75–6, 117–18
Malagasy crisis (March 2009): *bas quartiers* protestors, 91–2; citizen alienation from political system, 94–6, 146–7; coalition of the discontented, 79–83, 92; events, 72–3, 73–4; historical triggers, 74–7, 100; multiplicity of conflicts, 19, 78–9, 91; opposition from excluded political and economic cadres, 81–3, 88, 91, 97; violence, 72, 74, 76, 92, 97, 222n7; see also popular uprisings
Malagasy language, 17, 110, 133–4, 136
Malagasy Reconciliation Council (FFM), 148–9, 161, 167, 177–8
Mali, 2, 27, 207
Maputo agreement, 11, 105, 136, 137, 153
Marcus, Richard, 85, 86, 143
Marquardt, Niels, 120
Matlosa, Khabele, 57
Mauritania, 55, 62, 207
Mauritius, 113, 192–3, 194, 207
Mbeki, Thabo, 51–2
MDM (Movement for Democracy in Madagascar), 159, 230n12
mediation: between protestors and government, 10; conflicts between mediators and the sending organization, 8; international and regional organizations, 13; OAU Secretariat, 48, 49, 220n5

mediators: anti-African prejudice, 134, 135–6; competition and rivalry, 8, 129–32; consultations with supporters, 153; diplomats rather than mediators, 129; importance to outcome, 128, 139; Joint Mediation Team, 113, 130; knowledge of Malagasy culture and history, 132, 133, 139, 140, 141, 205; language issues, 110, 133–4, 136; minimal financial and logistical support, 212–13; as negotiators, 163–4; relations with Malagasy negotiators, 129, 130, 139; varied diplomatic and professional backgrounds, 108–10; *see also* Chissano, Joaquim
Menkerios, Haile, 115
mercenaries, 4, 47, 52, 72
military coups, 50, 52
mining industries, 93–4, 187
MONIMA (Nationalist and Independent Movement of Madagascar), 159, 230n12
mouvances, 100–12, 113; access to international networks, 106–8; fifth mouvance, 153; formation, 99–103; interests and strategies, 103–6; limitations, 111–12, 140, 152–3; membership, 11, 101–3; negotiation pressure, 156–7, 158–9, 160; *see also* Rajoelina mouvance; Ravalomanana mouvance; Zafy mouvance
Mozambique, 123
Mugabe, Robert, 9, 45, 71

Nathan, Laurie, 123
National Coordination of Civil Society Organizations (CNOSC), 155, 160
National Economic and Social Council (CONECS), 82, 88
National Federation of Malagasy Engineering Organizations (FNOIM), 82
National Solidarity Fund (FNS), 148, 161, 177
Ndadaye, Melchior, 48
negotiations: Antananarivo failure, 11; bilateral partners, 116–17, 140; contested 2001 elections, 75–6; diverging international approaches, 121–8, 140; four mouvances, 11, 100–12; international coercion, 163–8, 178; international and regional actors, 1, 112–15, 117–19; mouvance access to international networks, 106–8; mouvance interests and strategies, 103–6; mouvance limitations, 111–12, 140, 152–3; mouvance membership, 11, 101–3; pressure on remaining three mouvances, 156–7, 158–9, 160; protagonists and supporters, 152–3; reconciliation, 103; South African/French initiative, 138; subsidiarity principle, 168, 178; time pressures, 114, 132–3, 164; unequal access to financial resources, 110–12; *see also* amnesty; mediators; reconciliation
Neumann, Iver B., 35–6
New Partnership for Africa's Development (NEPAD) Secretariat, 62
newspapers, as research source, 16
Niger, 2, 48, 51–2, 207
Nkrumah, Kwame, 47
Norway, election aid, 173

OAU: early experiments with anti-coup norm, 46–50; Harare summit, 45; sovereignty repercussions of coups, 47; subcommittee on unconstitutional changes, 50–1, 52; suspensions, 53; system of mutual preservation, 28
OAU Assembly, 51; *see also* Lomé Declaration (2000)
OAU Central Organ, 50, 51
OAU Secretariat, 48–9, 54
Obasanjo, Olusegun, 51
Obote, Milton, 47
OIF (International Organisation of La Francophonie), 62, 113, 114–15, 192, 195–6
Onuf, Nicholas, 33–4
Open Society Institute, 62
ordonnance 2009-001, 72
Orford, Anne, 23–4, 35–6, 37
Other Sensibilities (AS), 159, 230n12
Ouédraogo, Ablassé, 113, 114, 129, 131, 132, 136, 167

INDEX

PACEM (Support Project for the Electoral Cycle 2012–2014), 173
Pan-African Parliament (PAP), 65, 68
Panos (NGO), 93
parliament: Ravalomanana's reforms, 85; transitional parliament, 144, 182, 183–4, 229*n1*
Pellerin, Matthieu, 102
Ping, Jean, 55, 121–2, 137, 138
political parties: new parties, 159, 183; Ravalomanana's reforms, 85, 91; *see also* AREMA; ESCOPOL (Space for Consultation of Political Organizations and Parties); TIM (I Love Madagascar) party
popular uprisings: early Madagascan, 75; leaders (providential man), 77; legitimacy, 69–70, 78; people's rights to express their will against oppressive systems, 64–5; *see also* Arab Spring; Malagasy crisis (March 2009)
post-coup intervention (general): ambiguous consequences, 201–2; by the AU, 205, 206–9, 207; legitimacy principles, 31, 33; neglect of rural needs and those not in formal political parties, 208; new subjectivities and power relations, 43–4; rationalities, 44; reconfiguration of power relations, 201; and return to constitutional order, 1, 2, 4–5, 199–200; as transboundary formation, 13–14, 18, 41–4, 199, 217
post-coup intervention (Madagascar): exclusion of economic questions, 213; importance of contextual and cultural aspects, 132, 133, 139, 140, 141, 205; overlapping mandates and responsibilities, 212; regional engagement, 192–7; as source of further conflicts, 19, 99, 141, 199; unimaginative solutions, 204, 217; *see also* mediators; negotiations
poverty, 182
power relations, 13–14, 36–7
presidential candidates, 151, 165–7
presidential powers, 143–6

protest movements *see* popular uprisings
Protestant Church of Jesus Christ (FJKM), 89–90
Protocol on Politics, Defence and Security (SADC), 114
providential man, 77, 189
PSC (Peace and Security Council): anti-coup document, 70; boundaries for Madagascar mediation, 113–14; decision-making on Madagascar, 121; on democratisation progress, 64; HAT member sanctions, 11, 166; indirect briefings, 122; Madagascar suspension, 10–11, 113; mandate, 5, 55; peace and security in Africa, 67; restoration of Madagascan constitutional order, 1, 139; sanctions mandate, 55, 57–8, 63
public opinion, 95–6, 182, 189
putschists *see* coup perpetrators

QIT Madagascar Minerals (QMM), 93, 94

Rabanirinirarison, Rindra, 183
Rajaonarimampianina, Hery, 11, 175, 189
Rajaonarivelo, Pierrot, 153, 159, 160
Rajoelina, Andry: anti-government protests, 72, 73; business interests, 80–1; election campaigning (2013), 175; election success (2018), 189; France's alleged support, 119–20, 137–8, 140; on international investments, 94; international links, 108, 224*n29*; lack of diplomatic experience, 109; political accord, 154; power-sharing agreement, 11; President of the Transition, 10–11, 72–3, 136, 143–4; public face of the protests, 80–1, 92; transitional election eligibility, 151, 165–6, 202
Rajoelina mouvance: dissolution, 153–4; financial resources, 110; formation, 102–3; negotiation interests, 104–5; negotiation strategy, 105–6
Rakotoarivelo, Mamy, 167
Rakotonandrasana, General Noël, 72

Rakotoniringa, Manandafy, 109
Ralambomahay, Toavina, 144
Rally of National Forces (RFN), 81
Rally of Political Forces (HPM), 101, 159
Ramaholimihaso, Madeleine, 88
Ramanantsoa, General Gabriel, 75
Ramaroson, André, 88
Ramaroson, Vice-Admiral Hyppolite, 72
Ramiaramanana, Patrick, 80–1
Randrianja, Solofo, 75, 87–8
Ranjeva, Raymond, 76, 182
Ratsimandrava, Colonel Richard, 75
Ratsirahonana, Norbert, 88, 109
Ratsiraka, Didier: buffer role in negotiations, 100; and Chissano, 106–7; contested 2001 election, 75–6; French support, 110; loses power (1993), 75; socialist presidency, 75; transitional election eligibility, 165–6; VIVA radio interview, 73
Ratsiraka mouvance: formation, 11, 101–3; negotiation interests, 103–5; negotiation pressures, 156–7, 158–9, 160; negotiation strategy, 105
Ratsiraka, Roland, 88
Ravalomanana, Lalao, 165–6
Ravalomanana, Marc: *Air Force One II* scandal, 73; anti-government protests, 10, 72–3, 73–4; anti-Ravalomanana 'coalition of circumstance', 79–83, 102, 159; and the church, 89–90; constitutional manipulation, 84–5; deinstitutionalization of political representation, 94–5, 184; economic interests, 83–4; economic reforms, 118; election (2001), 75–6; exile in South Africa, 10; and France, 120; hands over power (2009), 1, 10, 72; international networking, 106, 107–8; local government reforms, 86, 94–5, 222n5; managerial approach to politics and the state, 87–8; return to Madagascar, 146, 151, 165, 168, 189; SADC lobbying, 107–8, 124; transitional election eligibility, 151, 165–7

Ravalomanana mouvance: financial resources, 110; formation, 11, 101–3; language problems, 110; negotiating team, 109–10; negotiation interests, 104–5; negotiation pressures, 156–7, 158–9, 160; negotiation strategy, 105–6; SADC roadmap criticism, 145–6
Raveloson, Jean-Aimé, 183
Razafindrahavy, Edgard, 88
reconciliation: AU activities, 197; Committee for National Reconciliation (CRN), 81, 101, 146, 147; Malagasy Reconciliation Council (FFM), 148–9, 161; National Solidarity Fund (FNS), 148, 161; negotiations, 103; post-coup priority, 191; SADC roadmap, 146–9
regional organizations: and democracy promotion, 3; for conflict prevention and resolution, 65; effects of mediation, 13–14; guarantors of legitimate authority, 32; limited resources and internal divisions, 213; in Madagascar negotiations, 112–15, 117–19, 121–4; post-coup engagement, 192–7
research scholarship: abundant and accessible empirical material, 12; atheoretical treatment, 7, 14, 21–2; on AU reactions to coups, 7–8; AU's anti-coup norm, 2–3, 6; conceptual resources, 18, 22–3; fieldwork sources, 15; internal memoirs and letters, 16–17; interviews, 15–16; positionality of researcher, 17; primary documents, 16
responsibility to protect (R2P), 30–1
Reus-Smit, Christian, 24, 25, 38
rice, 83, 90
Rio Tinto, 93
Robinson, Jean-Louis, 177
Roindefo, Monja, 88, 159
Rosberg, Carl G., 26–7
rule of law, 48–9
rural regions, 94, 98, 188, 208
Russia, on transitional elections, 167

INDEX

SADC: and AU's anti-coup policy, 202; budgetary constraints, 137; evolving mediation role, 118–19; inability to provide leadership, 171–2; inaccessibility, 169–71; incomprehensible to Malagasies, 169; Madagascar integration, 118; Malagasy suspicion, 114; military cooperation, 191; pro-Ravalomanana, 114; Protocol on Politics, Defence and Security, 114; Ravalomanana lobbying, 107–8, 124; SADC-AU liaison office, 122–3, 124, 171, 191–2; summit decisions, 123, 168–9; troika meetings, 123–4, 169; unclear division of responsibilities, 168–9
SADC mediation office, 161
SADC roadmap: ad hoc and confrontational negotiations, 163–8; criticisms, 145, 160–1, 161–2; depoliticization of transitional institutions, 150–2; human rights, 149; international implementation, 161, 162, 172–3; pragmatic but arbitrary selection of signatories, 157–9; presidential powers, 143–6; reconciliation, 146–9; signatories, 159, 230n12; signature, 11
Salim, Salim Ahmed, 48, 49, 54, 210
Salomão, Tomaz, 168–9
sanctions: effectiveness, 11, 213; HAT members, 11, 166; Lomé Declaration, 53; Madagascar, 1, 121, 126–7, 194; PSC mandate, 55, 57–8, 63
Sankara, Thomas, 220n3
São Tomé and Príncipe, 48, 55
Sarkozy, Nicolas, 116
Saungweme, Sekai, 60
Schlichte, Klaus, 41
Scott, David, 30
Security Sector Reform (SSR), 89, 191, 197
SeFaFi (Observatory of Public Life in Madagascar), 82, 87, 88, 90, 93–4, 153, 174
Sending, Ole Jacob, 35–6
Seychelles, 113, 172, 192–3, 194, 195
Sierra Leone, 46

Simão, Leonardo, 135, 138, 145, 156, 157, 169, 172
social deprivation, 90, 97–8
social discontent, 79–83, 92
social inequality, 92
social policy, 33
socialism, 75, 76
Solidarity of Parliamentarians for the Defence of Democracy and National Unity (SPDUN), 81
Souaré, Issaka, 9
South Africa: and Madagascar, 123, 190–1; negotiations, 163; SADC troika presidency, 169, 170
sovereignty, 25–8, 31–2, 47, 201–2
Space for Consultation of Political Organizations and Parties (ESCOPOL), 154–5, 157, 159, 170, 230n12
SSR (Security Sector Reform), 89, 191, 197
state authority, and international organizations, 34–5, 215
Sturman, Kathryn, 9
Sudan, uprising (2019), 2, 70, 206, 207, 208
Swaziland, and Madagascar, 123
Switzerland, 113, 117, 173

Tajikistan, 39
Tanzania, 192
Tardelli, Luca, 38
Taylor, Charles, 220n3
Tesha, John, 135, 138
TGV (Young Malagasies Determined) party, 80, 159
Three National Forces (3FN), 81, 222n3
Tiko, 83–4
TIM (I Love Madagascar) party, 84, 85, 101, 159–60
time pressures, 114, 132–3, 164
Togo, 192, 207
Tomasz, Nuño, 135, 138
trade unions, 84, 93
transboundary formation: concept, 41–2; post-coup intervention, 13–14, 18, 41–4, 199, 217
Transition Authority *see* HAT (High Authority of the Transition)
transitional elections, Africa, 206–7, 207

transitional elections (2013): an end in themselves, 162; AU appreciation, 1; candidate numbers, 184; CENI-T (Independent National Electoral Commission for the Transition), 173, 174, 175, 177; corruption, 176; eligibility of presidential candidates, 151, 165–7; finances, 173, 175–6, 187; independent candidates, 185; observers, 173, 174, 175–6; OIF support, 196; SADC roadmap provisions, 144, 150; shortcomings, 175–9; support from political parties, 157–8; UN oversight, 161, 173; voter education, 173–4
transitional parliament, 144, 182, 183–4, 229n1
Tsiranana, Philibert, 75
Tsiranana, Pierre, 88
Tully, James, 22
Turkey, 192

UDR-C (Union of Democrats and Republicans for Change), 159, 230n12
Uganda, coup, 47
UN: arena of collective legitimization, 32–3, 35; electoral oversight, 161; internal divisions in Madagascar, 124, 131; limited intervention role, 115, 202; special advisor, 124; and the state, 35, 37
UN Department of Political Affairs (DPA), 115, 124
UN Development Programme (UNDP), 124, 173
UN Economic Commission for Africa (UNECA), 62
unconstitutional changes of government: AU's zero tolerance policy, 2, 9–10, 62–3, 198, 221n14; definitions, 4, 50, 52, 53, 68; expanding themes, 62–6; legal definitions, 68, 221n15; Lomé Declaration, 4–5; Madagascar, 10–12, 99–100; OAU subcommittees, 50–1, 52; see also constitutional manipulation
United Kingdom, 192
United States: bilateral partner, 113; Madagascar policy, 116; Rajoelina's participation in elections, 202; and Ravalomanana, 107; SADC roadmap, 167
Urfer, Sylvain, 90

Vandeginste, Stef, 5
Veit, Alex, 41
violence: anti-*dahalo* campaign, 188; Malagasy crisis, 72, 74, 76, 92, 97, 222n7
Vital, Camille, 176
VIVA media group, 80–1
Vohinahitsy, Jean-Eugène, 88, 159

Weber, Cynthia, 25
Weber, Max, 24
Wight, Martin, 29, 30, 32–3
World Bank, 113, 73, 86, 182, 186–7

young people, 80, 97

Zafimahova, Serge, 82
Zafy, Albert: buffer role in negotiations, 100, 113; and Chissano, 106–7; Committee for National Reconciliation (CRN), 81, 101, 146, 147; impeachment, 75
Zafy mouvance: financial constraints, 110–11; formation, 11, 101–2, 103; language problems, 110; negotiation interests, 103–5; negotiation pressures, 156–7, 158–9; negotiation strategy, 105; and reconciliation, 146–7; SADC roadmap criticism, 145
Zambia, and Madagascar, 123
Zanotti, Laura, 211
zero tolerance policy, 2, 9–10, 62–3, 198, 221n14

www.ingramcontent.com/pod-product-compliance
Lightning Source LLC
Chambersburg PA
CBHW072125290426
44111CB00012B/1780